FIRE & ICE

FIRE & ICE

ARCTIC CONVOYS 1941–1945

BRITANNIA NAVAL HISTORIES OF WORLD WAR II

BMT Press

Britannia Museum Trust Press

This edition first published in the United Kingdom in 2022 by Britannia Museum Trust Press, Britannia Royal Naval College, Dartmouth, TQ6 0HJ, United Kingdom.

PB ISBN 978-1-83801-076-8   **HB** ISBN 978-1-83801-077-5
© Britannia Museum Trust, 2022 © The Devonshire Press™ 2022

Publisher: Paul Honeywill
Series Editors: G. H. Bennett, J. E. Harrold, R. Porter and M. J. Pearce

 Cover image: Heavy seas view from the open bridge of HMS *Sheffield* during convoy JW 53. February 1943.

Typeset in Adobe Garamond Pro 11/14pt. Printed by Print on Demand

The historical documents reproduced here appear as unedited text, apart from minor changes made to date formats and corrections to typing errors found in the original.

© Richard Porter 2012

 # Britannia Royal Naval College

A majestic landmark, which towers above the harbour town of Dartmouth in Devon, Britannia Royal Naval College was designed by royal architect Sir Aston Webb to project an image of British sea power. A fine example of Edwardian architecture, the College has prepared future generations of officers for the challenges of service and leadership since 1905.

The Britannia Museum opened in 1999 to safeguard the College's rich collection of historic artefacts, art and archives and promote greater public understanding of Britain's naval and maritime heritage, as a key element in the development of British history and culture. It also aims to instil a sense of identity and ethos in the Officer Cadets that pass through the same walls as their forbears, from great admirals to national heroes to royalty.

http://www.royalnavy.mod.uk/The-Fleet/Shore-Establishments/BRNC-Dartmouth

Contents

Plans

The Arctic Star Medal   The Russian Ushakov Medal

'Despite everything, you, dear veterans, stood to the
end to deliver the much needed aid. We sincerely
admire, respect and thank you for this' what
Churchill called 'the worst journey in the world.'

Ambassador of Russia Andrei Kelin to the court of St. James's,
18 November 2020, rusemb.org.uk/ambarticles/571

Foreword

Vice–Admiral Sir Simon Lister KCB OBE

There is a real skill to summarising complexity, as any reader of the superlative Oxford Very Short Introduction series will attest. This Britannia History on the Arctic Convoys is of the same high standard – a masterpiece of brevity, relevance and accessibility; it brings to life the strategic context, the flow of events, and the titanic struggle for survival, let alone operational success, in northern latitudes. I am a little surprised, but grateful, for the chance to offer a foreword.

My own contact with Russia was inspired through the window of Russian language and culture that in turn led to two diplomatic appointments in Moscow, both falling at pivotal times for that society. This personal investment was initiated at school, nurtured at Dartmouth, and brought to maturity at the Defence School of Languages in the middle part of my career in the Royal Navy. Language has created both a lifelong interest in Russia, and a modest understanding of that nation; after a long naval career, I have come to understand Russia as an occasional and powerful ally, but more frequently, as a persistent and credible threat to our national security.

Visit the Commonwealth War Graves cemetery in Murmansk, and we quickly become aware of the sacrifice made by Allied Servicemen in the second war in this theatre. Dig a little deeper, and we find that Murmansk was established at the end of the first war at the insistence of the British to provide support to Russian allies in that war. After both conflicts, Anglo-Russian relationships rapidly deteriorated, part of a cycle that has repeated itself since Chancellor first established diplomatic and trading relations with Ivan the Terrible in the 16th century. Four centuries before the Arctic Convoys were established, valuable goods and services were flowing in each direction through the Barents and White Seas when the connection flourished, but were interrupted when relationships soured or the weather took charge. Our maritime forebears knew precisely what it took to survive and prosper inside the Arctic Circle.

My first contact with the Arctic Convoys was through Dervish '91, the fiftieth anniversary of the first convoy. Celebrated by many veterans visiting Murmansk and Archangel, I had the privilege to meet these modest, resilient and courageous men, intent on commemorating their comrades and their achievements, which, for many of them, had received insufficient recognition after the war. The convoy story, brought so clearly to life in this book, is one of strategic intervention, of extraordinary national and individual sacrifice, of operational collaboration fashioned rapidly with constrained resources, and of heroism in the face of extreme weather and high intensity combat. I suspect that a little research would show that these elements are the enduring qualities of naval warfare. This booklet therefore has much to tell us about the human capabilities needed to fight and win in these circumstances. I will single out the four that stand out for me.

A Shared Strategic Goal. The Arctic Convoys reflect the need to be able to work with enemies who become allies, and vice versa, and understand the strategic circumstances and imperatives that drive those choices. This strategic perspective and agility characterised Churchill's approach to Stalin and the Soviet Union. It is notable that our co-operation with the Soviet Union started before the US had entered the war, and continued to the end, reflecting British strategic national interests throughout. The intent and comradeship forged through the existence of a common foe survived the many operational set-backs and doubts on both sides, and speaks clearly to the need in these matters to have a clear, shared strategic goal and enduring commitment to its achievement.

Leadership of Effective Collaboration. The collaboration and inte-gration at a working level that was achieved in a short space of time was remarkable, given the suspicion and gulf of political outlook that existed at the outset. A British squadron of 'T' Class submarines operated from Polyarnoye for the duration of the war, and was sustained with Russian engineering support. When the Russians discovered that their own submarine atmosphere hydrogen removal device was much needed in the Royal Navy, the technology was immediately transferred (and was in use in the *Oberon* class some 50 years later). Meanwhile, the Russians were experiencing difficulties with their heavyweight torpedoes, and they approached the Royal Navy for assistance – it was immediately forth-coming. The Naval staff based at Polyarnoye formed a football team and competed in the Northern Fleet Football league, winning against the Harbour Defence team but losing to the Coastal Defence team. Wounded sailors arriving in Murmansk, a shattered city with little left standing, were treated by dedicated Russian doctors who understood the effects of frostbite and extreme exposure. Genuine collaboration and integration delivered a whole that was greater than the sum of its parts. Wise leaders understood this and drove teamwork hard, recognising that the rewards far outweighed the effort.

The Power of Deterrence. Deterrence is rooted in the tangible threat of loss following attack – and the need to disrupt it – appears throughout the North West Russia campaign. The effect of the *Tirpitz* presence in a Norwegian fjord on the progress of the campaign fully justified the extraordinary efforts by both the Royal Navy and the Royal Air Force to destroy her. The bravery and technical ingenuity shown by the 'X' craft crews, the Hurricane and Lancaster pilots operating in extreme conditions reflect the importance then and now of disrupting an enemy that presents a threat, even at long range when alongside. As I write this foreword, building the latest version of HMS *Glasgow*, a few miles from where her wartime predecessor was built, we reflect on the purpose of this new ship – to hold the latest generation of Russian submarines at risk in the North Atlantic. The deterrent effect of a ship which is able to hold the enemy at risk is an enduring and valuable aspect of naval power.

Military Linguists and their contribution to Operational Capability. Speaking the language of our allies and potential foes is a crucial capability to foster for the long term. During the Arctic Convoys, units quickly assembled linguists to assist. Just twenty years after the revolution, both sides were able to find sufficient interpreters to enable joint operations after a fashion. How challenging must have been those first encounters, before the standard procedures and specialist terminology had been exchanged and put to use? I have a naval linguist dictionary from the period, and can only imagine the value of this book to those attempting to bring allies together across the intermittent communications of the time, across the cultural divide, under the eye of Soviet political officers, intent on ensuring that Communist doctrine was not subverted by contact with the British. Interpreting at the 2001 Dervish ceremonies for the dwindling but stoic surviving veterans of both sides, I was struck by the vital role my wartime interpreter predecessors had fulfilled. This wartime period of collaboration was made effective by their efforts, and I am certain that linguists, expert in the specific military and naval lexicon of potential ally or foe, are an essential part of the deployable capability of the future Royal Navy. Linguists, stay current and step forward when the time comes, as it surely will.

I close by reflecting on my profound hope that the Russian people will, over time, pivot more to the West, repositioning themselves to enjoy the growth and prosperity that will come from more collaborative relations with their neighbours. It is a pivot I hope they will make without prejudicing their rich heritage, culture and identity. In the last four hundred years, during those brief periods of collaborative activity, the Royal Navy has played a vital role. The naval community should be ready for the next pivot when it comes, and do all it can to make it endure. I can think of no better way to honour the sacrifice made by many of our predecessors during their service in the Arctic Convoys.

Introduction

G. H. Bennett

Preamble

The following introduction was written before the Russian invasion of Ukraine on 24 February 2022. Writings on the Arctic convoys have been deeply affected by the politics of Anglo-Russian relations which have ranged from the wartime alliance from 1941 to 1945, to the bitter antagonisms of the Cold War era, and to a period of exploration of shared understandings about past relations from 1989 to 2022. The Russo-Ukrainian war marks another evolution in the relationship between Russia and the United Kingdom that will, no doubt, impact on the scholarship of the Arctic convoys especially with some Russian nationalists inferring that Russia fought alone during the "Great Patriotic War". One feature of that future evolution is already clear with the Russo-Ukrainian war serving as a powerful reminder of the importance of logistics as the determining factor in modern war. The Russian invasion of 24 February 2022 saw a vast army deployed across a large battlefront that is but a fraction of the size of that along which German and Russian armies fought between 1941 and 1945. The failure of the Russian military to achieve its initial military goals, because of a highly effective Ukrainian defence, and Russian difficulties in supplying its forces in the field along stretched supply lines, constrained by an inadequate road network, with complicating weather conditions, was a powerful echo of some of the factors at play in the fighting along the Eastern Front during the Second World War. The Russian withdrawal from Northern Ukraine in early April 2022, in order to regroup, re-equip and re-engage along the front in Luhansk and Donetsk placed the emphasis squarely on resupply with the West supplying Ukrainian forces with tanks, artillery, anti-tank and anti-air rockets along with other military equipment, and the Russians looking to China and beyond for resupply. The bigger the war, and the more drawn out the fighting, the more pivotal logistics, and the industrial output behind it, becomes. What was true between 1941 and 1945 can be glimpsed in May 2022 as the Russo-Ukrainian war moves into its next terrible phase.

Introduction

The organisation and defence of 78 convoys from the North Atlantic to the North Russian ports between August 1941 and May 1945, carrying badly needed supplies to the Soviet Union, offered the British and Americans a multi-faceted challenge.[1] The problems ranged from the complexities of inter-Allied coalition politics between powers of very different political and economic systems, to the human and nautical difficulties resulting from operating at the edge of the Arctic Circle in long hours of dark in the Northern Winter, or perpetual daylight in June-July at the height of the summer. The journey from British/Icelandic waters to North Russia, and back again, via a Northern route in Summer as the ice receded and a Southern Route in Winter (as long hours of darkness offered some relief from air attack), was difficult and dangerous even before the intervention of the German Armed Forces. Driven by ideological factors, the fighting on the Eastern Front following the German invasion of the Soviet Union on 22 June 1941 turned to absolute war in which 22 million Soviet citizens would lose their lives with a front-line stretching hundreds of miles from the Baltic to the Black Sea. In the hope of intercepting the convoys, the fjords of Norway after 1941 became the operating bases for some of the surviving heavy ships of the Kriegsmarine such as *Tirpitz* and *Scharnhorst*. They would be supported by bomber and torpedo bomber units of the Luftwaffe, together with a substantial force of Kriegsmarine submarines (some 240 would operate from Norwegian waters between 1940 and 1945 with forces at Hammerfest and Kirkenes specifically intended for use against the Arctic convoys). In popular understandings of the war at sea in Britain and the United States the life and death struggle to fight through the Arctic Convoys to their destinations in Russia has assumed almost mythic proportions: On their success depended the outcome of battles such as Stalingrad that would turn the tide of battle in the East against the German Armed Forces. The challenges faced on the "Murmansk Run" have come to epitomise the difficulties of defending convoys from sustained enemy attack, the challenges of harsh seas and extreme climates, and the heroism and determination of the sailors who maintained the global supply lines that allowed the Allies to win victory by 1945.

However, there are considerable conceptual and methodological issues that have prevented a proper appreciation of the Arctic convoys. The Arctic convoys cannot be viewed as a simply an offshoot of the

Atlantic Convoys. Indeed, the primary purpose of the establishment of that convoy route was political: To cement an alliance between Britain and the Soviet Union which would be joined later by the United States of America. Once established in 1941, the primary impetus to maintain the supply route to the North Russian ports came from inter-Allied politics, and the need to maintain a functional, if difficult, relationship with the Soviet Union. So strong was this impetus that the convoys continued to run all the way to 1945, despite the changing fortunes of war, despite significant losses of ships, crews and cargoes, and despite the wider impacts of the "Russia Run" on other theatres of operations such as the Atlantic and Mediterranean. Considerations about the value of Allied aid to the outcome of the land battles being fought on the Eastern front were secondary to the political needs of inter-allied politics and a thorny relationship between "Uncle Joe Stalin" and the west. Similarly, the wider strategic value of the Arctic front against the Germans, drawing significant forces away from other theatres, was not as fully recognised as it might have been at the time and, indeed, subsequently.

The outcome of some of the convoy operations between the German invasion of the Soviet Union in 1941 until the end of the war has added a further layer of complication in trying to arrive at a balanced analysis of the organisation, conduct and value of the Arctic convoys. Even before 1945 there were questions, and no little controversy, both domestically and internationally about the handling of the Arctic convoys. Post-war research, especially after the British records were opened to public scrutiny in the 1970s, has not stilled the controversy, with the politics of the Cold War adding a further level of antagonism to the debate on the "Russia Run". The significance, or otherwise, of Anglo-American aid to the Soviet Union became something of a political football between the historians of East and West during the cold war although there has been a growing consensus on the value of that aid since the 1990s and the fall of the Berlin Wall.

The naval challenges in maintaining the supply lines to North Russia are fully set out in the Naval Staff's Battle Summary No.22 'Arctic Convoys 1941-45' reproduced in this volume which was a work in progress from 1943 until the version reproduced here which dates from 1954. It is important to understand the contexts in which this history was produced, and evolved, and how that context began to shape the historiography of the Arctic Convoys. When the initial study was produced in 1943 it was driven by the urgent operational need to try and learn the lessons from a series of convoy battles, especially PQ 17, PQ 18 and convoy JW 51B. By 1946 the convoys to Russia were both a testament to the endurance and professionalism of sailors, but also a source of controversy and some potential embarrassment. The mauling of Convoy PQ 17 in July 1942 with only 11 merchant ships out of 34 reaching North Russia had been a disaster with the convoy scattering in the expectation of imminent attack by German heavy ships that were not there. If controversy surrounded the fate of PQ 17, stilled in the midst of war by censorship and the need to fight the war to a successful outcome, then an additional layer of awkwardness over the Arctic Convoys swiftly built up after May 1945 as a result of the developing cold war. In the context of the cold war the swift deterioration in relations between the Soviet Union and her former allies made the vast quantities of material sent to Russia between 1941 and 1945, at vast cost and considerable sacrifice, seem painfully ironic, if not rather embarrassing. The United States and Great Britain had helped to facilitate the survival, the growth and eventual dominance in Eastern Europe of the very rival against which they might have to fight the next war.

The repercussions of this awkwardness around the Arctic convoys manifested itself in various ways. It was not until 1950 that the Admiralty published the official dispatch on 'Convoys to North Russia, 1942' in *The London Gazette*, with the final version of the Battle Summary on the Arctic Convoys being produced in 1954, and incorporating material and perspectives based on study of the German archives.[2] In addition, and unusually, the updated summary incorporated clarifications and suggestions by a number of senior Royal Navy officers, together with the Air Historical Branch. The summary constituted a significant effort to frame the history of the Russian convoys, using multiple sources in case of question or controversy, and the Battle Summary sets out those sources carefully. That controversy, with suggestions of British blundering and incompetence, came with the publication in 1968 of David Irving's book on Convoy PQ 17 which caused a sensation.[3] In some quarters the book was considered little better than 'muck raking', and potentially libellous even if the research was otherwise diligent.[4] A court case followed (Broome versus Cassell & Co Ltd, 1970) in which Captain Jack Broome, who had commanded the escort group for PQ 17, successfully sued the publishers of Irving's book: The jury awarding the retired naval officer a then record of £40,000 in damages.[5] Controversy continued to surround the Russian convoys, and

PQ 17 in particular, even after the end of the cold war. The Arctic Star campaign medal, awarded to those who had served on the convoys was not created until 2012 and the following year, after public campaigning, the British Government relaxed its rules on the acceptance of foreign medals by British nationals to allow the Russian Medal of Ushakov (originally created in March 1944) to be given to British Arctic Convoy veterans.[6]

Initiating the Convoys to Russia

Relations between Britain and Russia had been less than easy from the start of the Bolshevik Revolution in 1917 to the point at which German forces invaded the Soviet Union in 1941. That history is an important means to understanding the depth of antagonism, particularly between the British and the Russians, that continued to fuel suspicions on both sides even after the powers became allies in 1941. In 1918 during the First World War British and French forces had landed in North Russia to safeguard the military supplies which had been sent to aid the war effort of the Czar against Germany, and then subsequently the Provisional Government, from March to November 1917. Alongside those land forces, a Royal Navy force primarily made up of C-Class cruisers and V and W-Class destroyers operated in the Baltic under the command of Rear-Admiral Edwyn Alexander-Sinclair. During 1918 relations between British forces and the Bolsheviks in North Russia deteriorated to the point where they were drawn into combat operations against each other, with the Royal Navy operating against the Red Navy in the Baltic. The British Government began to consider the possibility of a campaign to overthrow the Bolsheviks with additional British troops sent to other parts of what had been the Czar's Empire (40,000 to the Caucasus, 950 to the Trans-Caspian region, 1,800 to Siberia). Appeals to the Empire, to Allied and friendly governments resulted in the deployment of American, Canadian, Australian, Italian, Greek, Romanian and Japanese forces in Russia which were increasingly drawn into a Russian Civil War with White Russian forces also seeking to overthrow the "Reds". Over 900 British soldiers were killed before the intervention was abandoned and British forces withdrawn from Archangel (27 September) and Murmansk (12 October) in late 1919. Evacuations from other parts of Russia also took place (Caucasus 24 August) and the Royal Navy was involved in evacuating anti-Bolshevik forces from cities such as Odessa in late 1919 and early 1920.

The intervention of British forces in Russia, concerns about Communist subversion in Britain, left a lasting legacy of mistrust between Britain and Russia. Between the Russians and the Royal Navy the enmity was underpinned by the sinking by Royal Navy units of the Russian cruiser *Oleg*, and submarine depot ship *Pamiat Azova* with the Royal Navy also suffering damage to some larger ships and the loss of a number of smaller vessels such as three Coastal Motor Boats.[7] The murder of Naval Attaché Captain Francis Cromie by the Cheka during the seizure of the British Embassy in St Petersburg in 31 August 1918 likewise contributed to lasting antagonisms between the British and the Russians. Throughout the 1920s these were routinely fanned by fears of renewed military interventions in Russia, and Red Scares in Britain (the most notable of which involved the publication in 1924 of the Zinoviev letter, most likely with the involvement of the former head of the Department of Naval Intelligence, Admiral "Blinker" Hall). The evolution of Stalinism in the 1930s with its goal of socialism in one country (as opposed to revolutionary world socialism), and the entry into the League of Nations of the Soviet Union in 1934 in search of co-operation against the developing threat of Nazi Germany, did little to ease tensions between Britain and Stalin's Russia despite an Anglo-Soviet declaration in 1935 that there was no conflict of interest between the two governments on international policy. Five year plans, the collectivization of agriculture, and Stalin's relentless pursuit of enemies, resulted in mass starvation, trials of enemies accused of being in league with foreign enemies, and the totalitarianism of the NKVD and the gulag. The signature of the Molotov-Ribbentrop non-aggression pact between Russia and Germany on 23 August 1939 was seen as yet further evidence that the Soviet Union was not to be trusted. The Russian attack on Poland on 17 September in support of a German campaign which had begun on 1 September raised the question of an Anglo-French declaration of war on the Soviet Union, but the defeat of Poland on 6 October ended that possibility. The Soviet invasion of Finland on 30 November 1939 re-opened the possibility of an Anglo-Russian conflict but the negotiation of a peace treaty in March 1940, by which Finland ceded a considerable amount of territory to the Soviet Union (around 8% of the country), once again shut down that danger.

Despite the troubled history of Anglo-Soviet relations, and his own virulent anti-Communism, in May 1940 the new British Prime Minister (and former First lord of the Admiralty) Winston Churchill, tried to reach out to Stalin and to warn him of the dangers of Hitler. Veteran

British left wing politician Sir Stafford Cripps was sent to Moscow to try and win over Stalin. Warnings from Britain to the Soviet Union in the spring and summer of 1941, as German preparations for the invasion of Russia proceeded apace, were not heeded by Stalin who remained more wary of the British than Hitler, given the years of mutual antagonism since 1917. Nevertheless, when Germany attacked the Soviet Union on 22 June Churchill seized the chance to forge an alliance with the Soviet Union to overthrow Nazi Germany. In forging this alliance between two mutually distrustful parties, British aid to Russia, in the form of convoys, would be perhaps the vital initial underpinning as Soviet forces struggled to contain the Germans. Thus, the aid was both politically significant, as evidence of the British commitment to Russia, and also strategically important in helping Soviet forces to stand against the German onslaught. This combination of inter-Allied politics, and strategic support for Russia, would be at the heart of the convoys to Russia until 1945.

On the evening of 22 June, just hours after the German attack had begun, Churchill went on the radio to explain British policy in the light of the attack on the Soviet Union. He went to considerable pains, as a well-known anti-communist, to explain his reasons for the course Britain would now take towards the Soviet Union:

> The Nazi regime is indistinguishable from the worst features of
> Communism. It is devoid of all theme and principle except appetite
> and racial domination. It excels in all forms of human wickedness,
> in the efficiency of its cruelty and ferocious aggression. No-one has
> been a more consistent opponent of Communism than I have for
> the last twenty-five years. I will unsay no words that I've spoken
> about it. But all this fades away before the spectacle which is now
> unfolding. The past, with its crimes, its follies and its tragedies,
> flashes away. I see the Russian soldiers standing on the threshold of
> their native land, guarding the fields which their fathers have tilled
> from time immemorial.[8]

Reasoning that the destruction of the Soviet Union was but a precursor to the invasion of the United Kingdom Churchill went on to say that Britain would:

> give whatever help we can to Russia and to the Russian people. We
> shall appeal to all our friends and Allies in every part of the world to

take the same course and pursue it as we shall, faithfully and steadfastly to the end. We have offered to the Government of Soviet Russia any technical or economic assistance which is in our power and which is likely to be of service to them.[9]

Two days later, on Tuesday 24 June, Sir Anthony Eden (Foreign Secretary) similarly took great pains to outline that differences between the two countries would not stand in the way of effective co-operation and that the Russians had accepted offers of British assistance:

The political systems of our two countries are anti-pathetic, our ways of life are widely divergent, but this cannot and must not for a moment obscure the realities of the political issue which confront us to-day ... I can tell the House that I have now heard from His Excellency the Soviet Ambassador that his Government have accepted our offer to send military and economic advisors to Russia to co-ordinate our efforts in what is now, beyond doubt, a common task-the defeat of Germany.[10]

The Anglo-Russian alliance had begun in rather tentative circumstances, but with Russian forces sustaining massive casualties in the East, and without a foothold on the European continent, it was politically and strategically imperative to assist them on the battlefield with aid convoys, and by maintaining the strategic bombing offensive against Germany, especially after the Chiefs of Staff informed Churchill in early August that there was simply no question of launching any sort of offensive on the continent to relieve the pressure on the Russian armies in the East.[11] It helped that within seven days of the German attack the United States also began to give aid to the Soviet Union in the form of supplies for cash payment. In October 1941, following detailed negotiations in Moscow involving representatives of the Soviet Government and Lord Beaverbrook for the United Kingdom, and Averell Harriman for the United States, the provisions of Lend Lease Act were extended to give aid to the Soviet Union. This drew some hostile comment from certain quarters in the United States with, for example, the *Baltimore News Post*, carrying a cartoon image of Joseph Stalin sporting strap on angels' wings to indicate the magical transformation in perceptions of Russia that had seemingly taken place.[12] That aid, until after December 1941 and American entry into the Second World War, would have to be carried in

British ships to the Russian ports. Supplies would be delivered under an Anglo-American-Russian protocol that would run from mid-year to mid-year (First protocol was signed on 1 October to cover the period until the end of June 1942, with the second and subsequent protocols running from July to June).[13]

If getting supplies to Russia was vital in both a political and a military sense then there was the issue of how to get them there. Re-supply from the air was out of the question given the distances involved leaving the sea as the only means to deliver substantial amounts of aid. Convoys to the ports of Murmansk and Archangel in the North of Russia offered the most direct means of delivering aid to Soviet forces fighting on the Eastern front. There were, however, other means utilised that are frequently overlooked in the narrative of Anglo-American aid to the Soviet Union. For example, around half the aid by tonnage (17,499,861 long tons) sent to Russia reached the front after being landed in Vladivostock and transhipped by rail.[14] A further 25% of the aid came via the Persian Gulf, transhipped through Iran and into the Southern Soviet Union or across the Caspian.[15]

Evolution of the Russian Convoys: The Naval Perspective

During the course of the war the Russian convoys evolved through three distinct phases. In the first phase from 1 August 1941 to March 1942 the convoy run to Russia was established and the first deliveries of aid took place. During the second period from March 1942 to March 1943 the running of the convoys was keenly contested with serious losses of ships, men and materiel to the point that the Arctic lifeline was imperilled by the German Armed Forces. In the final phase the German threat against the convoys declined markedly as Soviet forces on the battlefield dealt hammer blows to German forces as they advanced steadily westwards towards Germany and to Berlin. Throughout, the geography of the route and the ice gave 'planners little or no choice in selecting routes and defense forces for each convoy'.[16]

Arctic Convoys Phase 1 August 1941 to March 1942

The first phase of Arctic convoy operations saw 13 convoys (114 merchant ships) being sent to North Russia with 100 ships making the return journey in 9 convoys.[17] The first convoy (code named Dervish) consisting of just six ships left Hvalfjord on 21 August, reaching

Archangel ten days later without incident. The German armies were so busy driving forward across the length of the Eastern front, capturing tens of thousands of Red Army prisoners in the process that the German Armed Forces appeared to attach little importance to the flow of Allied aid passing beyond the North Cape of Norway. On these first 13 convoys just two vessels were lost.

While Iceland was the departure point for these convoys their cargoes began their journey on the east coast of the United States and Scotland. Departing from Philadelphia, American ships bound for Russia would join with one of the convoys crossing the Atlantic, before breaking away and heading for Iceland. Here, at Reykjavik or Hvalfjord they would join British vessels that had been convoyed to Loch Ewe and Gare Loch in Western Scotland. Combined into one convoy they would then make the journey North Eastwards towards the North Cape of Norway and onwards to Russia. In some cases, the wait times for merchant ships arriving in Icelandic waters before starting the journey towards North Russia was considerable. One American vessel the 'Gateway City rode at her anchor chain for 107 days in Iceland while the crew, who were forbidden to go ashore lest they divulge matters of "military importance" to Axis spies, made skiffs out of dunnage and paddled around to other ships in the harbour, including the Russians'.[18]

That began to change, however, as the German offensive stalled in December 1941 amidst the start of one of the coldest winters of the Twentieth Century. The importance of stopping the flow of aid, which might tilt the military balance against the German armies fighting across thousands of miles of front, saw significant deployments with 260 Luftwaffe aircraft arriving in Norway along with the battleship *Tirpitz*, two heavy cruisers and supporting destroyers and submarines. The battlecruiser *Scharnhorst* followed later. With the 1942 campaign season likely to prove decisive the Luftwaffe and Kriegsmarine were called on by Hitler to do everything possible to help out the hard-pressed German armies by cutting Anglo-American aid shipments. This met with some resistance within the Kriegsmarine. For example, Admiral Döenitz, the head of the German submarine arm, objected to the dilution of the submarine effort in the Atlantic through the relocation of submarines to the Arctic.[19]

Arctic Convoys Phase 2 April 1942 to March 1943

During the months from April 1942 to March 1943 the Arctic convoys were keenly contested by the Germans as they sought victory on the Eastern front. On 28 June 1942 Army Group South launched "Case Blue" to take Stalingrad (an important node on the Soviet rail network and on the Volga river freight route) together with the oilfields of the Caucasus. Indeed, the fall of Stalingrad would end the flow of oil from the Caucasus to the Russian Armies in the North.[20] Beyond this, the successful capture of both objectives would threaten the aid corridor for American supplies to the Soviet Union through the Persian Gulf, along the Persian road and rail corridors and into the Southern Soviet Union via the land border or through the Caspian ports such as Baku.[21] With German land forces being steadily degraded by the fighting it was essential that Soviet strength was not further augmented by supplies via the Arctic convoys, the Persian corridor or through Vladivostock. There was also a sense of wider crisis as the North African campaign also hung in the balance, drawing badly needed resources from the German Armed Forces elsewhere, until defeat at the Second Battle of El Alamein from 23 October to 11 November 1942 saw a decisive turn of the tide against the Axis in North Africa. Problems in terms of the impact of the wider war on the situation in Russia were not entirely one way. The invasion of French North Africa under Operation Torch by United States forces (8-16 November 1942) drew merchant ships, escorts and resources away from potential availability for the Russian convoys, forcing a temporary lull.

Overall, during the period from April 1942 to March 1943 ten convoys incorporating 265 merchant ships were dispatched to the Soviet Union, along with 11 vessels sailing as independents. The losses were significant with sixty merchant ships failing to make port. On the return leg 22 ships were lost in nine convoys with 27 vessels travelling independently. One convoy, PQ 17 (27 June-10 July) was virtually destroyed losing 22 of its 36 merchant ships, plus one of the three rescue ships attached to the convoy,[22] after it was dispersed on 4 July (following signal from the Admiralty at 21.21hrs) in anticipation of an attack by major German warships at some point after 02.00 on 5 July. The danger of an attack was considerable as Milan Vego has set out in his 2016 article on 'The Destruction of Convoy PQ 17' in the *Naval War College Review*.[23] The weight of intelligence, and a build-up of attacks from aircraft and submarines, suggested to Pound that an attack on the convoy by German heavy units was developing).[24] In order to give the convoy time to scatter he gave the order before confirmation of imminent attack had been received. In fact, the German ships were not at sea, and eventually the order for the operation against the convoy was cancelled (5 July 21.32hrs), partly because with the convoy scattered the likely returns on a sortie were outweighed by danger to the German heavy ships, particularly from British and Russian submarines. In the event, the submarines of the Kriegsmarine, and the aircraft of the Luftwaffe (around 170), were more than enough to deal with the merchant ships of PQ 17 undefended by warships. The ruling of the House of Lords in the court case that resulted from the publication of David Irving's PQ 17 in 1968 gave an excellent summation of the causes of the disaster:

> It is sufficient to say that the primary cause of the disaster flowed from an order to the convoy to scatter, which made the ships in it an easy prey to the aircraft and submarines by which they were attacked. This order to scatter was issued by the Admiralty in Whitehall and was due to a faulty appreciation by the Naval Staff, in particular, as is now known, by the then First Sea Lord himself, that the German battleship *Tirpitz* was at sea, and to a decision, also by the then First Sea Lord, to take the responsibility for the order on himself rather than leave the decision to the discretion of the naval officers on the spot. The naval officers on the spot, including Admiral Hamilton in command of the Cruiser Squadron, and Captain Broome, had no option but to obey, and the convoy was thus left to fan out on individual courses covering a vast area of sea.[25]

The order for the convoy to scatter, the tragic repercussions and the sense that merchant ships had been abandoned to their fate, left a lasting mark. Within the American Merchant Marine PQ 17 became known as the "Fourth of July" Convoy whose ships had been "left alone" by the escorts.[26] Within the escorting forces there was a sense of shame, even if it had been at the behest of the Admiralty. For example, the signals officer on HMS *Offa* later recalled his horror as 'three ghastly signals arrived from the Admiralty… like something burning in your hand'.[27] On the bridge of the destroyer there was consternation:

We simply couldn't understand it. It was a most, most beautiful day, maximum visability and in naval tactics you only scatter a convoy when it is in danger of imminent danger of surface attack.... It was totally against our instincts ... So we debated what we should do ... We did consider pretending to be broken down and going back to join the convoy. We were doing this awful day and as we went away we heard the ships being bombed hit by submarines, torpedoed etc.[28]

The material losses were considerable as the convoy had been carrying 4,600 tanks and vehicles, 300 aircraft and 150,000 tonnes of general cargo. The losses, and the disruption to the convoy cycle, had ramifications in Britain, did a great deal of damage to inter-Allied relations, and raised questions over the Admiralty's handling of the convoy that would be exploited by later historians, most notably David Irving. Even today PQ 17 remains an on-going area of publication, documentary-making and debate. It continues to encapsulate the full horrors of the Arctic convoys with merchant seamen facing the extremes of climate, protracted enemy attack and the prospect of a freezing death in ice cold waters or sat in a water-logged lifeboat in the midst of sub-zero temperatures.

The Arctic convoys would be discontinued until 2 September 1942 when convoy PQ 18 departed (with a strong escort and aircraft carrier group in support) from Loch Ewe, Scotland. The convoy was successfully fought through to its destination, but a follow up convoy was not dispatched until December. The eagerness of the German Armed forces to continue to contest the route resulted in the Battle of the Barents Sea as convoy JW 51B, which had sailed from Loch Ewe on 22 December, encountered two German heavy cruisers and six destroyers on 31 December. Five ships from the 17th Destroyer Flotilla had joined the convoy on Christmas Day as reinforcement to the existing escort and in anticipation of a potential engagement with German surface ships. Six days later on New Year's Eve JW 51A was attacked by the heavy cruisers *Lützow* and *Admiral Hipper* supported by six destroyers (*Friedrich Eckholdt, Richard Beitzen, Theodor Riedel, Z29, Z30* and *Z31*). Skillfully handled against the German heavy ships the convoy's escort succeeded in protecting the merchant ships until the arrival of cruisers HMS *Sheffield* and HMS *Jamaica* (part of a covering force) persuaded German units to withdraw. British losses in the Battle of the Barents Sea amounted to one destroyer and a minesweeper with the Germans also losing a destroyer. Critically, no merchant ships had been sunk and on 4 January all 13 merchant vessels of the convoy arrived at the Kola Inlet.

Arctic Convoys Phase 3 April 1943-May 1945

During the final stage of the Arctic Convoy operations the balance tipped very rapidly in favour of the Allies. In April-May 1943 the tide of battle in the Atlantic turned decisively against the U-Boats with a rising tide of losses forcing their temporary withdrawal from the convoy lanes. This meant that Arctic convoys could be sailed with stronger escort forces including more destroyers, and with cruisers and capital ships (battleships and aircraft carriers) providing distant cover in case of potential intervention by German heavy ships.

At the same time the Germans lost their remaining heavy units in Norwegian waters with battlecruiser *Scharnhorst* being sunk on 26 December 1943 at the Battle of North Cape, and Battleship *Tirpitz* on 12 November 1944 in Tromsø Fjord following hits with tallboy bombs by RAF Lancasters from No.9 and No.617 Squadrons (attacks by Royal Navy submarines in September 1943, and the Fleet Air Arm in April 1944 had already reduced her to the status of little more than a floating gun battery).

During the final months of the war 18 outbound convoys (485 merchant vessels) suffered just five merchant ships lost, with 18 returning convoys comprising some 454 merchant ships losing just eight ships. The last convoy JW 67 left the Clyde on 12 May arriving at the Kola Inlet on 20 May with no losses from its 26 merchant ships.

Arctic Convoys Overall

During the course of 1941 to 1945 78 convoys had journeyed to and from the North Russian ports, and 85 merchant ships and 24 Allied warships had been lost including the cruisers HMS *Edinburgh* and HMS *Trinidad*. In terms of cargoes 4.5m metric tonnes of cargo had arrived in North Russia with 7,000 aircraft and 5,000 tanks. In trying to stop the flow of aid the Kriegsmarine had lost lost 38 ships (including 31 U-boats). During the course of the Arctic campaign there was a steady improvement in Allied fortunes and capabilities, partly aided by developments in the wider war. To meet the aerial threat merchant ships received enhanced anti-aircraft armament, and fighter cover improved from that provided by catapult assisted merchant ships (CAM Ships) to the provision of aircraft carriers in screening forces to provide fighter protection. Likewise, to safeguard against attack by the Kriegsmarine convoys were protected by anti-submarine trawlers and destroyers with covering forces which could include cruisers up to battleships such as HMS *King George V*. These vessels benefited from constant improvements in allied capabilities ranging from improved intelligence via ULTRA, long range photo-reconnaissance, improvements to radar, ASDIC, HF/DF and anti-submarine weapons such as hedgehog and squid.

The Germans, meanwhile, were handicapped by a reluctance on the part of Hitler and the navy to commit the remaining heavy ships of the Kriegsmarine, repeated damage to the *Tirpitz* which steadily reduced the capacity of the battleships and ultimately the collapse of the Eastern Front which resulted in the *Lützow* and other vessels being transferred to the Baltic to provide shore bombardment against the advancing Red Army. The capability of the Luftwaffe in Norway likewise gradually diminished, as squadrons were taken away to cope with other threats in the Mediterranean and on the Eastern Front.

Evolution of the Russian Convoys: The Diplomatic and Political Perspective

The Battle Summary which follows this introduction is written from the perspective of the naval professionals of the Royal Navy using the knowledge available up to 1954. Some of the writers and contributors to the study were aware of the significance of ULTRA, secret intelligence derived from German enigma code-breaking activities at Bletchley Park. That would remain classified secret until the 1970s so the potential importance of ULTRA to understanding Allied decisions around the Russian Convoys, and especially around Convoy PQ 17, could not feature in a publication circulating within the Royal Navy with only a 'Restricted' security classification. The authors also had only partial sight of some of the diplomatic context that lay behind the running of the convoys. Since diplomatic and political imperatives for both the Allies and Axis impacted on the conduct of the convoys this section charts the resultant pressures so that the naval and diplomatic stories of the Arctic convoys can be read in parallel.

Within hours of the German attack on the Soviet Union different parts of the British Government, especially the Ministry of Economic Warfare, had begun to evaluate likely Soviet needs in terms of supplies and shipping over the coming weeks and months. That process of intense planning and liaison, first between government departments, and later between the Allies intensified as Stalin pressed his new friends in the West for supplies.[29] Lord Hankey's Committee for the Co-ordination of Allied Supplies played a pivotal role in the early framing of British war supplies to the Soviet Union. The relationship between the Western Allies and the Soviet Union was, however, never easy and this would continue throughout the war with some members of the Soviet Government reacting almost personally to any delay, cancellation, loss or any other perceived inadequacy on the part of the British and Americans on meeting the Soviet Union's war requirements.

The desperate straits which the Soviet Union found itself in following the German attack on 22 June were challenging to say the least. Although a British-Soviet agreement was signed on 12 July 1941, which provided for mutual assistance and a commitment not to negotiate peace 'separately with the enemy', in the summer of 1941 Churchill could not dismiss the possibility of Stalin accepting a separate Russo-German peace.[30] Day-after-day, week-after-week the Soviet Armed Forces found themselves being driven back towards Moscow, Leningrad and through Ukraine and the Crimea. Soviet losses ran into the tens of thousands every week in the Summer and Autumn of 1941 for men killed, captured or wounded, with acres of territory being lost to the invaders. In time the cargoes delivered by convoy to the North Russian ports would make a material contribution on the battlefield, but in the meantime they could, at the very least, help to maintain Soviet morale as they suffered hammer blows at the hands of the German Armed Forces.

Churchill was determined to forge a good working understanding with Stalin. On 25 July 1941 the British Prime Minister wrote personally to Stalin to say that the Cabinet had approved the transfer to the Soviet Union of 200 Tomahawk P40 fighter aircraft even though it would 'seriously deplete' British stocks.[31] He ended his telegram with particularly warm words: 'We are watching with admiration and emotion Russia's magnificent fight, and all our information shows the heavy losses and concern of the enemy. Our air attack on Germany will continue with increasing strength'.[32] Reference to 'our air attack' was revealing as Churchill was already pushing the service ministries for their opinion on opening a second European front against Germany.

The signature of the Atlantic charter following the meeting between Churchill and Roosevelt at Placentia Bay of the coast of Canada (9-12 August) was the cause of some annoyance on Stalin's part. The conclusion of a separate agreement between the British and the Americans, constituting as it did a set of war aims between the democracies, did not seem to be entirely in the spirit of the British Soviet agreement of July.[33]

On 27 August 1941 the War Cabinet's Chiefs of Staff committee gave consideration as to whether it was possible to intervene on the European continent in order to relieve some of the pressure on Soviet forces in the East.[34] In September 1941 Lord Beaverbook, the Minister of Supply, arrived in Moscow as part of a British mission to the Soviet Union.[35] Churchill went to considerable lengths to explain to Stalin that Beaverbrook was a man he could do deals with: 'Lord Beaverbrook has the fullest confidence of the Cabinet, and is one of my oldest and most intimate friends'.[36] Stalin and Beaverbrook got on well to the extent that the latter rather fell under the spell of the Soviet leader. By the end of October Stalin was questioning why the British did 'not send a force to Archangel or the Ukraine' to join in the fight alongside the Red Army.[37]

As convoys began to arrive in late 1941 Churchill was anxious to ensure that there was no repeat of the First World War when Allied convoys arrived in North Russia only to languish in and around the ports without being transhipped to the front where they were needed. On 4 November he wrote to Stalin: 'I hope our supplies are being cleared from Archangel as fast as they come in. A trickle is now beginning through Persia. We shall pump both ways to our utmost'.[38]

During the winter of 1941-42 German opposition to the Arctic convoys became more of a problem and by late April 1942 the British were finding considerable difficulties in maintaining the cycle of convoys to and from Russia. Reducing the size of the convoy offered one potential route forward, as did reducing the convoy cycle down to three convoys every two months. It was eventually decided to reduce the size of convoys down to 25 ships so that they could be sufficiently well protected and kept manageable in the harsh conditions.[39] The logic of this would be that certain kinds of cargo would have to be prioritised. This in turn, led to a degree of political pressure to increase the size of convoys, and buoyed by the initial results of convoy PQ 15 (16 April to 5 May: 25 merchant ships – 3 lost) the Admiralty agreed to consider increasing the size of convoys to 35 vessels.[40] The decision was made partly under pressure from the United States Chief of Naval Operations Fleet Admiral Ernest J. King, who urged Admiral of the Fleet Dudley Pound (First Sea Lord) to run at least one more convoy in May to clear a backlog of cargoes and ships ('107 ships loaded or being loaded' in Allied ports) waiting for passage to Russia.[41]

PQ 16 (21-30 May), the convoy which followed the resolution of the 35-ship convoy debate, was badly mauled in a succession of aerial attacks which left seven ships sunk and three damaged with only 25 reaching the North Russian Ports in good order. As the scale of the attack on the convoy unfolded Stalin went out of his way to assure Churchill: 'With regard to the measures concerning protection of convoys you may rest assured that in this respect everything possible on our side will be done now and in the future'.[42] Despite the losses, with German forces renewing their advance in the summer of 1942 there could be no let-up in the cycle of convoys. Indeed, in early June President Roosevelt expressed to Churchill his 'great concern' at the situation on the 'Russian front'.[43] The severe mauling of convoy PQ 17 in late June/early July (rated as 'totally destroyed' at the Naval Conference on 26 August 1942), came at a moment of tension that had been building up over several months in terms of the fighting on the land, and the developing campaign in the Arctic.[44] It was blow of unexpected magnitude, at a moment of acute sensitivity, and in circumstances which invited Inter-Allied antagonism.

The Destruction of PQ 17: Allied Reactions

The fate of Convoy PQ 17 caused considerable disquiet in both London and Moscow, especially because it appeared by early July that the Germans might be planning an offensive to seize Murmansk.[45] On 9 July as the fate of the disaster was becoming clear the Soviet Ambassador in London visited Sir Anthony Eden, the Foreign Secretary. The ambassador was 'perturbed' at the scale of the losses even though Eden tried to suggest that German reports as to their successes against the convoy were always over-inflated by a considerable margin.[46] The pressure on Churchill for a reconsideration of the Russian convoys increased on 14 July when Jan Smuts, the South African Prime Minister, wrote to Churchill to warn that, while the obvious thing was to reinforce escort forces on the Arctic convoy routes, and to give Russia every assistance, it might be better not to 'put too many eggs into that basket'.[47] With growing concerns about sending a successor convoy, given the dangers, there was concern in the Foreign Office about how the Russians would react to postponement or delays to the convoy cycle.[48] There were a series of conversation between Churchill, the First Lord of the Admiralty and First Sea Lord about how to proceed.[49] When informed on 18 July that there would be a delay in resuming the convoys to North Russia Stalin expressed his anger. On 24 July the British Ambassador in Moscow warned that the Soviet Ambassador in London would deliver the response and that they could expect it to be: 'pretty hot'.[50] Indeed, it was:

> I received your message of 18 July. Two conclusions could be drawn from it. First, the British Government refuses to continue the sending of war materials to the Soviet Union via the Northern route. Second, in spite of the agreed communique concerning the urgent tasks of creating a second front in 1942, the British Government postpones this matter until 1943.

> Our naval experts consider the reasons put forward by the British naval experts to justify the cessation of convoys to the Northern ports of the USSR wholly unconvincing. They are of the opinion that with goodwill and readiness to fulfil the contracted obligations these convoys could be regularly undertaken and heavy losses could be inflicted on the enemy. Our experts find it also difficult to understand and to explain the order given by the Admiralty that the escorting vessels of the PQ 17 should return whereas the cargo boats should disperse and try to reach the Soviet ports one by one without any protection at all ...

> With regard to the second question, ie the question of creating a second front in Europe I am afraid it is not being treated with the seriousness it deserves. Taking fully in the account the present position on the Soviet-German front, I must state in the most emphatic manner that the Soviet Government cannot acquiesce in the postponement of a second front in Europe until 1943.

> I hope you will not feel offended that I expressed frankly and honestly my own opinion as well as the opinion of my colleagues on the question raised in your message.[51]

The situation was so awkward that within the circles of the British Government it was decided that it was better to postpone final decisions on the matter until a planned meeting between Churchill and Stalin in August.

This did not, however, prevent the Russians from continuing to press for more supplies. Raw materials such as aluminium and pig iron were in short supply, and machine tools had been lost to the German advance.[52] Churchill did his best to assuage Stalin's anger at the delay in aid when he arrived in Moscow on a converted B24 Liberator bomber on 12 August for his first summit with the Russian leader. The Prime Minister was painfully well aware of the strength of Stalin's opinion on the temporary suspension of the convoys. Equally he was worried by Admiralty concerns about whether the convoys could be fought through at reasonable cost, especially given the demands of convoying in the Atlantic, while meeting the needs of convoy operations to Malta, and in support of the Torch landings in North Africa.[53] At the Moscow Summit the latter was to prove Churchill's trump card. While he had to assuage Stalin that a delay to the convoy cycle was inevitable, and that there could be no immediate second front in Europe, he was able to surprise and delight the Soviet leader with news of imminent landings in North Africa.[54] The outcome of the meeting could not have been better as Sir Alexander Cadogan, the Permanent Under Secretary at the Foreign Office noted in a letter:

> Firstly – and most important – I think the two great men really made contact and got on terms. Certainly Winston was impressed, and I think that feeling was reciprocated. It's very difficult to get on terms through interpreters ... Anyhow, conditions have been established in which messages exchanged between the two will mean twice as much, or more, then they did before.[55]

The Russian government was also busy trying to assess the implications of PQ 17, and their appreciation of the situation was not helped by a report on 23 August into 'British and American Seamen in the Port of Archangel'. Published in *History Today*, after the end of the cold war, and written by the Deputy Head of the Department of Propaganda and Agitation of the Central Committee of the All-Union Communist Party, it drew on conversations with merchant seamen (British, American and Russian). The report depicted the behaviour of non-Russian seamen on the convoy in particularly harsh terms:

> The convoy sailed from a port in Iceland, was well armed and was accompanied by a large number of warships and aircraft. As soon as they sighted the first German reconnaissance plane, and then a bomber, the warships and aircraft started back for the shores of Iceland. The convoy dispersed ... and the German planes were offered the opportunity to shoot them down one by one. The crews

took no steps to defend the steamers and often abandoned them while they were undamaged, and there were cases when British submarines torpedoed British transport ships with cargo after the crews had got into lifeboats. Eleven Soviet seamen from the sunken ship Kiev witnessed how a ship peacefully rocking on the waves abandoned by its crew disappeared behind the horizon totally undamaged.[56]

In Soviet eyes the report, which contained significant inaccuracies, gross distortions and a constant criticism of the Anglo-Americans was confirmation of a lack of Allied commitment to the cause of Soviet victory, already fed by suspicions that the British and Americans could always find reason to deny this, or that, specific request for aid.

With considerable diplomatic fallout from the losses on Convoy PQ 17 there was considerable determination in London and Washington to ensure the success of Convoy PQ 18, set to depart from Loch Ewe in Scotland on 2 September. On 26 August President Roosevelt expressed his concern to the British Ambassador in Washington, Lord Halifax that not even the preparations for the Allied invasion of North Africa, could be allowed to interfere in ensuring that PQ 18 sailed with the heaviest possible escort.[57] The volume of material to be carried in the convoy was considerable as one Foreign Office official minuted: 'This convoy carries the whole of the British June quota together with the bulk allotment of ammunition for weapons already in the USSR and a large consignment (at least 1,200 tons) of aircraft spares on the new scale'.[58]

As PQ 18 was being fought towards its destination Churchill encouraged Stalin to support the convoy with whatever means were necessary. Stalin responded: 'I understand all importance of safe arrival of convoy PQ 18 in Soviet Union and necessity of taking measures for its defence. Difficult as it is for us to transfer at the present moment an additional number of long-range bombers for this task we have decided to do so'.[59] On its arrival, largely intact, there was considerable satisfaction at the success of the mission to fight through PQ 18. The official newspaper of the Communist Party, *Pravda*, carried the story under the headline: 'Fighting Alliance of Soviet and British Sailors'.[60] Nevertheless, the Admiralty and British Government were very tentative in their thoughts about running further convoys in the near future with their resourcing, and effective protection, imposing significant demands on the wider British and war efforts.[61] Indeed, with British forces heavily committed to Operation Torch planned for November 1942 it was considered unlikely that a further convoy could be sent through in the short term. Harry Hopkins, Franklin Roosevelt's personal trouble-shooter, warned Churchill on 23 September against potentially offending Stalin by extended delay to the next convoy.[62] Hopkins argued: 'what is said to Stalin now and what firm commitments we are prepared to make may well be [a] turning point in the war'.[63] The British Ambassador in Moscow expressed alarm at the idea that the next convoy might be delayed on 2 October. He argued that the postponing 'of the next convoy would create worst impression here and I do not believe that anything Maisky or I could say to [the] Soviet Government would convince them that we could not despatch it if we wanted to'.[64] This increased the diplomatic temperature between London, Moscow and Washington with the Russians protesting, providing cryptic responses and then falling silent.

The irritation between the Allies was palpable. Stalin on 13 October sent Churchill the briefest note acknowledging his telegram of 9 October.[65] With some sense of alarm the British ambassador in Moscow was left trying to find out what this terse communication meant.[66] Churchill wrote to Eden, British Foreign Secretary, on 25 October: 'I am meditating another telegram to Stalin, asking exactly what he means by his reply: "Thank you".[67] Three days later on 28 October, and still lacking clear communications from Moscow, President Roosevelt commented to Churchill: 'I am not unduly disturbed about our respective responses or lack of responses from Moscow. I have decided they do not use speech for the same purposes that we do'.[68]

The Convoys Restart JW 51A and JW 51B

It was not until December that the convoys to North Russia would be restarted. By late November, with the Torch landings and development of a bridgehead successful, the British and Americans were trying to put together a convoy.[69] Getting together a large convoy in the right place at the right time for dispatch to Russia would, however, prove very difficult given all the other demands, including the need to maintain the flow of goods across the Atlantic. This was explained to Sir Anthony Eden, the Foreign Secretary on 3 December.[70] The convoy would eventually sail in two halves. Convoy JW 51A sailed from Loch Ewe on 15 December with 16 merchant ships, a strong escort and a powerful covering force of cruisers and the battleship HMS *King George V*. Seemingly the convoy was not detected and it arrived safely at the Kola Inlet on 25 December. The successor convoy, JW 51B (15 merchant ships departing Loch Ewe on 22 December), would result in the Battle of the Barents Sea on 31 December 1942 with German forces being forced to withdraw from an action against the ships of the convoy following the arrival of British heavy units. The outcome of that withdrawal would have an added impact on the wider war at sea.

Impact of the Battle of the Barents Sea on the German High Command

If establishing and maintaining the flow of supplies to Russia convoys had caused considerable ructions within the higher political circles of the Allied High Command throughout 1941 and 1942, then by the start of 1943 it was the turn of the German High Command to experience the political fallout from Arctic convoy operations. Hitler had pressed the Kriegsmarine and Luftwaffe hard to do what they could to disrupt the flow of convoy traffic to North Russia. For him the war in the East was the inevitable and ultimate battle for Germany's national destiny: A fight between two nations underpinned by divergent political systems and by race. The failure to disrupt the convoy traffic in the latter part of 1942, and to repeat the success of German forces against PQ 17, was deeply troubling. Indeed, the failure of superior German forces in the Battle of the Barents Sea on 31 December 1942 against the destroyers of convoy JW 51B was a humiliation too far. For him it underlined a wider failure of the heavy surface ships of the Kriegsmarine. He was convinced that they represented poor value for the German war machine given their considerable cost and large crews, which limited their operational use to only those circumstances which were most favourable to their deployment. Their prestige value and Germany's difficulty in building replacements meant that they had to be used on relatively safe operations and, with the German submarine arm hard pressed to try and force a decision in the Atlantic, Hitler considered that the crews and resources might be better used elsewhere.

The Füehrer Naval Conference held on 6 January was Hitler's first opportunity after the Battle of the Barents Sea to make his displeasure known. Following a lengthy monologue on German naval history from 1870, Hitler demanded the decommissioning of the German heavy ships with their guns used to form new coastal batteries and their crews sent away to join the U-Boats and smaller surface vessels.[71] The head of the German Navy, Grand Admiral Raeder, refused Hitler's demands and resigned. His replacement on 20 January was Admiral Karl Dönitz (the head of the submarine arm). In many ways Dönitz was, as Jak Mallmann Showell has argued, a slightly odd choice to be the new head of the Kriegsmarine. Dönitz had little experience of the Naval High Command in Berlin because the U-Boat war had kept him in France since 1940.[72] Despite the fact that he was a submariner, Dönitz saw value in continuing to keep the heavy ships and he was eventually able to win over Hitler to keep them in operation. Nevertheless, the replacement of Raeder with Dönitz did have important consequences for the Kriegsmarine which would prove to be out of all proportion to the impact on the battlefield of the cargoes of the 15 merchant vessels of the convoy.

Of direct significance to the Arctic convoys was Dönitz's contention, which he was well placed to pursue after he took over the leadership of the Kriegsmarine, that a submarine deployed in the North was one less submarine which he could deploy to the critical battleground of the Atlantic sealanes. Even before the fall of Raeder Dönitz was pushing to redeploy submarines tasked against the Arctic convoys to Atlantic duties. As he explained to Raeder in December 1942:

> Between January 1 and November 30 1942 these boats [in the North] had sunk 262,614 tons in their own operations area. An equal number of boats in the Atlantic, however, had sunk approximately 910,000 tons during the same period. By employing these boats in the Arctic we had, therefore, sunk something like 650,000 tons less than we might have done ... Our failure to grasp the opportunity of achieving so potentially large a success adversely affected our war effort as a whole and was of great value to the enemy, particularly in view of the fact that these same freighters which traversed the Arctic also had to pass through the Atlantic.[73]

At Dönitz's urging as the new head of the German Navy, Hitler eventually gave permission to reduce the number of U-Boats operating against the Arctic convoys.

Beyond the Battle of the Barents Sea

Following the Battle of the Barents Sea, convoy JW 53 (26 ships leaving Loch Ewe on 15 February) was beset by heavy seas with storm damage causing 6 of the 28 ships to turn back. This caused some resentment in

Russian circles with the Russian ambassador to London attacking the Secretary of State for Transport, Lord Leathers.[74] The situation was complicated further by the fact that Leathers was already having to reduce the number of vessels allocated to convoy JW 54 from 15 to 10 because only some 210 tanks were ready to ship to Russia, as opposed to the 350 promised for delivery per convoy.[75]

The heat towards Lord Leathers and others over the conduct of the Arctic convoys did not only come from the Soviet side. For example, on 3 February 1943 in the House of Lords, Lord Beaverbrook, Lord Privy Seal outside the Cabinet and former Minister of Aircraft Production (May 1940-May 1941) and Minister of Supply (June 1941-February 1942), demanded greater support for the Soviet Union. He had been considerably impressed with the Soviet Union, with Stalin and the Russian people on a visit to Moscow in 1941. He argued in the House of Lords: 'Something much greater must be done ... so that Russia may win battles. We must get supplies there. It is no use saying that the convoy system is difficult, that the road is long, that the path is over the sea, and that ships are difficult to come by'.[76] This was quite a remarkable episode with a senior government official effectively attacking his own government over perceived inadequacies in the supplies being sent to aid Russia.

By the summer of 1943 the Soviet Union continued to request war materials, but were now able, in the light of experience and their own growing production, to be more selective in the types of aid they requested. Thus, in the summer of 1943 a plea for additional tanks was made in the form of a specific request for Valentine tanks, with any shortfall being made up by a particular mark of Sherman rather than Churchills, Centaurs or Matildas which were considered unsuitable for winter conditions.[77] Soviet armed forces had a very keen perception of what worked well within their own climate and within their armed forces. To some extent this eased relations between the Allies. The Soviets could find uses for tanks such as the Valentine (as second line infantry tanks) and Bell Airacobras P-39 fighters (a low altitude fighter suited to the Eastern front) while the British and Americans preferred other types.

Summer of 1943: Another Break in the Convoy Cycle

Interruption to the flow of convoys in the late summer of 1943 again brought complaints from Moscow that there was no reason why the convoys should be delayed and that with Russia pushing forward with offensives 'for the third successive month' that supplies were urgently needed.[78] By October 1943 Anglo-Russian relations had deteriorated to the point where a telegram from Churchill on 1 October met with a rather undiplomatic response. The British Ambassador in Moscow reflected that the 'message seems to have caught Stalin in [a] rough mood'.[79] Eden informed Churchill that he proposed to 'hand back the offensive message from Stalin' saying that he had 'no wish to receive it'.[80] The Admiralty meanwhile was very concerned not to over commit themselves with operations in the Atlantic and Mediterranean on-going, and with a need to set aside sufficient forces for the invasion of Western Europe in the summer of 1944.[81]

The sinking of the *Scharnhorst* in December 1943 brought mutual celebration in both London and Moscow. As soon as he had received confirmation of the sinking Churchill wrote to Stalin: 'The Arctic convoys to Russia have brought us luck. Yesterday enemy attempted to intercept with battle cruiser *Scharnhorst*. Commander-in-Chief Fraser with the *Duke of York* (35,000 ton battleship) cut off Scharnhorst's retreat and after an action sank her'.[82] As Churchill was aware the sinking of the German vessel had significant impacts in the strategic balance so far as the Russian convoys were concerned, although the RAF and Royal Navy were hesitant to decrease the number of aircraft covering the Arctic convoy routes.[83]

By January 1944 there were concerns in the Admiralty at the slow speed with which ships arriving in Russia were being unloaded.[84] This was resulting in ships missing the return convoys with further potential impacts on the convoy cycle, and the approach of D-Day in the Spring and Summer of early 1944 disrupted the convoy cycle once again. However, buoyed by the prospect of a new front in Western Europe Stalin was unusually appreciative. On 10 May he wrote to Churchill to express his appreciation of the 'organisation of the convoys which have delivered cargoes to Soviet northern ports'.[85] on 25 May 1944 Churchill wrote to Stalin to inform him that there were hopes to establish a new convoy programme but that 'I must see first what we lose in destroyers and cruisers in the sea part of Overlord'.[86]

Following D-Day, and the with German Armies subject to repeated offensives along the Eastern front there was considerable satisfaction at the apparent decrease in the threat to the Arctic lifeline to Russia. Indeed, on 12 November Churchill was able to send a telegraph to Stalin to inform him 'RAF bombers have sunk *Tirpitz*. Let us rejoice together'.[87]

The death of the *Tirpitz* did not, however, signal any kind of German abandonment of its positions in Norway on the flank of the Arctic convoys. While much of the attention of the Kriegsmarine focussed on the Baltic, and the battle to contain Soviet forces, the number of submarines in Norway remained considerable all the way to the end of the war. Their focus was, however, on the Battle of the Atlantic, and the defence of Norway, rather than interrupting the Arctic convoys. The outcome of the French campaign, and hopes to reinvigorate the Atlantic campaign with next generation submarines being produced by the German yards, placed an added emphasis on retaining the U-Boat bases in Norway.[88] The war would, however, draw to a close before the next generation submarines could enter service in sizeable numbers, with the last Arctic convoy sailing in May 1945.

Did the Supplies Carried by the Russian Convoys Make a Difference?

There can be no doubt that Allied convoys to Russia were enormously costly, but perhaps the ultimate question is to determine whether they made a difference to the outcome on the Eastern front and thus the war. The fact that there has been a heated, and long running debate around this question, marks the Arctic convoys out as unusual in terms of the scholarship of maritime operations. As David Morgan-Owen and Louis Halewood have noted recently: 'historians have so far only scratched the surface of the dynamic between economic warfare at sea and operational-level fighting on land'.[89] The scale of the amount of aid delivered is impressive. In November 1942 it was estimated that the following Anglo-American aid had reached Russia over the course of the previous twelve months: 'aircraft – 3.052; tanks 4,084; vehicles 30,031'.[90] Along with these impressive totals was 831,000 deadweight tons of miscellaneous cargo. This included:

> anti-tank guns, machine-guns, spares for aircraft and tanks, shells and small arms ammunition, as well as substantial quantities of various naval, military and air force stores of all kinds. There were also steel products and machinery, machine tools and electrical equipment, quantities of non-ferrous metals(including aluminium, brass, copper, zinc, nickel and tin), besides medical supplies and basic foodstuffs.[91]

With parts of the Soviet Union facing severe food shortages even before the German invasion of 1941, the importance of the latter (4.64 million long tons between 1941 and 1945) cannot easily be dismissed.[92]

These figures are as potentially significant as they are impressive. Just 9 days later Soviet forces would launch operation Uranus to cut off German forces in the City of Stalingrad. That offensive and the eventual surrender of German forces in Stalingrad in February 1942 would mark the turning point in the East, so the deliveries from November 1941 to November 1942 represented the critical period in which Soviet forces would turn the prospect of defeat into the prospect of eventual victory.

Like much else with the Russian convoys questions around the significance of the Allied contribution have been mired in historical controversy, influenced by the politics of the cold war. As Roger Munting noted in 1984 post-war Soviet analysts placed the level of Allied support for the Russian war effort at 'about twelve per cent of aeroplanes, ten per cent of tanks and less than two per cent of artillery', or around four percent of Soviet wartime production.[93] Munting noted that while the figures were widely accepted there were considerable problems in understanding their accuracy ranging from fluctuating exchange rates, the difficulty of comparing the military value on a like-for-like basis of Soviet and Allied equipment, the problem of comparing the significance of war deliveries against a background of a fluctuating war, and the fact that some of the information involved in the calculations had not been released by Soviet historians. His conclusion was that: 'It is nonsense to repeat the figure of four per cent of Soviet wartime production and disingenuous to disparage western aid – a feature evident in Soviet literature and one criticized even by Khrushchev'.[94] A balanced overall analysis would suggest that, while in certain areas such as the provision of tanks (around 13,000 tanks including 4,102 M4 Shermans were supplied by the United States and Britain to Russia),[95] Lend-Lease provided a useful supplement to the thousands of vehicles produced by the Soviet Union (around 12% of the armoured fighting vehicles used by the Red Army), in other areas the contribution was truly decisive. For example, while the Americans and British supplied around 19,000 aircraft to the Soviet Union (around 30% of the fighters and bombers utilised by the Red Air Force) the United States supplied 58% of the aviation gasoline, half of the TNT and 93% of the railway equipment. The overall figures also hide the fact while the vast majority of supplies reached the Soviet Union to support the Red Army drives of 1943 to

1945, and thus after the turning point of the Battle of Stalingrad, the supplies that reached North Russia in 1941 and 1942 were desperately needed by Red Forces being repeatedly defeated by the German Armed Forces.

Year	Tons of Supplies Delivered
1941	360,778
1942	2,453,097
1943	4,794,545
1944	6,217,622
1945	3,673,819
Total	17,499,861

In the aftermath of the cold war there has been a noticeable narrowing of the differences between Russian and Western historians with greater availability of sources and a desire to build bridges forging some sort of consensus around the idea that Anglo-American aid was more important than was generally recognised during the Soviet era, but that it cannot be considered absolutely crucial to the outcome on the Eastern Front. As Alexander Hill noted in an article in the journal *Military History* in 2007

> It would be difficult and unconvincing to argue that Lend-Lease aid "saved" the Soviet Union from defeat in 1941. Axis forces were, for instance, halted before Moscow with Soviet blood, and to a large extent with Soviet-manufactured arms and equipment. Nonetheless, as this article has suggested, Lend-Lease aid provided during the period of the First Moscow Protocol had a far more significant impact on the Soviet war effort and indeed on frontline capability both during and after the Battle for Moscow than the Soviet and indeed Western historiography would suggest.[96]

Likewise, from the Russian side since 1990 there has been an increasingly warm appreciation of the value of Anglo-American aid. On the 75th anniversary of the establishment of Anglo-American aid to the Soviet Union the Russian State News Agency RIA Novosti ran a story on its Russia Beyond web news site that highlighted the significance of the aid programme: 'Downplayed by the Soviet Union, the program was of vital importance to the USSR's war effort, as even Marshal Zhukov later admitted'.[97] The Russian commitment to celebrate the gallantry of those who took part in the Arctic Convoys, and to continue to award the Ushakov medal to the remaining handful of veterans, continues to be noteworthy.

Conclusion: The Less Tangible Contributions of the Arctic Convoys to Allied Victory

Beyond the significance of the Arctic Convoys to Allied victory at the diplomatic level, and in terms of their contribution to the equipment levels of the Red Army along the Eastern front, the accountancy of the Russian convoys also has to take on-board less tangible but equally significant contributions to victory. If Churchill, on the political level, was able to claim to Stalin that the heavy bomber offensive constituted a second front by air against Germany, drawing German fighting units and resources away from deployment on the Eastern Front, then the Russian convoys similarly constituted a seaborne front in the North. The Luftwaffe and Kriegsmarine deployed significant units to disrupt the convoy traffic that could have been utilised elsewhere. Submarines and surface ships deployed to Norwegian and Arctic waters were not operating against the Atlantic sealanes, off the coast of the United States, or further afield in the Indian Ocean. Likewise, Luftwaffe units based in Norway were not defending the Reich against streams of Anglo-American bombers or being used to support a hard-pressed German Army fighting along the Eastern front from the Baltic to the Black Sea. Similarly, the ability of the Royal Navy to operate close to Norway underlined its potential vulnerability to an Anglo-American landing, forcing the German Army to maintain substantial forces there instead of deploying them against Anglo-American and Russian armies. The Arctic front, and the German resources it tied down exemplified the seaborne threat which Anglo-American forces posed to the German Empire in Europe by 1943. With the Allies able to strike at almost any point on the coasts of Europe the German Empire was forced into defensive preparations across thousands of miles, while the Allies could pick and choose their moment and location at which to strike. The Arctic convoys demonstrate the utility of seapower to deliver significant strategic effects even while operations had to be conducted at the limits of human endurance in the harshest of climates, at the geographical extremes of the global battlefront.

Merchant Vessels Lost on the Arctic Convoys

American Vessels Lost (47)

Alamar
Alcoa Cadet
Alcoa Ranger
Andrew G. Curtin
Bellingham
Carlton
Christopher Newport
City of Joliet
Daniel Morgan
Edward H. Crockett
Effingham
Executive
Fairfield City
Graylock
Heffron
Henry Bacon
Honomu
Hoosier
Horace Bushnell
Horace Gray
Hybert
J L M Curry
John Penn
John Witherspoon
Kentucky
Mary Luckenbach
Massmar
Mormacsul
Oliver Ellsworth
Olopana
Oregonian
Pan Atlantic
Pan Kraft
Penelope Barker
Peter Kerr
Puerto Rican
Richard Bland
Silver Sword
Steel Worker
Syros

Thomas Donaldson
Thomas Scott
Wacosta
Washington
William Clark
William Hooper
William S Thayer

British Vessels Lost (36)

Aldersdale
Atheltemplar
Bolton Castle
Botavon
Cape Corso
Chulmleigh
Earlston
Empire Beaumont
Empire Byron
Empire Cowper
Empire Gilbert
Empire Howard
Empire Lawrence
Empire Purcell
Empire Ranger
Empire Sky
Empire Starlight
Empire Stevenson
Empire Tourist
Fort Bellingham
Goolistan
Gray Ranger
Harpalion
Hartlebury
Induna
Jutland
Lancaster Castle
Lowther Castle
Navarino
New Westminster City
Ocean Freedom

Ocean Voice
River Afton
Samsuva
Waziristan
Zaafaran

Russian Vessels Lost (11)

Dekabrist
Donbass
Ijora
Kiev
Krasny Partizan
Kuznetz Lesov
Rodina
Stalingrad
Sukhona
Tsiolkovsky
Ufa

Panamanian Vessels Lost (8)

Africander
Ballot
Bateau
El Capitan
El Occidente
Exterminator
Macbeth
Raceland

Dutch Vessels Lost (1)

Paulus Potter

Endnote

1. 37 Inbound from North Russia 42 Outbound.

2. 'Convoys to North Russia, 1942', Supplement to the *London Gazette,* 13 October 1950, Number 39041. pp.5139-5154.

3. David Irving, *The Destruction of Convoy PQ 17* (London: Cassell, 1968).

4. Angus Cunninghame Graham to Stephen Roskill, [undated] November 1968, Angus Cunninghame Graham papers, Churchill Archives, GBR/0014/ANCG II 4/1.

5. *See* 'Correspondence with solicitors, witnesses and potential witnesses, 1968-1974' and 'Legal Papers', Jackie Broome papers, Churchill Archives, GBR/0014/BRME 1-2, GBR/0014/BRME 3-4. For Boome's Action of PQ 17 *see* Jack Broome, *Convoy is to Scatter: The Story of PQ 17* (London: William Kimber, 1972).

6. 'Ushakov Medal for Arctic Convoy Veterans', Early Day Motion 630, tabled 24 October 2012, https://edm.parliament.uk/early-day-motion/44782/ushakov-medal-for-arctic-convoy-veterans, accessed 21 September 2021. Even today the Russian Embassy remains extremely grateful to those who had braved the enemy, the cold and the long distances to aid the Soviet Union in its hour of need as their website demonstrates: 'The Allied seamen showed true heroism in their long and perilous sea passages in convoys, being constantly attacked by enemy forces in the appalling weather conditions of the Arctic. The bravery of these men and women who unsparingly fought for the Victory will be always remembered and respected'.

   https://rusemb.org.uk/arcticalliedconvoys/&start=41&ps=10&ppp=15 [accessed 02/12/2021 and rechecked 14/05/2022].

7. The Bogatyr-class cruiser *Oleg* (6,975 long tons) was sunk on 17 June 1919 by torpedoes launched from Coastal Motor Boat *CMB-4* under the command of Captain Augustus Agar (he received the Victoria Cross for the action). *Pamiat Azova* was torpedoed and sunk the following month, on 18 August by *CMB-79* in Kronstadt Harbour.

8. Winston Churchill Broadcast on the Soviet-German War, 22 June 1941, https://www.jewishvirtuallibrary.org/churchill-broadcast-on-the-soviet-german-war-june-1941 [accessed 28 November 2021.]

9. Winston Churchill Broadcast on the Soviet-German War, 22 June 1941, https://www.jewishvirtuallibrary.org/churchill-broadcast-on-the-soviet-german-war-june-1941 [accessed 28 November 2021.

10. Sir Anthony Eden, adjournment debate, Parliamentary Debates [Commons], 24 June 1941, cols.971-4.

11. Brian P. Farrell, 'Yes, Prime Minister: Barbarossa, Whipcord, and the Basis of British Grand Strategy, Autumn 1941', *The Journal of Military History*, 57 (1993), pp.599-625. [604].

12. 'All Aid to Russia', *Baltimore News Post*, 10 October 1941, p.7.

13. Robert W. Coakley, 'The Persian Corridor as a Route for Aid to the USSR', in Kent Roberts Greenfield (ed.) *Command Decisions*, (Washington D.C.: United States Army Center of Military History, 1960). p.227.

14. T. H. Vail Motter, *The Persian Corridor and Aid to Russia: United States Army in World War II, Middle East Theatre*, (Washington D.C.: Centre of Military History, 1952), p.481.

15. Paul Kemp, *Convoy: Drama in Arctic Waters* (London: Arms and Armour Press, 1993), pp.235-237. Precise figures for all routes are given in T. H. Vail Motter, *The Persian Corridor and Aid to Russia*, p.481 (Persian Gulf, 23.8%; Vladivostock, 47.1%; Arctic Convoys, 22.7%; Black Sea, 3.9%; Soviet Arctic, 2.5%).

16. Milan Vego, 'The Destruction of Convoy PQ 17: 27 June-10 July 1942', *Naval War College Review*, 69 (2016), 83-141 [134].

17. For the details of individual convoys see Bob Ruegg and Arnold Hague, *Convoys to Russia 1941-1945* (Kendal: World Ships Society, 1992).

18. 'The Russia Run' in John Bunker, *Seafarers in World War II,* (Washington DC: Seafarers International Union in North America, 1951), 15-16 [16].

19. Admiral Karl Dönitz, *Memoirs: Ten Years and Twenty Days* (London: Cassell & Co, 2000), p.316.

20. 'War Cabinet, Weekly Resume of the Naval, Military and Air Situation', 6-13 August 1942, TNA: CAB66/27.

21. T. H. Vail Motter, *The Persian Corridor and Aid to Russia: United States Army in World War II, Middle East Theatre,* (Washington D.C.: Centre of Military History, 1952).

22. Merchant Ships of Convoy PQ17: *Alcoa Ranger* (US – sunk); *Azerbaijan* (USSR); *Bellingham* (US); *Benjamin Harrison* (US); *Bolton Castle* (British – sunk); *Carlton* (US – sunk); *Christopher Newport* (US – sunk); *Daniel Morgan* (US – sunk); *Donbass* (USSR); *Earlston* (UK – sunk); *El Capitan* (Panama – sunk); *Empire Byron* (British – sunk); *Empire Tide* (British); *Exford* (US – forced back to Reykjavík); *Fairfield City* (US – sunk); *Hartlebury* (British – sunk); *Honomu* (US – sunk); *Hoosier* (US – sunk); *Ironclad* (US); *John Witherspoon* (US – sunk); *Navarino* (British – sunk); *Ocean Freedom* (British); *Olopana* (US – sunk); *Pan Atlantic* (US – sunk); *Pan Kraft* (US – sunk); *Paulus Potter* (NL – sunk); *Peter Kerr* (US – sunk); *Richard Bland* (US – forced back to Reykjavík); *River Afton* (British – sunk); *Samuel Chase* (US); *Silver Sword* (US); *Troubador* (Panama); *Washington* (US – sunk); *West Gotomska* (US); *William Hooper* (US – sunk); *Winston-Salem* (US). Rescue Ships: *Rathlin* (British); *Zaafaran* (British - sunk); *Zamalek* (British).

23. M. Vego, 'The Destruction of Convoy PQ 17: 27 June-10 July 1942', *Naval War College Review* (July 2016).

24. Patrick Beesly, 'Convoy PQ 17: A Study of Intelligence and Decision-Making', *Intelligence & National Security*, 5 (1990), 292–322.

25. House of Lords ruling in Cassell and Company versus Broome and Another (HL23 February 1972), Jackie Broome papers, Churchill Archives, BRME 4/4.

26. 'PQ17' in Bunker, *Seafarers in World War II*, 25-27 [26].

27. Admiral Sir William O'Brien, https://www.youtube.com/watch?v=gorAbTLq7NY [accessed 5 December 2021]. See also 'Sir Admiral William O'Brien, The Times, 29 February 2016, https://www.thetimes.co.uk/article/admiral-sir-william-obrien-fhghdvhtj [accessed 5 December 2021].

28. Ibid.

29. *See* Lord Hankey Papers, 1941-42, TNA: CAB63/156-158.

30. Michael Reiman, *About Russia, Its Revolutions, Its Development and Its Present*, (Frankfurt Am Main: Peter Lang GmbH, 2015), p.137.

31. Churchill to Stalin, 25 July 1941, TNA: FO954/24B/353.

32. Ibid.

33. Reiman, *About Russia*, p. 138.

34. War Cabinet, Chiefs of Staff Committee, 27 August 1941, TNA: CAB79/13/49.

35. John Daniel Langer, 'The Harriman-Beaverbrook Mission and the Debate over Unconditional Aid for the Soviet Union, 1941', *Journal of Contemporary History*, 14 (1979), 463–482. Roger Munting, 'Lend-Lease and the Soviet War Effort', *Journal of Contemporary History*, 19 (1984), 495-510.

36. Churchill to Stalin, 21 September 1941, TNA: FO954/3A/6.

37. 'Military Aid for Russia (incorporating notes of conversation with Averell Harriman)', Memorandum by the Minister of Supply, 28 October 1941, TNA: CAB66/19.

38. Churchill to Stalin, 4 November 1941, TNA: FO954/24B/488.

39. Memorandum by William Averell Harriman (Advisor to President Roosevelt), 25 April 1942, TNA: FO954/3A/25.

40. Note for the Foreign Secretary on President Roosevelt's telegram, 27 April 1942, TNA: FO954/3A/30.

41. Churchill to Roosevelt, 30 April 1942, TNA: FO954/3A/44.

42. Stalin to Churchill, 28 May 1942, TNA: FO954/3A/70.

43. Roosevelt to Churchill, 12 June 1942, TNA: FO954/3A/71.

44. Conference of the C.-in-C., Navy with the Führer, 26 August 1942, Jak P. Mallman Showell, *Führer Conferences on Naval Affairs 1939-45* (London: Greenhill Books, 1990. p. 289.

45. War Cabinet, Conclusions, 8 July 1942, TNA: CAB85/26/33.

46. Eden to Sir Archibald Clark Kerr (British Ambassador in Kuibyshev), 9 July 1942, TNA: FO954/3A/82.

47. Smuts to Churchill, 14 July 1942, TNA: FO954/3A/83.

48. E. P. Donaldson (Foreign Office) to Eden, 21 August 1942, TNA: FO954/3A/95.

49. Ibid.

50. Sir Archibald Clark Kerr (British Ambassador in Kuibyshev) to Eden, 23 July 1942, TNA: FO954/3A/99.

51. Stalin to Churchill, 23 July 1942.TNA: PREM3/403/4.

52. Eden to Sir Archibald Clark Kerr (British Ambassador in Kuibyshev), 9 July 1942, TNA: FO954/3A/101.

53. 'Convoys to Russia', War Cabinet Memorandum WP (42) 344, by the First Lord of the Admiralty, 6 August 1942, TNA: CAB66/27/24.

54. On the 1942 Moscow Conference *see* Martin H. Folly, 'Seeking Comradeship in the "Ogre's Den": Winston Churchill's Quest for a Warrior Alliance and his Mission to Stalin', August 1942, Enter Text, 6 (2007), 276-303.

55. Cadogan to Lord Halifax (British Ambassador to Washington) 29 August 1942, TNA: FO1093/247.

56. 'Concerning British and American Seamen in the Port of Archangel', by Deputy Head of the Department of Propaganda and Agitation of the Central Committee of the All-Union Communist Party, 23 August 1942 reproduced in 'Through the eyes of Soviet Agitprop', *History Today*, September 1993, 21-27 [23].

57. Lord Halifax (British Ambassador in Washington) to Foreign Office, 25 August 1942, TNA: FO954/3A/118.

58. E. P. Donaldson (Foreign Office) to Eden, 21 August 1942, TNA: FO954/3A/115.

59. Stalin to Churchill, 9 September 1942, TNA: FO954/3A/122.

60. Sir Archibald Clark Kerr (British Ambassador in Kuibyshev) to the Foreign Office, 27 September 1942, TNA: FO954/3A/142.

61. E. P. Donaldson (Foreign Office) to Eden, 5 August 1942, TNA: FO954/3A/115.

62. Harry Hopkins to Churchill, 23 September 1942, TNA: FO954/3A/137.

63. Ibid.

64. Sir Archibald Clark Kerr (British Ambassador in Kuibyshev) to the Foreign Office, 2 October 1942, TNA: FO954/3A/147.

65. Stalin to Churchill, 13 October 1942, TNA: FO954/3A/175.

66. Sir Archibald Clark Kerr (British Ambassador in Kuibyshev) to the Foreign Office, 27 September 1942, TNA: FO954/3A/179.

67. Churchill to Eden, 25 October 1942, TNA: FO954/3A/185.

68. Roosevelt to Churchill, 28 October 1942, TNA: FO 954/3A/189.

69. E. P. Donaldson (Foreign Office) to Eden, 5 August 1942, TNA: FO954/3A/207.

70. E. P. Donaldson (Foreign Office) to Eden, 3 December 1942, TNA: FO954/3A/216.

71. Führer Naval Conference, 6 January 1943, Jak P. Mallman Showell, *Führer Conferences on Naval Affairs 1939-1945* (London: Greenhill Books, 1990), pp. 318-319.

72. Jak P. Mallmann Showell, *Dönitz, U-Boats, Convoys: The British Version of his Memoirs from the Admiralty's Secret Anti-Submarine Reports* (London: Frontline Books, 2013), pp. ix-x.

73. Dönitz, *Memoirs*, p. 316.

74. E. P. Donaldson (Foreign Office) to Eden, 25 February 1943, TNA: FO954/3B/330.

75. Lord Leathers (Secretary of State for Transport) to Eden, 9 February 1943, TNA: FO954/3B/310.

76. Lord Beaverbrook, Parliamentary Debates [Lords], 3 February 1943, cols. 930-934.

77. Minute for the Minister of Production 24 May 1943, enclosed in letter from E. P. Donaldson (Foreign Office) to Eden 24 May 1943, TNA: FO954/3B/461.

78. Sir Archibald Clark Kerr (British Ambassador in Kuibyshev), to the Foreign Office, 23 September 1943, TNA: FO954/3B/485.

79. Sir Archibald Clark Kerr (British Ambassador in Kuibyshev) to the Foreign Office, 14 October 1943, TNA: FO954/3B/503.

80. Eden to Churchill, 18 October 1943, TNA: FO954/3B/508.

81. Admiralty to Prime Minister, 26 September 1943, TNA: FO954/3B/486.

82. Churchill to Stalin, 27 December 1943, TNA: FO954/32B/422.

83. War Cabinet, Chiefs of Staff Committee, 5 January 1943, TNA: CAB79/69/3. War Cabinet, Chiefs of Staff Committee, 13 January 1944, TNA: CAB79/69/10. *See also* War Cabinet, Conclusions, 28 December 1943, TNA: CAB65/36/44.

84. Northern Department (Foreign Office) minutes, 3 January 1944, TNA954/3B/520.

85. Stalin to Churchill, 10 May 1944, TNA: FO954/3B/548.

86. Churchill to Stalin, 24 May 1944, TNA: FO954/3B/549. *See also* Stalin to Churchill, 28 May 1944, TNA: FO954/3B/550.

87. Churchill to Stalin, 12 November 1944, TNA: FO/954/26B/504.

88. Howard D. Grier, *Hitler, Dönitz and the Baltic Sea: The Third Reich's Last Hope, 1944-1945* (Annapolis [MD]: Naval Institute Press, 2007), pp. 189-191.

89. David Morgan-Owen, Louis Halewood, *Economic Warfare at Sea: Grand Strategies for Maritime Powers, 1650-1945*, (Liverpool: Liverpool University Press, 2020), p. 21.

90. Minute by E. P. Donaldson (Foreign Office), 10 November 1942, TNA: FO954/3A/198.

91. Ibid.

92. Roger Munting, 'Soviet Food Supply and Allied Aid in the War, 1941-45', *Soviet Studies*, 36 (1984), 582-593.

93. Roger Munting, 'Lend-Lease and the Soviet War Effort', *Journal of Contemporary History*, 19 (1984), 495-510.

94. Munting, 'Lend Lease', p. 506.

95. Lend-Lease Shipments: World War II, Section IIIB, (Washington D.C.: Published by Office, Chief of Finance, War Department, December 31, 1946), p. 8. and 'Russia (British Empire War Assistance)', House of Commons Debates, 16 April 1946, vol. 421, cc. 2513-9.

96. Alexander Hill, 'British Lend Lease Aid and the Soviet War Effort, June 1941 June 1942', *The Journal of Military History*, 71 (2007), 773-808. [808].

97. 'Lend-Lease: How American supplies aided the USSR in its darkest hour', 14 March 2016, https://www.rbth.com/defence/2016/03/14/lend-lease-how-american-supplies-aided-the-ussr-in-its-darkest-hour_575559 [accessed 16 December 2021].

Select Bibliography

Books

Beaumont, Joan. *Comrades in Arms: British Aid to Russia, 1941-1945* (London: Davis-Poynter, 1980).

Beitzell, Robert. *The Uneasy Alliance: America, Britain and Russia, 1941–1943* (New York: Knopf, 1972).

Beesly, Patrick. 'Convoy PQ 17: A Study of Intelligence and Decision-Making', *Intelligence & National Security*, 5 (1990), pp. 292–322.

Bennett, G.H. *Hitler's Ghost Ships: Graf Spee, Scharnhorst and Disguised German Raiders* (Plymouth: University of Plymouth Press, 2012).

Blond, Georges. *Ordeal below Zero: The Heroic Story of the Arctic Convoys in World War 2* (London: Souvenir, 1956).

Brookes, Ewart. *The Gates of Hell* (London: Jarrolds, 1960).

Broome, Jack. *Convoy Is to Scatter* (London: Kimber, 1972).

Brown, Peter C. *Voices From the Arctic Convoys* (Stroud: Fonthill Media, 2014).

Bunker, John, *Seafarers in World War II*, (Washington [DC]: Seafarers International Union in North America, 1951)

Burkett, Molly & Street, Robert. *Once Upon A Wartime* (Grantham: Barny Books, 2001).

Campbell, Ian, & MacIntyre, Donald. *The Kola Run: A Record of Arctic Convoys 1941-1945* (London: Muller, 1958).

Carse, Robert. *A Cold Corner of Hell: The Story of the Murmansk Convoys 1941-45* (New York: Doubleday, 1969).

Carter, William A. *Why Me, Lord? The Experiences of a U.S. navy Armed Guard Officer in World War II's Convoy PQ17 on the Murmansk Run.* (Millsboro [DE]: self-published, 2007).

'Convoys to North Russia, 1942', *Supplement to the London Gazette*, 13 October 1950, Number 39041. pp. 5139-5154.

Edwards, Bernard. *The Road to Russia: Arctic Convoys 1942* (Annapolis [MD]: Naval Institute Press, 2002).

Erswell, Charlie, *Surviving the Arctic Convoys: The Wartime Memoirs of Leading Seamen Charlie Erswell* (Barnsley: Pen and Sword, 2021).

Erwood, Peter. *A Long Night for the Canteen Boat: The Torpedoing and Salvage of HMS Cassandra December 11th 1944* (Fleet Hargate: Arcturus, 1996).

Evans, Mark Llewellyn. *Great World War II Battles in the Arctic* (Westport, [Conn.]: Greenwood, 1999).

Foxvog, Donald R. & Alotta, Robert I. *The Last Voyage of the SS Henry Bacon* (St Paul [MN.]: Paragon House, 2001).

French, John. *Catalina Over Arctic Oceans: Anti-Submarine and Rescue Flying in World War II.* (Barnsley: Pen & Sword Aviation, 2013).

Geroux, William. *The Ghost Ships of Archangel: The Arctic Voyage That Defied the Nazis* (London: Penguin Books, 2020).

Hall, Ivan. *Christmas in Archangel: A Memoir of Life in the Merchant Navy 1939-1946* (Victoria [B.C.]; Trafford, 2009).

Haynes, John L. *Frozen Fury: The Murmansk Run of PQ-13* (Baltimore [MD]: Publish America, 2010).

Herman, Fred. *Dynamite Cargo: Convoy to Russia* (London: Cassell; New York: Vanguard, 1943).

Hutson, Harry C. *Arctic Interlude: Independent to North Russia* (Bennington [VT.]: World War II Historical Society, 1997).

Irving, David. *The Destruction of Convoy PQ17* (London: Cassell, 1968).

Kemp, Paul. *Convoy: Drama in Arctic Waters* (London: Arms and Armour, 1993).

Kemp, Paul. *The Russian Convoys* (London: Arms & Armour, 1987).

Kerslake, S.A. *Coxswain in the Northern Convoys* (London: Kimber, 1984).

Konstam, Angus. *The Battle of the North Cape: The Death Ride of the Scharnhorst, 1943* (Barnsley: Pen & Sword Maritime, 2009).

Lend-Lease Shipments: World War II, Section IIIB, (Washington D.C.: Published by Office, Chief of Finance, War Department, December 31, 1946)

Llewellyn-Jones, Malcolm. *The Royal Navy and the Arctic Convoys: A Naval Staff History* (London: Routledge, 2007).

Lund, Paul, & Ludlam, Harry. *PQ17-Convoy to Hell: The Survivor's Story* (London: Foulsham, 1968).

McKay, John R. *Surviving the Arctic Convoys: The Wartime Memoir of Leading Seaman Charlie Erswell* (Barnsley: Pen & Sword Maritime, 2021).

Macleod, Donald J. *Survival against the Odds: The Story of Petty Officer Donald MacKinnon, Russian Convoy Survivor* (Aberdeen: Loch Roag Books, 2000).

Mallman Showell, Jak P. *Führer Conferences on Naval Affairs 1939-1945* (London: Greenhill Books, 1990).

Mallmann Showell, Jak P. *Dönitz, U-Boats, Convoys: The British Version of his Memoirs from the Admiralty's Secret Anti-Submarine Reports* (London: Frontline Books, 2013)

Mason, Alfred Grossmith. *Arctic Warriors: A Personal Account of Convoy PQ18* (Barnsley: Pen & Sword Maritime, 2013).

Mills, Morris O. *Convoy PQ13: Unlucky for Some* (Bramber: Bernard Durnford, 2000).

Morgan-Owen, David & Halewood,Louis, *Economic Warfare at Sea: Grand Strategies for Maritime Powers, 1650-1945.* (Liverpool: Liverpool University Press, 2020)

Moore, W. J. *Diaries and Memoirs of a Sailor* (Ilfracombe: Stockwell, 1983).

Ogden, Michael. *The Battle of North Cape* (London: Kimber, 1962).

Ommanney, Francis D. *Flat-Top: The Story of an Escort Carrier* (London: Longmans Green, 1945).

Pawlowicz, B. *ORP Garland in Convoy to Russia: The Record of a Polish Destroyer on Her Journey from Great Britain to Murmansk and Archangel in the Spring of 1942* (Mitcham: Surrey, 1943).

Pearce, Frank. *Last Call from HMS Edinburgh: A Story of the Russian Convoys* (London: Collins; New York: Atheneum,1982.

Pearce, Frank. *Running the Gauntlet: The Battles for the Barents Sea* (London: Fontana, 1989).

Pearce, Frank. *The Ship that Torpedoed Herself,* (Plymouth: Baron Jay, 1975).

Pearson, Michael. *Red Sky in the Morning: The Battle of the Barents Sea, 1942.* (Mechanicsburg [PA]: Stackpole, 2002).

Penrose, Barrie. *Stalin's Gold: The Story of HMS Edinburgh and its Treasure,* (London: Granada, 1982).

Pope, Dudley. *73 North: The Battle of the Barents Sea* (London: Weidenfeld & Nicolson; 1958).

Reeves, M. C. *Russian Convoys Sept. 1941–May 1945* (Garden Island [NSW]: Naval Historical Society of Australia, 1995).

Reiman, Michael. *About Russia, Its Revolutions, Its Development and Its Present*, (Frankfurt Am Main: Peter Lang GmbH, 2015).

Ruegg, Bob, & Hague, Arnold. *Convoys to Russia: Allied Convoys and Naval Surface Operations in Arctic Waters 1941-1945*, (Kendal: World Ship Society, 1992).

Schofield, B. B. *The Arctic Convoys* (London: Macdonald and Jane's, 1977).

Scott, Mark. *Eyewitness Accounts of the World War II Murmansk Run 1941-1945* (Lewiston [NY]: Edwin Mellen Press, 2006).

Smith, Peter C. *Arctic Victory: The Story of Convoy PQ18* (London: Kimber, 1975).

Swain, Henry. *Return to Murmansk* (London: Seafarer, 1996).

Taylor, J. E. *Northern Escort* (London: George Allen & Unwin, 1945).

Taylor, Theodore. *Battle in the Arctic Seas: The Story of PQ17* (New York: Crowell, 1976).

Thomas, Leona J. *Through Ice and Fire: A Russian Arctic Convoy Diary 1942* (Stroud: Fonthill, 2015).

Tye, Chris B. *The Real Cold War: Featuring "Jack in Joe's Land."* (Gillingham: self-published), 1994.

Wadsworth, Michael. *Arctic Convoy PQ8: The Story of Capt Robert Brundle and the ss Harmatris* (Barnsley: Pen & Sword Maritime, 2009).

Vail Motter, T. H. *The Persian Corridor and Aid to Russia: United States Army in World War II, Middle East Theatre* (Washington [DC]: Centre of Military History, 1952).

Walling, Michael. *Forgotten Sacrifice: The Arctic convoys of World War II* (London: Osprey, 2012).

Watts, A. J. *The Loss of the Scharnhorst* (London: Ian Allan, 1970).

Winn, Godfrey. *PQ17: A Story of a Ship* (London: Hutchinson, 1947).

Winton, John. *The Death of the Scharnhorst* (Chichester: Antony Bird, 1983).

Woodman, Richard. *Arctic Convoys 1941–1945* (London: John Murray, 2004).

Wragg, David. *Sacrifice for Stalin: The Cost and Value of the Arctic Convoys Re-assessed* (Barnsley: Pen & Sword Maritime, 2005).

Articles

Coakley, Robert W. 'The Persian Corridor as a Route for Aid to the USSR', in Kent Roberts Greenfield (ed.) *Command Decisions*, (Washington D.C.: United States Army Center of Military History, 1960). p. 227.

Farrell, Brian P. 'Yes, Prime Minister: Barbarossa, Whipcord, and the Basis of British Grand Strategy, Autumn 1941', *The Journal of Military History*, 57 (1993), pp. 599-625. [604].

Folly, Martin H. 'Seeking Comradeship in the "Ogre's Den": Winston Churchill's Quest for a Warrior Alliance and his Mission to Stalin', August 1942, *Enter Text*, 6 (2007), pp. 276-303.

Hill, Alexander. "British Lend Lease Aid and the Soviet War Effort, June 1941 –June 1942", *The Journal of Military History*, 71 (2007), pp. 773–808.

Langer, John Daniel, 'The Harriman-Beaverbrook Mission and the Debate over Unconditional Aid for the Soviet Union, 1941', *Journal of Contemporary History*, 14 (1979), pp. 463–482.

Munting, Roger. 'Soviet Food Supply and Allied Aid in the War, 1941-45', *Soviet Studies*, 36 (1984), pp. 582-593.

Munting, Roger, 'Lend-Lease and the Soviet War Effort', *Journal of Contemporary History*, 19 (1984), pp. 495-510.

'Through the eyes of Soviet Agitprop', *History Today*, September 1993, pp. 21-27.

Vego, Milan, 'The Destruction of Convoy PQ17: 27 June-10 July 1942', *Naval War College Review*, 69 (2016), pp. 83-141.

Arctic Marine Environment

Richard Porter

Maritime Operations in a Hostile Environment

Introduction

The marine environment is fundamentally hostile to human activity.

The principal elements of wind and precipitation are highly variable, with limited predictability, and can have significant impact on the conduct of naval operations.

High latitude maritime operations present exceptional conditions for those operating in their waters. But they differ in both hemispheres. The Antarctic is an ice-covered continent completely surrounded by water, while the Arctic is an ice-covered body of water largely surrounded by land. The ice hazards in the Southern Hemisphere are largely derived from floating ice that has broken off from the Antarctic Ice Sheet, while icebergs in the Northern Hemisphere are largely broken off from the Greenland ice sheet and glaciers.

Ice sheet and glaciers, while some floating ice has also broken off from the Arctic Ocean floating ice sheet. Icebergs therefore are much less of a hazard than in the Southern Hemisphere and largely confined to areas off the coast of Eastern Greenland.

Although there is clear evidence that the Arctic Ice Sheet is melting, which may be entirely due to natural causes, there is a mounting body of evidence that anthropogenic activities are accelerating the situation. The process could reverse, again due to natural causes as happened in the period from the 1940's to the 1960's.

This made navigating the Arctic Ocean adjacent to the European landmass even more difficult than was usually the case.

Therefore Naval Operations in the Arctic/North Atlantic Oceans have to deal with extremes of temperature and weather. The frequent storms producing high seas and the possibility of ice make these waters the most severe and treacherous in the marine environment.

The seasonal variations in the Arctic are barely perceptible and the spring and autumn are very short lasting only a few weeks, therefore the Arctic summer is considered to last from May to August and the winter from September to April.

The main effects are the very long hours of daylight in the summer, which renders any shipping vulnerable to attack by sea and air, the long winters with little daylight, while giving shipping some degree of protection from enemy attack brings its own problems dealing with the harsh winter weather.

Winston Churchill called these 'Arctic Convoys', "the worst journey in the world" (CWGC 2016.)

The North Atlantic Current

This feature has a marked effect on maritime operation in the North Atlantic/Arctic Ocean bordering the European landmass. It is also known as the 'North Atlantic Drift' and occasionally as the 'North Atlantic Sea Movement'.

All the worlds' major oceans have large circular currents, (that run clockwise in the Northern Hemisphere and anti-clockwise in the Southern Hemisphere) they are largely wind generated by the global wind systems and as such are relative stable oceanographic features. However the one in the North Atlantic has an almost unique feature, which warms the western coasts of Northern Europe. The North Atlantic Current (NAC) breaks away from the Gulf Stream, which forms the northern limb of this circular current and thus carries warm water that originated in the Gulf of Mexico northwards to the western coasts of the European landmass. Here it is responsible primarily for the 'warm' conditions that we enjoy in the United Kingdom, where other coastlines of the eastern seaboard of North America at the same latitude experience a much harsher climate, especially in the northern winter. It is also why the gardens at Inverewe can support a vast array of tropical plants even though they are situated on the west coast of the Scottish Highlands in Wester Ross. The NAC or Gulf Stream continues north where it becomes the Norwegian Current. It is driven by the global thermohaline circulation,[1] the North Atlantic Current is part of the wind-driven Gulf Stream, which goes further east and north from the North American coast across the Atlantic and into the Arctic Ocean. Thus the NAC is a most important factor is not only keeping the Norwegian coast ice free all the year round but also the coast across the top of Norway via North Cape to the Russian port of Murmansk. That was vital in the supply link to Russia for the Arctic Convoys, that could operate all the year round.

Therefore the North Atlantic Current ensures a sea route for the Arctic Convoys that supplied Russia during the hostilities in the latter half of World War II.

Climate and Weather in the Arctic Ocean

Almost all of the energy reaching the Earth's atmosphere and surface comes from the sun in the form of solar radiation. Variations in the amount of solar radiation reaching the Earth are a principal driver of global and regional climate. Latitude is the main factor at work and in the polar regions the solar radiation is spread over a much wider area than at lower latitudes, this results is a general decrease in temperature with increasing latitude. In addition the sun's rays fall on the polar areas at a much shallower angle, this not only reduces the temperature but also increases the reflectivity of the rays, coupled with the large areas of ice and snow that also reflect the sun's rays all combing to reduce surface temperature dramatically, producing the Arctic Climate.

Cold air subsides at the North Pole forming a high-pressure system, which in turn sees polar winds, which combined with the *coriolis effect* blow from the pole and are deflected towards the west which give rise to general polar originated winds known as the Polar Easterlies (winds always being named from the direction that they originate).

The ocean waters at the North Pole are very cold (0-4 degrees C) and because these waters normally freeze at those temperature and form ice, which in turn raises the salinity of the sea water (as only the fresh water component freezes). The increased salinity also increases the density of the water at the sea surface and it consequently sinks to become the water mass known as *North Atlantic Deep Water* (NADW). This water mass in the Arctic is consequently very cold, (0-4 degrees C) but it does not freeze because of its raised salinity.

Since sea-water has a salinity of 35 (35 parts per thousand, or ppth, of dissolved 'salts' and other elements and compounds) it reaches its maximum density at the freezing point, convection from the surface cooling continues until the whole mass of water is at -1.9 degrees C and then surface ice can form. The large volumes of sea water involved and the lower temperatures to which they have to be cooled mean that considerable heat transport to the atmosphere has to occur before the onset of freezing. This accounts for the delayed formation of sea ice compared with less saline waters of the same latitude. This also results in less severe winters in oceanic areas at high latitudes compared with continental interiors.

In the Arctic each summer about a third of each ice floe melts (an ice floe is just a term for floating ice), mostly from the top but some from the bottom of the floe, this gives a lower salinity to the surrounding sea-water and in the following winter a similar amount of ice is added to the underside of the floe. Therefore Arctic sea-ice tends not to be more than three years old.

The Polar Easterlies that blow across the Arctic Ocean have a long fetch and therefore they are capable of increasing the sea state and

HMS *Leamington*'s crew removes ice from the foc'st'le and bridge area with shovels and axes.

Snow covered deck of British light cruiser HMS *Scylla*. Nominated for duty as Flagship for Fighting Escort of Arctic Convoy PQ 18.

forming large swell waves. These winds also pick up moisture so heavy rain and snow showers are a feature, especially in the winter months. As they travel in a general southerly direction they move over progressively warmer waters, the moisture-laden air is often forced to rise, this will reduce the pressure locally and can give rise to the often deep lows known in Arctic waters, The resultant low pressure can develop into a *Polar Low*.

Polar Lows are usually small-scale and relatively short-lived low-pressure-systems (depressions) that can occur in the North Atlantic and Arctic Oceans. They typically have a diameter of no more that 600 nautical miles and exist for no more than a couple of days. They can be difficult to detect but are a distinct hazard to Arctic Ocean maritime operations.

The strong winds of the Arctic Ocean and consequent large swell waves produce sea spray, which could become a major hazard to the Arctic Convoys. In the early phases of Word War II Naval operations ships did not have the advantages of radar and sonar (ASDIC) as both were in their infancy and had yet to be developed sufficiently to be much use in detecting enemy forces at sea, consequently ships had to post lookouts at all times to warn of any possible attack from the enemy. The lack of enclosed bridges on ships meant that lookouts were exposed to strong winds, sea spray and precipitation.

In those Arctic temperatures, especially in winter the sea-spray would freeze before hitting the ship, even if not frozen the icy cold water would heighten the pressures on those exposed on board especially of fatigue and the uncomfortable conditions to which they were already enduring. Crew fatigue should not be under estimated, it is still a major factor affecting crews today and the effect on the crews of the Arctic Convoys must be difficult to imagine 80 years on.

The occurrence of fog is a common phenomenon in the Arctic and of course it affected the Convoys and the enemy equally. The poor visibility that fog brought made convoys far harder to find for German U-boats and the Luftwaffe, but it also made it significantly harder to navigate, particularly when in close proximity to ice. The low-lying nature of Arctic Sea Smoke[2] meant that the ships of the convoy could be shrouded from U-Boats but still vulnerable to attack from the air and would also have to reduce speed to avoid collisions.

The occurrence of Sea Smoke was the reason why HMS *Punjabi* unknowingly cut across the bows of HMS *King George V* in the fog and was cleaved in two (Evans, 2010, p89-93). Cloud cover, particularly when extensive and low, was generally a positive feature of the environment for the convoys. In clear skies the Luftwaffe was able to patrol large areas quickly, tracking and passing on the convoy's position.

Naval Operations in the Arctic Ocean

The tilt of the Earth's axis at approximately 23.5 degrees causes sunlight to fall at differing angles dependent on latitude. In the Arctic the low angle of the sun results in less atmospheric warming, but more importantly above the Arctic Circle (approximately 67.5 degrees North ie 90 degrees minus the 23.5 degrees of the tilt of the Earth's axis) the sun never rises above the horizon for the Arctic winter months and never sets or falls below the horizon in the Arctic summer months. In effect the winter months are in permanent dark conditions while the summer months are in permanent daylight. Obviously the weather conditions will affect visibility at sea but these conditions will have a profound effect on the safe operation of convoys.

There were many elements of the marine environment that made the journey of the convoys extremely hazardous, but the effects of daylight in particular were considered when planning convoys and use as made of the environment to advantage as much as possible. Consequently, over 75% of all convoys took place between November and April, using the greatly extended periods of darkness to conceal the ships' presence. The small number of convoys between May and October, whilst less than a quarter of the overall total, accounted for nearly 65% of overall losses as chronicled in the main body of the 'Battle Summary'.

Seasonal routing of the convoys became of paramount importance. In the summer the advantages of transiting further from land was lessened by the weeks of perpetual daylight, however this was offset by giving German warships and the Luftwaffe and the ever present U-Boat threat an advantage in being able to locate, track and attack the convoys. In the winter the near perpetual darkness gave precious cover for the ships with the advantage of hopefully remaining undetected for weeks at a time.

The combined effect of the sea ice, the weather and the sea state would result in fairly slow progress for the convoys. The large expanse of the Arctic Ocean means that there is a large *fetch*,[3] which would result in heavy seas, which in turn would slow the progress of the convoys, which was generally only about 8 knots but was often reduced to 5 knots in heavy seas. This would render the ships vulnerable to enemy attack but the German navy also had to contend with the same conditions.

Diesel powered German U-boats largely operated at the surface (as their dived endurance was limited), this enabled them to maintain a higher speed that when submerged (typically 20 knots at the surface as compared with 7 knots submerged) and this enhanced their ability to intercept a convoy once detected.

However the Arctic conditions made it difficult for them to target ships as wave height often obscured ships from view because of the low position of the U-boat.

The sea state could also give the convoys a further advantage over U-boats. Although the sea state often constrained the convoy's speed their greater length enabled them to proceed at a higher speed than the U-boats that were of shorter length and had a much smaller displacement. A typical U-boat having a length of about 87.5 metres compared to most warships having a length of 100 metres and up to 150 metres for a merchant ship.

Ships that did fall victim to attack would find the cold Arctic Ocean temperature very unforgiving at around 4 centigrade, at these temperatures survival times in the water are very limited, being only 30-90 minutes and with unconsciousness and exhaustion expected within 15-30 minutes, that is always assuming that the initial shock of the cold water did not claim victims earlier and for those who did survive wind chill would often reduce these survival ties dramatically.

Navigation was difficult and solely reliant on celestial navigation once out of sight of land, applying 'dead reckoning' which was often days old and inaccurate. Hampered by a lack of nautical twilight, either from the long sunlight or perpetual darkness, or a lack of visible stars owing to cloud cover, accurate position finding was very difficult for Allied and German vessels alike (Buchheim, 1978). Without accurate positional information, having been unable to take celestial fixes for the previous three days, the ships of QP 13 were led into an Allied minefield with the loss of 5 ships (Edwards, 2002, p. 96).

Although some ships of the convoys used gyrocompasses, a relatively well-established technology, many still relied on magnetic compasses. To steer an accurate true course, magnetic variation was applied. However, the further North the ship's position, the larger the correction and only an exact position would allow an accurate correction of the local variation. Without proper accounting for the variation, ships could take a far more circuitous route, or end up closer to the coast than intended.

In order to remain as covert as possible, ships often operated without lights to reduce the possibility of detection by aircraft and submarines. However, this, along with limited natural light, meant an ever-present risk of collision between ships in a convoy. The lack of daylight could assist the convoys in avoiding long-range detection, as U-boats were unable to see smoke columns. However, in good conditions and with the moon visible throughout the year, U-boats gained a significant advantage from the silhouettes caused by lunar illumination, which could be sufficient to use for targeting, whilst the conning towers of the U-Boats remained too low to be illuminated in the same way.

Early naval radar was a relatively short-range aid and would struggle to see contacts beyond 6 nautical miles, although it provided a useful guide and early warning, particularly at night and in fog. The radars that equipped some ships in the convoy were significantly affected by the sea state. When attempting to observe a small contact, such as a periscope or the conning tower of a U-Boat, these early radars would have struggled to pick up identifiable returns, although advances in the technology available towards the end of the war gave far better performance, particularly with the introduction of the 10cm radar.

Ice in the Arctic Ocean

As mentioned earlier the Arctic Ocean is an ocean surrounded by land but the polar area is covered by an ice cap formed of sea ice, as opposed to the Greenland ice cap, which is covered by land ice. The ice formed at sea is thinner than the ice formed on land but it nevertheless presents a significant problem to naval operations.

Land ice is only a problem when land glaciers reach the sea and the ice breaks away from the main glacier to form Icebergs, which can become a significant hazard to shipping. The extent of the ice would dictate the convoy's route. Routing close to the coast would increase the risk of detection and attack by German forces while routing close to the ice edge not only increase the distance to be navigated but also enforces a slow speed of advance. The risk of ice damage is also increased and six ships from PQ 14 were damaged significantly that they had to turn back and the tanker *Hopemount* damaged her propeller.

The various stages in the formation of sea ice from the onset of freezing to the eventual vast, relatively unbroken sheets known as pack ice are identified by many names and not always consistently. Common examples on British charts include:

Crevassed Glacier entering the Atlantic Ocean showing a floating ice-sheet and many small icebergs.

FRAZIL: First minute ice crystals form giving the sea an 'oily' appearance.

SLUSH: Ice crystals numerous and obvious.

PANCAKE: Ice crystals collect into large plates which have a raised, rounded edge from bumping into one another.

YOUNG: Continuous layer 5-20cm thick.

FIRST YEAR: Also Winter ice. Greater than 20cms thick but less than one year old.

MULTI-YEAR: Also Polar Ice. Thickness 2-4 metres.

PACK: Icefields of both hemispheres.

Pancake ice.

The icefields are in constant motion due to wind, wave and current action and this leads to considerable cracking and distortion. Where the icefield is under tension, the sheets break into pieces called 'ice floes'. The cracks may develop, particularly in the spring melt, into areas of usefully wide clear water known as:

LEADS: Channels or lanes which maybe navigable, particularly if air reconnaissance is available.
POLYNYA: Also know as 'Ice Clearings'. Large areas of clear water surrounded by ice.

Where the icefield is under compression the distortion may take several forms called 'pressure ice' as the following terms can be used:

TENTED: Slabs of ice pushed together and lifting to form an arch or 'tent'

RAFTED: Slabs of ice pushed over another.

HUMMOCKED: Haphazard distribution of mounds and hillocks.

RIDGED: More ordered distortion in the form of pressure ridges running in a particular direction.

Icefields can also drift for considerable distances on an oceanic scale. Thus the problem of ice floes in the Arctic Ocean and North Atlantic is ever present.

The last one to mention shows a general exception to the rules applied above:

FAST ICE: Ice that is not moving because it is either attached to a shore line or grounded in shoaling water.

Icebergs

Icebergs have a different origin to sea ice and as mentioned above they are derived from land-based glaciers when they enter the sea. They are occasionally known as 'land-ice'.

They derive from glaciers or ice sheets which discharge into the sea, a process known as 'calving'.

The two sources of icebergs produce different iceberg shapes. Those from glaciers are generally smaller and much more angular with a conventional mountain-like (berg) shape. Those from ice sheets generally have a flat-topped (tabular berg) shape and are much larger.

In the Arctic icebergs origination from glacial discharge appear to predominate because of the valley glaciers of Greenland and Spitzbergen. Once in the ocean they are usually readily seen and were more of a hazard to the convoys using the summer routes that ran closer to the Greenland coast and operated in the vicinity of Spitsbergen.

Arctic Ocean icebergs are often a darker colour than their counterparts in the Southern Hemisphere, this is partly because the Arctic derived icebergs contain more rock debris from glacial erosion on land but also because glacier ice is subject to higher pressures and consequently has less air entrained within it.

Icebergs eventually melt away mostly by floating into zones where they melt under the attack of warm air and a warmer sea. The subsurface melting may become quite vigorous to the point where an iceberg becomes unstable and turns over. As they dwindle away they are known as:

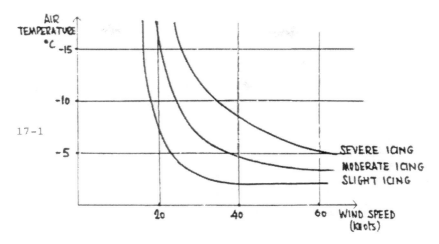

BERGY BIT: About the size of a house.

GROWLER: Less than 10 metres.

Ice Formation on Ships

The freezing of the sea spray onto the superstructure of ships was just one more major hazard that the crews of the Convoys had to endure and cope with.

The ice freezing onto the ships meant that it needed to be constantly chipped away to avoid the catastrophic effects of ice accretion. If left unattended the ice can soon increase the weight of the upper part of the ship by several hundred tons, This can have a drastic effect on a ship's stability, its manoeuvrability and greatly affect the ship's ability to float upright in the sea. Ice accumulation can affect the upper deck equipment and weapons, with guns being unable to move and the workings of machinery being frozen and unable to operate. Use of cold weather oils and greases went some way to ensuring that weapons and systems remained working. However, this wasn't assured, and a torpedo fired by HMS *Trinidad* turned back and damaged the ship when the gyroscope motor oil froze (Regan, 1993).

There are two types of ice that that form on ships, they are Rime Ice and Glaze Ice.

Rime Ice

Rime ice forms by the rapid freezing of small, super cooled water droplets when they come into contact with a solid surface. Since freezing

Top left Closeup of calving.

Bottom left Icebergs off the East Coast of Greenland.

is rapid, air is trapped between the droplets, making this kind of ice opaque, brittle and of low density and easy to remove.

Rime ice will form on ships in fog when the air temperature is below 0 degrees C. for example in Arctic Sea Smoke near the polar ice edge. The intensity of this type of icing is generally only slight due to the very small size of the fog droplets and hence presents few problems. However if the ship has been accreting ice for some time so that the effective cross section of standard rigging, for example, is much increased, then the effect of wind on the ship can be considerable.

Glaze Ice

Glaze ice is the most dangerous type of ice and forms when water strikes a surface that is well below freezing. The water spreads out on impact and freezes, trapping little or no air. Hence the ice formed is clear, dense and very difficult to remove. (This is very similar to the 'black ice' that forms on roads when rain freezes on or after impact).

Glaze ice forms on a ship's superstructure when spray freezes on impact. Its severity depends upon wind speed and the temperature of the air.

Wind

In order to produce any spray the wind strength must be above force 5.[4] The amount of spray then increases rapidly as the wind strength increases.

Temperature

Ice starts to form when the air temperature, and hence the temperature of a ship's superstructure, falls below the freezing temperature of sea-water. This is generally considered as being -2 degrees C, although it varies with salinity. When the air temperature falls below -8 degrees C all spray freezes on impact.

Therefore, it is the combination of low temperature and strong winds that cause the hazard. Significant icing will occur with winds in excess of 25 knots and with temperatures below -5 degrees C.

Slight, Moderate and Severe icing refer to the rate of ice accretion:

SLIGHT: 1.3 cms/24 hrs.
MODERATE: 4.6 cms/24h hrs.
SEVERE: 7.14 cms or more/24 hrs

Hazards from ice accretion include:

1. Increased weight of a ship.
2. Loss of steerage capability.
3. Reduced performance of radio and radar equipment.
4. Liability to become top heavy making a ship unstable, thus the ship's roll may become greater and more sluggish. Excessive icing may result in a capsize.

When ice is forming the best action would be to steam with the stern to the wind to reduce both spray and the relative wind speed, if possible. An alternative is to steam into wind but with minimum speed. This of course lengthens the voyage and makes the convoy more susceptible to enemy attack. Any other direction would result in an asymmetric accumulation of ice that would have a greater affect on the ship's stability. Research experiments have shown that a trawler at 30 degrees to the wind capsized with only 50% of the ice needed to capsize the same ship steaming into the wind.

In conclusion it may be come apparent that lessons learned from the Arctic convoys may become pertinent to modern day naval operations in the Arctic, certainly in terms of a fight to survive against the extreme natural conditions. With a significant reduction in ice expected from climate change, the waters remain cold nonetheless, this will probably affect submarines operations to a greater extent than those of surface ships.

References

Buchheim, L. G. (1978) *U-Boat War*, Collins: London.

CWCG (2016) *"The Worst Journey In The World" – A Brief History of the Arctic Convoys.* Commonwealth War Grave Commission [can be viewed online, viewed 29/4/17] http://www.cwgc.org/news-events/news/2016/8/the-worst-journey-in-the-world-a-brief-history-of-the-arctic-convoys.aspx.

Edwards, B. (2002) *The Road to Russia: The Arctic Convoys 1942-45*, Barnsley: Leo Cooper.

Evans, A. (2010) *Destroyer Down*, Barnsley: Pen & Sword Maritime.

Regan, G. (1993) *The Guinness Book of Naval Blunders*, Bath: The Bath Press.

Walling, M. (2012) *Forgotten Sacrifice: The Arctic Convoys of World War II*, Osprey Publishing: Oxford.

Woodman, R. (1994) *The Arctic convoys*, London: John Murray.

Endnote

1. This is the movement of seawater in a pattern of flow dependent on variations in temperature, which give rise to changes in salt content and hence in density.

   Thermohaline circulation plays an important role in supplying heat to the Polar Regions. Therefore, it influences the rate of sea ice formation near the poles, which in turn affects other aspects of the climate system (such as the albedo, and thus solar heating, at high latitudes).

2. Arctic Sea Smoke is also known as Steam Fog or Frost Fog. It is formed when light winds of very cold air, usually originating from nearby the ice caps or ice shelves flow over warmer water that has a layer of saturated air above it. It is generally thin and usually no more than about 10 metres thick above the sea surface but it has been observed up to 20-30 metres in thickness.

3. Three aspects of the wind determine the height of a wave on the sea surface, they are the speed of the wind, how long it has been blowing for and the fetch which is defines as the track of the wind over the surface of the earth, hence a large fetch or area over which the wind has blown the greater will be the wave that is created.

4. The Beaufort scale, which is used in marine forecasts, is an empirical measure for describing wind intensity based on observed sea conditions. The scale runs from 0 to 12.

   Force 12 has a maximum wind speed of 64 knots +. This is the maximum as wind speed cannot visually assessed above that speed. Force 5 has a wind speed of 17-21 knots (a knot being 1 nautical mph) with a probable wave height of 2 metres, it is referred to as a 'fresh breeze'.

Part I – Illustrations

Michael Pearce

Typical conditions on the upper deck of a warship escorting Arctic convoys – an ice-covered 20-inch signal lamp on the Town-class cruiser HMS *Sheffield*, December 1941.

The selection of photographs included in this section are nearly all in the public domain, augmented by some original WW2 prints from a private collection.

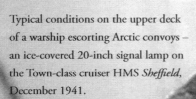

Allied Warships

Few campaigns of WW2 required the sustained effort and number of warships deployed as the Arctic convoys of 1941 to 1945, the escorting of which involved almost every type of naval vessel from modern battleships to requisitioned fishing trawlers. Their organisation was necessarily complex, as, often, the escort was divided into three layers of support. Firstly, a close escort of destroyers, corvettes, sloops, AA ships and anti-submarine trawlers that sailed with the merchant ships, despite their slow speed, to provide immediate anti-submarine and anti-aircraft defence. Secondly, a covering force of cruisers and destroyers able to reach the convoy and come to the assistance of the close escort within an acceptable time, as at the Battle of the Barents Sea on 31 December 1942. Thirdly, a more distant covering force of battleships, fleet carriers and heavy cruisers that could intervene if the convoy were to be attacked by Kriegsmarine capital ships, as at the Battle of North Cape on 26 December 1943, when the *Scharnhorst* was sunk.

In addition, a local escort force, based in North Russia, mainly consisting of minesweeping sloops, supplemented the convoys' close escort as they approached their destination, with a small number of Soviet ships and RAF and Russian air support.

From September 1942, a vital addition to the close escort of Arctic convoys was the escort carrier, carrying single-seat fighters, such as Hawker Sea Hurricanes and, later, Grumman Wildcats, together with anti-submarine strike aircraft such as Fairey Swordfish and, later, Grumman Avengers. These aircraft worked extremely well together, locating U-Boats and forcing them to submerge or sinking them, while the fighters also chased off or shot down Focke Wolf Fw200 Condor and Blohm and Voss Bv138 maritime reconnaissance aircraft. As more escort carriers came into service, two accompanied each convoy, while others, organised into operation-specific task groups, attacked U-Boat bases and German ships, airfields and defences in northern Norway.

1. *Top right* Ice-covered fore-turrets of battleship HMS *Anson* during the winter of 1942-43 when she was a 'distant cover' heavy escort for five Arctic convoys.

2. Battleship HMS *Anson* on trials in July 1942, firing her forward 14-inch 45-calibre main armament at the maximum elevation of 41 degrees, giving a range of 36,600 yards with a 1,590lb armour-piercing shell.

3. HMS *Anson* in Admiralty disruptive camouflage at Seidisfjord in Iceland, probably late August 1942 a few days before sailing as part of the covering force for PQ 18.

4. Cruiser HMS *Belfast* in 1943 wearing the revised 4-colour Admiralty camouflage scheme she wore during the Battle of North Cape.

5. HMS *Belfast* in heavy seas off Iceland, February 1943.

6. HMS *Belfast* in a kinder sea but with forecastle and forward triple 6-inch gun turrets coated in ice.

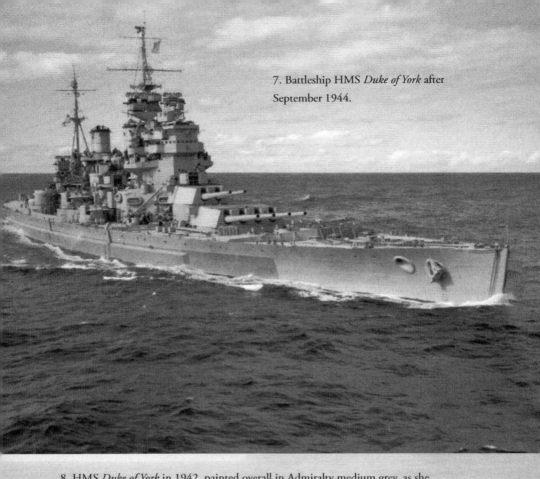

7. Battleship HMS *Duke of York* after September 1944.

8. HMS *Duke of York* in 1942, painted overall in Admiralty medium grey, as she appeared at the Battle of North Cape, 26 December 1943, when she was part of the covering force for JW 55B and sank the *Scharnhorst* in a night gunnery and torpedo action in rough weather.

9. HMS *Duke of York* in March 1943, emerging from refit at Rosyth Dockyard, showing forward quadruple 'A' and twin 'B' 14-inch turrets, with additional light AA guns grouped behind forecastle breakwater.

10. Battleship HMS *Howe* before May 1944 in Admiralty disruptive camouflage; the last of the five King George V class, commissioned 29 August 1942.

11. HMS *Howe* acted as 'distant cover' heavy escort for Arctic convoys, until transferring to the Mediterranean in time for the Operation Husky landings on Sicily in July 1943.

12. Colony class cruiser HMS *Jamaica*, 27 September 1943, showing the Admiralty disruptive camouflage scheme that she wore during the Battle of the Barents Sea on 31 December 1942.

13. HMS *Jamaica* refueling at sea, September 1944, showing the two forward triple 6-inch gun turrets, there were two similar turrets aft.

14. *Top left* HMS *Jamaica* in heavy northern seas, 1942 or early 1943.

15. Colony class cruiser HMS *Trinidad* in Kola inlet, April or May 1942, damaged by one of her own torpedoes that malfunctioned due to very low temperatures when launched at German destroyer *Z26* attacking PQ 13. *Z26* was sunk by gunfire from the *Trinidad* and destroyer HMS *Eclipse*.

16. HMS *Trinidad*, late 1941 or early 1942, in Hvalfjord, Iceland prior to Arctic convoy escort duty; she was sunk only seven months after commissioning.

17. HMS *Trinidad*, 15 May 1942, disabled by Ju.88s when limping home from Murmansk after temporary repairs to previous torpedo damage; the bomb and fire damage was so severe, she had to be torpedoed and sunk by destroyer HMS *Matchless*, seen alongside.

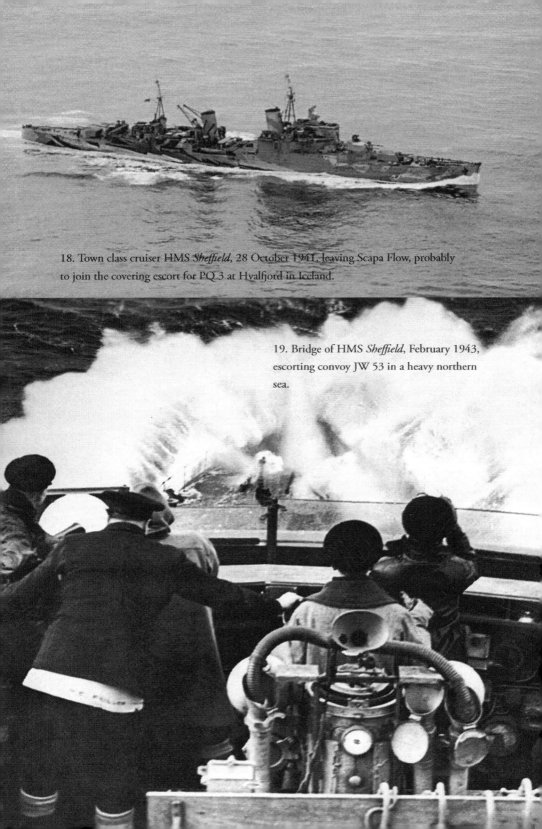

18. Town class cruiser HMS *Sheffield*, 28 October 1941, leaving Scapa Flow, probably to join the covering escort for PQ 3 at Hvalfjord in Iceland.

19. Bridge of HMS *Sheffield*, February 1943, escorting convoy JW 53 in a heavy northern sea.

20. HMS *Sheffield*, December 1941, anchored in the Kola Inlet off Murmansk after escorting PQ 5 or PQ 6. Fleet minesweeper HMS *Seagull*, used as a convoy escort, alongside.

21. HMS *Sheffield*, December 1941, in unusually calm northern waters, escorting the merchant ships of PQ 5 or PQ 6 seen astern.

22. County class heavy cruiser HMS *Suffolk*, June 1941, patrolling at the edge of the Arctic pack ice, the 8-inch guns of her two forward turrets are trained on either bow.

23. HMS *Suffolk*, October 1941, in a unique camouflage scheme; Polish destroyer *Burza* beyond her stern.

24. County class heavy cruiser HMS *Norfolk*, between June and December 1943 with full main armament of eight 8-inch guns but aircraft and catapult removed.

25. HMS *Norfolk*, April 1945, as flagship of 1st Cruiser Squadron for Operation Judgement II, a FAA strike on Kilbotn. 'X' turret removed after damage at the Battle of North Cape but light AA guns and radar equipment significantly increased. Seen from flight deck of escort carrier HMS *Searcher*.

26. County class heavy cruiser HMS *London*, late 1942. Reconstructed 1939-41, changing her 3-funnel profile, previously similar to HMSs *Suffolk* and *Norfolk*.

27. HMS *London*, early 1942, showing resemblance to smaller Colony class cruisers following 1939-41 modernisation.

28. Town class cruiser HMS *Edinburgh*, between Nov 1940 and December 1941. When escorting QP 11 she carried 4,570kg of Soviet gold in 465 ingots, worth over £224 million at 2022 values, as part-payment for war material delivered by the Arctic convoys. All but five ingots were salvaged from her wreck in the 1980s.

29. HMS *Edinburgh*, 30 April 1942 after being twice torpedoed by *U-456*; attacked by German destroyers *Hermann Schoemann*, *Z24* and *Z25* and torpedoed again on 2 May 1942 and totally disabled while under tow back to Murmansk. Her gunnery left the *Hermann Schoemann* in a sinking condition before the *Edinburgh* had to be scuttled by gunfire, depth charges and torpedo.

30. 'Dido' class cruiser HMS *Scylla*, brand new in the Clyde, June 1942, before sailing as flagship of PQ 18 escort. Armed with four twin 4.5-inch guns because of a shortage of 5.25-inch mountings, she was a highly effective AA and HQ ship, despite being nicknamed 'the toothless terror'.

31. 'O' class destroyer HMS *Obedient* armed with 4-inch AA guns, rather than the usual 4.7-inch destroyer armament. Damaged by heavy cruiser *Admiral Hipper* during the Battle of the Barents Sea, 31 December 1942.

32. *Top right* 'O' class destroyer flotilla leader HMS *Onslow*, 24 April 1943. Sank *U-589*, 14 September 1942, during PQ 18; seriously damaged engaging heavy cruiser *Admiral Hipper* during the Battle of the Barents Sea, 31 December 1942, protecting convoy JW 51B.

33. HMS *Onslow*, 4 February 1943, being cheered into Scapa Flow following temporary repairs at Murmansk, after the Battle of the Barents Sea when her Captain, Robert Sherbrooke, won the VC.

34. 'I' class destroyer HMS *Impulsive*, sank *U-457* on 16 September 1942 while escorting PQ 18.

35. Destroyer HMS *Achates* modified for escort work, with 'A' mounting replaced by a 'Hedgehog' anti-submarine mortar, 'Y' mounting by additional depth charges and aft bank of torpedo tubes by a 12pdr AA gun. Sunk 31 December 1942 by 8-inch gunfire of heavy cruiser *Admiral Hipper* at the Battle of the Barents Sea, while shielding ships of JW 51B with a smoke screen.

36. Tribal class destroyer HMS *Ashanti*, 1941-42, at Hvalfjord, Iceland; taken from fleet carrier HMS *Victorious*, County class heavy cruiser HMS *Kent* in left background.

37. Tribal class destroyer HMS *Eskimo*, September 1942, as part of the 'fighting destroyer escort' for PQ 18.

38. 'M' class destroyer HMS *Marne* in the Kola Inlet, North Russia, seen from a Soviet naval vessel.

39. 'M' class destroyer HMS *Martin*, early 1942 in pale Western Approaches camouflage; escorted convoys PQ 17 and PQ 18 but was sunk by *U-431*, 10 November 1942, NE of Algiers.

40. Destroyer HMS *Amazon*, refitted for escort duty with 'A' mounting replaced by a 'Hedgehog' anti-submarine mortar and 'Y' mounting by additional depth charges.

41. 'B' class destroyer HMS *Bulldog*, 17 September 1944, as an escort, 'A' mounting replaced by a 'Hedgehog' anti-submarine mortar, 'Y' mounting by additional depth charges and a 2pdr bow-chaser. Captured an Enigma machine from *U-110* May 1941 and sank *U-719*, 26 June 1944.

42. 'F' class destroyer HMS *Foresight*, 2 July 1942 after repairs to damage suffered during QP 11, defending disabled cruiser HMS *Edinburgh* from German destroyer attack 2 May 1942. Sunk 13 August 1942 after aerial torpedo damage during Operation Pedestal convoy to relieve Malta.

43. 'F' class destroyer flotilla leader HMS *Faulknor*, between June 1940 and July 1942, before her aft torpedo tubes were restored and a 12pdr AA gun substituted for the 4.7-inch 'X' mounting.

44. Destroyer flotilla leader HMS *Keppel*, March 1943, as an escort with cut-down after funnel, 'A' mounting replaced by a 'Hedgehog' anti-submarine mortar and 'Y' mounting by additional depth charges; in the pale Western Approaches camouflage scheme that was very effective in the Arctic. Leader of the close escort for PQ 17.

45. ex-US 'flush-deck' destroyer HMCS *Leamington*, early 1943, showing the severe winter icing conditions encounted in the Arctic and North Atlantic.

46. 'Hunt' class escort destroyer HMS *Middleton*, 4 August 1943. Escorted 10 Arctic convoys and the Operation Harpoon Malta convoy.

47. 'Hunt' class escort destroyer HMS *Ledbury*, escorted PQ 17 and JW 52; transferred to the Mediterranean between and was key in bringing the vital disabled tanker SS *Ohio* into Malta after the Operation Pedestal convoy.

48. 'Hunt' class escort destroyer HMS *Wheatland*, escorted five Arctic convoys before transferring to the Mediterranean.

49. Auxiliary AA Ship HMS *Alynbank*, late 1942. Former 'Bank' line freighter, built 1925, converted 1939-40 with a powerful AA armament of four twin 4-inch and two quad 2pdr mountings; sailed with PQ 16 and PQ 18, before transferring to the Mediterranean. Worn out by 1944 and expended as a blockship off the Normandy beaches.

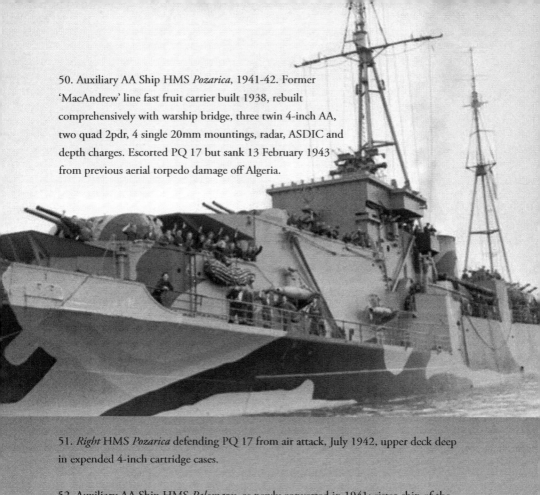

50. Auxiliary AA Ship HMS *Pozarica*, 1941-42. Former 'MacAndrew' line fast fruit carrier built 1938, rebuilt comprehensively with warship bridge, three twin 4-inch AA, two quad 2pdr, 4 single 20mm mountings, radar, ASDIC and depth charges. Escorted PQ 17 but sank 13 February 1943 from previous aerial torpedo damage off Algeria.

51. *Right* HMS *Pozarica* defending PQ 17 from air attack, July 1942, upper deck deep in expended 4-inch cartridge cases.

52. Auxiliary AA Ship HMS *Palomares*, as newly converted in 1941; sister-ship of the *Pozarica* and given a similar conversion. Escorted PQ 17 before transfer to Mediterranean; converted to Fighter Direction Ship, 1943, after bomb damage off Algiers.

53. Auxiliary AA Ship HMS *Ulster Queen*, former Belfast to Liverpool fast ferry, given a similar extensive conversion and armament to the *Pozarica*, except with 10 20mm oerlikon mountings. Escorted PQ 15 and PQ 18, then AA guardship in the Kola Inlet. Converted to Fighter Direction Ship 1943.

54. Anti-submarine trawler HMS *Ayrshire*, Hvalfjord, Iceland. Built 1938, requisitioned 1939, escorted Atlantic convoys, then PQ 17 and PQ 18. When PQ 17 was ordered to scatter, the Ayrshire's CO led 3 merchant ships north into the pack ice, camouflaged them with white paint found aboard one and brought them safely to Archangel.

55. Improved 'Dido' class cruiser HMS *Black Prince*, February/March 1944, escorting JW 57 or RA 57; photographed by an aircraft from escort carrier HMS *Chaser*.

56. Improved 'Dido' class cruiser HMS *Bellona* and escort carrier HMS *Queen*, April 1945, in rough weather off northern Norway; photo taken from flight deck of escort carrier HMS *Searcher*.

57. 'Halcyon' class fleet minesweeper HMS *Harrier*, escorted first Arctic convoy, PQ 1, Operation Dervish, in September/October 1941; refitted for Arctic service, escorted PQ 8 then based in Murmansk/Archangel 1942/43 as part of convoy Local Escort Force.

58. HMS *Halcyon*, fleet minesweeper, nameship of her class, 12 October 1942, escorted first Arctic convoy, PQ 1, Operation Dervish, in September/October 1941; escorted PQ 8 then based in Murmansk/ Archangel 1942/43 as part of convoy Local Escort Force; escorted PQ 17/QP 13, July 1942.

59. 'Halcyon' class fleet minesweeper HMS *Bramble*, 12 July 1939; based in Murmansk/ Archangel 1941/42 as part of convoy Local Escort Force.

60. HMS *Bramble*, photo taken during PQ 17 in July 1942. Escorted JW 51B and was sunk with all hands, 31 December 1942, when engaging heavy cruiser *Admiral Hipper* and destroyer *Friedrich Eckholdt* at the the Battle of the Barents Sea.

61. *Top left* Escort carrier HMS *Trumpeter*, March 1945, in the Kola Inlet, North Russia, in the few days between arriving with JW 65 and sailing with RA 65; note thick ice around her motor boat.

62. Escort carrier HMS *Searcher* pitches into a heavy sea, April 1945, two Wildcat VI fighters of 882 NAS lashed down on her flight deck.

63. *Bottom left* 'Flower' class corvette HMS *Honeysuckle*, March 1945, in thick ice, Kola Inlet, North Russia, alongside escort carrier HMS *Trumpeter* for refueling after escorting JW 65 and before sailing with RA 65.

64. HMS *Searcher*, one of the very few escort carriers operated as a fighter carrier, carrying 20-24 Wildcats; photo shows six Wildcat VI stowed forward, wings folded.

65. Escort carrier HMS *Nabob*, 23 August 1944, down by the stern and listing, limping back to Scapa Flow under her own power from northern Norway; limited flying continued. The ship's company of HMS *Nabob*, apart from FAA personnel, was provided by the RCN.

66. HMS *Nabob* docked after return from northern Norway with a hole 32 feet across made by an acoustic torpedo from *U-354* on the evening of 22 August 1944.

67. Escort carrier HMS *Campania*, early 1944; British-built escort carriers like the *Campania* were mainly deployed to the Arctic, as their riveted hulls were considered less prone to cracking in very low temperatures than welded US-built Lend-Lease ships.

68. HMS *Campania*, late 1944/early 1945, in the Kola Inlet, clearing snow and ice from flight deck prior to flying.

69. British-built escort carrier HMS *Nairana*, February 1945, pitching into heavy seas, while escorting JW 64 and RA 64, photo taken from cruiser HMS *Bellona*.

70. Escort carrier HMS *Fencer*, May 1944; snow and ice clearance underway while escorting RA 59. Swordfish of 842 NAS and Wildcats of 881 or 842 NAS on flight deck.

71. HMS *Nairana* in kinder seas June 1944.

72. Fleet carrier HMS *Victorious*, March 1942, in Norwegian waters as part of heavy covering force for PQ 12 and PQ 13; Fairey Fulmars on deck, County class heavy cruiser HMS *Berwick* astern.

73. HMS *Victorious*, showing the advantages of her enclosed bow while pitching into heavy northern seas.

74. Escort carrier HMS *Avenger*, March/April 1942, in USN camouflage before handover to RN under Lend/Lease. The first escort carrier to sail with an Arctic convoy when she escorted PQ 18 in September 1942.

75. Escort carrier HMS *Striker*, late 1944/early 1945, three Swordfish of 824 NAS ranged to fly and two Wildcats of 898 or 824 NAS with wings folded.

76. 'Flower' class corvette HMS *Bluebell*, on the River Tyne. Escorted Atlantic convoys, then 11 Arctic convoys. Sunk 17 February 1945 off Kola Inlet by acoustic torpedo from *U-711* that detonated her depth charges, leaving only one survivor. *U-711* was sunk on 4 May by a FAA strike on Kilbotn.

77. 'Flower' class corvette HMS *La Malouine*, 1942, ordered by the Marine Nationale of France but taken over by the RN, without a change of name when France surrendered in June 1940. Escorted PQ 17 in July 1942 before transferring to the Mediterranean.

78. 'Type VII' 'Gnevny' class Soviet destroyer *Gremyaschi*. Class designed with Italian assistance but their marginal structural strength, stability and sea-keeping qualities were taxed by demanding Arctic conditions; sister-ship *Sokrushetelni* broke in two and sank in a storm on 21 November 1942.

79. 'Type VII' 'Gnevny' class Soviet destroyer *Razumny* sailed from the Soviet Pacific Fleet around Siberia via the Northern Sea Route in June 1942, joining the Northern Fleet based in the Kola Inlet to escort Allied convoys until end of WW2.

80. 'Sims' class destroyer USS *Wainwright*, part of the PQ 17 covering force, detached to the convoy to refuel, 4 July 1942, but was interrupted by several large-scale torpedo bomber attacks, which the *Wainwright*'s aggressive and accurate gunnery drove off.

81. *Top right* Battleship USS *Washington*, May 1942, Hvalfjord, Iceland, showing six of her nine 16-inch 45 calibre guns; heavy cruisers USS *Wichita* and HMS *Kent* beyond. Covered PQ 17, then transferred to the Pacific; sank Japanese battleship *Kirishima* in a night gunnery action November 1942.

82. Heavy cruiser USS *Wichita*, April 1942 anchored in Scapa Flow, carrier USS *Wasp* in background. The *Wichita* covered PQ 16, QP 12 and PQ 17 before transferring to North Africa and then to the Pacific.

83. RN 'X' craft midget submarines inflicted such severe damage on the battleship *Tirpitz* at Kaafjord in Operation Source, September 1943, that she was under repair until April 1944. Photo shows *XE7*, a slightly modified boat designed for Far East service.

84. 'T' class submarine HMSub *Trident* at her launch in Birkenhead, 7 December 1938.

85. HMSub *Trident* torpedoed the heavy cruiser *Prinz Eugen* on 23 February 1942, almost blowing off her stern; repairs lasted until October 1942. Photo shows the *Trident* on 19 March 1942, returning alongside depot ship HMS *Forth* in Holy Loch.

86. 'T' class submarine HMS *Tuna* sank Type VIIC U-Boat *U-644* on 7 April 1943, SE of Jan Mayen Island. Shown alongside depot ship HMS *Forth* in Holy Loch, 26 August 1943.

87. RN submarines in Holy Loch, late 1942: alongside, *Sturgeon* (L), *Tigris* (R); middle distance, *Graph* (ex-*U570*), furthest away, *P42* (later named *Unbroken*).

88. Norwegian submarine HNorMS *Uredd*, 6 February 1943, setting out on her 9th patrol, a clandestine mission off the occupied Norwegian coast; she was sunk with all hands in a German minefield only four days later.

89. Free French submarine *Junon* spent most of 1942 patrolling off occupied Norway and on clandestine missions, landing British and Norwegian commandos, before transferring to the Mediterranean.

90. 'Black Swan' class escort sloop HMS *Cygnet*, 1944/45; escorted JW 56A/B and RA 56, then detached to Atlantic convoys March to August 1944, sinking *U-962* in defence of SC156 on 8 April 1944 with sister-ship HMS *Crane*; then escorted 13 more Arctic convoys.

91. 'Black Swan' class escort sloop HMS *Peacock* in 1945; escorted JW 59B and RA 59A, taking part in the sinkings of *U-354* on 24 August 1944 and *U-394* on 1 September 1944, before being transferred to Atlantic convoy escort duty.

Kriegsmarine Warships

WW2 started some years too early for the Kriegsmarine, as only the first two huge battleships of the ambitious 'Z' Plan had been laid down and these were soon scrapped on their building slips. The plan would have provided Nazi Germany with a surface fleet that, on paper and at least in battleships, offered the possibility of meeting the Royal Navy and Marine Militaire on something like equal terms. However, the Kriegsmarine began WW2 with only three 'armoured ships', always known to the British as 'pocket battleships', and two battlecruisers/fast battleships. Meanwhile, urgent efforts were made to complete the *Bismarck* and *Tirpitz*, two large battleships, superior to any RN capital ship, unrivalled in power and unsurpassed in size in the European theatre. The German navy therefore reverted to its traditional role of 'a fleet in being', encouraged by Hitler's reluctance to risk his surface warships, after losing the *Graf Spee* after only three months of war and the *Bismarck* on her maiden war cruise. Nevertheless, this defensive strategy tied down large numbers of British capital ships and cruisers to contain German surface warships in Norway, particularly after the commencement of large-scale convoys carrying war materials to north Russia through Arctic waters. Failures of German heavy ships to stop these, particularly the Battle of the Barents Sea, destroyed Hitler's faith in his navy and induced one of his periodic rages in which he ordered the scrapping of the Kriegsmarine's surface fleet and accepted the resignation in protest of Grand Admiral Erich Raeder, although his successor, Karl Dönitz, persuaded Hitler to retain them.

Kriegsmarine heavy cruisers and destroyers were plagued with machinery problems, often caused by the ambitious adoption of very high pressure boilers that performed disappointingly in wartime operating conditions, while many destroyers suffered from insufficient structural strength and poor sea keeping abilities in demanding Arctic conditions.

Kriegsmarine U-Boats were efficient and effective with well-trained crews and were, with Luftwaffe aircraft, the main threat to Allied Arctic convoys, eventually countered by escort carriers.

92. The powerful, well-protected
Bismarck class battleships, posed
a potent threat, initially to
Atlantic convoys and, after the
Bismarck's early loss, to Arctic
convoys by the mere presence
of the *Tirpitz* in Norwegian
fjords.

93. Battleship *Tirpitz*, between September 1942 and July 1943; starboard side in dazzle camouflage off Bogen in Ofotfjord, near Narvik, the port side wore an entirely different camouflage scheme at this time.

94. *Tirpitz*, 17 July 1942, moored off Bogen, protected by anti-torpedo nets.

95. *Tirpitz*, October 1942, in Ofotfjord with escorting destroyers, showing port side 'splinter' camouflage scheme.

96. *Tirpitz*, hit by 1,600lb armour piercing bombs in Kaafjord from FAA Fairey Barracuda dive bombers in Operation Tungsten, launched 3 April 1944, the day after completion of damage repairs from 'X' craft midget submarine mines, 22 September 1943.

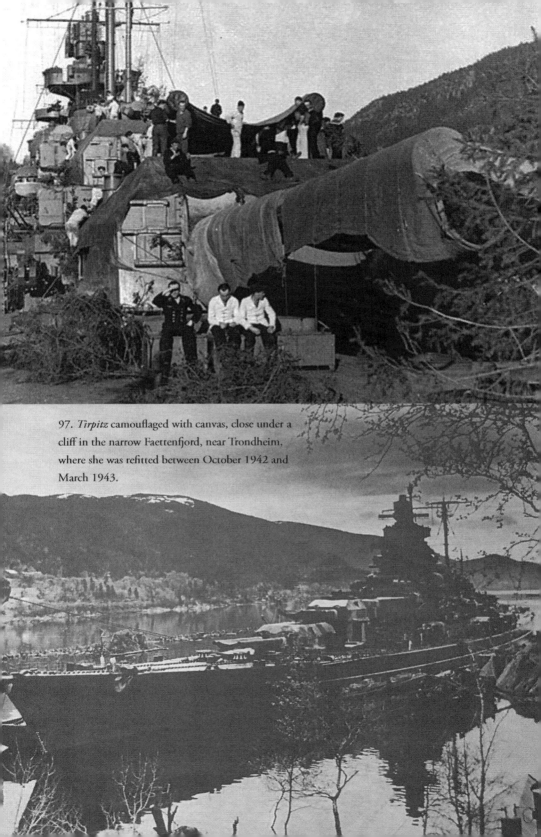

97. *Tirpitz* camouflaged with canvas, close under a cliff in the narrow Faettenfjord, near Trondheim, where she was refitted between October 1942 and March 1943.

98. *Tirpitz* firing her aft main armament of 15-inch guns that were used in action against a surface target only once, on 7 September 1943, when she and the *Scharnhorst* bombarded Spitzbergen.

99. *Top left* Elaborate efforts were made to camouflage the *Tirpitz* from Allied aircraft, including the use of local trees and foliage, with many yards of canvas to break up her outline.

100. *Tirpitz*, probably in Kaafjord between July 1943 and March 1944, when the mainmast was extended and radar installations altered.

101. Battlecruiser or fast battleship *Scharnhorst* immediately after completion of refit in November 1939, to raise the forecastle and fit an 'Atlantic bow' to improve sea-keeping, install a funnel cap and move the mainmast aft, giving her an elegant profile.

102. *Scharnhorst* in a seaway about June 1940; even after the 'Atlantic bow' was fitted, low freeboard made her a wet ship, often shipping heavy seas that found their way below and caused damage. Arado Ar196 floatplane visible on catapult forward of mainmast.

103. *Scharnhorst*, late 1940, wearing short-lived 'Baltic' camouflage stripes on the hull.

104. *Scharnhorst*, ice build-up around forecastle area with 11-inch (28cm) guns of forward triple turret depressed, presumably to aid ice clearance.

105. Heavy cruiser (formerly 'armoured ship') or 'Pocket Battleship' *Admiral Scheer*, June 1942, Ofotfjord; camouflage scheme applied late May 1942 and carried in this form only until early July 1942 when dark grey on the funnel and bridge tower was replaced with a lighter shade. Arado Ar196 floatplane visible on catapult aft of funnel.

106. *Admiral Scheer*, 22 February 1942 *en route* to Trondheim, Norway; seen across the stern of heavy cruiser *Prinz Eugen* that was torpedoed and badly damaged by HMSub *Trident* the following day, note swastika aerial recognition marking on red deck panel.

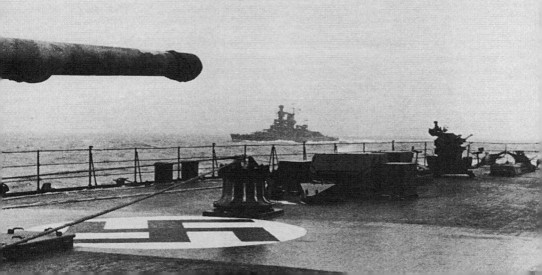

107. Capsized wreck of the *Admiral Scheer* in Kiel, mid-1945; sunk by Avro Lancasters of 1 and 3 Groups RAF, April 1945. Partially scrapped post-war, the remains of the wreck were buried when Kiel's inner harbour basins were filled in and built over.

108. The *Admiral Scheer* rolling heavily in a seaway; note tail of Arado Ar196 floatplane on catapult and secondary armament on upper deck.

109. 'Armoured ship' (later heavy cruiser) or 'Pocket Battleship' *Deutschland*, 1938, deployed to the Spanish Civil War 'neutrality' patrol with red, white and black national colour stripes on 11-inch turrets and a newly fitted low funnel cap. Heinkel He.60c biplane floatplane on catapult between bridge and funnel, later replaced by Arado Ar196.

110. *Lützow* formerly *Deutschland*, mid-1942 in Langfjord, Norway; reclassified from 'armoured ship' to heavy cruiser early 1940 when renamed, larger funnel cap fitted early 1942.

111. *Bottom right Lützow*, June 1942, camouflaged off Bogen in Ofotfjord, near Narvik. Sailed to attack PQ 17, 3 July 1942, but ran aground in fog and returned Narvik. Repaired in Kiel, August to October 1942, before Battle of the Barents Sea, 31 December 1942.

112. *Lützow*, 11/12 April 1940, down by the stern, under tow for Germany after being torpedoed by HMSub *Spearfish*. Centre 11-inch gun missing from fore-turret following damage from Norwegian shore batteries at Drøbak, Oslofjord early on 9 April 1940.

113. Heavy cruiser *Admiral Hipper,* April 1942, camouflaged in Trondheim, Norway. Sailed, 3 July 1942, with *Tirpitz, Lützow* and *Admiral Scheer* to attack PQ 17, Operation Rosselsprung, but sortie cancelled when they were detected.

114. *Admiral Hipper* in dry dock at Brest, February/March 1941, before returning to Germany via the Denmark Strait, N Atlantic and Norway for 7 month refit in Kiel.

115. *Admiral Hipper*, summer 1942, Trondheim, Norway; wore a similar camouflage scheme during the Battle of the Barents Sea, 31 December 1942.

116. *Admiral Hipper* follows the *Tirpitz*, accompanied by 6 destroyers, out of Trondheim to attack PQ 17, 3 July 1942, in Operation Rosselsprung, but sortie cancelled when they were detected.

117. Unusual bow view of the *Admiral Hipper*, summer 1942, Trondheim.

118. *Bottom right Prinz Eugen* between 24 February and 15 May 1942 in Lofjord making temporary repairs to severe stern damage when torpedoed by HMSub *Trident* off Trondheim on 23 February. Repair ship *Huascaras* alongside to starboard, heavy cruiser *Admiral Scheer* in foreground.

119. Heavy cruiser *Prinz Eugen*, late 1940 or early 1941; the 'Baltic' camouflage was painted over at Grimstadfjord near Bergen on 22 May 1941, immediately before she broke out into the Atlantic with the battleship *Bismarck*.

120. *Prinz Eugen*, February/March 1942, in Lofjord, down by the stern, after being torpedoed by HMSub *Trident*.

121. *Bottom left* Aft view of the *Prinz Eugen*, May 1942 with damaged stern cut away and plated over, making a broad transom; two temporary rudders manually actuated from the aft capstan, enabled her to reach Kiel under her own power.

122. *Prinz Eugen*, February/March 1942, showing extent of torpedo damage to starboard side of stern.

123. *Prinz Eugen*, February/March 1942, showing extent of torpedo damage to port side of stern.

124. Type '1934A' destroyer *Friedrich Ihn*, pre-WW2; hull numbers on German destroyers indicated flotilla positions. Damaged by heavy weather in 1942 when escorting the *Tirpitz* in her unsuccessful sorties to attack convoys PQ 12/QP 8 and PQ 17.

125. Type '1934A' destroyer *Paul Jacobi*, pre-WW2; escorted the *Tirpitz* in the unsuccessful sortie to attack convoys PQ 12/QP 8, March 1942, and then the damaged *Prinz Eugen* to Kiel in May 1942

126. Type '1934A' destroyer *Theodor Riedel*, pre-WW2; seriously damaged by grounding 3 times: 8 June 1938, 12 August 1940 and 2 July 1942 when escorting the *Tirpitz* to attack PQ 17. At the Battle of the Barents Sea, 31 December 1942.

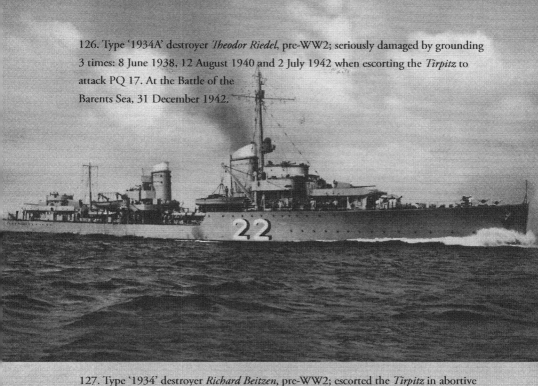

127. Type '1934' destroyer *Richard Beitzen*, pre-WW2; escorted the *Tirpitz* in abortive sortie to attack PQ 17, July 1942; took part in the Battle of the Barents Sea, helping to sink minesweeper HMS *Bramble*, 31 December 1942.

128. Type '1934A' destroyer *Hans Lody*, 8 June 1940, sinking empty troop ship SS *Orama* off Norway. Ran ashore 2 July 1942 and severely damaged when sailing to escort the abortive *Tirpitz* attack on PQ 17.

129. Type '1934A' destroyer *Hermann Schoemann*, pre-WW2; escorted the *Tirpitz* in the unsuccessful sortie to attack convoys PQ 12/QP 8, Mar 1942. 1 May 1942, part of destroyer attack on PQ 14 and disabled cruiser HMS *Edinburgh*; critically damaged by the *Edinburgh*'s 6-inch gunfire and scuttled with her own depth charges.

130. Type '1936' destroyer *Karl Galster*, pre-WW2; sole survivor of a class of 6, her sisters were sunk at the Battles of Narvik in April 1940. Ran ashore 2 July 1942 and severely damaged when sailing to escort the abortive *Tirpitz* attack on PQ 17.

131. Type '1934A' destroyer *Friedrich Eckholdt*, pre-WW2. Sank minesweeper HMS *Bramble* at the Battle of the Barents Sea, 31 December 1942, but blundered into cruiser HMS *Sheffield* at 4000 yards in poor visibility and was sunk with all hands by rapid 6-inch salvoes.

132. Type '1936A' destroyer flotilla leader *Z28*, early WW2; 1942, carried out mine laying off N Russia; July 1942 nominated for abortive attack on PQ 17; early March 1943 ran aground N Norway.

133. Type '1936A Mob' destroyer *Z31* in Norwegian waters; took part in the attack on JW 51B, 31 December 1942, and the subsequent Battle of the Barents Sea, without damage. Damaged by Allied shore batteries, 8 September 1943, during bombardment of Spitzbergen.

134. Type '1936A' destroyer *Z26*; part of destroyer force searching for PQ 13, 29 March 1942, sunk by gunfire of cruiser HMS *Trinidad* and destroyer HMS *Eclipse* during a snowstorm.

135. Type '1936A' destroyer *Z24*; based in Tromsø late 1941; 17 December 1941, searched for QP 6, briefly engaging RN minesweepers *Speedy* and *Hazard* in fog. 28 March 1942, part of attack on PQ 13, engaging cruiser HMS *Trinidad*. 1 May 1942, part of attack on QP 11 and disabled cruiser HMS *Edinburgh*, rescuing survivors from *Hermann Schoemann*.

136. Type VIIC *U-288*, sunk when attacking JW 58 south of Bear Island, 3 April 1944, in combined attacks by Wildcat, Swordfish and Avenger aircraft from RN escort carriers *Activity* and *Tracker*.

137. *U-288*, 3 April 1944, under attack with depth charges by Swordfish of 819 NAS from escort carrier HMS *Activity*.

138. U-Boat depot ship *Black Watch*, *U-711* and cargo ship *Senja* under attack at Kilbotn 4 May 1945. 28 Wildcats of 882, 846 and 853 NAS, and 16 Avengers of 846 and 853 NAS from escort carriers *Searcher*, *Trumpeter* and *Queen*, sank all three German ships, while heavy AA ship *Thetis*, former Norwegian coastal battleship *Harald Haarfagre*, visible in left foreground, was damaged.

139. *Black Watch*, former Olsen Lines passenger vessel built in 1939, became Kriegsmarine depot and HQ ship in 1940. Some sources suggest she was renamed *Generalleutnant Eduard Dietl* after that officer's death in an air crash 23 June 1944. Sunk by FAA air attack 4 May 1945.

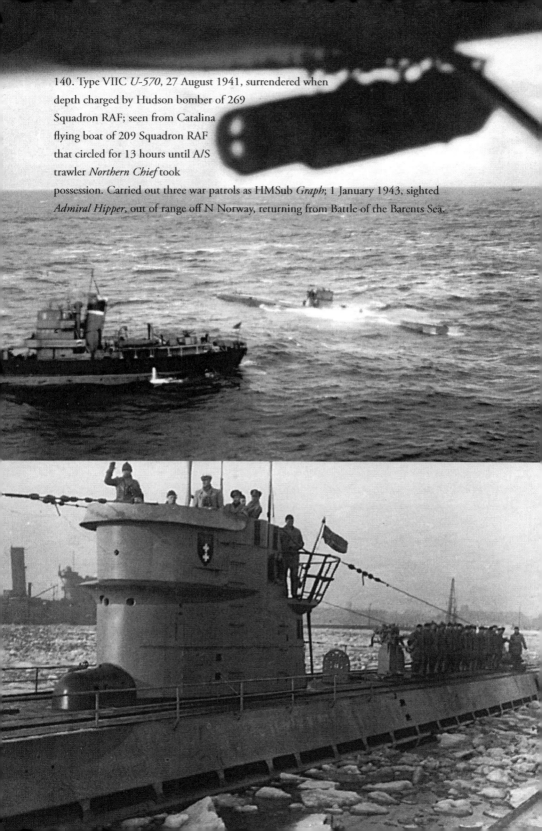

140. Type VIIC *U-570*, 27 August 1941, surrendered when depth charged by Hudson bomber of 269 Squadron RAF; seen from Catalina flying boat of 209 Squadron RAF that circled for 13 hours until A/S trawler *Northern Chief* took possession. Carried out three war patrols as HMSub *Graph*; 1 January 1943, sighted *Admiral Hipper*, out of range off N Norway, returning from Battle of the Barents Sea.

141. Type VIIC. *U-278*, December 1943/January 1944, on passage from Kiel to Bergen; carried out 5 war patrols in Arctic waters; torpedoed new destroyer flotilla leader HMS *Hardy* escorting JW 56A, SE of Bear Island, causing her to be scuttled, 30 January 1944.

142. Type VIIC *U-711*, duck emblem on conning tower. Torpedoed corvette HMS *Bluebell* escorting RA 64, 17 February 1945, in Kola Inlet, leaving only 1 survivor. *U-711* sunk in FAA raid on Kilbotn, 4 May 1945.

143. *Bottom left* Type IXD2 *U-864*, Winter 1944/45; heavy AA ship, *Arcona*, in background. 9 February 1945, left Bergen for Japan with strategic materials and specialist personnel. Sunk by HMSub *Venturer* in the only action where one submarine torpedoed another while both were submerged.

144. *Top left* Type VIIC *U-255*, 15 July 1942 in Narvik, flying 4 victory pennants and the flag of the SS *Paulus Potter* after PQ 17; sank 11 merchant vessels in WW2; also sank destroyer escort USS *Leopold* in March 1944, south of Iceland.

145. Type VIIC *U-251*, July 1941, Narvik; 3 May 1942 sank damaged freighter *Jutland* from PQ 15 in Barents Sea; 10 July 1942 sank damaged and abandoned freighter *El Capitan* from PQ 17 in Barents Sea.

146. Type VIIC *U-354*, carried out 11 war patrols in Arctic waters, damaging escort carrier HMS *Nabob* and frigate HMS *Bickerton* with acoustic torpedoes, 22 August 1944, the *Bickerton* was scuttled; two days later, *U-354* was sunk by escorts of JW 59. Shown March 1944 in U-Boat pen Trondheim.

147. Type VIIC *U-378*, carried out six war patrols in Arctic waters, then two in the Atlantic; sank Polish destroyer *Orkan* 8 October 1943 but sunk 12 days later by Wildcat and Avenger aircraft from escort carrier USS *Core*.

148. S-boat depot ship *Adolf Lüderitz* 1942, camouflaged against cliffs in Semskefjord, north of Kirkenes. Hitler ordered S-boats to be stationed in northern Norway to counter any Allied landings, not to attack Arctic convoys, which were largely out of range and the prevailing weather was too bad. In Semskefjord, the *Adolf Lüderitz* used her comprehensive radio installation as a repeat station for shortwave radio transmissions from U-boats in the area. Inset – *Adolf Lüderitz* when new.

Aircraft

Early Arctic convoys to North Russia had to rely on the initially limited AA armament of escorts to provide protection against determined Luftwaffe attacks, mainly by Junkers Ju.88 and Heinkel He.111, and had little chance of deterring more distant Blohm and Voss BV138 and Focke Wulf 200 Condor shadowers from reporting a convoy's position, course and speed to direct air and U-Boat attacks. However, between April and August 1942, limited air cover for Arctic convoys was provided by 'Catapult Aircraft Merchant' (CAM) ships, merchant ships fitted with a rocket powered catapult to launch a single Hurricane fighter over the bows. Launching the "catafighter" was a matter of fine judgement as it had limited flying time and needed to ditch after its single mission, with the pilot bailing out over the convoy, unless it was near enough to fly to a Russian airfield. From September 1942, escort carriers became available and the first to accompany an Arctic convoy, PQ 18, was HMS *Avenger*, carrying 12 Sea Hurricanes and 3 Swordfish. Although 13 merchant ships from PQ 18 were sunk, the Germans lost 4 U-Boats and 44 aircraft, mainly torpedo bombers with their highly trained crews. Aircrew from both sides who were shot down or ditched, needed to be rescued very quickly before they froze to death in the icy Arctic seas, something that was often not possible for the Luftwaffe. By 1944, escort carriers became more numerous and their air groups better equipped to carry out destructive and disruptive air strikes, on German ships, U-Boat bases and airfields in Norway, in addition to directly escorting the convoys to North Russia.

Hawker Hurricane fighters, initially flown by the RAF, were based at Vaenga airfield near Murmansk, from September 1941 to provide air cover for convoys, but were handed over to Soviet personnel by November 1941. In September 1942 RAF Handley Page Hampden torpedo bombers flew to Vaenga to cover the final stage of PQ 18 and, in October 1942, these, too, were transferred to Russia, to be replaced by Soviet torpedo bombers as they became unserviceable.

149. Fairey Swordfish of 816 NAS on escort carrier HMS *Tracker*, being readied for an anti-submarine patrol in late 1943.

150. Fairey Swordfish of 813 or 825 NAS on escort carrier HMS *Campania* 1944/45; as snow and ice is cleared from the flight deck.

151. Grumman Wildcats VI of 882 NAS on escort carrier HMS *Searcher*, ranged for take off for the Operation Judgement II raid on Kilbotn, May 1945. Note single drop tanks under starboard wings.

152. Wildcat VI (JV768) of 882 NAS and Fairey Firefly NF1 night fighter of 746A NAS (one of two carried) securely storm-lashed down, with engine and cockpit covers in place against wind-driven spray as escort carrier HMS *Searcher* rolls heavily off northern Norway, April 1945.

153. Wildcat VI of 882 NAS returns to escort carrier HMS *Searcher*, after Operation Judgement II strike on U-Boat base at Kilbotn, northern Norway, 4 May 1945.

154. Wildcat VI JV719 of 882 NAS, piloted by Sub Lt J F Pullen RNVR, makes an almost perfect landing on HMS *Searcher*, 26 March 1945, despite significant starboard tailplane damage sustained in combat with a Messerschmitt Bf109 during Operation Prefix, an anti-shipping strike on Trondheim.

155. Three Wildcat VI of 882 NAS securely lashed down to the flight deck of escort carrier HMS *Searcher* during a driving snow storm off northern Norway, April 1945.

156. Wildcat VI on the snow-covered flight deck of escort carrier HMS *Campania*, 1944/45.

157. Hawker Sea Hurricanes of 802 and 883 NAS, with non-folding wings lashed down on the camouflaged flight deck of escort carrier HMS *Avenger*, 1942.

158. Grumman Avenger of 846 NAS catches an arrester wire and lands on escort carrier HMS *Trumpeter* in late 1944 or early 1945.

159. Avenger of 846 NAS burns on the quarterdeck of escort carrier HMS *Tracker*, 1 April 1944, after hitting the round-down when landing after an ASW patrol, escorting convoy JW 58. The fire was quickly extinguished but the pilot did not survive. The *Tracker* had re-equipped with
Avengers in January 1944.

160. *Top right* Grumman Hellcat of 800 NAS, with drop tank under fuselage, takes off from escort carrier HMS *Emperor* on 3 April 1944 for the Operation Tungsten strike on the *Tirpitz* in Kaafjord.

161. Hellcats of 800 NAS ranged on the flight deck of escort carrier HMS *Emperor* for the Operation Tungsten strike against the *Tirpitz*, 3 April 1944. Astern are the carriers *Furious*, *Searcher* and *Pursuer*.

162. Hawker Hurricane IIB of No 134 Squadron RAF at Vaenga airfield, Murmansk, with typically suspicious Soviet sentries. No 134 and No 81 Squadron RAF formed 151 Wing to provide fighter cover for Arctic convoys in September and October 1941, flying 365 sorties before handing their aircraft over to Soviet personnel.

163. Hurricane IIB fighters of No 81 Squadron RAF at Vaenga airfield in September or October 1941. 15 crated Hurricanes were transported to North Russia in the first Arctic convoy, Operation Dervish, while a further 24 flew in from the old carrier HMS *Argus*.

164. *Top right* Avro Lancaster heavy bomber of 9 or 617 Squadron RAF over Kaafjord, 15 September 1944, during Operation Paravane, an attack on the *Tirpitz* with 'Tallboy' 12,000lb bombs. A direct hit and several near misses rendered the battleship unfit for further operations. Sunk at Tromsø by several 'Tallboy' bombs, 12 November 1944.

165. Consolidated Catalina MkII flying boat of 240 Squadron RAF at Stranraer, Scotland, March 1941. Coastal Command Catalinas operated from Vaenga and Lakhta airfields in North Russia until 1944, flying anti-submarine patrols in support of Arctic convoys.

166. Fairey Barracuda carrier-borne dive bombers flying over Langfjorden *en route* for Kaafjord to carry out the first strike of Operation Tungsten against the *Tirpitz*, 3 April 1944.

167. *Top right* Barracudas and Vought Corsair fighters on fleet carrier HMS *Formidable*, before an Operation Goodwood strike against the *Tirpitz* during in August 1944; armourers man-handling 1,600lb bombs to load onto the Barracudas. County class heavy cruiser HMS *Berwick* astern.

168. 12 Fairey Albacore torpedo bombers ranged on fleet carrier HMS *Victorious*, 9 March 1942, for the only attack by carrier-borne aircraft on the *Tirpitz* at sea. The attack, made during her unsuccessful attempt to intercept Arctic convoys PQ 12 and QP 8, scored no hits but one torpedo missed by only 10 yards.

169. Hurricane MkIIC. The Hurricane's high-performance Rolls-Royce Merlin engine was designed to use 100 octane aviation spirit and struggled when run on the standard Soviet 95 octane fuel.

170. *Top right* Handley Page Hampden TB1 torpedo bomber in Soviet Naval Air Force markings, 1942/43. Operation Orator flew 32 Hampdens of 144 Squadron RAF and 455 Squadron RAAF to Vaenga airfield in September 1942 to cover PQ 18 from attack by German heavy warships, 24 survived the flight and were gifted to the Soviet Navy in October 1942 when RAF/RAAF personnel returned home.

171. Hurricane MkIIC, supplied under Lend/Lease, in Soviet markings, with four wing-mounted 20mm Oerlikon cannon. A development of the MkIIB, the first Lend/Lease-supplied Hurricane variant with only six wing-mounted .303 machine guns, which was thought under-armed and under-armoured by the Russians who increased both.

172. Hampden TB1 torpedo bombers, known as 'the balalaika' by the Russians because of the unusual fuselage shape, carried a single torpedo and served until mid-1943, when the surviving aircraft were worn out; with spares unobtainable they were replaced by Ilyushin DB-3 and IL-4.

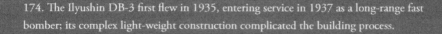

173. Ilyushin DB-3T in 1942, with torpedo mounted beneath fuselage; torpedo bomber variant was first built in 1938.

174. The Ilyushin DB-3 first flew in 1935, entering service in 1937 as a long-range fast bomber; its complex light-weight construction complicated the building process.

175. The Ilyushin IL-4, developed from the DB-3 with construction simplified; entered production in January 1940.

176. The IL-4 torpedo bomber variant could carry 3 torpedoes but, like the bomber from which it was developed, was considered weak in defensive armament.

177. German torpedo bombers, probably Heinkel He.111 H6, attacking convoy PQ 18, September 1942, seen from escort carrier HMS *Avenger*, their primary target.

178. Heinkel He.111 H6 torpedo bombers attacking convoy PQ 17, July 1942; rescue ship *Rathlin* in foreground.

179. Heinkel He.111 H6 torpedo bomber releasing one of the two torpedoes carried on external racks beneath the fuselage.

180. Heinkel He.111 H6 torpedo bomber being loaded with a second torpedo; the first is already mounted below the fuselage.

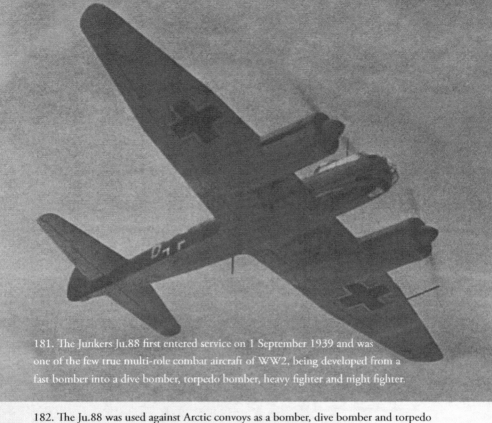

181. The Junkers Ju.88 first entered service on 1 September 1939 and was one of the few true multi-role combat aircraft of WW2, being developed from a fast bomber into a dive bomber, torpedo bomber, heavy fighter and night fighter.

182. The Ju.88 was used against Arctic convoys as a bomber, dive bomber and torpedo bomber and was effective in all those roles. The torpedo bomber version was designated Ju.88 A-17 and carried two torpedoes abreast on external racks under the fuselage as in the Heinkel He.111 H6.

183. Junkers Ju.87D 'Stuka' dive bombers in formation near Kandalaksha, on the Kola Peninsula near Murmansk, June 1944.

184. The Ju.87 'Stuka' dive bomber was an accurate and highly effective dive bomber that also had ground attack and anti-tank versions but its slow speed and poor manoeuvrability made it vulnerable to fighter opposition unless strongly escorted.

The Ju.87 first saw service in 1937 as part of the German 'Condor Legion' in the Spanish Civil War.

185. Heinkel He.115 B1 floatplane torpedo bomber; torpedo being loaded into the internal weapons bay at the Grossenbrode Torpedo School on the Baltic coast of Schleswig-Holstei

186. The He.115 was a highly effective floatplane with fine handling characteristics, good stability and reasonable performance; a successful torpedo bomber, mine layer and reconnaissance bomber, although vulnerable to attack from high-performance fighters.

187. A closer view from the port side of a He.115 BI floatplane being loaded with a torpedo at the Grossenbrode Torpedo School.

188. The He.115 B2 variant was modified for Arctic service with the underside of the floats reinforced with steel ice runners to enable it to fly from ice or compacted snow.

189. *Top left* An Arado Ar196 floatplane being recovered for hoisting aboard the heavy cruiser *Prinz Eugen* below one of her 4 triple torpedo tube mountings.

190. The Arado Ar196 was the standard catapult-launched reconnaissance floatplane carried by large German surface warships from 1939; armed with 20mm cannon, it handled well in the air and on the water.

191. The Blohm and Voss BV138 twin-boom flying boat was named the 'Sea Dragon' but nicknamed 'the flying clog' after the hull shape. A robust, reliable and highly effective long-range maritime patrol and reconnaissance aircraft used to shadow Arctic convoys.

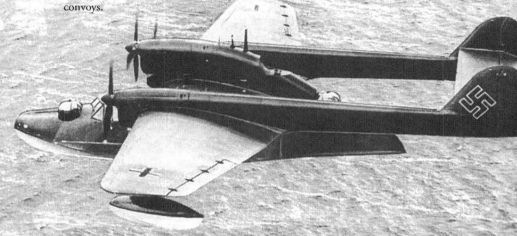

192. *Below right* The BV138 was powered by three Jumo 880hp 6-cylinder 12-piston horizontally opposed 2-stroke diesel engines that gave long range and the ability to refuel at sea from U-Boats.

193. The Focke Wulf FW200C 'Condor' long-range maritime patrol bomber, developed from a pre-war commercial airliner, was a serious threat to Allied shipping before escort carriers and CAM ships. A fundamentally weak rear spar caused frequent structural failure of the aft fuselage. Largely replaced by the BV138 from mid-1941.

194. The Messerschmitt Bf109 first saw action in 1937 in the Spanish Civil War but remained the standard German fighter throughout WW2, being built in larger numbers (almost 34,000) than any other fighter aircraft.

195. Progressive development of the Bf109 throughout WW2 resulted in variants from A to K and ensured that it remained competitive with Allied fighters until 1945.

196. The Messerschmitt Bf110 heavy fighter did not live up to initial high expectations because of a lack of manoeuvrability compared with single-seat fighters but escorted bombers and torpedo bombers attacking Arctic convoys and became an effective night fighter.

Merchant Ships

From PQ/QP 1 in September 1941, to JW/RA 67 in May 1945, 78 convoys were fought through Arctic waters, to and from north Russia, comprising 1576 civilian-manned ships, of which 103 were lost from all causes. The merchant vessels convoyed flew many national flags; apart from the UK, US and Soviet Union, there were ships from Panama, Norway, Belgium, Honduras, Poland and the Netherlands. Armed only with single 4 or 5-inch guns and light AA weapons, most of the merchant ships were mismatched, slow and unwieldy, both when heavily laden outbound and then in ballast on their return voyage, giving the convoy commodores a demanding task to keep the ships together in formation, particularly when under attack, in appalling Arctic weather and mountainous seas.

197. RFA *Black Ranger*, Admiralty oiler, refuelled convoy escorts on PQ/QP 1, PQ 16, QP 14, PQ 18, JW/RA 64 and JW/RA 66.

198. Matilda Mk II infantry tanks being loaded at Liverpool for convoying to north Russia, possibly in PQ 3, 17 October 1941.

199. SS *Charles R McCormick*, neutral in April 1940 but held in Norway during German invasion and had her cargo of vehicles confiscated before being allowed to sail. Later, with hull lettering painted out, sailed to Murmansk in PQ 18 and returned in QP 15.

200. SS *Empire Stevenson*, sailed with PQ 5 but torpedoed and sunk in PQ 18 by German aircraft north of Bear Island, 13 September 1942.

201. Panamanian SS *El Occidente*, torpedoed and sunk by *U-435* when part of QP 10, 13 April 1942.

202. SS *Induna*, straggled from PQ 13 during bad weather, torpedoed and sunk by *U-376*, 30 March 1942, NE of the Kola Inlet.

203. SS *Goolistan*, straggled from QP 15 in a storm, torpedoed and sunk by *U-625*, 23 November 1942, between Bear Island and Spitzbergen, there were no survivors.

204. Soviet MV *Kuznetz Lesov*, also a straggler from QP 15 after a storm, torpedoed and sunk by *U-601*, 23 November 1942, 3 hours after the SS *Goolistan*, there were no survivors.

205. SS *Empire Lawrence*, CAM ship, catapult-mounted Hurricane fighter forward. Part of PQ 16, bombed and sunk by Luftwaffe aircraft east of Bear Island, 27 May 1942, when her Hurricane had ditched after shooting down a German bomber.

206. Convoy PQ 17 in tight formation, before being given the order to scatter.

207. SS *Pan Atlantic*, Passing under the Cape Cod vertical lift Canal Railroad Bridge in Bourne, Massachusetts, 23 January 1938. Bombed and sunk by Junkers Ju.88, 6 July 1942, west of Narvik, when part of PQ 17.

208. SS *Empire Tide*, June 1942, CAM ship, catapult-mounted Hurricane fighter forward, in Hvalfjord, Iceland. Part of PQ 17, reached Archangelsk carrying many survivors and returned to UK; survived WW2.

209. SS *Hartlebury*, part of PQ 2 and PQ 11; when she joined PQ 17, all 4 of her sister-ships had been sunk in action. Torpedoed and sunk by *U-355*, 7 July 1942, in Kara Sea.

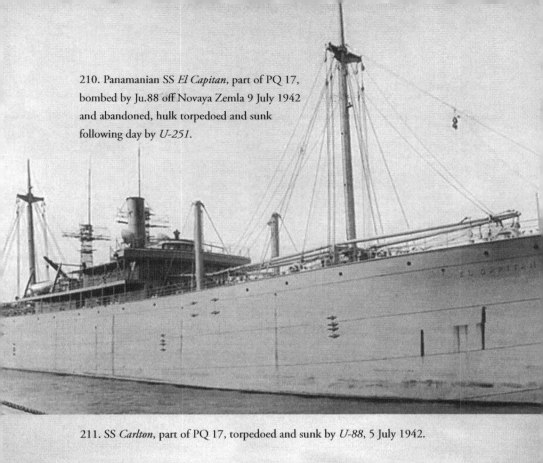

210. Panamanian SS *El Capitan*, part of PQ 17, bombed by Ju.88 off Novaya Zemla 9 July 1942 and abandoned, hulk torpedoed and sunk following day by *U-251*.

211. SS *Carlton*, part of PQ 17, torpedoed and sunk by *U-88*, 5 July 1942.

212. SS *Honomu* under her former name of *Edmore*; torpedoed and sunk by *U-456* in the Barents Sea, 5 July 1942 when part of PQ 17.

213. SS *William Hooper*, Liberty ship, part of PQ 17, torpedoed by Heinkel He.111, 4 July 1942 and abandoned, hulk sunk by gunfire of *U-334* later that day.

214. SS *Christopher Newport*, Liberty ship, part of PQ 17 on her maiden voyage, torpedoed by Heinkel He.115 floatplane, 4 July 1942 and abandoned, hulk torpedoed and sunk by *U-457*. Pictured sinking with back broken.

215. SS *Patrick Henry*, the first Liberty ship of 2,710 built, took part in PQ 18 and survived WW2.

216. MV *Atheltemplar*, tanker, part of PQ 18, torpedoed by *U-457*, 14 September 1942, and abandoned, burning fiercely. Capsized hull sunk by gunfire of *U-408* later that day.

217. SS *Empire Beaumont*, part of PQ 18, reached Archangelsk but torpedoed and sunk there by Heinkel He.111, 13 September 1942; she was less than 3 months old.

218. SS *Mary Luckenbach*, part of PQ 18, torpedoed in the Barents Sea by a Junkers Ju.88 that was shot down but detonated her cargo of over 1,000 tons of TNT.

219. SS *Mary Luckenbach*, totally destroyed by an immense explosion, killing all 65 aboard; surrounding ships were badly shaken by the shock wave and showered with falling debris. Photo taken from escort carrier HMS *Avenger*.

220. Convoy RA 53 leaving the Kola Inlet, 1 March 1943, merchant ships riding high in ballast, photo taken from escorting destroyer, probably HMS *Inglefield*.

221. SS *Executive* under her former name of *Carenco*, part of RA 53, torpedoed and sunk by *U-255*, 5 March 1943.

222. SS *Fort Bellingham,* part of JW 56A, torpedoed by *U-360*, 26 January 1944, but carried on as a straggler until torpedoed and sunk by *U-957* later that day.

223. SS *Empire Tourist,* part of RA 57, torpedoed and sunk by *U-703*, 4 March 1944, off the Kola Inlet.

224. A Liberty ship, as yet unidentified, probably part of RA 64, contending with the high seas and storms of February 1945, conditions almost unprecedented, even in the Barents Sea.

225. January 1945, ships of JW/RA 63 steaming through 'frost-smoke' in a relatively quiet northern sea; both these convoys completed their voyages without loss.

226. A Liberty ship, as yet unidentified, in RA 64. On 18/19 February 1945, winds in the Barents Sea gusted to force 11, with exceptionally high seas, worsening on 22 February with force 12 winds reaching 90 knots and temperatures many degrees below freezing.

227. Liberty ship SS *Henry Bacon*, her steering damaged by huge seas, was 55 nm astern of RA 64 on 23 February 1945 in moderating weather, when Junkers Ju.88s torpedoed her; she claimed 5 shot down by her gunners before she sank, the last Allied ship sunk by the Luftwaffe in WW2.

228. SS *Fort Hall*, Canadian-built; convoy Commodore's ship in JW 55A when new and also part of JW 64. Survived WW2.

229. *Bottom right* SS *Rathlin*, as a convoy rescue ship: booms at bows deployed scrambling nets at 90° to ship's side; forward well-deck cranes lowered overboard 2-man rescue baskets; sloped racks of rafts on bridge front. Shot down FW200 Condor during PQ 17; also in PQ 18 and 22 other convoys, rescuing 634 survivors.

230. SS *Copeland*, before conversion to convoy rescue ship. Sailed with PQ 18, credited with shooting down one bomber and damaging two others; part of QP 15 and 71 other, mainly Atlantic, convoys.

231. SS *Syrian Prince*, before conversion. Convoy rescue ships were small, nimble freighters with AA guns, enhanced lifesaving equipment, a naval-manned hospital and operating theatre, plus enlarged galleys, accommodation, messing facilities, clothing stores, and sanitary facilities, for around 150 survivors, though many rescued far more.

PART II

The original documents that form the core of this title, are two of the official Naval Staff History Battle Summaries issued as classified internal documents for instructional purposes within the Royal Navy during or just after WW2. They may therefore contain occasional inconsistencies but the original documents have not been edited, in order to preserve their historical authenticity. Therefore, historical content appears as unedited text, apart from minor changes made to date formats and corrections to typing errors found in the original.

BR. 1736 (44)

NAVAL STAFF HISTORY SECOND WORLD WAR

BATTLE SUMMARY No. 22

ARCTIC CONVOYS

1941–1945

(Historical Section), Naval Staff, Admiralty, S.W.1

THE CONTENTS OF THIS BOOK ARE BASED ON INFORMATION AVAILABLE UP TO AND INCLUDING NOVEMBER 1954

Admiralty
7th December 1954

TSD 296/52

BR 1736 (44) Naval Staff History, Arctic Convoys 1941-1945, having been approved by My Lords Commissioners of the Admiralty, is hereby promulgated for information.

B.R. 1736 (15) dated 1944 is hereby superseded, and all copies are to be destroyed in accordance with B.R.1.

By Command of Their Lordships

Foreword
November 1954

Battle Summary No. 22, Russian Convoys, 1942, was originally written in 1943. It then dealt with eight out of the sixteen which were run in 1942, after the strengthening of the German forces in Norway in the spring of that year.

In the present edition, the story has been re-written so as to include the 1942 convoys previously omitted, with a view to giving a connected account of the increasing enemy pressure and the countermeasures evolved to meet it as it developed. A chapter has also been added dealing more briefly with the convoys run from 1943 to 1945, when the commitments of the German Air Force elsewhere and the timidity (and gradual destruction) of their surface forces practically confined the attacks on the convoys to the submarine.

Chapters I, IV, V and VI deal with the convoys which formed the subject of the previous battle summary; they have been expanded and where necessary amended. Chapters II, III, VII and VIII contain entirely new matter. A considerable amount of information about the German intentions and operations, derived from documents captured at the end of the war, has been embodied. New plans including such information have been produced.

Admiral of the Fleet Lord Tovey, Admirals Sir Henry Moore, Sir Louis Hamilton, Sir Robert Burnett, Captains A. W. Clarke, C. T. Addis and the late Rear-Admiral J. W. Clayton have been good enough to clarify certain aspects of operations in amplification of contemporary records; J. C. Nerney, Head of the Air Historical Branch, kindly made available information derived from captured documents of the German Air Force. Since by far the greater number of merchant ships in the convoys were American or British, and their defence was almost entirely a British commitment, it is felt that the title 'Russian Convoys' is in the nature of a misnomer, and the book has therefore been re-named Arctic Convoys 1941-45.

'the worst
journey
in the
world.'

Attributed to Winston Spencer Churchill,
Navy News, 15th December 2020

Introduction 1954

On 22nd June 1941, Germany invaded Russia. That same evening Mr. Winston Churchill broadcast a speech pledging all possible British assistance to the USSR against the common enemy.

At that time there existed only two practicable routes by which supplies from Britain could reach Russia, viz. to Murmansk and the White Sea port of Archangel in the north, and via the Cape of Good Hope to the Persian Gulf, and thence overland for more than 1,000 miles, in the south.

The first convoy for Archangel sailed towards the end of August 1941, and throughout the winter of 1941-42 the service was maintained with little opposition from the enemy and with surprisingly light losses. With the coming of spring, conditions changed and the maintenance of the North Russian convoys became one of the most bitterly contested operations of the maritime war.

* * * * *

In order to assess the place of these convoys to Russia in the Allied strategy, it will be convenient to glance at the worldwide situation at this time. Almost everywhere the spring of 1942 marked the nadir of Allied fortunes. In the Far East, the Japanese had so far carried all before them; Singapore fell on 15th February, Java surrendered on 9th March; Rangoon had been occupied, and the fate of Burma and north-east India was in the balance. Some four thousand miles further east, Japanese landings had taken place in east New Guinea; Australia felt herself gravely menaced. In the Middle East a German advance of some 300 miles in Cyrenaica took place in the first week of February; Admiral Cunningham's Mediterranean Fleet, seriously weakened by recent casualties, was hard put to it to protect the vital convoys to Malta, then undergoing savage air attack. The Battle of the Atlantic had entered its grimmest phase; U-boats sank a higher tonnage of merchant shipping in the quarter ending March 1942 than in any previous period, and this was on the increase. Only in Russia had the Axis received a check, where their armies, having failed to deal Russia a knock-out blow in the autumn, had been caught unprepared for the rigours of a winter campaign and suffered heavy punishment at the hands of the Russians.

The Allied forces were indeed stretched to the uttermost, particularly at sea. Serious casualties had been suffered recently by the British Navy[1] and at the same time a new fleet had to be formed for service in the Far East. Some critical months must yet elapse before the damage inflicted on the American Fleet at Pearl Harbor could be made good. The air requirements of the Navy and Army were far from being met and the policy of subordinating such requirements to the bombing of enemy cities was the subject of vigorous protest by the Commanders-in-Chief, Home Fleet and Mediterranean.[2]

Reviewing the dismal picture, the Joint Staff Mission in Washington laid down three main defensive tasks,[3] viz.:–

To keep Russia effectively in the war.
To prevent Germany and Japan from joining hands in the Indian Ocean area.
To check the Japanese advance on India or Australia.

The first task – keeping Russia effectively in the war – was deemed the most important. There were two contributions that the Allies could make to this end, namely the successful defence of the Middle East (in default of which the whole Russian position would be undermined), and the delivery of a continuous flow of munitions and aircraft to Russia. The safe passage of these supplies thus became a cardinal feature of Allied strategy, and it is against this background that the operation of the convoys to Russia in 1942 must be viewed.

* * * * *

It so chanced that in the autumn of 1941 Hitler began to have serious misgivings about the security of his northern flank in Norway, and by the end of January 1942 he had convinced himself that a major Allied operation against this region – with the possible support of Sweden and Finland – was in preparation. He therefore decided to transfer the main surface forces of his Navy to this area. 'Every ship that is not stationed in Norway is in the wrong place,' was his dictum – a view with which Grand Admiral Raeder, the Commander-in-Chief of the Navy, was in agreement. The battleship *Tirpitz* had already been sent to Trondheim on 16th January, and on 12th February the battlecruisers *Scharnhorst* and *Gneisenau*, with the 8-inch cruiser *Prinz Eugen*, made their celebrated dash from Brest through the English Channel, as a preliminary to her. Both battlecruisers[4] were seriously damaged by mines, which delayed them in German ports for repairs, but the *Prinz Eugen*, with the battleship *Scheer*, proceeded to Trondheim between 20th and 23rd; the former, however, was torpedoed on passage by the submarine *Trident* and put out of action for nine months. In addition, 20 per cent of operational U-boats was allocated to the defence of Norway.[5]

Meanwhile, the Commander-in-Chief of the German Fleet had represented the heaviest concentration of ships in Norwegian waters would be ineffective unless the Luftwaffe were correspondingly increased, and as a result certain torpedo bomber squadrons were transferred to the north. Thus it came about that just at the time the northern route to Russia became of crucial importance to the Allies, the measures taken by the enemy primarily for defence against an imaginary invasion disposed strong forces most favourably for attacking it.

* * * * *

The protection of the convoys to North Russia was a responsibility of the Home Fleet, then commanded by Admiral Sir John Tovey. It presented him with an inherently difficult problem. A glance at the chart (Plan 1) shows the strategic disadvantages under which he laboured. He had to provide for their safety on passage to and from a destination some 2,000 miles distant. The route, which was open to U-boat attack throughout its entire length, was limited to the westward and northward by ice and to the eastward and southward by an enemy-occupied coast, well provided with anchorages whence surface forces could operate at will, and airfields from which aircraft could dominate 1,400 miles of its furthest east, and therefore most vulnerable, waters. The whole route, moreover, including the terminal ports at each end, lay within the range of enemy air reconnaissance, for which he was not lacking in resources, and at two points was crossed by German routine meteorological flights. British shore-based air support was confined to what could be given from Iceland and Sullom Voe.

Quite apart from enemy interference were the great navigational difficulties in these Arctic waters – strong and uncertain currents, frequent gales, which would disperse the convoys and drive the ships many miles from their routes; no sun sights or W/T beacons to enable them to check their positions.[6] And ice, in one form or another, was an ever present menace.

During the winter of 1941-42, owing to the paucity of enemy forces in the area and the long hours of darkness in the high northern latitudes, the commitment did not involve a very serious strain on Home Fleet resources. By the end of February, however, the problem was becoming much more complicated. In the first place, there was the recent arrival of the two heavy ships, the *Admiral von Tirpitz* and the *Admiral Scheer*, at Trondheim, where they were equally well placed either for a breakout into the Atlantic to attack the vital trade routes – always the main preoccupation of the Commander-in-Chief, Home Fleet – or for attack on the Russian convoys. He was thus compelled to face both ways, as it were, and that with a depleted fleet, owing to imperative calls from other theatres of war. The nights were shortening and daylight hours were already long enough to allow the enemy surface ships and aircraft a fair chance of attack,[7] especially as in March and April the ice barrier lies further south than at any other time of the year, thus forcing the convoys to pass south of Bear Island and within some 250 miles of the Norwegian coast. Furthermore, a large increase in the scale of the Russian convoys had been decided on and the two scheduled to sail at the beginning of March were larger than hitherto. Clearly big ship cover would have to be provided in future; but the U-boat threat necessitated destroyers for screening the capital ships, whose radius of action, except in emergency, was thus limited by the endurance of the screen.

Gradually, as the year advanced, further measures for the protection of the convoys had to be devised. From April onwards the escorts were strengthened: more destroyers and some smaller vessels, as well as anti-aircraft ships and submarines, and on one occasion an escort aircraft carrier. These operations threw such a heavy strain on the Home Fleet that destroyers and corvettes, minesweepers and trawlers had to be attached to it from other commands to assist in the work. Submarines, too, were employed on patrol in support; they were stationed sometimes off the German bases in Norway, sometimes in zones placed across the enemy's line of approach to the convoy, their positions shifting as the convoys proceeded east and west. Reconnaissance by aircraft of Coastal Command within the limits of their endurance contributed to the work of the ships.

* * * * *

The ensuing battle summary traces the fortunes of the convoys to North Russia. After the first winter the campaign against them passed through three phases, viz.:–

March 1942 to the end of that year.
The years 1943 and 1944.
December 1944 to the end of the war.

(*a*) From March 1942 to the end of the year, the convoys had to face very heavy air and U-boat attack, as well as attacks by surface forces. The vulnerability of the route to air attack has already been mentioned, and the U-boat attack was more difficult to counter than in the Atlantic. Not only was there a shortage of escort vessels, but the difficulty of re-fuelling the destroyers prevented them hunting the U-boats to a kill and restricted their efforts to keeping them away from the convoys. The German surface forces fortunately were handled with marked timidity; had they been used resolutely to attack in the Barents Sea, it is difficult to see how the convoys could have continued. As things were, they only sank three merchants ships,[8] all of them stragglers. Each passage during this opening phase was full of incident and very heavy losses were incurred during the summer months.

(*b*) During the years 1943 and 1944 the German Air Force was too pre-occupied in other theatres to interfere much with the convoys, and though the surface remained until damage to the *Tirpitz* and the sinking of the *Scharnhorst* end of 1943, the only form of attack the convoys had to endure was U-boats. For this reason it is unnecessary to record each of these passages in detail. During the summer months of these two years the convoys were suspended. Gradually the development of HF DF, increasingly large A/S escorts, and above all the inclusion of escort carriers as they became available, gained the upper hand, and the U-boats suffered severely.

(*c*) In December 1944, after an absence of two years, the German Air Force torpedo bombers once again took a hand in the attacks and at about the same time the U-boats adopted new and more formidable tactics. Though the menace never acquired anything approaching the proportions of that of 1942 several of these latter convoys had exciting passages, which are again dealt with in detail.

Endnote

1. Casualties to capital ships and aircraft carriers had been particularly unfortunate. In the Mediterranean the *Ark Royal* and the *Barham* had been sunk in November 1941, and the *Valiant* and *Queen Elizabeth* severely damaged by limpet mines in December; the *Prince of Wales* and *Repulse* were sunk that month off Malaya.

2. M.051479/42. At about the same time, General Wavell, then C.-in-C. India, cabled: – 'It certainly gives us furiously to think when, after trying with less than 26 light bombers to meet attack which has cost us three important warships [*Dorsetshire*, *Cornwall* and *Hermes*] ... and nearly 100,000 tons of merchant shipping, we see that over 200 heavy bombers attacked one town in Germany'.

3. JSM No. 155, 1905Q, 1/4/42.

4. While repairing in Kiel, the *Gneisenau* was further damaged in an air raid on the night of the 26th and 27th February, this time so seriously that she was paid off and, as things turned out, never re-commissioned.

5. Hitler wished the whole U-boat fleet to be transferred to Norway, but this the Naval Staff found impracticable, both as regards operational requirements and bases. Maintenance and repair facilities were very poor in the Norwegian ports.

6. It is remarkable that in the whole 3 3/4 years during which the convoys were running, only six ships were lost as the result of navigational errors. One merchant ship (independently routed) was shipwrecked on Spitzbergen; four merchant ships and HMS *Niger* were sunk in the British minefield north of Iceland, owing to a large iceberg being mistaken for North Cape, Iceland.

7. In latitude 73° N., 1st March, civil twilight (sun 6° below horizon) commences at approximately 0615, LMT; evening twilight ends 1800. From 19th April to 6th May and 5th to 22nd August, twilight lasts all night, while between 6th May and 5th August the sun is continually above the horizon.

8. One other merchant ship which sailed independently, not in convoy, was sunk by surface craft – a total of four in four years.

Chapter I

Convoys PQ 1–12, QP 1–8: August 1941–March 1942
(All times are Zone minus 1.)

1

The first[1] of the convoys to Russia sailed for Archangel 21st August 1941: seven ships carrying stores and the ground staff for some Hurricane aircraft that were to work with the Russians. From this small beginning developed the regular service of military supplies to North Russia in which 21 convoys outward and 16 homeward bound had sailed with varying fortunes by the end of 1942.

At the outset the Germans seem to have under-estimated[2] the importance of this traffic; no interference was attempted except by a few submarines and destroyers, and weak air forces based on Bardufoss and Banak in Northern Norway. In these circumstances, the convoys sailed with a cruiser and a couple of destroyers as ocean escort, and in addition some trawlers or minesweepers for one or two days at either end of the voyage; later on, the local escort at the eastern end was reinforced by Russian destroyers.

With the coming of winter, the long nights, rough weather and bitter cold were in themselves a protection in those Arctic regions, where aircraft could not fly and spray froze guns and instruments, so that a ship could seldom steam at high speed without losing efficiency. Up to March 1942 there were lost only one merchant ship (SS *Waziristan*), out of 158[3] that sailed, and one escorting ship – the destroyer *Matabele* – both sunk by U-boats. One other ship, SS *Harmatrid*, was torpedoed but reached harbour in tow. Arduous though the service was, and calling for a high degree of endurance from both ships and crews, the voyages of these early convoys[4] presented no features of special interest so far as enemy action was concerned. For this reason they need not be considered further.

2

Convoys PQ 12 and QP 8 (Plans 1 and 2) were the first convoys to run under the less favourable conditions which came into being after February 1942. Each convoy consisted of 15 merchant ships[5] and was due to sail from Iceland and Murmansk respectively on 1st March.

On 26th February the Commander-in-Chief, Home Fleet, signalled to the Admiralty his proposals for their passage:—

'The following factors affect protection of North Russian convoys.

It seems probable that air and U-boat attacks will be concentrated on the eastern part of the route and that surface forces will operate to westward, where there is more sea room, although not further from base than the approximate longitude of Jan Mayen Island.

The protection of these convoys is a major commitment for the Home Fleet; but in it lies a hope of bringing enemy surface ships to action. On the other hand the operation covering northern passage and the time spent in northern waters must be the minimum.

The area in which the danger of surface attack is greatest is between longitude 5°W. and 14° E.[6]

To economise the use of our heavy forces as cover, the passage of the outward and homeward convoys through this danger area should be synchronised; and they should sail on the same date at minimum intervals of 14 days, which would allow the escort of a PQ convoy to take over the next QP convoy.

Such a programme would involve Home Fleet heavy forces being in northern waters during about five days in every 14; and it cannot be managed with the present number of destroyers, if a proper screen is to be provided for capital ships and an escort of two destroyers to each convoy. Another four destroyers will be required.

I intend normally to cover these convoys with two capital ships, and sometimes with carrier also.

With the 14-day cycle, it may prove the time during which the northernmost passages are to a large extent uncovered is too long.'

The Commander-in-Chief proposed sending his second in command, Vice-Admiral A. T. B. Curteis, with the *Renown* and *Duke of York*, a cruiser and a screen of destroyers, to cruise in support of the convoys during their passage 5° W. and 14° E., while he stayed at Scapa himself

PLAN I

The Thousand I⁵

Hope I.

German Air Striking Force

Barents Sea

Bear I.

Admiralty Peninsula

Sukhoi Nos

C. Stolbovoi

Moller B.

N. Gusini Nos

Byelushka Bay

Matochkin Str.

NOVAYA ZEMLYA

Kara Strait

North C.

Porsanger Fd

HAMMERF

BANAK

VADSO

Varanger Fd

Altenfiord

TROMSO

KIRKENES

PETSAMO

Kola Inlet

BARDUFOSS

MURMANSK

VAENGA

Kolguev

R. Pechora

ARVIK

IOKANKA

C. Kanin

DEN

White Sea

FINLAND

U·S·S·R

Gulf of Bothnia

ARCHANGEL

CONVOYS TO
NORTH RUSSIA
THEATRE OF
OPERATIONS

Gulf of Finland

LENINGRAD

G. of Riga

TSO/NS (1062)

217

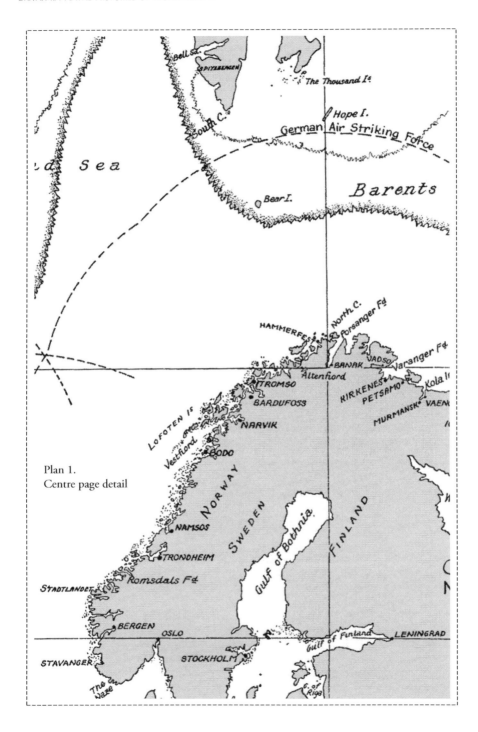

Plan 1.
Centre page detail

with the third capital ship, *King George V*, the aircraft carrier *Victorious*, and another cruiser. There he would be ready to join Vice-Admiral Curteis or 'to deal with a possible break out' of German ships into the Atlantic, according to the information he received, he should put to sea himself, he considered, only if he learnt that the enemy were on the move or if the air reconnaissance[7] of Trondheim failed. He thought it unlikely that the *Tirpitz* would risk fighting Admiral Curteis, whose force 'was well able to look after itself'; on the other hand his own force might gain an opportunity of getting between the enemy and their base and of forcing an action. Moreover, he wished to husband his strength against the summer, when he expected the *Tirpitz* to be reinforced by the *Scharnhorst* and *Gneisenau*, which had lately arrived in Germany from Brest. The employment of the whole capital ship strength of the Home Fleet, whenever Russian convoys were at sea, would 'lead to a steady decline in its efficiency' by interrupting refits and leave.[8]

But the Admiralty preferred a full concentration of force. This would ensure superiority over the German surface ships, besides ensuring the presence of the fighter protection provided by aircraft in the *Victorious*, which they considered very important, although the enemy's air strength in Norway was still small and Admiral Tovey had instructed Vice-Admiral Curteis to keep 250 miles from the coast except to sink or damage enemy ships of war. Their Lordships told the Commander-in-Chief they took 'full responsibility for any break out of German ships which may occur while you are covering PQ and QP convoys'.

The Commander-in-Chief therefore arranged to rendezvous with Vice-Admiral Curteis, who was then at Hvalfjord (near Reykjavik), in 71° N. 3° E.[9] on 6th March, when Convoy PQ 12 was expected to be passing to the northward of this position.

To comply with this, the Vice-Admiral sailed from Hvalfjord on 3rd March, with the *Renown* (flag), *Duke of York*, *Kenya* and six destroyers,[10] and the Commander-in-Chief left Scapa with the K*ing George V*, *Victorious, Berwick* and six destroyers[11] the next day. The junction was effected at 1030, 6th March, and the *Kenya* was then detached to join the convoy and accompanied it to Murmansk.

The strength of the battle fleet was then as follows:–

King George V, Duke of York, Renown, Victorious, Berwick and nine destroyers.[12] With this force the Commander-in-Chief cruised some 50 miles to the southward of PQ 12.

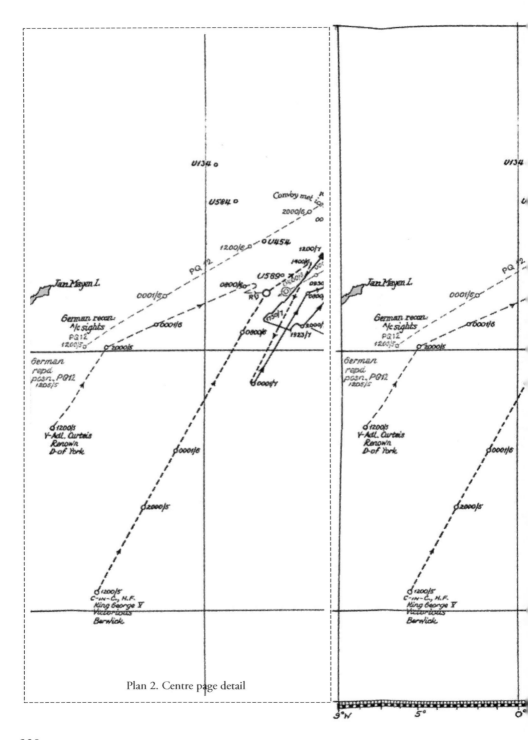

Plan 2. Centre page detail

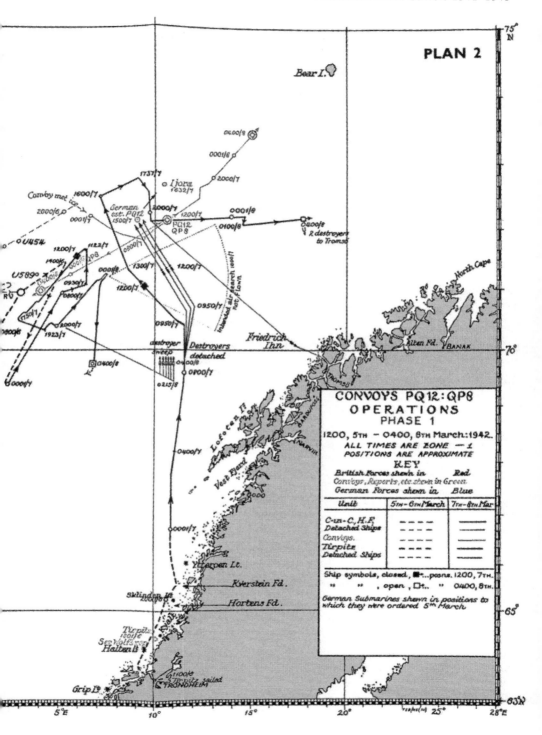

PLAN 2

CONVOYS PQ12:QP8
OPERATIONS
PHASE 1

1200, 5TH – 0400, 8TH March.:1942.
ALL TIMES ARE ZONE — 1
POSITIONS ARE APPROXIMATE

KEY
British Forces shown in   Red.
Convoys, Reports, etc. shown in Green.
German Forces shown in   Blue

Unit	5th–6th March	7th–8th Mar
C-in-C, H.F. Detached Ships	– – – –	————
Convoys.	– – – –	
Tirpitz Detached Ships	– – – –	————

Ship symbols, closed, ■...posns. 1200, 7TH.
  "   "   , open , □... "   0400, 8TH.

German Submarines shown in positions to
which they were ordered 5TH March

3

Convoy PQ 12 (Plan 2) had sailed from Reykjavik on 1st March – 15 merchant ships and an oiler under Commodore H. T. Hudson, RNR, with a local escort of trawlers. The minesweeper *Gossamer* and four minesweeping whalers were to have overtaken the convoy on the 4th, but two whalers only joined, the others passing the convoy without sighting it.[13] Early on the 5th, however, the destroyers *Oribi* (Commander J. E. H. McBeath, SO) and *Offa* relieved the local escort 100 miles south of Jan Mayen Island, and later in the day the *Kenya* (Captain M. M. Denny) joined, having been sent by Vice-Admiral Curteis.

Soon afterwards the convoy was located and shadowed for some time by a German aircraft.

Next morning (6th) the *Kenya* parted company to rejoin Vice-Admiral Curteis, being sent back after his junction with the Commander-in-Chief to provide close cover all the way to Murmansk. That same evening came the news that the *Tirpitz* or an 8-inch cruiser had sailed from Trondheim and was steering to the northward up the Norwegian coast.[14]

This news came from the *Seawolf* (Lieutenant R. F. Raikes) one of the submarines stationed off the coast. Aircraft of Coastal Command had been maintaining a reconnaissance of Trondheim since the end of February, with special extra patrols to seaward from 4th to 7th March. On the 5th and 6th, however, the reconnaissance had failed, while the day patrol on the 6th was discontinued in the afternoon, apparently for lack of aircraft. But the submarines *Trident* and *Seawolf* were patrolling outside the northern approaches to Trondheim, the *Trident* evidently sighted the enemy at about 1700, the 6th, too far off to see what they were or to make a report. Half an hour later, the Seawolf sighted flying boats 'wave-hopping' towards her and faint smoke to the southward and then the foretop and funnel of a large ship steaming fast up the coast ten miles inshore. Two hours later, Lieutenant Raikes brought the *Seawolf* to the surface to make a report, having hoped in vain that the enemy might wait until dark before leaving the approaches and so enable him to attack. His signal, timed 1801/6, but made at 1940, called the enemy a battleship or an 8-inch gun cruiser; but he says in his written report, 'I was certain in my own mind that it was the *Tirpitz*' and indeed it was.[15]

Before the German battleship could endanger its passage, Convoy PQ 12 had to contend with other difficulties. In the evening of 6th March, the convoy encountered ice and had to turn from a north-easterly to a south-easterly course. It was luckily loose pack ice only, according to Captain Denny of the *Kenya*, though serious enough to make him remark that 'after experience with PQ 12, I would never take a convoy anywhere near ice, accepting almost any other risk in preference.' A merchant ship and one of the whalers parted company that evening; the *Oribi*, meeting more ice in the night, was considerably damaged. Next morning, the 7th, however, the convoy was able to return to its proper course and there began a curious game of hide and seek in varying visibility[16] and arctic squalls – the *Tirpitz* searching for the convoys, particularly PQ 12 but usually to the southward of its track and the Home Fleet hunting the *Tirpitz*, but always to the south-west of her area of operations. The four groups were within 100 miles of each other most of the day and both the *Tirpitz* and each convoy had narrow escapes from being located;[17] but the only contact hat occurred was between a German destroyer and a straggler from the homeward bound convoy, QP 8.

QP 8, consisting of 15 ships, escorted by two minesweepers and two corvettes,[18] had sailed from Murmansk on 1st March, the same day PQ 12 left Iceland. The cruiser *Nigeria* (flag Rear-Admiral H. M. Burrough, Commanding 10th Cruiser Squadron), sailed next day, to provide close cover, but did not succeed in finding the convoy and eventually went alone to Scapa. On 4th March, QP 8 encountered a heavy gale which scattered the convoy; all ships, however, except two – the *Ijora* and *Larrinaga* – had reformed by noon the next day. Another gale dispersed the convoy on the 6th, but, except for the two original stragglers, all ships managed to reform next forenoon. These gales caused considerable delay, putting the convoy some 100 miles to the eastward (about 12 hours steaming) of its scheduled position.

At noon, 7th March, Convoys QP 8 and PQ 12 passed each other in a snowstorm in 72° 09' N. 10° 34' E., approximately 200 miles south-west of Bear Island – 'a perfect gridiron was executed' wrote Captain Denny, 'in visibility one mile.' Some two hours later the *Kenya* sighted smoke on the horizon to the northward, the visibility being then at a maximum, so she left PQ 12 in order to investigate, standing out for half an hour or so at high speed. The stranger appeared to be 30 miles off, steaming at seven knots to the south-west, a course similar to that of the homeward bound convoy; she was evidently 'harmless' and almost certainly a straggler from that convoy. Captain Denny therefore turned back to his own charges, rejoining them at 1515. Then, at 1600, he received a signal from the Admiralty[19] saying that enemy surface forces might be near his convoy – a possibility the *Seawolf*'s report had foreshadowed the night before – and ordering him to steer north unless he had other orders from Admiral Tovey. At 1640, accordingly, the convoy turned to course 360°, the *Kenya* having closed the Commodore to give the instruction by loud-hailer. 'No sooner was this wheel executed,' than Captain Denny learnt that a leading telegraphist had read a signal timed 1632 from the *Ijora* through the ship's company wireless set on the mess deck, the message stating that she was being 'gunned' by a man-of-war in 72° 35' N. 10° 50' E., though the position was doubtful. It was more than likely that the *Ijora* was the ship whose position and course had been observed by her funnel smoke two hours earlier; she would be now some 35 or 40 miles to the westward of Convoy PQ 12; and its northerly course might lead the convoy straight into the arms of the raider.

Captain Denny assumed that the Admiralty and the Commander-in-Chief knew nothing of the convoy's departure from its route to avoid the icefield and its consequent loss of distance the previous night and they probably supposed it to be west of the enemy. He had also in mind the danger of meeting ice again to the northward, 'trapped against which the convoy would become anybody's meat.' Consulting then with the Commodore and with Commander McBeath of the damaged *Oribi* he decided to turn away to course 060° without signal at 1800, when it would be nearly dark. Meanwhile, he sent up the *Kenya*'s Walrus aircraft at 1720 to search for an hour between the bearings 270° and 210° from the convoy; and he told the *Offa*, his only completely serviceable destroyer, '*Tirpitz* is believed to be out. If my aircraft finds her or any other warship, I shall send you to locate and shadow.' Her service was not required. The Walrus returned soon after 1800, having found the sector of search clear to a depth of 45 miles. Reassured by this report, Captain Denny altered back an hour later to course 040° for the night, as 'it would help the general situation if the convoy was brought gradually nearer to its official track.'[20]

4

The report of Convoy PQ 12 being at sea had not come as a surprise to the German naval authorities, as they had estimated that convoys would be sailing at the beginning of March; this expectation seemed to receive confirmation when on the 1st air reconnaissance found that the warship and larger steamers which had been sighted at Murmansk on 27th February were no longer there and search for the PQ convoy to Russia was carried out to the north-west of Norway as thoroughly as the limited number of aircraft available permitted. It was not until 1205, 5th March, that it was sighted. It was reported as consisting of 15 steamers of between 5,000 and 10,000 tons, escorted by one cruiser, two destroyers and two smaller escort vessels, course 030°, speed six knots, in position 69° 44' N. 9° 7' W.[21] Measures to intercept this convoy were at once put in train; four U-boats then at sea to the west of Bear Island were ordered to form a line across its estimated track some 200 miles to the north-east of Jan Mayen Island,[22] and at the same time preliminary orders were sent to the 'battle group'[23] (Plan 2).

The final decision to use the latter required the assent of the Führer; this was obtained the following day and at 1100, 6th March, the *Tirpitz* wearing the flag of Vice-Admiral Ciliax (who had recently distinguished himself by bringing battlecruisers through the English Channel) and three destroyers[24] left Trondheim and set course to the northward in search of PQ 12, which it was calculated should be in about 72° 10' N. 9° E. at 1500, 7 March.[25]

'the British will always be able to have on the spot within a short time the support of aircraft carriers, destroyers and cruisers, whereas our own escorts, because of their low fuel capacity and bad sea-keeping qualities will (in an operation lasting several days) become only a burden.'[26]

5

No further reports of the convoy's position, either from aircraft or U-boats, reached the German Admiral after leaving Trondheim, so at 0850, 7th March, he detached his three destroyers to sweep to the N.N.W. (342°, i.e. directly towards the estimated 1500 position of PQ 12); an hour later, being then in approximately 70° 28' N. 11° 30' E, he himself in the *Tirpitz* altered course to port to search further to the north-westward[27] (Plan 2). Actually at this time PQ 12 was some 95 miles almost right ahead of the destroyers (bearing 343°), while – all unknown to the Germans – Admiral Tovey was 110 miles to the westward of the *Tirpitz*, bearing 290° and steering a converging course (360°).

Admiral Tovey, after his junction with Vice-Admiral Curteis, had spent the remainder of the 6th March cruising to the southward of the convoy route. At midnight, 6th and 7th March, he was about 90 miles S.S.W. of PQ 12 and had just turned to course 030°, when he received the *Seawolf*'s report of the *Tirpitz* timed 1801/6, relayed by the Admiralty. Reviewing the situation, the Commander-in-Chief judged that PQ 12, which had been located on the 5th, was the enemy's quarry, rather than QP 8, which so far as was known had not been sighted since leaving Kola Inlet; he also considered it probable that the move of the *Tirpitz* was really defensive, based on the possibility of PQ 12 being a troop convoy, bound for North Norway. He accordingly continued to steer 030° throughout the night and at daylight informed his force that there appeared to be at least one enemy ship at sea and that the *Victorious* would be required to make an air search to the southward of PQ 12, keeping a striking force ready.

It was a cold, misty morning, with overcast sky, drizzle and snow squalls; visibility was logged in the *King George V* as six miles and the surface temperature at just below freezing point. At 0800, the fleet raised steam for full speed and turned to course 070°, the Commander-in-Chief giving his intentions in the following signals:–

> To *Renown* and *Victorious*, 0806/7: 'If an unexpected contact is made. *Victorious* is to disengage at once; *Renown* is to disengage if *Tirpitz* is met.'

> To *Victorious*, 0812/7: 'Prepare to carry out search in sector 065° to 115° to depth 120 miles flying off 1000. Intend to steer 070° until 1000 then 030°, 15 knots. If you do not like weather conditions, reduce depth of search.'

> To Captain (D), *Onslow*, 0821/7: 'Be prepared to deliver a close range attack, if sudden contact is made.'

> 'By great misfortune', however, 'for this search would almost certainly have located the *Tirpitz*, severe icing conditions were experienced and no air reconnaissance was possible all day.'[28]

After an hour and a half – at 0930 – the fleet turned north, in the vain hope of escaping the fog, but conditions did not improve and at 1130 it steered away to the south-west 'to search for clearer weather and to reach a central position covering both convoys.'[29]

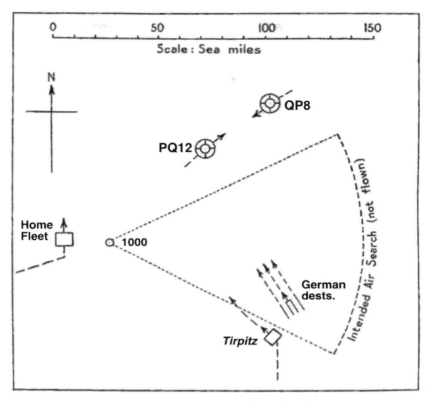

Figure 1. Convoys PQ 12, QP 8: situation 0950, 7th March 1942

The Commander-in-Chief considered PQ 12 comparatively safe in the short visibility to the eastward, whereas the enemy might find QP 8 to the westward; he did not know that the latter had been held up by gales and that it was still a long way to the east of him. He also had to bear in mind the security of his own force. Though his radar was working most efficiently, it could not differentiate between an enemy ship, a merchant ship from either convoy, the *Kenya* or the *Nigeria*, any of which might be picked up, whereas the enemy had the advantage of knowing that any ship detected must be hostile. A chance torpedo hit or two on the 'unwieldy unit'[30] of three capital ships, the *Victorious* and the *Berwick* would be extremely serious, for the fleet was nearly 1,000 miles from a base, its destroyers must soon part company to refuel and there were German submarines and aircraft within easy call to attack a damaged ship in tow.

Meanwhile the *Tirpitz* on her north-westerly course had been

227

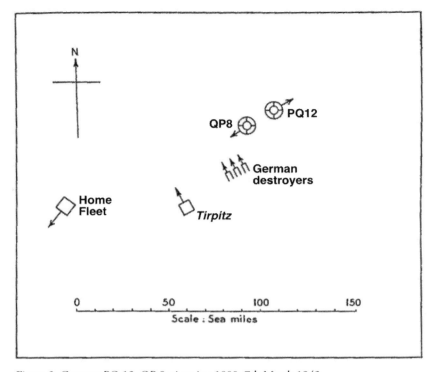

Figure 2. Convoys PQ 12, QP 8: situation 1800, 7th March 1942

gradually closing the fleet. Admiral Ciliax had intended to fly off two aircraft at 1100 on reconnaissance, but, like Admiral Tovey earlier in the forenoon, was prevented by the weather from doing so. Had this search been flown, its report might well have proved unexpectedly interesting, for he had no idea that the Home Fleet was at sea.[31] As things fell out he passed some 60 miles to the eastward of it at 1300; at the same time he hauled more to the northward and the distance between the two forces began to open rapidly.

The two convoys had passed each other an hour previously; PQ 12 for the time being was out of danger from the enemy, but QP 8 on a W.S.W. course was only 50 miles north-east of the *Tirpitz* and much nearer the German destroyers sweeping to the N.N.W. spread about five miles apart. The easterly one (*Z25*) must have passed less than ten miles ahead of this convoy shortly before 1400, but no contact occurred. At 1545, however, smoke was sighted bearing 010°; this proved to be from the straggler *Ijora*, which was sunk by the *Friedrich Ihn* at 1713, but not before she had transmitted a distress signal with 'accurate position'[32] at

1632. As she sank the *Tirpitz* hove in sight to the westward; having intercepted the *Ijora*'s, signal, Admiral Ciliax had turned to close the position, in the hope that the remainder of the convoy would be somewhere in the vicinity.

The destroyers rejoined the flag at 1728 and the Admiral then decided to make to the eastward, where he thought he would be better placed to intercept the convoy later on, should it have been diverted or turned back on the strength of the *Ijora*'s signal, as seemed probable. But the destroyers required fuel, which it had been planned they should take from the *Tirpitz* that night and the weather conditions among the ice floes were far from propitious; he therefore first shaped course to the southward, hoping to find better. These hopes were not fulfilled and at 2035 course was altered to 086°, the *Friedrich Ihn*, which was running very short, being detached to Tromsø. The other two destroyers followed her at 0400, 8th and the *Tirpitz* continued the search alone.[33]

The Home Fleet, meanwhile, had maintained its south-westerly course throughout the afternoon of the 7th March. At 1632 the *Ijora*'s distress signal was intercepted, but 'the position was incompletely received and could have been either 72° 35′ N. 10° 50′ East, well astern of the estimated position of this convoy[34] or 67° 35′ N. 10° 50′ West, a shorter distance ahead.'[35] Shortly afterwards, a DF bearing, possibly of an enemy surface vessel, pointed to the former position – nearly 200 miles north-east of the fleet – as did the supposition that PQ 12, which should have been in this neighbourhood, was the enemy's objective. 'I thought it probable' – the Commander-in-Chief subsequently wrote – 'that if this bearing was of the *Tirpitz*, who I am convinced was highly nervous of being in such waters, she would consider her position compromised and return immediately to her base.' Acting on this assumption, he turned to the E.S.E. at 1750, but there was no certainty that the DF bearing was actually of the *Tirpitz*, so he decided to send Captain Armstrong (D17) with six destroyers to the south-eastward to try to intercept, should she be coming south, while he himself with he Fleet stood towards Bear Island, in case she remained in the north. Course was altered to 040° at 1923, but before the destroyers had left several signals from the Admiralty indicated that the *Tirpitz* was prepared to remain at sea for a long time and to operate well to the eastward of Bear Island and also that the enemy was not aware that the Home Fleet was at sea; under these circumstances the Commander-in-Chief held back the destroyers and stood on to cover PQ 12.

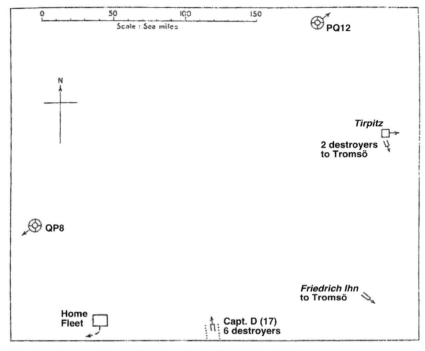

Figure 3. Convoys PQ 12 QP 8 situation 0400 8th March 1942

At 1940, however, another DF bearing of the same unit showed that she was moving south at high speed, so Captain Armstrong with his six destroyers[36] was detached at 2009. The destroyers reached the starting point of their search, 69° 30' N. 11° E., at 0215, 8th March and, spreading two miles apart, swept north at 15 knots until 0600. They sighted nothing. Captain Armstrong then turned to the westward having orders to go to Seidisfjord for fuel, passing through 70° N. 00°.

The battle fleet, in default of further news, turned back at midnight 7th/8th, steaming to the southward at 24 knots in order to arrive within air-striking range at dawn, should the flotilla have found the enemy. At 0400, 8th, however, the Commander-in-Chief decided he had missed his quarry, so turned away at 0415 towards Iceland 'to collect some destroyers;' for unless he had good hopes of meeting the *Tirpitz*, he did not wish to remain in possibly submarine infested waters without a screen.

This may be considered the conclusion of the first phase of the operations of the Home Fleet and *Tirpitz* in connection with PQ 12.

6

Thus the situation at 0400, 8th March, was as follows: Convoy PQ 12 'approximately 90 miles to the south-westward of Bear Island, was steering 040°' almost directly for the island.

Ninety miles to the south-eastward the *Tirpitz* was on an easterly course, soon to alter to the northward and search the waters to the south and west of Bear Island. About 250 miles to the south-westward of the *Tirpitz* the Home Fleet was just about to shape course for Iceland, under the impression that the *Tirpitz* had abandoned her operation. QP 8 was about 270 miles to the W.S.W. of the *Tirpitz* and was practically clear of danger, making about nine knots to tire westward.

Both the *Tirpitz* and the Home Fleet were bereft of destroyers, each Admiral having had to part with them on account of their fuel requirements.

7

After parting with the last two destroyers at 0400, 8th March, the *Tirpitz* continued on her easterly course until 0700 when she turned north for the estimated convoy route; this was reached at 1045, in about 73° 23' N. 20° 9' E. and turning in the supposed direction of the convoy, she commenced zigzagging on a line of advance 255°,[37] passing some 55 miles south of Bear Island at about noon (Plan 3).

Actually at this time PQ 12 was on a northerly course, about 75 miles to the north-westward of her. During the night of the 7th/8th the convoy had held its course 040° towards Bear Island. No more had been heard of the *Ijora* or the enemy; but soon after midnight another signal came from the Admiralty telling the convoy to steer to pass north of Bear Island, if ice permitted – a very considerable diversion from the original route. At daylight, 8th, therefore, course was altered further to the northward, Captain Denny warning the Commodore not to take the destroyers through ice. The weather and information about the icefield, however, soon determined the two senior officers to disregard the Admiralty signal and they altered course to the south-east a little after mid-day, intending to cross the meridian of Bear Island to the southward after dark that evening. About 1530, between snowstorms, they sighted the island 40 miles off to the north-east and the icefield at the same time. At dusk, 1700, they ran into the fringe of the ice. It took the convoy three hours to work clear and reform, whereupon, to avoid further damage to the *Oribi*, Captain Denny detached her to make her own way to Murmansk,

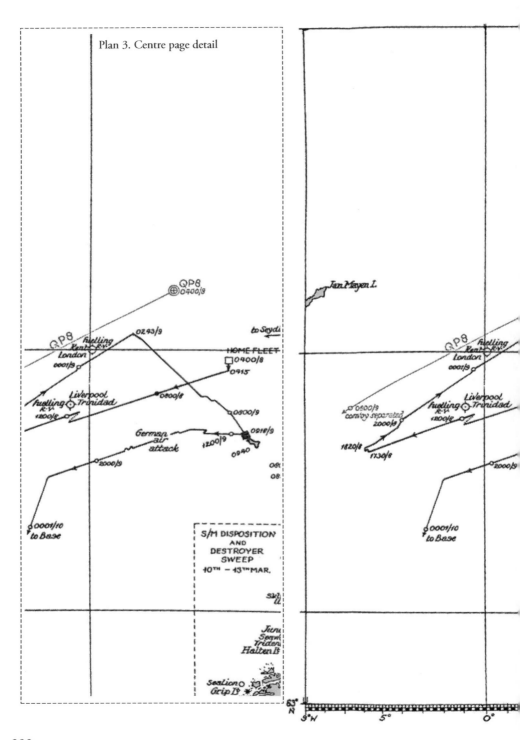

Plan 3. Centre page detail

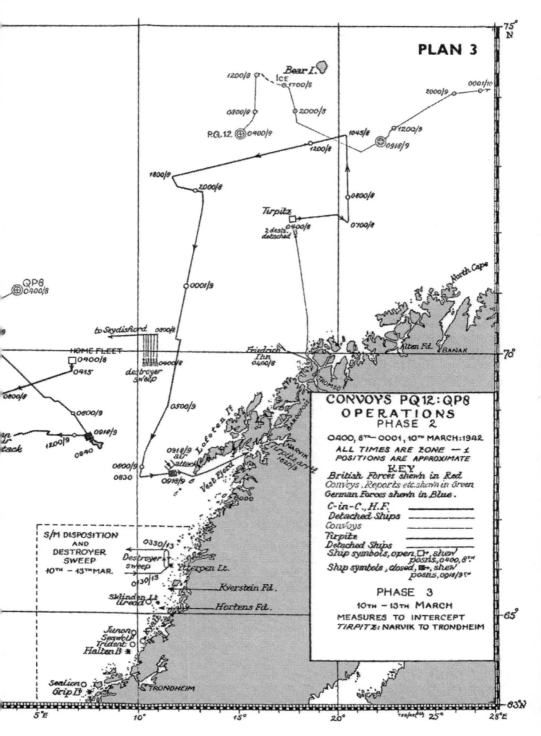

PLAN 3

Bear I.
ICE
1200/8
1700/8
0800/9
2000/8
P.Q.12. 0400/8
1045/8
1200/8
0918/9
1800/8
2000/8
0800/8
Tirpitz
0400/8
2 destr.
detached
0700/8
0001/9
2000/9
0001/10

QP8
0400/8

to Seydisfjord 0500/9
HOME FLEET 0400/8
0415
0400/8
destroyer
sweep
0500/9
Friedrich
Ihn
0400/8
North Cape
TROMSO
Alten Fd.
BANAK
0600/9
0800/9
0918/9
1200/9
0240
0918/9
air
attack
0800/9
0830
0918/9
Lofoten Is.
Vest Fjord
NARVIK
TIRPITZ dep'd
1020/9
BODO

CONVOYS PQ12: QP8
OPERATIONS
PHASE 2
0400, 8TH – 0001, 10TH MARCH: 1942
ALL TIMES ARE ZONE — 1
POSITIONS ARE APPROXIMATE
KEY
British Forces shewn in Red.
Convoys, Reports etc.shewn in Green
German Forces shewn in Blue.

C-in-C., H.F. ————
Detached Ships ————
Convoys ————
Tirpitz ————
Detached Ships ————
Ship symbols, open □+, shew
posns,0400, 8TH
Ship symbols, closed ■+, shew
posns, 0918/9TH

PHASE 3
10TH – 13TH MARCH
MEASURES TO INTERCEPT
TIRPITZ: NARVIK TO TRONDHEIM

S/M DISPOSITION
AND
DESTROYER
SWEEP
10TH – 13TH MAR.
Destroyer
Sweep
0330/13
0330/13
Yterpen Lt.
Kvernstein Fd.
Skjinden Lt.
Uredd
Hortens Fd.
Junon
Seywolf
Trident
Halten I.
Sealion
Grip I.
S.TRONDHEIM

5°E
10°
15°
20°
25°
28°E

75°
N
76°
70°
65°
63°N

which she reached two days later. The convoy went on, keeping as far north as the ice allowed; but at 2000 it was still 40 miles to the S.S.W. of Bear Island and only about 110 miles to the north-east of the *Tirpitz*, which was then just about to abandon the search and return to base.

Admiral Ciliax continued to steer 255° throughout the afternoon. He had received no further news of the convoy's movements, but at 1120, 8th, a signal from Group Command North gave new areas further to the westward where they thought it was more likely to be found. The Admiral inferred from this that they wished him to continue the search throughout the 9th; he therefore ordered the destroyers to rejoin him in 72° 10' N. 21° 42' E. at 0700, 9th and at 1800, being then about 170 miles south-west of Bear Island, he hauled round to the south-eastward meaning to stand off to the southward of the convoy route, the same as the previous night.

But at 1816 Group Command North informed him that it was quite possible that the convoy had turned back after being sighted by the German aircraft on the 5th, leaving the decision to him whether to continue the operation or not; and at 2025 that evening, he signalled that he was returning to base and ordered the destroyers to meet him at the original rendezvous west of Vestfjord. Ten minutes later the *Tirpitz* altered course to 191° and headed for the Norwegian coast.[38]

8

While the convoy and the *Tirpitz* had been manoeuvring within 120 miles of each other in the Bear Island area during most of the 8th March, Admiral Tovey had been steering for Iceland at 24 knots. That evening, when the fleet had run nearly 300 miles to the westward, an Admiralty message suggested that the *Tirpitz* was still in the far north; he accordingly altered course back to the north-eastward at 1820, intending to search south of Bear Island the following day (Plan 3).

The Commander-in-Chief had been unable to communicate with the Admiralty during the 7th and 8th, but it was now essential to inform them of his intentions and of the fact that he had no screen. Accordingly, at 1830, 8th, he broke wireless silence[39] to do so and at the same time asked the Admiralty to operate the cruisers and destroyers of the Home Fleet, owing to his great difficulties of communication. He thought that the approach of the heavy ships to Bear Island might well drive the *Tirpitz* south once more and give the light forces a chance to intercept. The Admiralty had already ordered the *Kent* and *London*, *Trinidad* and

Liverpool to positions[40] 190 miles east and south of Jan Mayen Island[41] ready to refuel destroyers and were collecting and sailing all other available destroyers in Iceland, Scapa, Rosyth and Loch Ewe.

During the night, however, further information from the Admiralty indicated that the *Tirpitz* was on her way south and at 0240, 9th March, the fleet altered course to 120° for the Lofoten area, working up to 26 knots. The enemy was then 200 miles to the eastward and it was impossible to reach a position close enough to launch a dawn air attack, but a searching force of six Albacores was flown off at 0640, followed by a striking force of 12, armed with torpedoes, at 0730. They left the *Victorious* encouraged by a signal from the Commander-in-Chief: 'A wonderful chance, which may achieve most valuable results. God be with you.'

9

The *Tirpitz* was sighted by an aircraft of the searching force at 0800 in about 67° 45' N. 9° 10' E., some 80 miles from the fleet. She was steaming to the southward at high speed, with one destroyer in company – the *Friedrich Ihn* which had rejoined her at 0650. At 0815, when in 67° 57' N. 8° 58' E., a hostile aircraft was sighted. Admiral Ciliax decided to make for the coast as quickly as possible; he only waited to fly off an aircraft to give some fighter protection, then turning to course 082° headed for Vestfjord. This alteration was duly reported by the shadowing aircraft, though the observer made the new course 040°.

At 0842 the striking force sighted her 20 miles off to the south-east in the direction of the sun. They climbed from a height of 200-300 feet from the water to hide above the cloud belt, which lay between 2,000 and 3,000 feet up; and the squadron commander ordered the sub-flights to act independently. They flew in on her port quarter, with a 35-knot wind on their port bow, overtaking her with a relative speed of some 30 knots.[42] The squadron commander meant to fly beyond the enemy and to come down out of the clouds to attack from ahead. Unluckily, at 0917, as they were about to pass over her, the leading aircraft came to a large break in the cloud. They were seen by the Germans and after some little delay both ships opened fire. Her delay in opening fire and its inaccuracy, encouraged the belief that the *Tirpitz* was not ready, so the squadron commander decided to attack at once.[43]

He led his sub-flight down in a shallow dive, dropping the torpedoes off the port bow of the *Tirpitz* at a height of 70 to 100 feet above the water and at a range he believed to be 1,000 yards, though it was probably twice that distance. The ship turned wide to port; and the next three aircraft, crossing astern from her other side, dropped their torpedoes off her port quarter at long range minute after the first attack. The other two sub-flights, further to starboard, attacked several minutes later, being held up by the slow rate of approach and the ship's turn away. Before they fired, the *Tirpitz* had time to turn back to her old course, bringing the aircraft on her starboard bow. Two were shot down, whether before firing or after is not known; the remaining four dropped their torpedoes at short range, but at somewhat fine angles of track. There were no hits.[44] It was a bitter disappointment; for the chances had seemed unusually promising. The *Tirpitz* had no defending aircraft,[45] no guns save own and those of a single destroyer and she was steaming into the wind aircraft had good visibility and clouds to cover their flight to the position of attack; conditions, said Captain Bovell of the *Victorious*, were ideal. But they attacked from astern and from to leeward, instead of holding on for a position ahead and to windward and thus gave up the advantage of attaining the maximum relative speed in the final approach.

As the airmen went back to their ship they saw the *Tirpitz* steer away for the mouth of Vestfjord, making smoke.[46]

10

Meanwhile, the Home Fleet had turned back to the north-west at about 1000, on reaching a position 170 miles from the enemy airfield at Bodø and 240 miles from Bardufoss. The last of the surviving Albacores landed on at 1045 and as soon as he had gathered the airmen's impression of the *Tirpitz's* movements and intentions, the Commander-in-Chief steered to the westward (Plan 3). He decided against further reconnaissance for the time being, feeling sure the *Tirpitz* was making for harbour and because the Albacores could not face the German fighters at Bodø; moreover, Coastal Command aircraft were patrolling already between Bodø and Trondheim. He decided to find a destroyer screen, return to the eastward and make an air search up the coast of Norway in the night, in case the *Tirpitz* should be on the way to Trondheim, while destroyer striking forces operated by the Admiralty worked southward of the fleet. Unfortunately, nothing came of this plan. The fleet was shadowed on the 9th from 1015 onwards by heavy Blohm and Voss aircraft, too powerful to be deterred by the Fulmar, fighters in the *Victorious*. At 1545, in about 68° 30' N. 3° 30' E., three Ju.88 bombers appeared one of which dropped its bombs near the *Victorious*, though gunfire and fighters drove off the others.[47] This attack delayed the fleet and though four destroyers[48] joined at 1900 it was then too late to return to the coast that night. The weather too, was unsuitable for night flying from a carrier and accordingly the Commander-in-Chief shaped course for Scapa, where he arrived on the night of the 10th, having been joined by eight more destroyers[49] on the way.

This was not yet the end of the operation, for there was still a chance of intercepting the *Tirpitz* on her way from Vestfjord to her base. The Norwegian authorities informed the Admiralty that, if she went south along the coast in the Inner Lead, she might come out into the open water as far north as Kverstein Fjord, failing which she must certainly come out through Hortens Fjord and pass one side or the other of the Sklinden Light. It was therefore decided to increase the number of submarines in the northern approaches to Trondheim from two to four, stationing one also off the Grip Light to the southward and to carry out a sweep by destroyers off the coast north of 66° N. in the night of 12th-13th March.

Captain Scott-Moncrieff sailed accordingly from Scapa in the evening of the 11th with eight ships – *Faulkner, Fury, Intrepid, Icarus, Bedouin, Punjabi, Eskimo* and *Tartar* – in time to begin the sweep at 0200, the 13th. The *Punjabi* had to return with her steering gear disabled; otherwise the sweep was carried out as arranged, but the flotilla had not the luck to sight anything. The submarines were equally unfortunate. They had been expecting the *Tirpitz* every day since the 9th and on the 11th Admiral Horton told them, 'I know how trying this waiting is, but the chances of *Tirpitz*'s passing are still very good. He may try Inner Leads, but would have to come out in vicinity of Sklinden Channel Stick it!' When the time came, in the afternoon of the 13th, it was thick weather, with snow reducing the visibility to under a mile. The *Tirpitz* passed at high speed, close to the *Trident*, unseen and undistinguishable by hydrophone from her screening destroyers. She may well have passed within reach – given clear weather – of some of the other submarines to the northward; for all except the *Uredd* had depth charges scattered near them and she also sighted two destroyers within a few hundred yards.

The convoys, in the meanwhile, had continued their passages unmolested. QP 8 reached 69° N. 6°40'W., north of Iceland, without incident at 0800 9th March, when it divided, some ships continuing in company with the corvettes to Reykjavik, while the others went independently to Akureyri and the minesweepers to Scapa.

PQ 12 too, when clear of the ice, had an uneventful passage. On the 9th, the *Offa* detected a patrolling aircraft by her radar, but 'exceptionally thick and persistent sea smoke rising many feet into the air,' combined with a change of course for two hours, prevented discovery, while intercepted signals showed that the *Tirpitz* was no longer likely to be a danger, for she had been attacked that morning off the Lofoten Islands by aircraft from the *Victorious*. On the 12th the convoy arrived at Murmansk.

The only ship lost was the whaler *Shera*, which capsized on 9th March, after following the convoy from Iceland without finding it; three of her crew were rescued by another whaler then in company, the *Svega*, which arrived at Murmansk on the 11th. Three merchant ships had parted with the convoy 'during the voyage: the *Kiev* on 3rd March, *El Occidents* on meeting ice on the 6th and the *Sevzaples* on the 11th during the convoy's last encounter with the icefield. The first two ships arrived on the 10th at Iokanka. The third reached Murmansk on the 14th, having joined the whaler *Stefa*, a straggler since the 6th; these two proceeded together and on the 13th the *Stefa* shot down an aircraft that tried to bomb her consort 100 miles east of Murmansk. The convoy may have been reported by a submarine on the 9th; but Captain Denny remarked that the weather was extremely favourable for an unobserved passage, that the Arctic sea smoke gave very effective cover against submarines, at the low clouds made high-level bombing generally impracticable. Admiral Tovey regarded the safe passage of the convoy as 'an example of the of the virtue of keeping wireless silence'; for the enemy's sole indication of the position came from the aircraft near Jan Mayen Island on the 5th. He also remarked that:–

> 'the situation following the *Ijora* incident ... reveals a possible source of confusion resulting from an order given from a distance to steer a definite course, even though it is generally understood to be a discretionary order.'

11

The operations described in the foregoing sections provided both British and German with food for thought. Writing to the Admiralty on 14 March 1942, the Commander-in-Chief, Home Fleet, discussed at length the problem posed by the presence of the German heavy ships at Trondheim. While admitting that the reasons for this concentration were not yet fully established, he was strongly of the opinion that they were mainly defensive and that their policy was at all costs to avoid action with our heavy forces.

> 'The *Tirpitz*, by her existence, contains very large British and United States forces and prevents their transfer to the Far East or the Mediterranean. She is so valuable an asset to all the Axis Powers that I am convinced that the enemy will not willingly expose this unique and irreplaceable ship to any unnecessary risk. The promptitude with which she entered the nearest harbour, when attacked by the aircraft from the *Victorious* and the evident alarm with which the enemy views the completion of her passage to Trondheim,[50] support my conviction. The raid from which she was returning may have been prearranged; but it is more likely to have originated from the accidental air sighting of PQ 12, south of Jan Mayen Island and the enemy's fear that this convoy might carry the first flight of an invasion force. I have no doubt that she was feeling extremely unhappy in the far north and I do not believe that she would willingly have accepted action with any British capital ships. Her experiences during this operation were not such that she is likely to repeat it.'[51]

On these grounds he still preferred the dispositions he had originally proposed for running Convoys PQ 12 and QP 8 and pointed out that the instructions contained in Admiralty signal 0135 3rd March, viz., that the protection of the convoys was his object and that he was to provide fighter protection for all capital ships within range of enemy shore-based aircraft, compelled him to operate his three capital ships and the *Victorious* as one unit – a risky proceeding in those submarine-infested distant waters, where the destroyers' endurance forced him to operate for long periods without a screen.[52] He remarked that throughout the whole of the operations he had been 'seriously embarrassed' by these instructions. In his opinion the sinking of the *Tirpitz* was 'of incomparably greater importance to the conduct of the war than the safety of any convoy' and on receipt of definite information that she was at sea, he must be at liberty to take her destruction as his object, without regard to the latter. After pointing out that the dispositions and movements required to effect the one were seldom, if ever, the same as for the other, he requested an assurance that Their Lordships were in agreement with this view.[53] As regards the convoys, he considered that 'by far the most serious threat' came from U-boats and aircraft, against which our scale of defence was at that time quite inadequate.

The German Staff, though their reasoning was not quite the same, came to much the same conclusions as the Commander-in-Chief, Home Fleet, with regard to the employment of the *Tirpitz*; three months were to elapse before she was again risked against the convoys and then she was so fettered by cautious instructions, as to render her direct intervention highly unlikely.

> 'The *Tirpitz* operation had not resulted in any direct success. Only sheer good fortune had saved the ship from damage by enemy ships, torpedo-bombers and submarines. But the operation clearly revealed the weakness of the German Navy's position in the north. Vice-Admiral Ciliax pointed out that operations by single ships without adequate air cover in an area patrolled by the British Fleet offered slight prospects and were not worth a great risk. Grand Admiral Raeder stressed the risk involved in such operations in view of the lack of aircraft carriers and the weakness of the Luftwaffe. He queried whether the use of capital ships in this way was consistent with their main task of defence against invasion ... The lesson derived from the *Tirpitz* operation appeared to be that caution must be used in the employment of warships, if they were to be kept in a fit state to repel an invasion.'[54]

But at this time Hitler realised the important influence the seaborne supplies to North Russia were exercising on the operations of the Army on the Eastern front and directed that every available method was to be used to restrict the traffic. He also ordered the submarine offensive in northern waters to be intensified, the Luftwaffe to be increased and the aircraft carrier *Graf Zeppelin*, on which work had been stopped, to be completed forthwith;[55] in addition the cruiser *Seydlitz* and liner *Potsdam* to be converted into auxiliary carriers.

The Navy thus found itself committed to two objectives: ships had to be ready to repel a possible invasion and at the same time they were to develop the maximum offensive against the convoys. As a compromise the Naval Staff decided to keep the *Tirpitz* in reserve for the former, while using the remaining forces, especially destroyers, for attack on the convoy traffic.

Chapter II

Convoys PQ 13, QP 9: March 1942
(All times are Zone minus 1.)

12

The next pair of convoys – PQ 13 and QP 9 – sailed on 20th and 21st March respectively. The new decisions by Hitler and the German Naval Staff[56] were already in operation, and increased air and U-boat attacks were planned; but surface operations were to be limited to destroyers. This, of course, was not known to the British; indeed, there were indications in the contrary direction, as the *Hipper* was passing up the coast of Norway, apparently to reinforce the ships at Trondheim.

At the Admiralty, the Commander-in-Chief, Home Fleet's views were still under consideration, and the measures for the protection of these convoys did not differ much from those for PQ 12 and QP 8. Cover against surface attack by the heavy ships in Trondheim was provided over the western part of the route by the *King George V, Duke of York, Renown, Victorious, Edinburgh, Kent* and 11 destroyers, under Vice-Admiral Curteis, wearing his flag in the *King George V.*

It was not possible materially to strengthen the close escorts, which consisted of two destroyers, a minesweeper and two trawlers for the eastbound convoy and one destroyer and two minesweepers for the westbound; but one cruiser accompanied each convoy as close cover, while another, the *Nigeria*, cruised west of Bear Island in support. Three destroyers[57] and five minesweepers from Vaenga reinforced the escorts off the Murmansk Coast; no air support was available outside the immediate vicinity of Kola Inlet.

Before the convoys sailed the Commander-in-Chief issued the following directions to the escorts:–

'I wish it to be clearly understood that, in the event of a Russian convoy being attacked by a force overwhelmingly superior to the

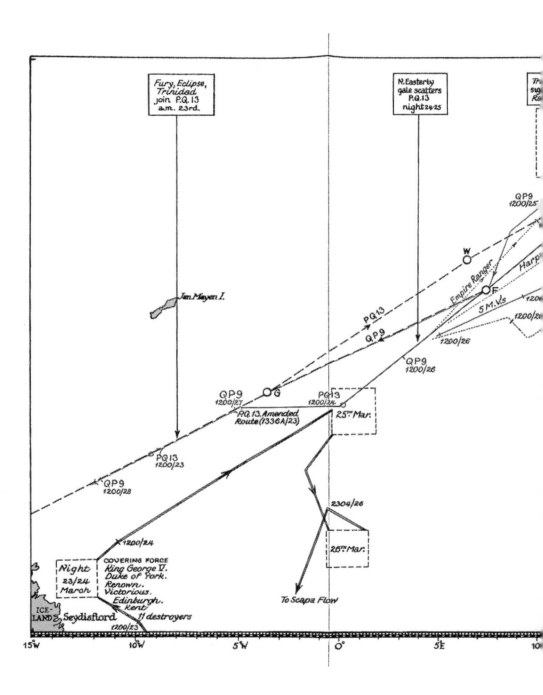

Fury, Eclipse,
Trinidad
join P.Q.13
a.m. 23rd.

N.Easterly
gale scatters
P.Q.13
night 24/25

Tr
su
Ra

QP9
1200/25

W

Empire Ranger

Harp

F

5 M.V.s

120

1200/2

1200/26

Jan Mayen I.

PQ13

QP9

QP9
1200/26

QP9
1200/27

G

PQ13
1200/24

PQ13
1200/23

PQ.13.Amended
Route (1336A/23)

25TH Mar.

QP9
1200/28

2304/26

26TH Mar.

X 1200/24

COVERING FORCE
King George V.
Duke of York.
Renown.
Victorious.
Edinburgh.
Kent.
11 destroyers

To Scapa Flow

Night
23/24
March

ICE
LAND   Seydisfiord
1200/23

15 W   10 W   5 W   O°   5 E   10

242

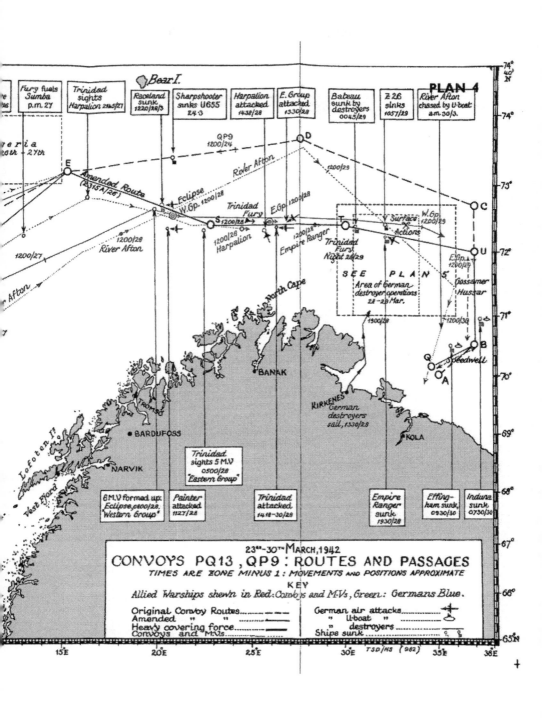

PLAN 4

Bear I.

| Fury fuels Sumba p.m. 27 | Trinidad sights Harpalion 2145/27 | Raceland sunk 1220/18/3 | Sharpshooter sinks U655 24·3 | Harpalion attacked 1438/28 | E. Group attacked 1330/28 | Bateau sunk by destroyers 0045/29 | Z 26 sinks 1057/29 | River Afton chased by U-boat a.m. 30/3 |

QP9 1200/24

D

Amended Route (0315A/26)

E

River Afton

1200/23

Eclipse W.6p. 1200/28

Trinidad Fury

E.6p 1200/28

W.6p 1200/29

C

S 1200/28

T

V Surface Actions

U

1200/28 Harpalion

1200/28 Empire Ranger

Trinidad Fury Night 28/29

SEE PLAN 5

E.6p. 1200/29

Gossamer Hussar

1200/27

River Afton

SEE PLAN

Area of German destroyer operations 28–29 Mar.

1500/29

1200/30

B

Speedwell

Afton

North Cape

Q

Y

A

BANAK

KIRKENES German destroyers sail, 1330/28

KOLA

TROMSÖ

BARDUFOSS

| Trinidad sights 5 M.V 0500/28 "Eastern Group" |

NARVIK

| 5 M.V formed up: Eclipse, 0300/28, "Western Group" | Painter attacked 1127/28 | Trinidad attacked 1418–30/28 | Empire Ranger sunk 1930/28 | Effingham sunk 0930/30 | Induna sunk 0730/30 |

CONVOYS PQ13, QP9: ROUTES AND PASSAGES
23ᴿᴰ–30ᵀᴴ MARCH, 1942
TIMES ARE ZONE MINUS 1: MOVEMENTS AND POSITIONS APPROXIMATE

KEY
Allied Warships shewn in Red: Convoys and M.Vs, Green: Germans Blue.

Original Convoy Routes.............
Amended   "   ".............
Heavy covering force.............
Convoys and M.Vs.............

German air attacks.............
  "   U-boat   ".............
  "   destroyers   ".............
Ships sunk.............

15°E   20°E   25°E   30°E   730/HS (982)   35°E   36°E

74° 40' N
74°
73°
72°
71°
70°
69°
68°
67°
66°
65°N

243

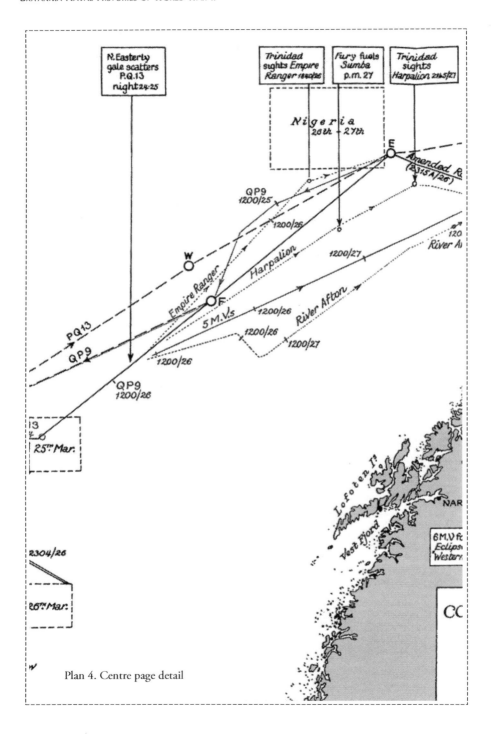

Plan 4. Centre page detail

escort, the primary object of the escort is to ensure the enemy being shadowed to enable them to be brought to action by our heavier forces or submarines, or to be attacked after dark, or under more suitable conditions by the escort itself. Any delaying action is to be taken with this primary object in view.'[58]

Convoy PQ 13's passage was full of incident. Dispersed by a violent gale in the early days of the voyage, its widely scattered groups and units suffered attacks by aircraft, destroyers, and U-boats. QP 9, on the other hand, had little to contend with except the weather, and one eminently satisfactory encounter with a submarine.

13

Convoy PQ 13 consisting of 19 ships escorted by the destroyer *Lamerton*,[59] the trawlers *Blackfly* and *Paynter* and three armed whalers[60] sailed from Iceland on 20 March and shaped course for a position (X) about 140 miles south of Jan Mayen Island (Plan 4).

The westbound convoy, QP 9, also 19 ships, was delayed 24 hours on account of a report of U-boats off the entrance to Kola Inlet, and did not put to sea until 1900, 21st. The ocean escort consisted of the minesweepers *Sharpshooter* (Lieut. Commander D. Lampen, SO), *Britomart* and the destroyer *Offa*.[61] The convoy ran into short visibility from the start, which afforded protection from the attentions of both friend and foe; the *Kenya*, which sailed the next day to provide close cover, never made contact throughout the passage. A gale of wind, force 3-9, sea 7, with heavy snowstorms, was encountered during the 23rd and 24th March. That evening the *Sharpshooter* rammed and sank a U-boat,[62] which she sighted 300 yards off in a snow squall. She sustained damage herself, but was able to continue under her own steam independently, turning over the convoy to the *Offa*. The remainder of QP 9's passage was uneventful and calls for no further remark, the convoy arriving intact on 31st March.

Convoy PQ 13 reached position X during the afternoon of 23rd March and was joined by the destroyers *Fury* (Lieut. Commander C. H. Campbell SO) and *Eclipse* (Lieut. Commander E. Mack) from Seidisfjord. Close cover was provided by the *Trinidad* (Captain L. S. Saunders) which made contact at 2030, 23rd, and then cruised to the south and east of the convoy during the night. A strong south-westerly wind had accelerated the passage and the convoy was some 40 miles ahead of its scheduled position when sighted by the *Trinidad*. On reaching the meridian 5° W. course was altered to the eastward in compliance with Admiralty instructions amending the route,[63] in order to avoid a U-boat area; by noon, 24th it was in 69° 20' N. 0° 20' E., making good knots. So far all had gone well.

That night, however, a gale sprang up from the north-east and by the forenoon of the 25th it was blowing force 8, with visibility varying 'up to 2 miles.' For the next 36 hours the gale continued unabated;[64] by dawn, 27th, the convoy was widely scattered,[65] and not a single merchant ship was in sight from the *Trinidad* or either of the escorting destroyers.

Away to the south-west, the weather had so retarded the advance of the heavy ship covering force, besides damaging the *Victorious* and *Tartar*, that the Vice-Admiral, seeing no chance of being able to reach the area where surface attack was probable, had decided to return to harbour and shaped course for Scapa Flow at 2304, 26th March.

Throughout the 27th short visibility and heavy weather made it difficult to find the scattered units of PQ 13. The *Trinidad* searching the area about 100 miles south-west of Bear Island, where she was joined by the *Nigeria* (Flag, Rear-Admiral, 10th Cruiser Squadron), sighted none of them until the evening, when two ships were located. The *Eclipse* some 180 miles to the southwestward had one ship in company. The *Fury* spent most of the afternoon finding and fuelling the whaler *Sumba* in response to an urgent appeal[66] received at 1127. This she completed at 2041, and then steered to rejoin the convoy, falling in with SS *Harpalion* at 0710, 28th, with whom she remained in company.

By this time the weather was moderating and the situation was approximately as follows. The convoy was strung out over about 150 miles. Furthest east was SS *Empire Ranger* by herself, some 80 miles due north of North Cape at 0800; about 40 miles astern of her was a group of six merchant ships and an armed whaler, and 35 miles astern of this group the *Harpalion* with the *Fury*, while a further 65 miles astern were six merchant ships with the *Eclipse*, *Paynter* and *Sumba* in company. Four merchant ships and an armed whaler were straggling.[67]

The *Trinidad*, having spent the night sweeping to the eastward along the convoy route, sighted the *Empire Ranger* at 0830, and then turned and swept back along the track, with the intention of concentrating with the *Fury* and *Eclipse*, in view of the possibility of surface attack of which warning had been received from the Admiralty.[68] The *Harpalion* and *Fury* were sighted at 1125, and 20 minutes later, with the latter in company, course was again altered to the eastward. Meanwhile, the convoy had been located by the enemy air reconnaissance.

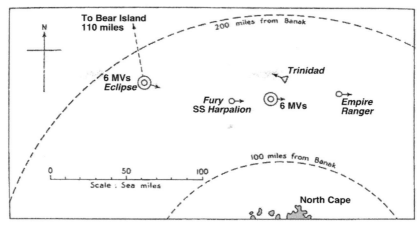

Figure 4. Convoy PQ 13: situation 1000, 28 March 1942

14

The forenoon of the 28th March was clear and sunny, with occasional snow patches. At 1007 the *Trinidad* sighted a shadowing aircraft,[69] which she engaged ineffectively at long range. The enemy wasted no time; within about an hour their bombers arrived on the scene, and that afternoon three destroyers sailed from Kirkenes in search of the convoy.

Throughout the remainder of the day, air attacks were carried out at intervals (Plans 4 and 5). The eastern group of six merchant ships with the *Silja* was dive bombed twice, the Panamanian SS *Ballot* being so shaken by near-misses that she dropped astern and started to abandon ship, though she subsequently reached port under her own steam. At 1127 the *Paynter* was attacked; the *Trinidad*, after being narrowly missed by three bombs from an aircraft which dived out of cloud at 1318, was persistently dive-bombed by Junkers 88 between 1418 and 1430; eight minutes later, SS *Harpalion* reported being bombed. Fortunately, none of these attacks inflicted serious damage: but a straggler, the *Raceland*, was sunk, and about 1930 the *Empire Ranger* reported herself sinking and abandoning ship in position 72° 13' N. 32° 10' E. The trawler *Blackfly* was sent to this position, but was unable to find any survivors.

During the hours of darkness,[70] 28th and 29th March, the *Trinidad* and *Fury* cruised to the southward of 72° 25' N. 30° E. (position T) in order to cut off the enemy destroyers, should they attack either main group of the convoy. Course was altered to the E.N.E. at 0200, in order to close the leading group of merchant ships, and to locate HMS *Oribi* and two Russian destroyers – the *Sokrushetelni* (Captain (D)) and

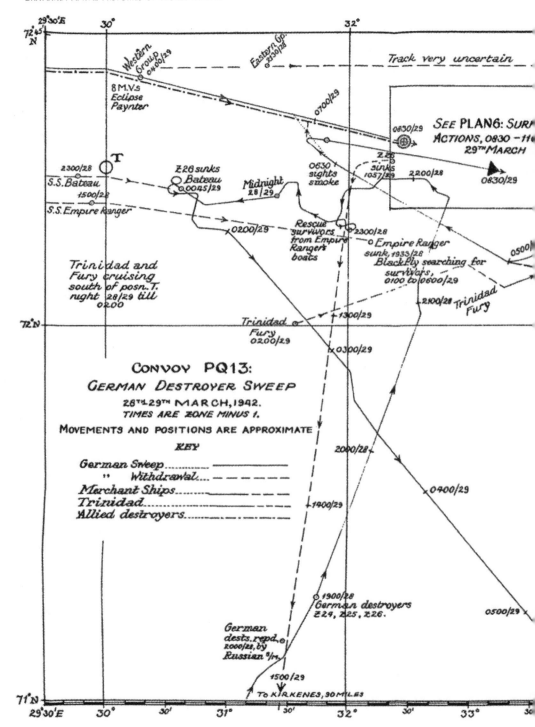

CONVOY PQ13:

GERMAN DESTROYER SWEEP

28TH-29TH MARCH, 1942.
TIMES ARE ZONE MINUS 1.

MOVEMENTS AND POSITIONS ARE APPROXIMATE

KEY

German Sweep	———
" Withdrawal	- - - - -
Merchant Ships	—·—·—
Trinidad	············
Allied destroyers	—··—··—

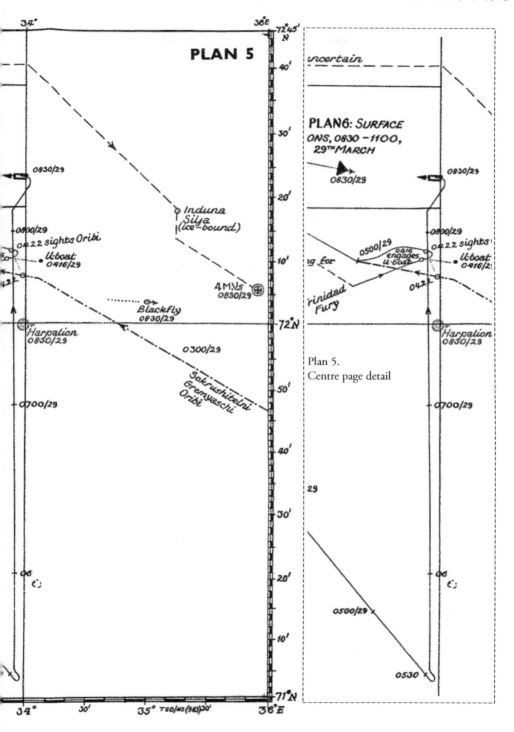

PLAN 5

0830/29

0500/29

0422 sights Oribi

U-boat
0416/29

Induna
Silya
(ice-bound.)

4 M.Vs
0830/29

Blackfly
0830/29

Harpalion
0830/29

0300/29

Sokrushitelni
Gremyaschi
Oribi

0700/29

06

PLAN 6: *SURFACE*
ONS, 0830 –1100,
29ᵀᴴ MARCH

0830/29

uncertain

0830/29

0500/29

0422 sights

0500/29
engages
U-boat

ng for

U-boat
0416/2

0422

Trinidad
Fury

Harpalion
0830/29

Plan 5.
Centre page detail

0700/29

29

06

0500/29

0530

72°45′
N

40′

30′

20′

10′

72°N

50′

40′

30′

20′

10′

71°N

34°   30′   35° 7 SO/NS (98) 30′   36°E

Gremyaschi – from Vaenga Bay, which were due at position T at 0800. These were met at 0422, just as the *Trinidad* was engaging a U-boat,[71] and course was then shaped to the westward to close the *Eclipse*'s group. Shortly afterwards the wreckage from the *Empire Ranger* was passed, and four boats – well found and with ample supplies – were examined by the *Oribi*; the absence of survivors led to the conjecture that they had been rescued by some ship during the night.[72]

The convoy group, then consisting of eight merchant ships, with the *Eclipse, Paynter* and *Sumba*, was sighted at 0630. Leaving the two Russians and *Oribi* with this group,[73] the *Trinidad* and *Fury* altered course at 0700 – being then in position 72° 29' N. 31° 48' E. to 105° at 20 knots to seek the eastern group. This group had become reduced to four ships. One ship, as already mentioned, had straggled the day before as the result of the air attacks; another, the *Induna*, with the *Silja* (which had run short of fuel) in tow, got caught in heavy ice during the night and did not get clear until the following afternoon.

15

Meanwhile the German surface striking force, consisting of the destroyers *Z26* (SO), *Z25* and *Z24* had left Kirkenes at 1330, 28th March, and shaped course to the northward[74] (Plan 5). At 2145, being then in approximately 72° 20' N., 32° 50' E. (about 50 miles east of position T) course was altered to the westward to sweep along the estimated route of the convoy, at 15 knots, the destroyers being spread 3 miles apart. An hour later they came across the *Empire Ranger*'s boats and picked up her survivors.

Continuing to the westward, they sighted the straggler SS *Bateau* at 0035, 29th, in 72° 20' N., 30° 40' E.[75] (12 miles to the eastward of position T). *Z26* promptly sank her by torpedo and gunfire. From survivors they learned of the convoy's vicissitudes in the storm, and the strength of its escort – which was given as two cruisers and four destroyers. The Germans remained in this vicinity for about an hour, and then, apparently thinking they were too far to the northwest,[76] at 0140 set course 140°, and swept to the south-eastward at 25 knots until 0530, when they turned to due north up the meridian 33° 55' E.

By 0820, 29th, they were once more on the estimated convoy route in approximately 72° 22' N., 34° E., and they altered to 270°, 17 knots, to sweep along it. This course took them directly towards the *Trinidad* and *Fury* (then only about 17 miles to the westward), which, it will be

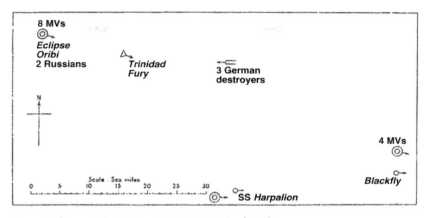

Figure 5. Convoy PO 13: situation 0820, 29 March 1942

remembered, had left the western group at 0700 and were steering to the eastward at 20 knots to support the eastern group. The two forces were thus closing each other on almost reciprocal courses at a rate of 37 knots. The weather, which had earlier been fine, with the sky almost free from cloud and the visibility extreme, was then deteriorating and the visibility rapidly shortening.

16

The visibility had fallen to two miles when at 0843 the *Trinidad's* radar picked up an echo bearing 079° 6 ½ miles; two minutes later the bearing changed to 092° 4 ½ miles–apparently three ships. 'I thought,' wrote Captain Saunders, subsequently, 'they might be ships of the convoy, but ... I was surprised that three should be in this position. At 0849A in position 72° 21' N., 33° 32' E.[77] shapes were sighted in the mist, which were identified as three foreign destroyers on approximate course 330°. Fortunately, I had already located the Russian destroyers and I was able to open fire without challenging at the leading destroyer at 0851 ...' (Plan 6).

The enemy replied almost at the same moment. By 0852 the leading destroyer (*Z26*) had been frequently hit and was blazing amidships; fire was then shifted to the second destroyer, which was thought to be hit,[78] but after half a minute the wheel was put hard to starboard to avoid torpedoes which might have been fired; two in fact passed up the port side just afterwards while the ship was turning, and the action ceased for the time being.

251

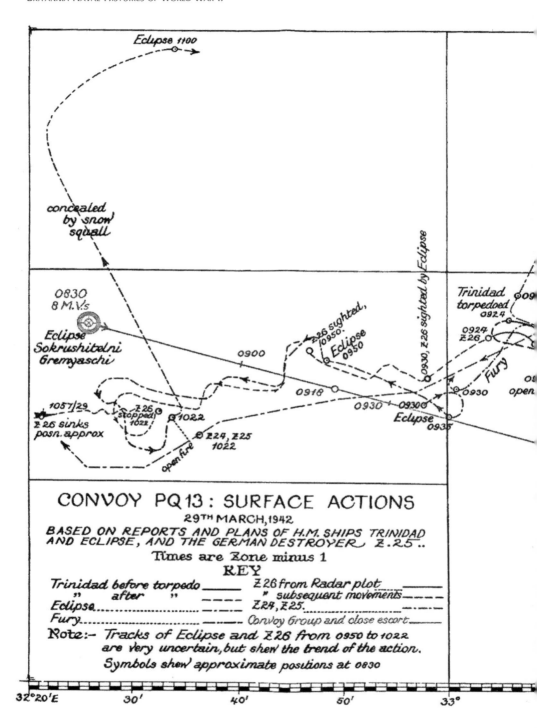

CONVOY PQ13 : SURFACE ACTIONS

29TH MARCH, 1942

BASED ON REPORTS AND PLANS OF H.M. SHIPS TRINIDAD AND ECLIPSE, AND THE GERMAN DESTROYER Z.25..

Times are Zone minus 1

KEY

Trinidad before torpedo _____   Z26 from Radar plot _____
    "   after   "   ‒ ‒ ‒   "   subsequent movements ‒ ‒ ‒ ‒
Eclipse .... ‒ .. ‒   Z24, Z25 ....
Fury .... ‒   Convoy Group and close escort ____

Note:‒ Tracks of Eclipse and Z26 from 0950 to 1022 are very uncertain, but shew the trend of the action. Symbols shew approximate positions at 0830

32°20'E   30'   40'   50'   33°

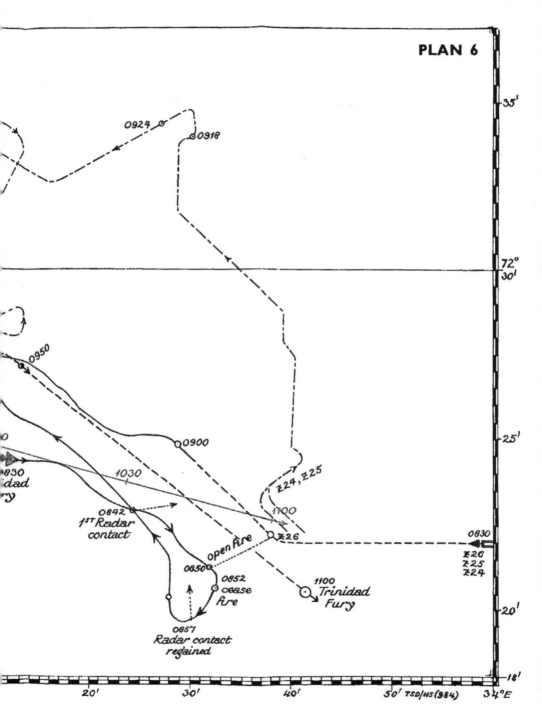

PLAN 6

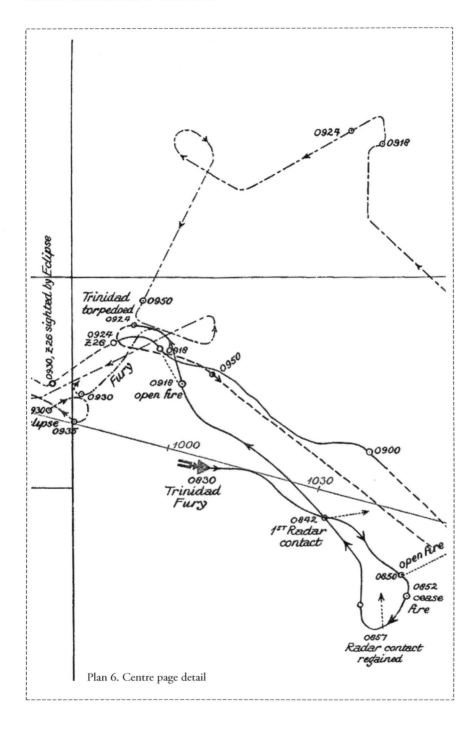

Plan 6. Centre page detail

Z26, severely damaged, made to the north-westward; the other two German destroyers, who had not sighted the enemy through the mist, turned to the north-eastward to avoid torpedoes,[79] thus becoming separated from their leader, whom they failed to rejoin for an hour.

Meanwhile, the *Trinidad* with the *Fury* astern had steadied on 360°. At the same time radar contact was regained with *Z26*, bearing 358°, 7,200 yards; speed was increased and course altered to port as necessary to close. At 0917 the outline of the destroyer was sighted fine on the port bow. The *Trinidad*, hauling slightly to starboard to open A-arcs and cross under her stern, immediately opened fire at a range of 2,900 yards. The enemy endeavoured to avoid the salvoes which were falling all round her by a 'continuous and violent zigzag;' she did not return the fire and was 'apparently too heavily damaged to fire torpedoes, although still able to steam.'[80] At 0922 the *Trinidad* fired a torpedo at her, which appeared to be running true on a relative bearing Red 080°; two others fired half a minute later failed to leave the tubes owing to icing. Meanwhile, the enemy was suffering severe punishment and all seemed to be going well when at 0923 a torpedo broke surface 200 yards on the *Trinidad*'s port bow;[81] the wheel was put hard to port, but it was too late and she was hit on the port side between 71 and 79 stations. The ship listed 17° to port, speed dropped to eight knots, all communication from the compass platform failed, and steering had to be shifted to the after-steering position.

Z26 made off to the south-westward and was soon lost to view, pursued by the *Fury*, which from her station astern of the *Trinidad* had hitherto not sighted the enemy. This course took them close north of the approaching convoy. Visibility was then about six cables; the destroyers of the escort were 'zigzagging furiously around in order to maintain a decent speed,'[82] when the *Eclipse* sighted a warship (*Z26*) bearing about 020° just visible in the mist. One of the Russian destroyers opened fire, but the *Eclipse*, mistaking her for the *Trinidad*, refrained from doing so. 'At this moment (about 0930) *Fury* appeared out of the snow ahead at high speed and for some minutes chaos reigned in the destroyer screen ...'[83] The *Fury* actually fired two salvoes at the *Eclipse* before recognition. She then turned back to rejoin the *Trinidad*, and the *Eclipse*, 'as there seemed altogether too many destroyers around the convoy,'[84] hauled round to the westward at 15 knots to follow the ship which had passed to port of the convoy a few minutes before.[85] The *Eclipse* had not gone far when her radar picked up an echo distant two miles, which she closed keeping the bearing about 20° on the port bow. Slowly the range decreased; at 0950 a ship was dimly sighted through the snow half a mile off. She was again taken for the *Trinidad*, but when the range was down to 800 yards she was recognised as a Narvik class destroyer and promptly engaged.[86] The luckless *Z26* quickly increased speed and strove to get away.

There followed a running fight in a snowstorm, the German making smoke and altering away whenever the *Eclipse* worked up on his quarter and opened A-arcs.[87] The damage previously inflicted by the *Trinidad* prevented her replying to the British fire except with occasional shots which did no harm. 'Conditions were very severe. Spray, which swept over guns and bridge, immediately froze on anything it touched; gundecks were icy and gun wells full of water and ice. Use of binoculars by bridge and director personnel was almost impossible.'

This went on for half an hour, until at 1020, having by then been hit six times by 4.7-inch shells, *Z26* came to a stop, her stem almost awash and listing to port. The *Eclipse* was just about to fire her remaining torpedo into her,[88] when suddenly *Z24* and *Z25* hove into sight about two miles on her disengaged beam. They were an unwelcome sight. At the same time the snow stopped and visibility increased rapidly. The Germans immediately opened fire, and the *Eclipse* made off at high speed to the north-westward, eventually reaching cover in a snow squall at 1035, but not before she had been hit aft by two shells at 1028 and holed above the waterline forward by two others which burst close alongside under the flare; her main aerials were also shot away.[89] The enemy made no attempt to follow, but stood by the sinking *Z26*, which capsized at 1057. After rescuing survivors, they set course at high speed for Kirkenes, where they arrived without incident that evening.

The *Eclipse* found herself in unseaworthy condition, short of fuel, and with nine casualties in urgent need of attention; she accordingly shaped course independently for Murmansk,[90] where she arrived next day with only 40 tons of oil remaining.

17

The *Trinidad*, meanwhile, after the explosion of the torpedo had turned to the south-eastward and was steering 130°, 6 knots, when the *Fury* rejoined her. Speed was slowly increased as much as due regard for the strain on her bulkheads permitted. At about 1100 the group of merchant ships screened by the Russian destroyers was overhauled and the *Oribi* was ordered to join the *Fury* as A/S screen; early in the afternoon the *Harrier*[91] also joined the screen. During the forenoon the list on the *Trinidad* had been gradually reduced and by this time she was on an even keel and making good between 12 and 14 knots. Late that night, however, priming with salt water in the feed water compelled a reduction of speed to 2 to 4 knots, and threatened to stop her altogether. The ship was then (2315) in 70° 18' N., 34° 55' E. – some 70 miles from the entrance to Kola Inlet – and a signal was sent to the SBNO, North Russia, asking him to arrange for the assistance of tugs and also air protection. By 0200, 30th March, however, it was found possible to maintain a speed of seven knots.

By the early morning the wind, which had been freshening all night, was blowing hard from the northward, with a considerable sea. Once the ship broached to, and stern way had to be gathered to bring her stern into the wind and her head to the proper course. On the whole she weathered it well, and reached Kola Inlet at 0930, 30th. There tugs were met, but their assistance was not required and three hours later the *Trinidad* and *Fury* anchored at Rosta.

18

To return to the convoy (Plan 4). During the 29th March the various groups and stragglers pursued their way unmolested, turning to the southward on reaching the 37th meridian; short visibility and low cloud gave protection from air attack and they were not yet in the area chosen by the enemy for submarine attack.

The western group of eight ships, escorted by the two Russian destroyers and the *Oribi*, after their fleeting glimpse of *Z26*, passed clear to the southward of the other two enemy destroyers while they were searching for their leader. The four ships of the eastern group by the time the surface actions were over, were about to alter course to south near position U.

The *Induna* and *Silja* did not get clear of the ice until 1500 that afternoon; they estimated they were then in approximately 72° N., 38° E., and shaped course direct for Murmansk. Five hours later the tow parted and the *Silja* disappeared in a squall. Efforts to find her proved unavailing[92] and the *Induna* continued her voyage alone. At 0720, 30th, she was torpedoed by a U-boat and sank 40 minutes later;[93] it was hard luck, after her strenuous efforts on the *Silja*'s behalf. An hour after the *Induna* sank, the same fate overtook SS *Effingham* – one of the eastern group – some 45 miles to the south-westward; and that afternoon Commodore Casey in the *River Afton*, which had been proceeding independently after her experiences in the gale, was chased by a U-boat for some hours in the same area.

No further enemy interference was met with, except an unsuccessful air attack on the ships of the 'western' group off Kola Inlet, in the course of which SS *Tobruk* claimed to have shot down two aircraft. By the night of the 30th all the surviving 14 ships had arrived except one, which did not reach port until early on the 1st April.

Nineteen ships had left Reykjavik on 20th March; five had been lost on passage. Considering the dispersal caused by the gale,[94] and the scale of the enemy attacks perhaps these losses were not excessive; nevertheless, they exceeded 25 per cent and could not be viewed without concern – especially at a time when lengthening hours of daylight and the position of ice were increasingly favouring the enemy.

19

The attacks on Convoy PQ 13 and the continued movement northward of enemy surface, air and U-boat reinforcements:–

'showed clearly the importance attached by the enemy to the stopping of this traffic. Further representations to the Admiralty were therefore made and some destroyers and corvettes from the Western Approaches were promised for the next convoys. The Russians also agreed to receive a mission from Coastal Command to help in organising their oversea reconnaissance and fighter protection.'[95]

The Commander-in-Chief also recommended that the number of the convoys should be reduced during the next few months, when the German airfield conditions and air reconnaissance would be improving, while the convoy routes would still be restricted by ice, though he realised that political considerations would probably dictate an increase rather than the decrease he suggested.

The Germans regarded the results of their operations against PQ 13 as a 'notable success,' but the loss of *Z26* was considered too high a price for the one merchant ship sunk by surface craft. This led to a difference of opinion between the Naval Staff and the Flag Officer, Northern Command, the former holding that the situation must be met by the exercise of greater caution in the use of surface ships against the convoys, while the latter considered that the only solution lay in the employment of a capital ship as cover for the destroyers. At this time, shortage of fuel prevented this being done; and there the matter rested for the next couple of months.[96]

20

Six weeks after her encounter with *Z26* the *Trinidad* was still at Murmansk, her repairs then nearing completion, when on 7th May a stoker engaged in cleaning out debris from the furnace of a boiler in 'A' boiler room made an interesting find. This debris had come from the forward part of the boiler room in the earlier stages of clearing away wreckage from the effects of the torpedo hit on 29th March. His find consisted of the whisker of a torpedo pistol, which was speedily identified by its markings and shape as being part of a pistol fitted to one of the torpedoes in the port tubes of the *Trinidad* at the beginning of the action. Beyond a shadow of doubt the *Trinidad* had torpedoed herself.

This startling denouement was the subject of enquiry by a Board subsequently convened at Plymouth. The Board found that the torpedo had been properly prepared in all respects except for cold weather running; for this the necessary oils had not been available. The precise cause of its erratic behaviour could not be determined with certainty, many possibilities of a highly technical nature being involved. On the whole it seemed fair to ascribe it to the effect of the bitter cold on the torpedo's mechanism, e.g., solidification of the engine and gyro oil.

No blame was attributed to the *Trinidad*. As the Commander-in-Chief, Home Fleet, later wrote, 'it was cruel hard luck that his (Captain Saunders') ship should have been put out of action by one of his own torpedoes ...'

Chapter III

Convoys PQ 14–16, QP 10–12: April–May 1942
(All times are Zone minus 2.)

21

The heavy attacks on Convoy PQ 13 described in the last chapter left no doubt in the mind of the Commander-in-Chief, Home Fleet, that the enemy was:–

> 'determined to do everything in his power to stop this traffic.
> The U-boat and air forces in Northern Norway had been heavily reinforced, the three remaining destroyers were disposed offensively at Kirkenes and the heavy forces at Trondheim remained a constant, if reluctant, threat.'[97]

As a result of his representations, sufficient destroyers, corvettes and trawlers to bring the close escort of each convoy up to ten were transferred from the Western Approaches Command early in April. The Russians were requested to help in the Barents Sea by reinforcing the escort and by disposing submarines to the south of the convoy route to discourage surface raiders. They were also asked to provide long range fighter or A/S air escort over this part of the route and to bomb the enemy airfields; but in the words of Sir John Tovey, 'little response was forthcoming.'[98] Apart from the considerably increased close escorts, the measures for the defence of the next pair of convoys, which sailed in the second week of April, were much the same as those for the previous pair.

Heavy cover was provided by the *King George V*, wearing the flag of the Commander-in-Chief, *Duke of York* (flag V.A.2), *Victorious, Kent* and eight destroyers, while the *Norfolk* cruised in an area about 130 miles to the southwest of Bear Island, whence she could support either convoy during this part of their passages. Convoy PQ 14,[99] consisting of 24 ships, under Commodore E. Rees, sailed from Iceland on 8th April, escorted by the minesweepers *Hebe* and *Speedy* and four trawlers and steered for a position about 120 miles, 200° from Jan Mayen Island, where they were to be joined by the *Edinburgh* (flag Rear-Admiral SSPQ Bonham-Carter) which was to provide close cover and the remainder of the escort – five destroyers and four corvettes[100] – under Commander M. Richmond, HMS *Bulldog*, on the 11th. The convoy, however, ran into thick drifting ice during the night of the 10th/11th and was delayed and scattered. Thick weather added to the difficulties; 16 of the merchant ships never regained contact and, with several of the escort,[101] which had been damaged by ice, returned to Iceland. Only eight ships continued the passage. These were located by the enemy on the 15th and ineffective bombing attacks occurred at intervals throughout the day. These were intensified and together with submarine attacks continued throughout the 16th and 17th; but the weather favoured the defence and the only loss occurred on the 16th, when the Commodore's ship, the *Empire Howard*, was hit by two torpedoes from a U-boat and blew up. Commodore Rees was not among the survivors and the Vice-Commodore, Captain W. H. Lawrence, Master of the *Briarwood*, took over the direction of the convoy. Early on the 17th two Russian destroyers reinforced the escort and the minesweepers *Niger, Hussar, Gossamer* and *Harrier* joined next day. The surviving seven ships of PQ 14 arrived at Kola on 19th April.[102] This was not the end of their troubles, repeated air attacks being made on them on the days following their arrival; no ships were hit, but unloading was delayed.

Convoy QP 10 consisting of 16 ships under Commodore Casey, escorted by the destroyers *Oribi, Punjabi, Fury, Eclipse* and *Marne*, a minesweeper and two trawlers, with the *Liverpool* providing close cover, sailed from Kola on 10th April. Two Russian destroyers and the *Harrier, Gossamer* and *Hussar* accompanied them as far as 30° E. longitude. The convoy was heavily attacked by aircraft and U-boats during the three days passage between Kola and Bear Island. Several ships suffered damage and four were lost: the *Empire Cowper* by bombs on the 11th, the *Kiev* and *El Occidents* torpedoed by U-boats on the 12th and the *Harpalion*, after having had her rudder blown off by air attack on the 13th, was sunk by gunfire from the escort. The enemy did not, however, have it all his own way, six aircraft being shot down and one damaged by the fire of the convoy and escort.[103] Dense fog, followed by a westerly gale, put an end to the enemy activities on the 13th and though the weather moderated next day and their reconnaissance aircraft regained contact, no further attacks developed and augmented by six stragglers from PQ 14 which were met, the convoy arrived at Reykjavik on 21st April. No interference

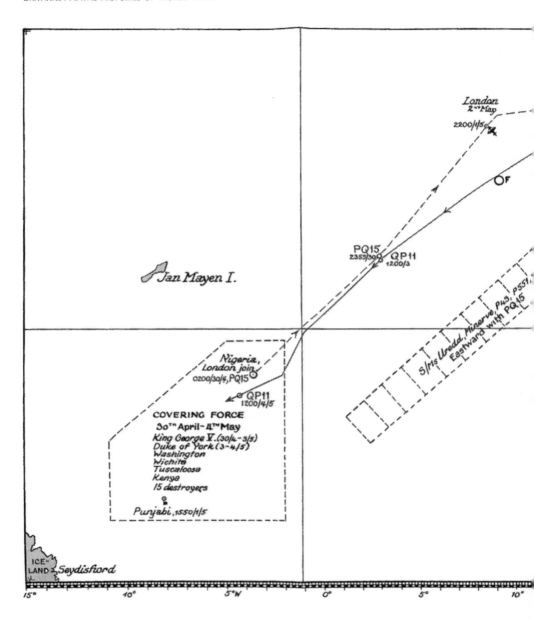

by enemy surface craft was experienced by either of these two convoys. Actually, the three operational German destroyers had put to sea on the 12th April and again on the 13th, with QP 10 as their objective; but on each occasion the operation was cancelled on account of weather.

As a result of these operations, the Commander-in-Chief, Home

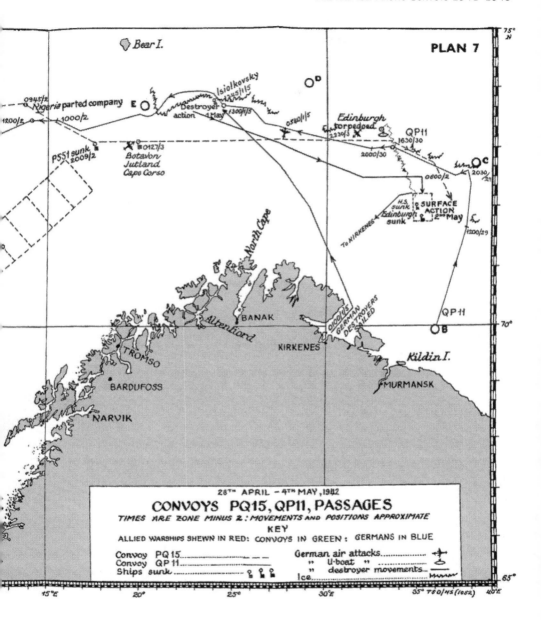

Bear I.

PLAN 7

O D

Isiolkovsky
1245/115

Destroyed
action 1 May 1300/3

Nigeria parted company E O

0945/2

1200/2 1000/2

PS51 sunk
2009/2

X B012/3
Botavon
Jutland
Cape Corso

0590/115

Edinburgh
torpedoed
2230/3

2000/30

QP11
1650/30

2030/
2 O C

Edinburgh

0800/2

To KIRKENES

H.S.
sunk
Edinburgh
sunk

SURFACE
ACTION
2nd May

1200/29

DIOO/15
GERMAN
DESTROYERS
SAILED

North Cape

BANAK

QP 11

O B

70°

Altenfiord

KIRKENES

Kildin I.

TROMSO

BARDUFOSS

MURMANSK

NARVIK

28TH APRIL – 4TH MAY, 1942
CONVOYS PQ15, QP11, PASSAGES
TIMES ARE ZONE MINUS 2: MOVEMENTS AND POSITIONS APPROXIMATE
KEY
ALLIED WARSHIPS SHEWN IN RED: CONVOYS IN GREEN: GERMANS IN BLUE

Convoy PQ15	German air attacks
Convoy QP 11	" U-boat "
Ships sunk	" destroyer movements
	Ice

75°
N

70°

65°

TS 0/HS (1052)

15°E   20°   25°   30°E   35°   40°E

Fleet, again suggested that if the next pair of convoys could not be postponed until the ice moved north, they should be reduced in size. This, however, could not be accepted and these two convoys, PQ 15 and QP 11, contained 26 and 13 ships respectively.

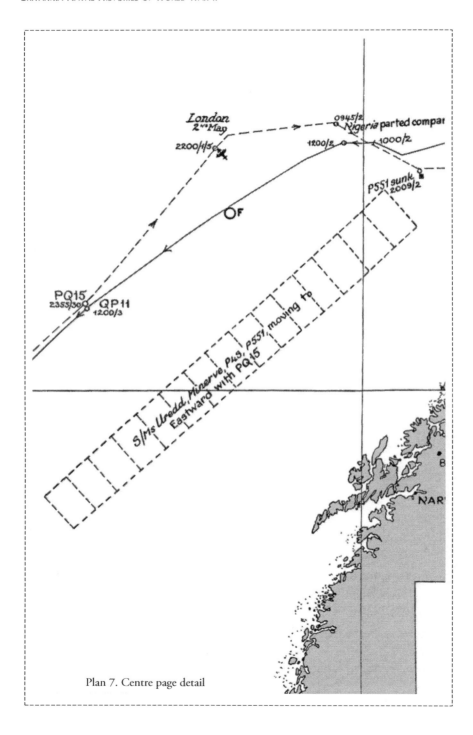

Plan 7. Centre page detail

22

Convoys PQ 15 and QP 11 sailed at the end of April. Two innovations were made in the defensive measures. The first was the addition of an A.A. ship to the close escort of PQ 15; a submarine, the *Sturgeon*, also accompanied this convoy as far as 5° E. The other was forced on us by the inability of the submarines to maintain the patrols off the approaches to Trondheim, as hitherto, owing to the lengthening hours of daylight. They were therefore disposed in 'shifting zones' about 150 miles[104] from the Norwegian Coast, moving to the north and east according to the progress of the east going convoy.[105]

Apart from these differences, the dispositions were much the same as those for Convoys PQ 14 and QP 10. The London reinforced the close covering forces while they were to the westward of Bear Island and distant cover was provided by a mixed force of British and American ships – the first occasion in the war on which United States ships operated as part of the Home Fleet.[106]

Convoys PQ 15 and QP II were fortunate in their passages. Despite unfavourable ice conditions, air and surface attack and a heavy concentration of U-boats in the Barents Sea, only four ships were lost out of the 39 at sea in the two convoys. The covering forces, however, did not come off so well, a cruiser, a tribal destroyer and a submarine being lost during the operations and three destroyers and a battleship damaged.

23

Convoy QP 11, consisting of 13 ships, left Kola Inlet on 28 April[107] (Plan 7). Captain W. H. Lawrence, Master of SS *Briarwood*, acted as Commodore. The close escort consisted of six destroyers, the *Bulldog* (Commander Richmond SO) *Beverley, Beagle, Amazon, Foresight* and *Forester*, four corvettes and a trawler. Close cover was provided by the *Edinburgh* (Captain H. W. Faulkner), wearing the flag of Rear-Admiral Bonham-Carter. Minesweepers accompanied the convoy until the evening of the 29th and the Russian destroyers *Sokrushitclni* and *Gremyaschi* were to reinforce the escort as far as 30° E. longitude.

The convoy was sighted and reported by enemy aircraft and U-boats on the 29th, but no attacks took place that day. The following afternoon, however, the *Edinburgh*, then zigzagging at high speed some 15 miles ahead of the convoy,[108] was struck by two torpedoes from a U-boat.[109] Her stem was blown off and steering gear wrecked, but she was able to steam at slow speed. The explosion was seen from the convoy and the

Foresight and *Forester* were detached to her assistance, followed shortly afterwards by the two Russian destroyers. Escorted by them, she started the 250-mile return passage to Murmansk.

The presence of the destroyers prevented *U-456*, the submarine that had done the damage, from repeating her attack. But she continued to shadow and report the *Edinburgh*'s movements. These reports tempted the Flag Officer, Northern Waters, contrary to his previous intentions,[110] to send the three destroyers at Kirkenes to attack Convoy QP 11 with its depleted escort; and at 0100[111] that night, the *Hermann Schoemann, Z24* and *Z25* put to sea and steered to the northward.

Convoy QP 11, meanwhile, continued its passage. At 0540, 1st May, being then about 150 miles to the E.S.E. of Bear Island it was unsuccessfully attacked by four torpedo aircraft;[112] at the same time a U-boat was sighted and forced to dive by the *Amazon*. Frequent HF DF bearings indicated that four U-boats were keeping pace with the convoy on different bearings and at 0820 course was altered 40° to starboard (i.e. to 320°) in an endeavour to shake them off. Then ice was sighted in large quantities ahead; this was found to extend some 20 miles to the southward of the route and course was again altered to the westward.

The forenoon passed without incident. The weather was moderate, wind N.N.E., force 3; frequent snow squalls caused the visibility to vary between ten and two miles.

At 1345 the convoy was on course 275°, skirting heavy drift ice to starboard, when the Snowflake reported three radar contacts bearing 185°; at the same moment the *Beverley*, screening on the port bow, reported enemy in sight, bearing 210°. The enemy proved to be three large destroyers. In the course of the next four hours they made five separate attempts to reach the convoy, each of which was foiled by the aggressive tactics of the escorting destroyers[113] despite their great inferiority in gun power to the Germans.[114]

24

On receipt of the *Beverley*'s sighting report, Commander Richmond who was on the starboard bow of the convoy, moved across to the threatened flank and ordered the destroyers to concentrate on him. The convoy (with the corvettes) at once carried out an emergency turn of 40° to starboard, the destroyers making smoke to cover it.

At 1400 the *Bulldog* turned towards the enemy on a south-westerly course, with the destroyers in line ahead in the order *Beagle, Amazon* and

Beverley. The Germans were at this time in line of bearing formation, about 10,000 yards distant, heading towards the convoy; at 1407, both sides opened fire, the Germans turning together to starboard to open 'A' arcs and the British destroyers to port to a similar course (Plan 7). Both sides fired torpedoes; none of them found its mark, but a track was seen to pass close astern of the *Bulldog*. After three minutes (1410) the Germans turned away and the British destroyers returned towards the convoy, making smoke. In this brief engagement the *Amazon* was hit, her steering gear, telegraphs and one gun being put out of action; but she managed to keep control and was stationed at the rear of the line.

A quarter of an hour after this action ceased, the convoy suffered its only loss, when a Russian ship which was straggling was hit by one of the torpedoes fired by the enemy destroyers and sank rapidly; survivors were rescued by the trawler *Lord Middleton*.

Commander Richmond, meanwhile, was keeping his destroyers between the convoy and the estimated position of the enemy. At 1433 they were again sighted, bearing 160°, about 15,000 yards off and the second attack developed. The British destroyers again steered for them and at 1440 fire was opened at 12,000 yards range; no hits were obtained by either side, but after five minutes the enemy turned away and the British once more retired on the convoy. By this time the convoy was well within the ice and 'in order to maintain touch the destroyers were led through lanes of open water as opportunity offered, bearing in mind that sufficient sea room to manoeuvre in action must be maintained. This presented a nice problem.'[115]

About an hour elapsed before the enemy's next attempt. Then, at 1558, he was sighted six miles away coming in from the eastward, bearing 115°. Commander Richmond repeated his tactics and both sides opened fire at 1600; the *Bulldog* was straddled several times and slightly damaged, but after ten minutes the enemy turned away under smoke to the southward and the British again closed the convoy, by then spread out over a distance of some seven miles, as it picked its way through the heavy drift ice in single line formation.

Shortly before 1700 the Germans were again sighted, following a radar report from the *Snowflake*, this time bearing 146°, 20,000 yards; the *Bulldog* led round towards them, fire was opened at 1658 and after seven minutes the enemy made smoke and turned away.

Half an hour later the Germans made their fifth and last attempt to breakthrough; fire was exchanged between 1736 and 1742, when they

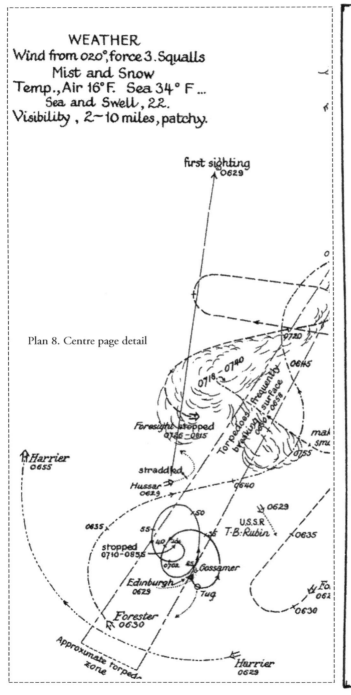

WEATHER
Wind from 020°, force 3. Squalls
Mist and Snow
Temp., Air 16° F.   Sea 34° F ...
Sea and Swell, 22.
Visibility, 2~10 miles, patchy.

first sighting
0629

Plan 8. Centre page detail

0720

0745

0740

0718

Torpedoes frequently breaking surface 0645-0658

0658

Foresight stopped 0746-0815

main smo

0755

Harrier
0655

straddled

Hussar
0629

0640

0629

x50

0635

55

35

U.S.S.R.
T.B. Rubin

0635

stopped
0710-0855

40

45

0701

45

Gossamer

Edinburgh
0629

Tug

Fo.
062

0630

Forester
0630

Approximate torpedo zone

Harrier
0629

WEATHER
Wind from 020°, force 3. Sc
Mist and Snow
Temp., Air 16° F.   Sea 34
Sea and Swell, 22.
Visibility, 2~10 miles, p

Foresig

Harrier
0655

stradd

Hussar
0629

0635

55

40

stopped
0710-0855

Edinburgh
0629

Forester
0630

Approximate torpedo zone

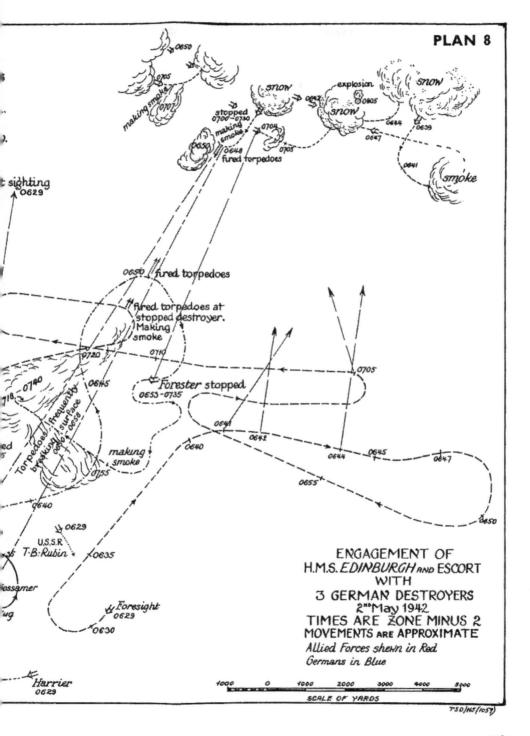

PLAN 8

0650
0705
0700
making smoke
snow
explosion
0605
snow
snow
0652
0644
0644
0639
stopped
0700–0730
making
smoke
0704
0647
0650
0703
0641
0648
fired torpedoes
smoke

t sighting
0629

0650 fired torpedoes

fired torpedoes at
stopped destroyer.
Making
smoke
0720
0710
0705
0740
0645
Forester stopped
0653–0735
18
Torpedoes frequently
breaking surface 0610–0650
0641
0642
0640
0655
0644
0645
0647
making
smoke
0755
0640
ed
0629
U.S.S.R.
T.B: Rubin
0635
ossamer
ug
Foresight
0629
0630

Harrier
0629

ENGAGEMENT OF
H.M.S. *EDINBURGH* AND ESCORT
WITH
3 GERMAN DESTROYERS
2ⁿᵈ May 1942
TIMES ARE ZONE MINUS 2
MOVEMENTS ARE APPROXIMATE
Allied Forces shewn in Red
Germans in Blue

1000   0   1000   2000   3000   4000   5000
SCALE OF YARDS

TSD/HS/1057

once more turned away.[116] The British held on towards them for a few minutes until the rear destroyer disappeared into the smoke to the south-east.[117] This was the last seen of them; shortly afterwards they were ordered to attack the damaged *Edinburgh*, some 200 miles to the eastward and altered course accordingly. Commander Richmond of course could not know this and for the next three hours he kept his force cruising between the supposed direction of the enemy and the convoy, while the latter was breaking its way through the ice. By 2155, 1st, it was in open water and the destroyers resumed their screening stations.

The remainder of the passage was uneventful; PQ 15 was sighted making to the eastward at 1000, 2nd May and QP 11 duly arrived at Revkiavik at 0700, 7th.

25

In the meantime, while convoy QP 11 was being subjected to the attacks described in the last section, the damaged *Edinburgh* had been making the best of her way towards Murmansk. The first torpedo had hit her on the starboard side forward, causing considerable flooding; the second hit right aft and virtually blew her stern off. She had lost her rudder and the two inner shafts, but could steam at about 8 knots with the outer propellers (Plan 8).

The *Foresight* (Commander J. S. Salter SO), *Forester* and the two Russian destroyers arrived about an hour after she was hit. An attempt by the *Forester* to tow her failed; with no stern and seven feet down by the bow, she came rapidly into the wind as soon as she gathered headway and parted the tow. Further attempts to aid her were then delayed while the destroyers hunted a U-boat that was sighted on the surface four miles away.

During the night of 30th April/1st May some progress at about three knots was made, by the *Edinburgh* taking the *Foresight* in tow and using her to control the steering. At 0600, 1st, however, the two Russian destroyers reported that they must return to harbour for fuel and parted company. U-boats were known to be about and in these circumstances Admiral Bonham-Carter deemed it essential that both the remaining destroyers should be used for screening. So the *Foresight* was cast off and the *Edinburgh* struggled on, steering as best she could with her engines. Left to her own devices, a persistent swing to port could only be countered by gathering sternway every few minutes and the speed of advance fell to two knots.[118] Thus she proceeded for about 23 hours. That no U-boat succeeded in attacking during this anxious period is the measure of the alertness of the *Forester* and *Foresight*.

That afternoon the *Bulldog's* report of the German destroyer attacks came in; the probability of their shifting their attentions to the *Edinburgh* was at once realised and Admiral Bonham-Carter gave the following instructions:–

'In event of attack by German destroyers, *Foresight* and *Forester* are to act independently, taking every opportunity to defeat the enemy without taking undue risks to themselves in defending *Edinburgh*. *Edinburgh* is to proceed wherever the wind permits, probably straight into the wind. If minesweepers are present they will also be told to act independently retiring under smoke screen as necessary.[119] *Edinburgh* has no RDF or Director working.'

At 1800, 1st May, the Russian escort vessel *Rubin* joined and six hours later the minesweepers *Hussar, Harrier, Gossamer* and *Niger* arrived with a Russian tug. Disappointingly, she was not powerful enough to tow. Eventually, at 0530, 2nd May, the *Edinburgh* was again making about three knots under her own power and holding a fairly steady course (150°) steered by the tug line on the starboard bow and the *Gossamer* acting as a drogue on the port quarter. The remaining two minesweepers,[120] the *Rubin* and the two destroyers settled down to an endless chain patrol around them.

The wind was N.N.E., force three; as usual there were frequent snow squalls and the visibility varied from ten to two miles. Despite the fact that U-boats were known to be taking up positions to intercept and the probability of destroyer attack, there seemed to be a chance of making port. But it was not to be.

At 0627 gunfire from the *Hussar*, then on the starboard quarter, heralded the approach of an enemy, which proved to be the three destroyers. The *Hussar* was almost immediately straddled and fell back on the *Edinburgh*.

There ensued a series of individual actions, ships engaging whenever visibility permitted. The Germans kept about seven miles to the N.N.E. of the *Edinburgh*, making full use of snow squalls and smoke to get within torpedo range and it was seldom that more than one of them was in sight at the same time.

At the first alarm the *Edinburgh* cast off the tows and went on to her maximum speed–about eight knots. Unable to steer, she circled round to port, sometimes rapidly, sometimes on a wider curve, firing with 'B' turret whenever it could be directed from the bridge on to a fleeting target. The minesweepers[121] remained near her, engaging the enemy with their one gun salvoes whenever they appeared and looking out for U-boats. The *Foresight* (Commander Salter) at once steered for the gunflashes (030°) at 24 knots, while the *Forester* (Lieut. Commander G. P. Huddart), which was two or three miles to the westward, went on to 30 knots and steered to join her.

First blood on either side was drawn by the *Edinburgh*, which opened fire on the *Hermann Schoemann* at about 0636. Her first salvo fell within 100 yards; the German increased speed to 31 knots, made smoke and turned away, but the second salvo scored a hit, which put both engines out of action and destroyed all control instruments. This fortunate hit had a marked effect on the events of the day; she came to a stop and remained virtually out of action, while from then onwards the efforts of her consorts were largely directed towards succouring and screening her.[122]

Meanwhile the *Foresight* had sighted an enemy destroyer – *Z24* – 10,000 yards off, steering straight towards her, just as the *Edinburgh* opened fire at 0636; four minutes later (0640) the range was down to 8,000 yards and Commander Salter opened fire on *Z24*, altering course to the eastward to open 'A' arcs. From '0640 to 0648 all three enemy destroyers were playing hide and seek in the snow and their own smoke screens: targets were engaged as and when they came into vision,'[123] the ranges varying between 6,000 and 8,000 yards.

The *Forester* was also fighting under much the same conditions, but she stood on to the northward when the *Foresight* turned to open her 'A' arcs. At 0650 she fired torpedoes; almost at the same moment she received three hits. One in No. 1 boiler room brought her to a standstill, one put 'B' gun out of action and killed the Commanding Officer and one on 'X' gun shattered its breech mechanism. Three minutes later (0653) torpedoes were seen passing under the ship in the direction of the *Edinburgh*.[124] She was then about five miles north-west of the *Foresight*, which had just (0648) altered away from the enemy to the westward, in order to close the *Edinburgh*; seeing the *Forester* stopped and on fire, Commander Salter steered to her assistance. The *Forester* with her sole remaining gun was engaging the stationary *Hermann Schoemann*, some three miles to the northward and shifting to the other destroyers whenever they appeared. The *Foresight* had closed to within half a mile by 0700 and then turned to an easterly course, so as not to foul the *Forester*'s range and engaged one of the destroyers which had been firing on her.

Just at this time (0702) the *Edinburgh* was torpedoed. The torpedoes were seen breaking surface as they approached; there was nothing she could do to avoid them but it looked as if her eccentric gyrations would take her clear. Her luck was out, however; one torpedo running deep struck her port side amidships at a point practically opposite one of the former hits. She immediately listed to port and gradually came to a standstill. The ship was 'open from side to side.' It was clear that she might break in two and sink at any moment and Admiral Bonham-Carter ordered the *Gossamer* alongside to take off the wounded and passengers. The *Edinburgh* nevertheless continued to engage the enemy whenever they appeared – her shooting was described by the *Z24* as 'extraordinarily good,' and twice deterred her from going to the *Hermann Schoemann*'s assistance – but the list was increasing and when it reached 17° her guns would no longer bear. The Admiral then directed Captain Faulkner to abandon ship.

Meanwhile the *Foresight* after engaging her opponent for five minutes, again turned to the westward and seeing the *Forester* being heavily straddled, passed between her and the enemy, drawing their fire.[125] At 0714 Commander Salter altered course to close the range and a few minutes later fired a salvo of torpedoes (which missed) at the *Hermann Schoemann*. Just afterwards he came under a heavy concentration of fire from *Z24* and *Z25* at 4,000 yards range, he increased to full speed and tried to get away under smoke, but received, four hits one of them in No. 3 boiler, which brought the ship to a standstill at 0724 in a welter of steam and smoke with only one gun still in action.

The *Edinburgh*, *Foresight* and *Forester* were thus all stopped with their gun power much reduced; there seemed nothing to prevent the two comparatively undamaged German destroyers from sinking each of them separately and afterwards dealing with the slow, lightly armed minesweepers at their leisure. But though they made repeated attacks on the destroyers with heavy but fortunately inaccurate fire, they did not press home their advantage. Their main concern was with the *Hermann Schoemann*; already three attempts by the *Z24* to go alongside and take off her ship's company had been foiled by British gunfire and they let the opportunity pass.

Ten minutes after the *Foresight* stopped, the *Forester* managed to get under way (0735); at the same time the two German destroyers again opened fire on her, but they soon disappeared into smoke, emerging a few minutes later to concentrate on the *Foresight*. This gave the *Forester* an opportunity to repay the debt she owed for the respite the *Foresight* had afforded her earlier in the day and, zigzagging between her and the enemy, she covered her with a very efficient smoke screen. This was the close of the action. Shortly afterwards the *Z24* got alongside the *Hermann Schoemann* and took off about 200 survivors;[126] the latter – already in a sinking condition – was then scuttled and the *Z24* and *Z25* (which had received a hit in her wireless room) withdrew at high speed to the north-westward and were lost to view by the British at about 0820.

Meanwhile the *Foresight* had effected temporary repairs and by 0815 was proceeding slowly on the port engine. The *Edinburgh* had been abandoned by 0800, the *Gossamer* taking about 440 men and the *Harrier*, in which Rear-Admiral Bonham-Carter hoisted his flag, about 350,[127] while the *Hussar* screened them with smoke; but she was settling very slowly and the enemy might reappear at any moment. Attempts by gunfire and depth charges from the *Harrier* to hasten her end had little effect and the *Foresight* was ordered to sink her with her one remaining torpedo. This she did and all ships then shaped course for Kola Inlet, where they arrived without further incident next day (3rd May).

By sinking the *Edinburgh*, the enemy achieved his object. But it may be claimed that the offensive spirit and skilful tactics of the British gained a moral victory and incidentally saved the remainder of the force from disaster. To Admiral Bonham-Carter it seemed inexplicable that the enemy did not press home their attacks; in his opinion, they had a good chance of sinking all the British ships had they shown any real determination, unless indeed they had themselves suffered very serious damage of which he was not aware. A suggestion of the Commanding Officer of the *Harrier* that they might have mistaken the minesweepers for destroyers at the range and visibility prevailing was not far off the mark, their identification according to the log of the *Z24* being five destroyers – of the *Tribal, Jervis* and *F* or *H* classes and one American. It was a matter for regret that the two heavily armed Russian destroyers,[128] which had been ordered to return to the *Edinburgh* after fuelling, did not arrive in time to take part in the action.

Considering the odds against the *Foresight* and *Forester*, their casualties were not excessive, the former losing Lieutenant R. A. Fawdrey

(1st Lieutenant) and seven ratings killed or died of wounds and 11 ratings wounded, the *Forester* her Commanding Officer, Lieutenant-Commander Huddart and 12 ratings killed and nine ratings wounded. In addition one officer and two ratings belonging to the *Lancaster Castle*, who were embarked in the *Foresight* were wounded and her master (Captain Sloan) was killed.

26

While the attacks on Convoy QP 11 and the *Edinburgh* were taking place in the Barents Sea, Convoy PQ 15 from the westward was entering on the critical stages of its passage.

This convoy, consisting of 25 ships including for the first time a CAM ship,[129] the *Empire Morn*, had left Reykjavik on 26th April (two days before the departure of QP 11) escorted by the *Bramble* (Captain J. H. F. Crombie SO) and three other minesweepers and four A/S trawlers.[130] The remainder of the close escort, comprising the destroyers *Somali, Matchless, Venomous, St. Albans, Boadicea, Badsworth*, the submarine *Sturgeon* and the A.A. ship *Ulster Queen* together with the oiler *Gray Ranger* and *Ledbury* (Force Q) joined from Seidijfjord on the 28th and the cruisers *Nigeria*, wearing the flag of Rear-Admiral Burrough and the *London* on the 30th.

Heavy cover for both PQ 15 and QP 11 was provided by the *King George V*, wearing the flag of the Commander-in-Chief, the US battleship *Washington* (flag, Rear-Admiral Giffen), the *Victorious, Kenya*, US cruisers *Wichita* and *Tuscaloosa* and ten destroyers, of which four were American. This force left Scapa between 27th and 28th April and cruised to the southward of the convoy routes. An unfortunate accident occurred on 1st May, when in very short visibility the *Punjabi* came into collision with the *King George V* and was cut in half. Her depth charges exploded and the stern sank rapidly; the foremost part remained afloat some 40 minutes, enabling five officers and 201 ratings to be taken off. The *King George V*, damaged both by the collision and the explosion of the depth charges, left the covering force for Scapa next day on the arrival of the *Duke of York* (flag, V.A.2) from Hvalfjord to take her place.[131]

Convoy PQ 15 was located some 250 miles to the south-westward of Bear Island by an enemy aircraft shortly before midnight, 30th April; but short visibility and frequent snow squalls gave considerable cover and it was not until 2200, 1st May (just as Convoy QP 11, some 200 miles to the eastward, was resuming its interrupted passage after the destroyer attacks) that it was molested. Then six Ju.88s carried out an ineffective bombing attack, losing one of their number in doing so.[132]

At midnight 1st/2nd May, the *London* was detached to cruise to the westward of Bear Island. The *Sturgeon* and Force Q had already left the convoy in the course of the day; and at 1000, 2nd, the *Nigeria* parted company in 73' 48' N., 13° 40' E., subsequently joining the *London* and with her covering the later stages of QP 11's passage.[133]

The departure of the *Nigeria* left Captain Crombie, HMS *Bramble*, the Senior Officer of the escort. Shortly afterwards QP 11 was sighted; the *Somali* was detached to communicate and returned with a somewhat gloomy forecast of what probably lay ahead – awkward position of ice, attack by enemy destroyers and torpedo bombers and concentration of U-boats.

Half an hour later enemy shadowing aircraft made contact and from then onwards until longitude 36° E. was reached, PQ 15 was continuously under observation by one or more aircraft or submarines.[134]

That evening, 2nd May, an unfortunate incident occurred. At 2009, in 73° 1' N., 17° 32' E., the *St. Albans* and *Seagull* obtained a contact and carried out an attack on a submarine, which forced her to the surface. She proved to be the Polish submarine *P551* and was so badly damaged that she had to be sunk by gunfire after survivors had been taken off. As she was nearly 100 miles out of her position and in waters where U-boats were expected to be operating, no blame could possibly be attached to the *St. Albans* and *Seagull*.

Five hours later (0127, 3rd May), being then in 73° N., 19° 40' E., the convoy was attacked by torpedo aircraft. The visibility was four miles, frequently closing down to less and the half light of the Arctic night, combined with haze, made the aircraft very difficult to see; nor were they detected by radar. Six aircraft came in low on the starboard bow; two were shot down and one crashed later, but they sank three ships – the *Botavon* (Commodore), *Jutland* and *Cape Corso*. Commodore Anchor and 137 survivors were picked up by escorting craft.

From about noon, 2nd May, to the afternoon of the 4th the convoy was constantly shadowed by U-boats, but they did not succeed in attacking. Escort vessels made several promising attacks on submarine contacts, but no U-boat was sunk.

A bombing attack took place at 2230, 3rd May, the convoy then being in 73° N., 31° 15'E. Slight damage from a near miss was suffered by the trawler *Cape Palliser*; one Ju.88 was shot down. This was the last air attack PQ 15 had to face; visibility deteriorated in the evening of the 4th and a southeasterly gale sprang up bringing heavy snow. This provided excellent cover for the remainder of the passage and the convoy arrived at Kola at 2100, 5th May.

27

Before the next pair of convoys sailed, the last act in the unfortunate story of the *Trinidad* was played out.

Having effected temporary repairs[135] at Murmansk she undocked on 2nd May, the intention being for her to proceed to Hvalfjord and thence to the United States for permanent repairs. On 5th May Rear-Admiral Bonham-Carter hoisted his flag in her, intending to sail on the 9th; but there were indications of a northward movement by the German heavy ships at Trondheim and her departure was postponed until the situation was cleared up by air reconnaissance.[136]

A force of four cruisers – the *Nigeria, Kent, Norfolk* and *Liverpool* – and four destroyers[137] under Rear-Admiral Burrough was disposed west of Bear Island to cover her passage; the battlefleet, consisting of the *Duke of York* (flag Commander-in-Chief), *Victorious, London*, USS *Washington, Tuscaloosa* and 11 destroyers provided distant cover further to the south-westward.

The *Trinidad*, escorted by the *Somali* (Captain J. W. Eaton, Captain (D) 6). *Matchless, Foresight* and *Forester*, left Murmansk in the evening of 13th May. She was reported by enemy aircraft at 0730 the following morning; low cloud, short visibility and snow showers afforded cover during the forenoon, but the weather cleared later. Air escort which had been promised by the Russians[138] for the first 200 miles failed to materialise and German shadowing aircraft made contact at Intervals throughout the day. There were also several U-boat alarms and ice restricted movement to the northward. By 1852, 14th, there were four shadowing aircraft circling the ships and from then onwards homing signals were almost continuous.

Air attacks developed shortly before 2200 that evening, when Ju.88s started dive bombing the *Trinidad* and destroyers. There was a light westerly wind, the sea was calm and visibility was variable; the sky was 9/10 covered with low strato cumulus clouds. After about 25 bombing attacks, in which no hits were obtained though all ships experienced near misses, about ten torpedo bombers came in at 2237. Eight minutes later (2245) a lone Ju.88 dived out of the clouds close on the starboard quarter of the *Trinidad* and released its bombs from a height of about 400 feet. One bomb hit the starboard side of the bridge structure and burst on the lower deck, just before the part of the ship damaged on 29th March, starting a fire which spread rapidly between decks and over the bridge; a second bomb – either a hit or a very near miss – flooded 'B' magazine and adjacent compartments and blew in a temporary patch abreast the marine's mess deck.[139] The ship listed 14° to starboard, but was still able to steam at about 20 knots; torpedoes then just arriving from the torpedo bombers were avoided, as were other torpedoes a quarter of an hour later, but at 2315 the fire and smoke compelled Captain Saunders to stop the ship in order to reduce the draught which was fanning the flames. By midnight it had to be recognised that the fire was out of control and in view of the distance from the nearest port, the presence of U-boats and the certainty of further air attacks, the decision was taken to abandon ship. The wounded and passengers had already been taken off by the *Forester* and the remainder were then embarked in the other three destroyers.[140] Admiral Bonham-Carter, who transferred to the *Somali*, then found himself for the second time in a fortnight under the necessity of giving the sad order to sink one of HM ships. This was done by three torpedoes from the *Matchless* and at 0120 15th May the *Trinidad* sank in 73° 35' N., 22° 53' E.

The destroyers then joined Rear-Admiral Burrough's force and steered for Iceland. They were shadowed by enemy aircraft until 2000, 15th May, when about 25 Ju.88s attacked with bombs; no hits were scored by either side. This attack took place over 350 miles from the nearest airfield, which meant that in future the convoys must expect to be attacked from the air during five days of their passage.

Rear-Admiral Bonham-Carter's experiences in the *Edinburgh* and *Trinidad* left no doubt in his mind as to the hazards and dangers to which the convoys to North Russia were exposed. 'I am still convinced,' he wrote, shortly after the loss of the *Trinidad*:–

'that until the aerodromes in North Norway arc neutralised and there are some hours of darkness that the continuation of these convoys should be stopped. If they must continue for political reasons, very serious and heavy losses must be expected. The force of the German attacks will increase, not diminish. We in the Navy are paid to do this sort of job, but it is beginning to ask too much of the men of the Merchant Navy. We may be able to avoid bombs and torpedoes with our speed, a six or eight knot ship has not this advantage.'

These views were endorsed by the Commander-in-Chief, Home Fleet, who had repeatedly expressed his anxiety and more than once suggested that the convoys should at least be reduced in size. The compelling pressures that rendered their maintenance – and increase in size – a necessity at this time have since been revealed by Mr. Winston Churchill;[141] and so it came about that PQ 16, the next to leave Iceland, was larger than any heretofore, though it was the most unfavourable period of the whole year.

28

With all the German destroyers in Northern Norway either sunk or damaged, the threat of destroyer attack on the convoys had temporarily disappeared and it was no longer necessary to risk cruisers to guard against it. How serious that risk was had just been underlined by the loss of the *Edinburgh* and *Trinidad*. The dispositions for the passages of PQ 16 and QP 12 were therefore changed. Four cruisers – the *Nigeria* (flag, Rear-Admiral Burrough), *Kent*, *Norfolk* and *Liverpool*, with the destroyers *Onslow*, *Oribi* and *Marne* – provided close cover west of Bear Island against the pocket battleships,[142] while the battlefleet[143] cruised north-east of Iceland ready to deal with the *Tirpitz*, should she come out in support.

Two submarines, the *Trident* and *Seawolf* accompanied PQ 16 and the submarine cover off the coast of Norway remained as before, five British and three Russians being employed.

All the merchant ships in PQ 16 carried balloons and some degree of anti-submarine protection as far as longitude 10° E. was given by four flying boats from Iceland.

As regards the westbound convoy, the Senior British Naval Officer, North Russia, was authorised to adjust the sailing of QP 12 up to 24 hours either way, in order to take advantage of weather unsuitable for enemy air reconnaissance.

The Russians promised to assist the passage of these two convoys with a large scale air offensive by 200 Army bombers on the airfields in Northern Norway, but as things turned out this offensive was limited to one attack by 20 aircraft after the main series of German air attacks on the convoy had been completed.[144]

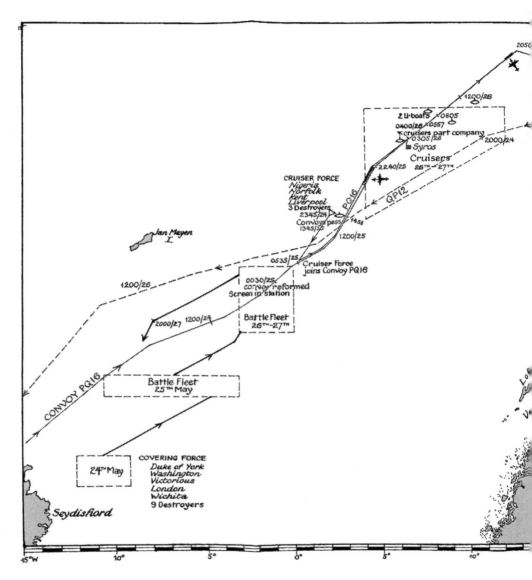

29

Convoy PQ 16 (Plan 9), consisting of 35 ships under Commodore Gale in the *Ocean Voice*, sailed from Hvalfjord on 21st May, escorted by the *Hazard* (SO) and four trawlers.[145] Two days later it was joined by the A.A. ship *Alynbank*, the submarines *Trident* and *Seawolf*, four corvettes[146] and Force 'Q' (the oiler *Black Ranger* with the *Ledbury*), all from Seidisfjord.

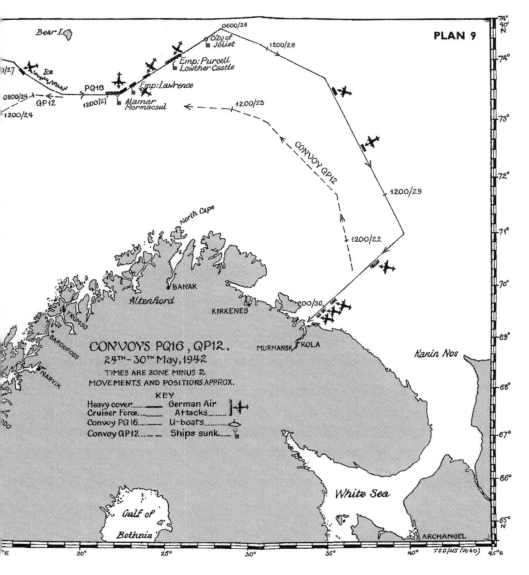

CONVOYS PQ16, QP12.
24TH – 30TH May, 1942
TIMES ARE ZONE MINUS 2
MOVEMENTS AND POSITIONS APPROX.
KEY
Heavy cover........ German Air
Cruiser Force....... Attacks........
Convoy PQ 16........ U-boats.........
Convoy QP12....... Ships sunk.....

PLAN 9

Rear-Admiral Burrough flying his flag in the *Nigeria* sailed from Seidisfjord that day (23rd May) with the *Onslow, Oribi, Marne* and destroyer escort for PQ 16, being joined later by the *Norfolk, Kent* and *Liverpool* from Hvalfjord. At about 1900 the force was sighted and reported in 67° N., 11° 30' W. by an enemy aircraft. Dense fog was encountered quite suddenly at midnight 23rd/24th May and shortly afterwards the destroyer escort, consisting of the *Ashanti* (Commander R.

281

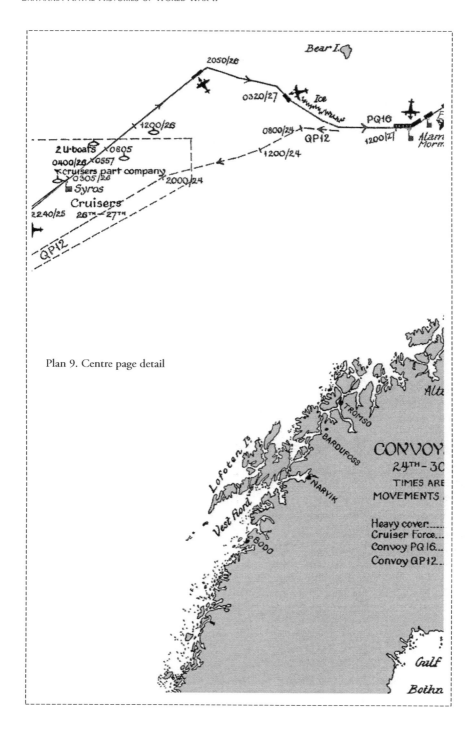

Plan 9. Centre page detail

G. Onslow, SO), *Martin, Achates, Volunteer* and ORP *Garland* was detached to join PQ 16, the remainder of the force standing on to the north-eastward for a position whence it could also cover QP 12 approaching from the eastward.

Commander Onslow's force had considerable difficulty in locating PQ 16, which had become divided into two sections in the fog and it was not until 0030, 25th, that the detached portion of the convoy rejoined and the whole convoy was proceeding with the screen in station.[147]

At 0535, 25th, Rear-Admiral Burrough's force which, after reaching a position approximately half way between Convoys PQ 16 and QP 12 (71° 30'N., 2° 30' E.) had turned to the westward, joined Convoy PQ 16. The cruisers formed in two divisions between the 4th and 5th and the 5th and 6th columns respectively and the destroyers reinforced the convoy screen.[148]

An hour later the first enemy shadower, a Focke Wulf, started circling the convoy and from this time until its arrival at its destination five days later, PQ 16 was continuously shadowed, except for a short period of thick weather on the 29th May. The day passed fairly quietly. All the destroyers had completed with fuel by noon and Force 'Q' was detached in the afternoon. Convoy QP 12 was sighted at 1400 and reported having sighted a U-boat at 0700 in 71° 40'N., 5° E. An hour later, the *Martin* sighted a U-boat seven miles on the starboard beam of PQ 16 and carried out an attack.

Between 2035 and 2230 25th May the convoy experienced the first air attack of a running fight which was to last until 1740, 30th – a period of five consecutive days. Seven torpedo bombers (He.111) and about six Ju.88s attacked from a clear sky. The Hurricane was launched from the *Empire Lawrence*; it set one He.111 on fire and severely damaged another. The pilot, Pilot Officer A. J. Hay, was wounded and picked up by the *Volunteer*. Two Ju.88s were shot down. The only damage to the convoy was a fractured steam pipe in the *Carlton* due to a near miss. She was subsequently detached to Iceland in tow of the *Northern Spray*.[149]

The day closed with an ineffectual attack by 12 Ju.88s between 2315 and 2330.

The 26th May started inauspiciously with the loss of a merchant ship – the *Syros* – which was torpedoed by a U-boat at 0305; 28 survivors out of a company of 37 were rescued by trawlers. Half an hour later the cruisers parted company. There was only one air attack on this day – an ineffective effort by eight torpedo bombers and three Ju.88s at 1800 –

but U-boats were sighted at frequent intervals and chased away or attacked with depth charges. The last encounter took place at 2300, after which no more were met with during the remainder of the passage, though DF signals received up to the 29th indicated their continued presence over the horizon.

After an air attack which did no harm at 0320, 27th May, course had to be altered to the south-eastward for a couple of hours to avoid heavy pack ice. At 1115 there started a series of attacks by a large number of Ju.88s which continued with little respite until 2130; six merchant ships were lost and three, in addition to the *Garland*, suffered damage. The *Alynbank* recorded attacks by 108 aircraft on this day,[150] and 120 sticks of bombs or torpedoes were heard to explode. The dive bombing attacks were pressed well home from broken cloud at 3,000 feet and the enemy was assisted by an intermittent filmy haze at about 1,500 feet, which made them very difficult to see.

The first casualty occurred at 1310, when SS *Alamar* was hit by two bombs and set on fire; five minutes later the *Mormacsul* was damaged by two near misses. Both ships sank at 1330, survivors being rescued by escort craft. Between 1405 and 1410, five direct hits sank the *Empire Lawrence* and another started a fire in the *Stary Bolshevik*, which was successfully fought by her crew for 36 hours; near misses damaged the *Empire Baffin*, ORP *Garland*[151] and the *City of Joliet*; the latter so badly that she had to be abandoned next morning. Great courage and determination was shown by the smaller escort vessels in rescuing survivors from the ships sunk, though subjected to deliberate heavy dive-bombing while doing so.[152]

Soon after these attacks, ice conditions allowed a more northerly course and at 1435[153] Commander Onslow ordered the convoy to steer 060°; there appeared to be more cloud in that direction and he also hoped that the increased distance from the enemy's airfields would diminish the weight of the air attacks next day. During the rest of the afternoon there was a lull in the action – except for one ineffective attack by eight Ju.88s – until 1945, when heavy dive bombing recommenced, accompanied by attacks by torpedo aircraft. The *Empire Purcell* was hit by bombs and later blew up, the *Lowther Castle* was torpedoed and sunk and the Commodore's ship, the *Ocean Voice*, received a direct hit which set her on fire and tore away 20 feet of her side plating abreast No. 1 hold within two feet of the water line. Fortunately the sea remained calm.

'I had little hopes of her survival,' wrote Commander Onslow subsequently, 'but this gallant ship maintained her station, fought her fire and with God's help arrived at her destination.'[154]

There were no further attacks after 2130 that day; but two Blohm and Voss floatplanes could be seen ominously circling the horizon. The situation appeared far from rosy. Five ships had been lost, the *City of Joliet* was settling by the bows and the *Ocean Voice* appeared unlikely to remain afloat much longer. The *Garland* was so seriously damaged that she was detached later in the evening to make her own way to Murmansk at high speed. 'With another three days to go and 20 per cent of the convoy already lost,' to quote Commander Onslow:–

'I felt far from optimistic. The question of ammunition began to worry me badly. I ordered all ships to exercise strict economy and restricted controlled fire in the *Ashanti* to one mounting at a time. We were all inspired however by the parade ground rigidity of the convoy's station keeping, including *Ocean Voice* and *Stary Bolshevik* who were both billowing smoke from their foreholds ...'[155]

But the worst was over. Apart from the *City of Joliet* which succumbed to her injuries and sank early on 28th May, there were no further losses. That forenoon three Russian destroyers, the *Grozni* (SO), *Sokrushitelni* and *Kuibishev* joined the escort – a very welcome addition to its A.A. fire power. Only one ineffective air attack carried out by four Ju.88s at 2130 occurred that day.

Early on 29th May, six torpedo bombers and two Ju.88s attacked, again without success. That evening six minesweepers[156] under Captain Crombie (Capt. MS1) joined in 70° 58' N., 39° 27' E.; under their escort, with the *Alynbank* and *Martin*, six of the merchant ships were detached to Archangel. At 2330, while the two sections were still in sight of each other, the Murmansk section was attacked by 18 and the Archangel section by 15 Ju.88s; no damage was suffered by the ships.

The departure of the *Alynbank* with the Archangel section added to the anxieties of Commander Onslow, as it left him without any long range radar set with his convoy. U-boats were known to be just over the horizon waiting for a favourable opportunity to attack, so he could not keep the screen constantly in their anti-aircraft stations, as he wished to do. However, luck was with him; no submarine attacks took place and three bombing attacks on 30th May (at 0800, 1020 and 1245), in which two Ju.88s were destroyed, failed to do any damage. From then onwards, Russian Hurricanes gave air cover and at 1600 that afternoon Convoy PQ 16 passed Toros Island, 'reduced in numbers, battered and tired, but still keeping perfect station.'[157]

While PQ 16 was undergoing this protracted ordeal, Convoy QP 12 (Plan 9) was having a singularly uneventful passage. This convoy, consisting of 15 ships,[158] which included the CAM ship *Empire Morn*, sailed from Kola Inlet on 21st May, escorted by the destroyers *Inglefield* (Captain P. Todd SO), *Escapade, Venomous, St. Albans, Boadicea* and *Badsworth*, the A.A. ship *Ulster Queen* and four trawlers. The escort was reinforced by four minesweepers until the evening of the 22nd and by two Russian destroyers until the meridian 30° E. was reached at 1000, 23rd. Though the visibility was generally good during the 22nd and 23rd, the convoy was not sighted until homing signals; the pilot, Pilot Officer J. B. Kendell, RAF, unfortunately lost his life through his parachute failing to open when he baled out. Enemy aircraft continued shadowing until the afternoon; but no air attacks developed. Nor were there any submarine attacks, though U-boats were known to be in the vicinity. Thick weather aided the convoy in avoiding their attentions and QP 12 duly arrived at Reykjavik intact[159] and undamaged early on 29th May.

30

As the result of his experiences with PQ 16, Commander Onslow made several suggestions most of which were adopted for later convoys. As a counter to air attack he recommended that either an auxiliary carrier or a large number of C.A.M. ships should be included in each convoy and stressed the importance of using fighters against shadowers; additional A.A. ships to be provided (the fire of the *Alynbank* was the greatest deterrent against dive attacks); as many of the escorting destroyers as possible to have good A.A. armament; and as many long range radar sets as possible to be included in the convoy. In the case of PQ 16, after the *Empire Lawrence* was sunk, the *Alynbank* was the only ship with such a set.

He considered that a high powered salvage tug with good fire fighting appliances might have saved the *Empire Purcell* and suggested that one should accompany future convoys; also special rescue ships, as the trawlers and corvettes became badly overcrowded with survivors.

He also recommended that reserves of ammunition for both escorts and merchant ships should be carried in the convoys and built up at Kola Inlet.

The submarines detailed for escort duty should be of a class with sufficient speed to enable them to regain station quickly after diving for air attack.

The Commander-in-Chief, Home Fleet, was agreeably surprised that in the face of such a scale of attack four-fifths of the ships of this large convoy reached their destination. 'This success was beyond expectation' he wrote:–

> 'it was due to the gallantry, efficiency and tireless zeal of the officers and men of the escorts and to the remarkable courage and determination of those of the merchant ships. No praise can be too high for either.'

Severe though the ordeal of PQ 16 had been, the enemy had not had it a their own way. Commander Onslow would have been gratified could he have read Admiral Dönitz's, Commander-in-Chief, U-boats, war diary on the operation:–

> 'My opinion as to the small chances of success for U-boats against convoys during the northern summer ... has been confirmed by experience with PQ 16. Owing to the difficult conditions for attack (constant light, very variable weather and visibility, abnormally strong convoy escort, clever handling of the convoy, appearance of Russian aircraft forcing the U-boats to dive on sighting our own aircraft as well) the result, in spite of shadowing and a determined set-to by the boats, has been one steamer sunk and four probable hits. This must be accounted a failure when compared with the results of the anti-submarine activity for the boats operating ... *U-436, U-703* have depth charge damage, unfit to dive to greater depths. Three more boats have slight depth charge damage, the effects of which ... will probably mean some considerable time in the dockyard.
>   This success of the anti-submarine forces is the more serious in the light of the bad dockyard situation in Norway and at home and it will probably mean that ordinarily far more than 50 per cent of all the boats detached to the Northern area will be unfit for service, if further operation against PQ convoys is undertaken ...'

After exploring various aspects of the problem Admiral Dönitz concluded, 'The German Air Force would seem to be a better means of attacking convoy's in the north in the summer,' and suggested 'that these facts be taken into account rather more than they have been hitherto when U-boat operations in the north are planned.'[160]

The German Air Force greatly over-estimated the effects of their attacks on PQ 16 and claimed to have destroyed the whole convoy. Something seems to have gone badly wrong with their reconnaissance, for they were convinced that the convoy had dispersed as the result of the first attack[161] in the evening of 25th May. The lesson they drew from this attack was that the A.A. defence could be dissipated and confused by high level dive bombing closely integrated with the launching of torpedoes from a height of about 300 feet. The method adopted for the torpedo attack, which was known as the 'Golden Comb,' was for the aircraft to approach in a wide line abreast and to drop their torpedoes simultaneously. It was also decided to attack at twilight with the ships silhouetted against the lighter sky. By June, 42 torpedo aircraft had arrived in Northern Norway and these tactics were assiduously practised.[162]

CHAPTER IV

Convoys PQ 17, QP 13: June–July 1942
(All times are Zone minus 2.)

31

Nearly a month elapsed between the arrivals of convoys PQ 16 and QP 12 at the end of May and the sailing of the next pair of convoys. This was owing to the necessity of calling on the Home Fleet to contribute forces to an operation for the supply of Malta,[163] which left insufficient destroyers for running the convoys to Novell Russia. When these were resumed, the story of Convoys PQ 17 and QP 13 was one of unrelieved gloom. PQ 17's losses amounted to a major disaster. Out of the 33 merchant ships that cleared Iceland only 11 completed their voyage; 66 per cent succumbed to the German Air Force and submarines. QP 13 was not molested by the enemy, but, as though some malign fate was brooding over these operations, lost five ships in an Allied minefield off Iceland.

The disaster to PQ 17 was the subject of considerable criticism on both sides of the Atlantic, as well as by the Russians. It will therefore be convenient to take stock of the situation as it appeared to those responsible for the sailing and protection of the convoys at this date.

At the Admiralty, the problem had been continually under review. The risks were by no means underestimated; but however great, political considerations compelled their acceptance. Nor, for similar reasons, could the palliatives suggested by Sir John Tovey, viz., temporary suspension or smaller convoys, be agreed to; American munitions for Russia were piling up and Russia was clamouring for the munitions.

Hitherto, it could be claimed, the defence had on the whole kept pace with the increasing severity of the attack. There had been serious losses, but they had been confined to acceptable limits. Nevertheless, those best qualified by personal experience to judge viewed the prospect of continuing the traffic during the summer months with grave misgiving. It was difficult to see how the problem could be solved if the enemy chose to supplement his air and U-boat offensive by using his heavy ships for surface attack in the Barents Sea.

This was precisely what the German Naval Staff had decided to do. By the beginning of June the fuel situation (hitherto a limiting factor) had sufficiently improved to permit operating the heavy ships, a course repeatedly recommended by the Flag Officer, Northern Waters and concurred in by Admiral Schniewind, the Commander-in-Chief afloat, who, while unwilling to become involved with Allied heavy ships, was not happy about the effect on morale of his forces lying idly in the fjords, while the U-boats and aircraft were committed to the attack. Fortunately, the approval of Hitler himself was necessary for the employment of the heavy ships; his reluctance to expose them to risk and the restrictions imposed by him were sufficient seriously to hamper their operations.[164]

This, of course, was unknown to the British, though, as already mentioned, it was suspected – at any rate so far as the *Tirpitz* was concerned – by the Commander-in-Chief, Home Fleet.[165] But there were indications in June that the enemy intended at last to bring out his main units to attack the next eastbound convoy to the eastward of Bear Island and this threat formed the main preoccupation of the Admiralty at the end of that month.

32

The Germans, it will be remembered, had four heavy ships in Norway, the *Tirpitz* and *Hipper* at Trondheim and the *Scheer* and *Lützow* at Narvik; the Trondheim group included four and the Narvik group six destroyers.

The strategic situation, wrote Admiral Tovey in his despatch:–

'was wholly favourable to the enemy. His heavy ships would be operating close to their own coast, with the support of powerful shore-based air reconnaissance and striking forces and protected, if he so desired, by a screen of U-boats in the channels between Spitzbergen and Norway. Our covering forces, on the other hand, if they entered these waters, would be without shore-based air support, one thousand miles from their base, with their destroyers too short of fuel to escort a damaged ship to harbour.'[166]

He went on to remark that apart from Allied submarine attacks off the enemy coast 'a more favourable disposition could be brought about only by inducing the enemy heavy ships to come further to the westward to deliver their attacks.'[167] Accordingly, he proposed that the eastbound convoy, on reaching longitude 10° E., should put back for 12 to 18 hours, unless it was known that the German ships were still in harbour or the weather prevented shadowing from the air. He hoped that 'this temporary turn back would either tempt the German heavy ships to pursue, or cause them to return to harbour, or compel them to cruise for an extended period among our submarines' – of which, including Russians, a dozen were stationed between Bear Island and the coast of Norway. The Admiralty did not agree to this, though their instructions[168] 'envisaged the possibility, under certain circumstances of the convoy being temporarily turned back by the Admiralty; but not of this turn being timed to achieve the object'[169] the Commander-in-Chief had in view. The Admiralty instructions also laid down that the safety of the convoy against surface attack to the westward of Bear Island must be met by our surface forces and to the eastward of that meridian must be met by submarines; and that the cruiser covering force was not intended to go east of Bear Island, unless the convoy was threatened by the presence of a surface force which the cruisers could fight,[170] or in any case to go beyond 25° E.

This plan did not altogether meet the Commander-in-Chief's views, which from the first appearance of the German heavy ships in Norway had differed in several respects from those of the Admiralty as to the tactical dispositions best calculated to achieve the object;[171] but he was seriously perturbed to learn in the course of a telephone conversation with the First Sea Lord that under certain circumstances the Admiralty contemplated ordering the convoy to scatter.[172] All the latest experience[173] had pointed to the vital necessity for ships to keep well closed up for mutual support against the heavy air attack that was certain, weather permitting, to take place and he strongly deprecated such an order being given, except as a last resort in the actual presence of attack by overwhelming surface forces.

In the event the sailing of the *Tirpitz* and other heavy ships resulted in disaster to PQ 17, though they themselves were never within 300 miles of the convoy.

The dispositions adopted were very similar to those for PQ 16 and QP 12. Four cruisers under Rear-Admiral L. H. K. Hamilton, the *London* (flag), *Norfolk*, *Tuscaloosa* and *Wichita*, with the destroyers *Somali*, *Wainwright* and *Rowan* were to provide close cover as far as Bear Island, while the Commander-in-Chief in the *Duke of York*, with the

Washington (flag, Rear-Admiral Giffen), *Victorious* (flag, Vice-Admiral Sir Bruce Fraser),[174] *Nigeria* (flag, Rear-Admiral Burrough), *Cumberland* and 14 destroyers provided distant cover to the northeast of Jan Mayen Island.

There was also a diversion in the shape of a pretended convoy, consisting of five ships of the 1st Minelaying Squadron and four colliers, escorted by the *Sirius, Curacoa* and some destroyers and trawlers, This force assembled at Scapa several days before the main operation was tor begin and sailed on 29th June (two days after PQ 17 left Iceland). Having passed the Shetlands west- about, the force steered eastward as far as 61° 30' N., 1° E., hoping to be seen and reported by enemy aircraft, after which it turned back for Scapa. The sailing of the Battle Fleet was arranged for the same day as this pretended convoy to give an impression of supporting it, while 'diversionary bombing' in Southern Norway was also arranged – all to suggest that a raiding force was bound there. As it happened, though the movement eastward was carried out twice – on 30th June and 1st July – the Germans did not observe it.

During June arrangements had been made to base a few Catalinas of Coastal Command in North Russia and between 1st and 3rd July five of these proceeded to Archangel, carrying out reconnaissance patrols on the way. They then maintained a series of cross-over patrols, designed to cover the waters between Altenfjord and the convoy as it drew to the eastward.

33

While the Admiralty and the Commander-in-Chief, Home Fleet, were concerting the measures described, the German naval authorities were maturing their plan. Hitler had been informed on 1st June of the proposal to use the surface ships against PQ 17; he was assured that the operation would only take place if it could be safely assumed that no superior enemy forces would be met with and that adequate air cover could be provided.[175] Eventually he approved, but with the proviso that before the ships sailed the Allied aircraft carriers' disposition must be ascertained so that they could be attacked by the Luftwaffe.

This proviso was tantamount to cancelling the operation, as it would have delayed the sailing of the ships too long. Grand Admiral Raeder therefore decided that the operation should be carried out in two phases: on the convoy being located, the ships should transfer to sortie ports in the extreme north, there to await the Führer's final sanction and orders to proceed.

On 14th June, Admiral Schniewind issued his orders for the operation, which was known as Rosselspring (Knight's move). On confirmation of PQ 17's approach, the Trondheim squadron was to move to Vestfjord and the Narvik squadron to Altenfjord. As soon as the convoy had passed 5° E., the two German squadrons were to proceed to a rendezvous 100 miles north of North Cape and thence to attack the convoy to the eastward of Bear Island between 20° E. and 30° E.

Great importance was attached to early reports of the convoy. For this reliance was placed on air reconnaissance and U-boats. Out of the ten operational U-boats available, three were sent to patrol the north-eastern sector of Denmark Strait as early as 5th June and by 18th June all had been disposed on the estimated convoy route.

34

Meanwhile, Convoy PQ 17 (Plan 10) had sailed from Reykjavik on 27th June. The route was longer than hitherto, the ice having receded sufficiently for it to run north of Bear Island, thus increasing the distance from the enemy air bases; moreover, all ships were bound for Archangel, Murmansk having been virtually destroyed by bombing.

The convoy consisted of 35 merchant ships under Commodore J. C. K. Dowding, escorted by the *Halcyon, Britomart, Salamander* and four A/S trawlers. One merchant ship grounded while leaving harbour and another was damaged by drift ice in Denmark Strait and had to put back. The oiler *Gray Ranger*, which was included in the convoy, was also damaged by ice.

The close escort joined from Seidisfjord on 30th June. It consisted of six destroyers, the *Keppel* (Commander J. E. Broome SO), *Leamington, Wilton, Ledbury, Fury, Offa*; four corvettes, the *Lotus, Poppy, Dianella*, FFS *La Malouine* and the submarines *P614* and *P615*. Two A.A. ships, the *Palomares* (Act. Captain J. H. Jauncey) and the *Pozarica* (Act. Captain E. D. W. Lawford) joined at the same time; there were also three rescue ships, the *Zaafaran, Rathlin* and *Zamalek* and Force '0', the oiler *Aldersdale* and the *Douglas*. The latter force after fuelling the escorts of PQ 17 was to transfer to QP 13 (which had left Russia the same day as PQ 17 left Iceland) and eventually proceed to a rendezvous to fuel the destroyers with the battlefleet. Owing to the ice damage sustained by the *Gray Ranger*, she exchanged duties with the *Aldersdale*, the latter accompanying PQ 17 throughout its voyage.

First contact with the enemy occurred on 1st July, when ships of the escort attacked U-boats sighted on the surface several miles from the

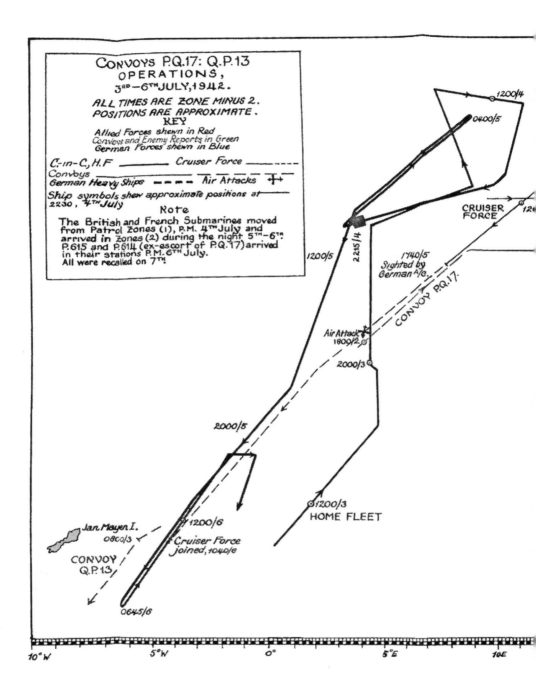

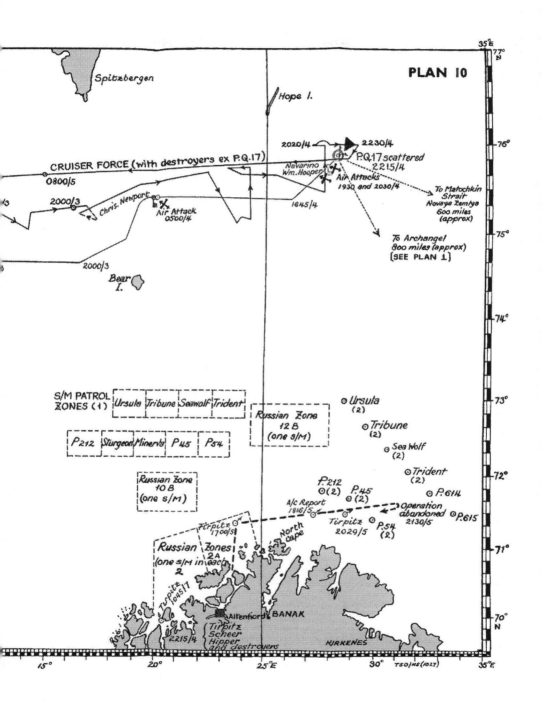

PLAN 10

Spitzbergen

Hope I.

2020/4   2230/4

CRUISER FORCE (with destroyers ex P.Q.17)   P.Q.17 scattered
                                              2215/4
0800/5   Navarino
                              Wm. Hooper
2000/3   Air Attacks
                                              1930 and 2030/4
        Chris. Newport   1645/4
                        X   To Matochkin
                        Air Attack   Strait
                        0500/4   Novaya Zemlya
                                                            600 miles
                                                            (approx)

                                              To Archangel
2000/3   800 miles (approx)
                                              [SEE PLAN 1]

        Bear
        I.

S/M PATROL
ZONES (1)   Ursula Tribune Seawolf Trident   ⊙ Ursula
                                                         (2)
                                      Russian Zone
                                         12 B   ⊙ Tribune
     P.212 Sturgeon Minerva P.45 P.54 (one s/m)   (2)

                                                       ⊙ Sea Wolf
                                                          (2)

     Russian Zone   ⊙ Trident
        10 B   (2)
     (one s/m)   P.212
                                     ⊙(2)   P.45   ⊙ P.614
                                            ⊙(2)
                          A/c Report   Operation
                          1816/5   abandoned ⊙ P.615
                                     Tirpitz ⊙   2130/5
                          Tirpitz ⊙ 2029/5 P.54
                          1700/5   ⊙(2)
                                    North
     Russian Zones 2A   Cape
     (one s/m in each)
            2

            Tirpitz ⊙   Altenfiord BANAK
            1045/5
                          Tirpitz
                          Scheer
                          Hipper
            2215/4   and destroyers   KIRKENES

TSO/MS(1027)

15°   20°   25°E   30°   35°E

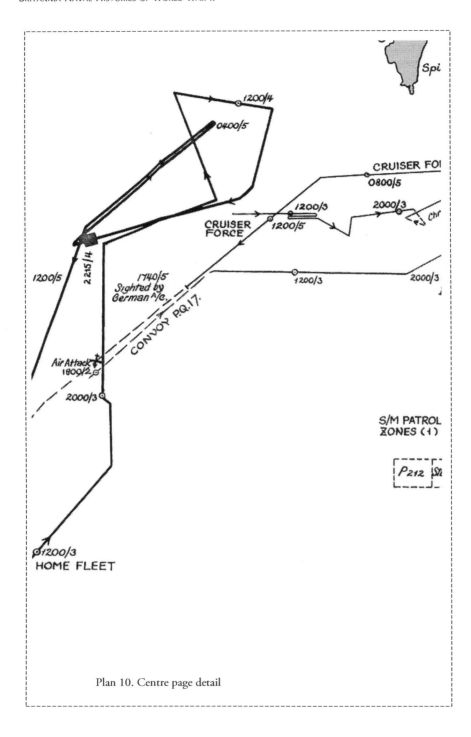

1200/4

0400/5

CRUISER FO

0800/5

CRUISER
FORCE

1200/3

1200/5

2000/3

Chr

1200/5

2 215/4

1740/5
Sighted by
German A/c.

CONVOY P.Q.17.

1200/3

2000/3

Air Attack
1800/2

2000/3

Spi

S/M PATROL
ZONES (1)

P212 S

1200/3
HOME FLEET

Plan 10. Centre page detail

convoy, both in the morning and the afternoon.[176] At noon, too, that day the first shadowing aircraft came on the scene. Others appeared next day; thenceforward, except during brief spells of fog, the convoy was shadowed from the air almost continuously.

During 1st July the weather was fine and calm and all the escorting destroyers were fuelled. Early on the 2nd, Force 'Q' was detached to rendezvous with Convoy QP 13; the two convoys passed each other that afternoon in about 73° N., 3° E. At about the same time convoy PQ 17 had to turn away to avoid torpedoes fired by a U-boat, which was attacked by the *Fury, Wilton, Lotus* and *Ayrshire.*

The same evening, Convoy PQ 17 suffered its first attack from the air. Nine torpedo aircraft approached at about 1800 in 73° 30' N., 4° E., with a surface visibility of ten miles; some, without attempting to penetrate the screen dropped torpedoes, which exploded wide of the convoy. One aircraft was shot down, probably by the US destroyer *Rowan,* then on her way from Rear-Admiral Hamilton's force to fuel from the *Aldersdale.*

By this time the cruiser force had overhauled the convoy and was standing to the northward, as the Admiral had decided to steer a course parallel to the convoy some 40 miles away, beyond the vision of shadowing aircraft, in order to 'keep the enemy guessing' concerning his whereabouts. He considered that the *Tirpitz* might attack the westbound convoy in order to draw the British battlefleet south, while the *Lützow* and *Scheer* made for Convoy PQ 17: 'the longer, therefore, I remained unseen the greater my chance of bringing the pocket battleships to action.'[177]

That night (2nd) the convoy ran into fog, which persisted until the forenoon of 3rd July, enabling the change of course for the long stretch past Bear Island into the Barents Sea to be made unseen at 0700. This apparently threw the shadowing aircraft off the scent for several hours. U-boats were still about, however and the escorting destroyers chased three away during the afternoon.

By this time Rear-Admiral Hamilton was beginning to feel that he was on the wrong side of the convoy, because the German ships might attack in thick weather and escape unscathed and that the time had come to disclose his position. Accordingly, he stood towards the convoy, sighting first the shadowing aircraft and then the convoy, some 20 miles off, at about 1630. Thinking his ships had been seen by the shadowers, though actually they had not, he then opened out to his former distance.

Soon afterwards a signal came from the Admiralty to say that air reconnaissance showed the edge of the icefield to be much further north than had been supposed. Rear-Admiral Hamilton, therefore, sent the London's aircraft to tell Commander Broome to pass 70 miles north of Bear Island, anticipating an Admiralty signal to similar effect and again with orders for the convoy to keep 400 miles from Banak air station. The convoy duly altered course to the northward, though not so much as Rear-Admiral Hamilton wished, for Commander Broome was impressed with the importance of making progress eastward, as the best means of getting the convoy through, which the Admiralty had pointed out in their instructions.

The cruisers again closed the convoy at 2215 that night, when it was some 30 miles north-west of Bear Island. This time the shadowers reported them, 'which pleased me considerably' said Rear-Admiral Hamilton, because he had just heard that German ships were on the move. The weather had prevented air reconnaissance of the Norwegian ports for several days; but in the afternoon of 3rd July the British aircraft were able to report that the *Tirpitz* and *Hipper* had left Trondheim, though the Narvik reconnaissance had once more failed. Admiral Tovey was already steering with the battlefleet for a cruising area 150 to 200 miles north-west of Bear Island, from which the *Victorious* could send aircraft to defend the convoy on the 4th, if German ships attacked it. Rear-Admiral Hamilton decided to continue with the convoy, using the discretion allowed to him by the instructions.

Actually the preliminary moves of the German plan had started the previous afternoon (2nd July), when the *Tirpitz* and *Hipper* left Trondheim for Gimsoystraumen in the Lofoten Islands near the entrance to Vestfjord and the *Scheer* and *Lützow*[178] left Narvik for Altenfjord. The *Lützow* did not get far, as she grounded in Tjelsund while leaving Ofotfjord and could take no further part. The remaining ships arrived at their destinations on the 3rd, but three of the destroyers[179] of the *Tirpitz* group grounded on arrival and returned to Trondheim a day or so later.

By the early morning of 4th July, Convoy PQ 17 was about 60 miles north of Bear Island. There it sustained its first loss. Just before 0500 a single aircraft torpedoed – 'through a hole in the fog' – the *Christopher Newport*, leading ship of one of the columns; she had to be sunk, while a rescue ship embarked her crew.

About midday, 4th, the Admiralty gave Rear-Admiral Hamilton leave to go east of longitude 25° E., should the situation require it, but subject to his discretion and to contrary orders from Admiral Tovey.[180] The latter, who had no information that seemed to justify the change of plan, instructed the cruisers to withdraw when the convoy was east of that meridian, or earlier at the Rear-Admiral's discretion, unless the Admiralty assured him that he could not meet the *Tirpitz*.[181] This signal crossed one sent by Rear-Admiral Hamilton at 1520 in which he stated that he was remaining in the vicinity of the convoy until the enemy surface situation clarified, but certainly not later than 1400, 5th July. At 1809 he replied that he intended withdrawing to the westward about 2200 that evening, on completion of fuelling destroyers.[182] Another signal from the Admiralty reached him about 1930, telling him that further information might be available shortly and to remain with the convoy pending further instructions.[183] At this time he was keeping some 10 to 20 miles ahead of the convoy, which he had closed early in the afternoon, zigzagging across its line of advance.[184]

Meanwhile the convoy, though constantly shadowed, had had a fairly quiet day. At 1645 course was altered from 090° to 045° on Rear-Admiral Hamilton's orders, in order to open the distance from Banak airfield to 400 miles. At 1930 there came a half-hearted attack by a few bombers, whose nearest bombs 'fell through the cloud ahead of the convoy' between the *Keppel* and USS *Wainwright* (come from the cruiser force to oil). It was meant to be a combined torpedo and bombing attack; half a dozen He.115 aircraft had been circling the horizon for some time and a torpedo exploded harmlessly outside the convoy. Commander Broome remarked that the *Wainwright*'s 'Fourth of July enthusiasm,' as she 'sped round the convoy worrying the circling aircraft' with long range fire was largely the cause of the enemy's failure.

A more serious torpedo attack was made an hour later, the anti-aircraft ship *Palomares* detecting 25 aircraft coming up from astern at 2020. They attacked from the starboard quarter, flying fast and low. Their leader showed great determination, hitting the *Navarino* in the middle of the convoy with two torpedoes, before he crashed in flames just ahead of the *Keppel*. The remainder were not so bold. 'Had they kept up with him, dividing and generally embarrassing the A.A. fire,'[185] wrote Commander Broome, 'many ships would have been sunk.' As it was, they only succeeded in torpedoing two other ships, the *William Hooper*, rear ship of the port wing column and the Russian tanker *Azerbaidjan*. The *Navarino* and *William Hooper* had to be sunk, but on closing the *Azerbaidjan* Commander Broome found her 'holed but happy, capable of 9 knots, with the female part of the watch busy hoisting boats;'[186] she eventually reached harbour. Commander Broome remarked on the good shooting of the escort and the convoy; four aircraft[187] were thought to have been brought down, including one by the *Offa* and one by the *Wainwright*. The three rescue ships with the convoy proved their value by picking up survivors quickly and efficiently.

Rear-Admiral Hamilton watched the air attacks, much surprised at the Germans for leaving his ships alone, though they were well in sight. He remarked on the vital importance of shooting down shadowing aircraft. There was little chance of doing so however, though Commander Broome considered afterwards that perhaps he ought to have used for this purpose his only Hurricane aircraft, in the CAM ship *Empire Tide*.

It was at this juncture that the threat of potential danger from the German heavy ships had its effect, though there was still no certain news of their whereabouts. It will therefore be convenient to consider the general situation at this time.

35

The situation at what proved to be the critical moment of PQ 17's passage was thus as follows. The convoy, then about 130 miles north-east of Bear Island, had just come through the heavy air attack remarkably well; the convoy discipline and shooting had been admirable and a substantial toll had been taken of the enemy. A feeling of elation prevailed; in the words of Commander Broome, 'My impression on seeing the resolution displayed by the convoy and its escort was that, provided the ammunition lasted, PQ 17 could get anywhere.'

Rear-Admiral Hamilton was still covering the convoy some ten miles to the north-eastward, with orders from the Admiralty to continue to do so until further orders; but for this, he had intended parting company in about an hour's time in accordance with the Commander-in-Chief's latest signal.

Some 350 miles to the westward the heavy covering force was cruising in the area south-west of Spitzbergen.

Turning to the Germans, the approval of the Führer for sailing the heavy ships to the attack had not yet been obtained; but the Naval Staff, fearing it might be delayed too long, had sanctioned the *Tirpitz* force joining the pocket battleships at Altenfjord and this had been done the previous night (3rd/4th July). Admiral Tovey's covering force had been sighted some 300 miles south-west of the convoy early on 3rd July; since

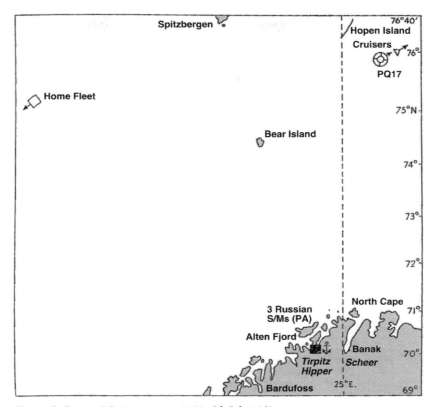

Figure 6. Convoy PQ 17: situation 2100, 4th July 1942.

then nothing had been seen of it and in view of Hitler's stringent orders that the carriers were to be located and put out of action before launching the operation, Grand Admiral Raeder decided that nothing further could be done for the present. There they remained until the afternoon of 5th July.

At the Admiralty the situation was being watched with increasing anxiety. It had been known since 3rd July that the heavy ships had left Trondheim and in the afternoon of the 4th that the northern squadron had left Narvik; but none of the ships had been located. That evening the First Sea Lord called a staff meeting to consider the situation. It was appreciated that an attack might develop any time after 0200 next morning, 5th. If the attack was pressed home in full strength while Rear-Admiral Hamilton's cruisers (two of which were American) were still present, it seemed it could only result in their destruction, in addition to that of the convoy. Against such an attack, the more widely the merchant ships were dispersed, the better seemed their chances of escape. Once the alarm had been given, the enemy raiders would not wish to spend more time than necessary in the neighbourhood,[188] rounding up odd groups and ships. But an 8-knot convoy takes some appreciable time to scatter effectively and the matter was further complicated by uncertainty as to the extent to which the ice would permit manoeuvring to the northward, i.e. away from the probable direction of the attack. On the other hand, the convoy was still some 800 miles from its destination. Air and U-boat attacks had already started and were certain to continue on a heavy scale. Once scattered, the isolated groups and units of the convoy would present comparatively easy targets and heavy casualties had to be expected.

Shortly after 2100, 4th July, the decision was taken: the cruisers must withdraw and the convoy must scatter immediately.

36

The Admiralty decision was conveyed to Rear-Admiral Hamilton in the following three signals:—

'Most immediate. Cruiser force withdraw to westward at high speed.' (2111 B/4)
'Immediate. Owing to threat from surface ships, convoy is to disperse and proceed to Russian ports.' (2123 B/4)
'Most immediate. My 2123/4. Convoy is to scatter.' (2136 B/4)

To the Rear-Admiral, these signals could only mean that the further information the Admiralty had been hoping for at 1858[189] had indeed come in and was of such a nature as to render imperative the drastic measures now ordered. Actually, the emphasis on the use of high speed by the cruisers was due to reports of a massing of enemy submarines between 11° and 20° E.; and the order to scatter was intended merely as a technical amendment of the term 'disperse' (used in the previous signal).[190] This could not be known to the recipients and the cumulative effect of the three signals – especially as the last had a more urgent priority marking than the middle one – was to imply that pressing danger was actually upon them. As Commander Broome put it, he expected to see the cruisers open fire and the enemy's masts appear on the horizon at any moment. In this belief he decided to take the destroyers of the escort to reinforce the cruiser force and ordered the two submarines to stay near the convoy when it scattered and to try to attack the enemy, while the rest of the escorting ships were to proceed independently to Archangel.

At 2215, 4th July, Commander Broome passed the signal to scatter (Plan 10) to Commodore Dowding, the convoy being then in 75° 55' N., 27° 52' E. and he himself with the destroyers steered to join Admiral Hamilton. The decision to leave PQ 17 and the remaining escort ships at such a moment was described by Commander Broome as the hardest he had ever had to make; but in the circumstances that seemed to have arisen it was clearly the right one to comply with the Commander-in-Chief's standing instructions[191] and was approved both by Rear-Admiral Hamilton at the time and subsequently by the Commander- in-Chief.[192]

Rear-Admiral Hamilton received the Admiralty orders at 2200. The *Norfolk* had then just flown off her aircraft on an ice patrol; he therefore stood on to the eastward for half an hour while endeavours were made to recall it. These were without success,[193] and at 2230 the force turned to a westerly course, steering to pass to the southward of the convoy, i.e., between it and the probable direction of the enemy. The visibility was extremely variable with numerous fog patches 'made all the more interesting by the presence of growlers.'[194] An hour later the merchant ships, by that time on widely divergent courses, were passed; there we will leave them for the present, while the cruiser force reinforced by Commander Broome's destroyers, withdrew to the westward at 25 knots.

Rear-Admiral Hamilton was much concerned at the effect the apparent desertion of the merchant ships might have on morale.

'Assuming, as we all did assume, that the scattering of the convoy heralded the imminent approach of enemy surface forces, we were – in the eyes of all who did not know the full story – running away and at high speed.'[195]

Had he been aware that the Admiralty had no further information of the enemy heavy units than he himself possessed, he would have remained in a covering position until the convoy was widely dispersed, when he could have parted company in a less ostentatious manner.

He personally regarded the dispersal of the convoy 800 miles from its destination during the all-daylight period as too hazardous and would have preferred to have kept it in formation and resorted to smoke screening tactics (in which he had specially exercised his ships) had the enemy surface forces appeared, as had been done by Rear-Admiral Vian in the Mediterranean three months previously.[196]

The whole episode emphasises the necessity for the Admiralty to keep the Senior Officer conducting an operation fully primed with all the information germane to it they possess and whatever executive orders they may decide to send him in an emergency, to follow them up as soon as possible with the intelligence (or, as in this case, the lack of intelligence) on which they were based. It also illustrates the difficulty in which a junior and detached Admiral may be placed when receiving directions from two superior authorities (in this case the Admiralty and the Commander-in-Chief) both of whom have information not imparted to him.[197]

37

As time went on with no further developments Rear-Admiral Hamilton became more and more puzzled as to what could have led to the sudden scattering of the convoy. But whatever the reason, the orders for his own force were peremptory, so he maintained his westerly course at 25 knots. Thick fog was encountered soon after midnight, which persisted with brief intervals until 0630, 5th July. Commander Broome, equally mystified by the course of events, soon began to feel that his place was with the merchantships; but he thought Rear-Admiral Hamilton was acting on fuller information than he himself possessed and expected him to send the escort destroyers back to their erstwhile charges the moment he deemed it advisable. As soon as the fog lifted sufficiently for visual signalling he informed the Rear-Admiral of his last hurried instructions to PQ 17 and requested that they should be amplified or amended as necessary.[198]

Actually Rear-Admiral Hamilton, who was still under the impression that the enemy surface forces were in close proximity, argued that once the convoy had scattered they would leave it to their air forces and submarines to deal with (as in fact they did); but he credited them with more enterprise than they possessed and expected them to transfer their attentions to his own force. Reinforced by Commander Broome's destroyers, he felt he could fight a delaying action and had a good chance of leading the enemy within reach of the *Victorious*'s aircraft and possibly the Commander-in-Chief's heavy ships.

At 0700, being then in 75° 40' N., 16° E.,[199] Rear-Admiral Hamilton reduced to 20 knots and at 0930, on crossing the meridian 13° E., he altered course to 230° in the direction of Jan Mayen Island. It was not until that forenoon that the situation as regards the enemy heavy ships was made clear to him.

Meanwhile, he had to decide what to do with Commander Broome's destroyers. The merchant ships were widely scattered and it seemed the destroyers:–

'could do little except screen individual ships, if they could find them. In view of their fuel situation and the difficulties they would have in finding an oiler, I considered that, with the possibility of offensive action by the battlefleet and *Victorious* against the enemy heavy ships, the most useful service the destroyers could perform would be with the battlefleet.'[200]

Accordingly, he ordered them to fuel from the *London* and *Norfolk*. By 1630, the *Ledbury, Wilton, Rowan* and *Keppel* had been completed; and Rear-Admiral Hamilton, who had received no further instructions since the order to withdraw the previous evening, continued to steer 230° at 20 knots. Throughout the day the weather was 'brilliant' and the visibility extreme; but nothing was seen of the enemy until 1740, when a Focke Wulf made contact and reported the force (correctly) in 74° 30' N., 7° 40' E. Having been located, Rear-Admiral Hamilton broke wireless silence and at 1830 informed the Commander-in-Chief of his position, course and speed and the composition of his force. This was the first intimation received by Sir John Tovey that Commander Broome's destroyers were still with the cruisers – a circumstance which he regretted.[201]

The Commander-in-Chief, having spent 4th July cruising about 150 miles north-west of Bear Island, had turned to the south-westward in the early morning of the 5th and was then on his way back to Scapa some 120 miles south-west of Rear-Admiral Hamilton. Shortly afterwards there came news at last of the German heavy ships. The Russian submarine *K21* reported the *Tirpitz, Scheer* and eight destroyers in 71° 25' N., 23° 40' E. (some 45 miles N.W. of North Cape) steering 045° at 1700, 5th July and claimed to have hit the *Tirpitz* with two torpedoes.[202] An hour or so later, at 1816, a reconnoitring aircraft reported 11 strange ships in 71° 31' N., 27° 10' E., steering 065°, 10 knots; and lastly submarine *P54*, which with the other Allied submarines, was shifting her original station further east,[203] reported the *Tirpitz* and *Hipper*, escorted by at least six destroyers and eight aircraft in 71° 30' N., 28° 40' E., steering 060°, 22 knots at 2029. She had sighted the enemy's smoke over an hour earlier and had tried to close within attacking range, on the surface, until forced by aircraft to dive and then at full speed under water; but the enemy passed her ten miles off. The *Trident*, on her way to the outer patrol line, having received the aircraft report timed 1816, stretched south-east beyond her station till midnight, 5th/6th, reaching as far as 32° 25' E., but saw nothing of the enemy, though the visibility was at its maximum.[204] Nothing more was heard of the German ships for two days.

Actually, their cruise was of short duration. Hitler's permission to launch the operation had only been obtained that forenoon (5th) and the executive order to proceed to sea was given at 1137. Rear-Admiral Hamilton's cruisers were then known to be moving to the westward and Admiral Tovey's covering force was some 450 miles alike from the convoy and the North Cape; it seemed there would be no special danger, provided the German force could approach the merchant ships unseen and engage them (or as short a time as possible. But the Allied sighting reports off North Cape from 1700 onwards were intercepted and the Naval Staff calculated that Admiral Tovey would be able to close sufficiently to launch an air attack before they got back to harbour, if they continued operations against the merchant ships after 0100, 6th. Air and U-boat attacks were taking a heavy toll – they accounted for a dozen ships that day – and it did not seem that the few stragglers which might fall to the surface craft were worth the effort. At 2132, 5th July, orders were given to abandon the operation, much to Admiral Schniewind's regret and twenty minutes later the force, then in 71° 38' N., 31° 5' E., reversed its course and returned to Altenfjord.

During the night of 5th/6th July the Admiralty made three signals to the Commander-in-Chief, Home Fleet, suggesting that the *Tirpitz* might be 'reluctant to go as far as the convoy' if the battlefleet was sighted steering to the eastward; and that aircraft from the *Victorious* might be able to attack her, if she had been damaged by the Russian submarines. The latter appeared to Admiral Tovey unlikely, for it seemed certain that the *Tirpitz*, especially if damaged, would not be sailed down the Norwegian Coast until adequate fighter cover and seaward reconnaissance were available. However, arrangements were made for the fleet to reverse its course if the approach of enemy aircraft was detected and at 0645, 6th July, course was altered back to the north-eastward. An hour later an enemy aircraft passed over the fleet above the clouds; endeavours to attract its attention by gunfire and fighters were unsuccessful. That forenoon Rear-Admiral Hamilton's force joined the fleet (1040). But the weather was unsuitable for air reconnaissance and Admiral Tovey felt there was nothing to be gained by continuing to the north-eastward. Rear-Admiral Hamilton's cruisers with eight destroyers, were detached to Seidisfjord at 1230 and the battlefleet turned to the southward again shortly afterwards. All ships reached harbour on the 8th.

The last news of the enemy ships came on 7th July, when a British aircraft working from Vaenga, near Murmansk, reported the *Tirpitz*, *Lützow*[205] and *Hipper* with some destroyers, followed by an oiler from a neighbouring fjord, turning out of Langfjord in Åmøy[206] (70° N., 20° 30' E.). By this time the British heavy ships were well on their way home, but an attempt to attack the enemy once again was made by submarines. Anticipating their return to Narvik, the *Sturgeon* and *Minerve* had been ordered on 6th July to leave the main patrol line and to patrol off the mouth of Vestfjord on the 7th and 8th, one at a time, in case the *Tirpitz* should pass outside the Lofoten Islands, owing to her heavy draught and possible damage. Nothing came of this, however, nor of a further patrol carried out by the *Sturgeon* on the night 9th/10th, close inshore in the Inner Lead some 70 miles north of Trondheim, in case any German ships should be going to that port; and the *Tirpitz* and her consorts duly arrived at Narvik without incident.

38

To return to Convoy PQ 17 (Plan 11). The sudden order to scatter came to Commodore Dowding as an unpleasant surprise. Like Rear-Admiral Hamilton and Commander Broome, he did not doubt that it heralded the immediate appearance of enemy heavy ships and as the escorting destroyers parted company to join the cruisers, he signalled to the *Keppel*: –

> 'Many thanks; goodbye and good hunting,' to which Commander Broome replied 'It is a grim business leaving you here.'

It was indeed a grim business and the gravity of the situation was clear to all; whether attack by surface craft developed in a few minutes or by aircraft and submarines during the next few days, the plight of the individual merchant ships – deprived of mutual support and of their escort – was parlous in the extreme.

The convoy scattered 'as laid down ... in perfect order, though it must have been apparent to the ships that had to turn to the south-west that they were heading towards where most trouble might be expected.'[207]

BARENTS SEA
MOVEMENTS OF SHIPS
EX- CONVOY P.Q.17.
4TH-28TH JULY, 1942.

NOTE

Positions are very rough, many dead
reckonings being much in error, e.g.,
Daniel Morgan and Fairfield City
were together when sunk, but their
respective D.R.s place them 90 miles apart.
Nothing is known of position of S.S.Carlton,
sunk by U-boat.

KEY

🔺......Ship Sunk.   ✈......Air attack
                          ......U-Boat attack

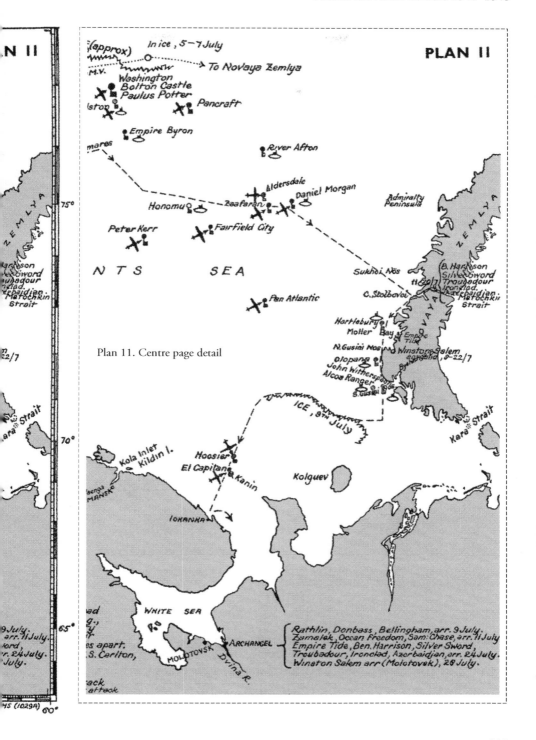

Plan 11. Centre page detail

The merchant ships proceeded mostly alone, or in groups of two or three. The anti-aircraft ships *Palomares* and *Pozarica* each took charge of a group, each collecting also two or three minesweepers or corvettes to act as a screen; they joined company next day, 5th July and steered for Novaya Zemlya. The *Salamander* accompanied two merchantmen and a rescue ship. The *Dianella*, escorting the submarines, stood by them until clear of the convoy, when they separated to patrol in its wake, while the corvette went on by herself. At first the different groups spread on courses ranging from north to east, a few steering afterwards for Archangel, most seeking shelter in Novaya Zemlya. But less than half the merchant ships reached even 'horrid Zembla's frozen realms,' for 17 in addition to the oiler *Aldersdale*[208] and the rescue ship *Zaafaran* were sunk during the next three days by bombing aircraft and U-boats. The bulk of the losses took place on the 5th while the ships were still in the far north, six being sunk by bombs[209] and six torpedoed by submarines[210] in an area roughly from 74° to 77° N. and from 35° to 45° E.[211] One ship was bombed on the 6th.[212] Four[213] were torpedoed off the south-west coast of Novaya Zemlya between the evening of the 6th and the early morning of the 8th, all possibly by the same submarine.[214]

By the 7th July, most of the escort, the rescue ship *Zamalek* and five merchant ships, the *Ocean Freedom, Hoosier, Benjamin Harrison, El Capitan* and *Samuel Chase*, had reached Matochkin Strait. Commodore Dowding, whose ship the *River Afton* had been sunk by a U-boat on the 5th, arrived in the *Lotus*, which had rescued him and 36 survivors, including the Master, Captain Charlton, after 3 ½ hours on rafts and floats. After a conference on board the *Palomares*, these merchantmen were formed into a convoy and sailed that evening, escorted by the two A.A. ships, the *Halcyon, Salamander, Britomart, Poppy, Lotus, La Malouine* and three trawlers.[215] The *Benjamin Harrison* soon got separated in a fog and returned to Matochkin Strait,[216] but the remainder were all in company when the weather temporarily cleared during the forenoon of 8th July and course was shaped to pass east and south of Kolguef Island.

It was an anxious passage; much fog and ice were encountered and U-boats were known to be about. From time to time boatloads of survivors from ships already sunk were met with and picked up – a reminder of the fate that might be in store for any of them.

During the night of the 9th-10th some 40 bombers carried out high level attacks on the little convoy, apparently guided by submarines the previous evening. The attacks lasted four hours: the *Hoosier* and *El Capitan* were sunk by near misses some 60 miles north-west of Cape Kanin. Four aircraft were believed to be shot down. The attacks ended about 0230, 10th July and half an hour later two Russian flying boats appeared.

The surviving ships arrived at Archangel the following day, 11th July; 'NOT a successful convoy. Three ships brought into port out of 37' to quote the concluding sentence of Commodore Dowding's report.

Things were not quite so bad as that, however. The rescue ship *Rathlin* with two merchant ships, the *Donbass* and *Bellingham* had arrived on the 9th, having shot down an aircraft the day before and before long news of other ships sheltering in Novaya Zemlyan waters began to come in.

At his special request, Commodore Dowding, despite all he had been through, left Archangel in the *Poppy* on 16th July, in company with the *Lotus* (Lieutenant H. J. Hall RNR SO) Escorts and *La Malouine*, to form these merchant ships into a convoy and bring them back to Archangel. After a stormy passage they arrived at Byelushya Bay on the 19th; there 12 survivors from the *Olopana* were found. During the day the coast was searched between South and North Gusini Nos; in the evening the *Winston Salem* was found aground south-east of North Gusini Nos and later the *Empire Tide* at anchor in Moller Bay. The next morning Matochkin Strait was entered. There five merchant ships from PQ 17 were found at anchor – the *Benjamin Harrison, Silver Sword, Troubadour, Ironclad* and *Azerbaidjan* – besides a Russian icebreaker, the *Murman* and trawler, the *Kerov* and HM trawler *Ayrshire* (Lieutenant L. J. A. Gradwell, RNVR).

The latter had done fine work, in collecting the *Silver Sword, Troubadour* and *Ironclad* soon after the convoy scattered. With them she steered a northerly course close east of Hope Island, until ice was encountered, when course was altered to the eastward. In the evening of 5th July, Lieutenant Gradwell decided to enter the ice to avoid detection, camouflaging the ships by painting them white and penetrated some 20 miles into the icefield, where they remained until the 7th, when they continued their voyage to Novaya Zemlya, arriving at Matochkin Strait on the 11th. None of the ships had a large scale chart and in an attempt to sail for Archangel, the *Ironclad* ran aground twice and the *Troubadour* once. Both ships were refloated by the efforts of the *Ayrshire* which then managed to pilot them some 20 miles up the strait, where they remained well camouflaged and unmolested.

Commodore Dowding wasted no time. A conference was held that forenoon and in the evening all ships sailed,[217] the Commodore leading in the Russian icebreaker *Murman*. The *Empire Tide*, which had a lot of survivors from sunken ships on board, joined the convoy from Moller Bay early on 21st July. The *Winston Salem* was still aground, with two Russian tugs standing by.

Much fog was encountered during the passage, which apart from one or two U-boat alarms was uneventful. The escort was reinforced by the *Pozarica, Bramble, Hazard, Leda, Dianella* and two Russian destroyers on 22nd July and the convoy arrived safely at Archangel on the evening of the 24th.

Four days later (28th July) the *Winston Salem*, having been re-floated under the superintendance of the American Naval Attache, Captain S. D. Frankel, who flew to Novaya Zemlya in an antique Catalina, arrived at Molotovsk. This was the last ship of the ill-fated Convoy PQ 17 to reach harbour, making a total of 11 survivors all told out of 35 merchant ships and one oiler that set out from Iceland. Air attack had destroyed 13 (besides the *Zaafaran*) at a cost of six aircraft.[218] Submarines had sunk 10[219] without loss to themselves; two had fallen by the wayside and were still in Icelandic waters.

It is to be noted that, with the exception of three ships, these heavy losses occurred after PQ 17 had ceased to be a convoy and the ships had scattered. A Russian admiral is said to have observed that the *Tirpitz* had achieved her object simply by making the convoy an easy prey for submarines and aircraft.

This was the opinion of the Commander-in-Chief, Home Fleet:–

'The order to scatter the convoy,' he wrote, 'had, in my opinion, been premature; its results were disastrous. The convoy had so far covered more than half its route with the loss of only three ships. Now its ships, spread over a wide area, were exposed without defence to the powerful enemy U-boat and air forces. The enemy took prompt advantage of this situation, operating both weapons to their full capacity …'[220]

In point of fact, the episode raises once again the exceedingly difficult problem of how far the Admiralty, with its overall responsibility and superior Intelligence organisation, ought to exercise executive control over the 'man on the spot'. In this instance it is hard to resist the conclusion that it would have been better to have kept Sir John Tovey and Rear-Admiral Hamilton informed of precisely what was known of the enemy surface craft movements and left them to decide what to do. It is certain, for example, that of the three authorities the Rear-Admiral alone was aware of the existing weather conditions – with all their variations from thick fog to extreme visibility or flat calm to full gale – and on this score was in the best position to assess the chances of evasion or a successful defence.

39

The disastrous passage of Convoy PQ 17 tended to throw into the background the fortunes of the westbound convoy, QP 13. This convoy of 35 ships sailed in two parts from Archangel and Murmansk, joining up at sea on 28 June under Commodore N. H. Gale. Its escort consisted of five destroyers, the *Inglefield* (Commander A. G. West, SO), *Achates, Volunteer, Intrepid* and ORP *Garland*, the A.A. ship *Alynbank* and eight smaller craft.[221]

Thick weather prevailed during most of the passage, but the convoy was reported by enemy aircraft on 30th June while still east of Bear Island and again on 2nd July. No attacks developed, however and that afternoon Convoy PQ 17 was passed, to which the enemy then transferred their attentions.

After an uneventful passage, Convoy QP 13 divided off the north-east coast of Iceland on 4th July in compliance with directions from the Admiralty,[222] Commodore Gale with 16 merchant ships turning south for Loch Ewe, while the remaining 19 ships continued round the north coast of Iceland for Reykjavik. Captain J. Hiss, master of the United States ship *American Robin*, was nominated as Commodore of this section on parting company. At 1900, 5th July, Captain Hiss's convoy formed in five columns and escorted by the minesweepers *Niger* (Commander A. J. Cubison SO) and *Hussar*, the Free French Corvette *Roselys* and the trawlers *Lady Madeleine* and *St. Elstan*,[223] was approaching the north-west corner of Iceland. The weather was overcast, visibility about one mile; wind N.E., force 8; sea rough. No sights had been obtained since 1800, 2nd July and the position was considerably in doubt.

At 1910, Commander Cubison suggested that the front of the convoy should be reduced to two columns in order to pass between Straumnes and the minefield to the north-west of Iceland. This was the first the Commodore had heard of the existence of the minefield.

Soon afterwards, Commander Cubison gave his estimated position at 2000 as 66° 45' N., 22° 22' W.[224] and suggested altering course to 222° for Straumnes point at that time. This was done. About two hours later (2200), the *Niger*, which had gone ahead to try and make a landfall, leaving the *Hussar* as a visual link with the convoy, sighted what she took to be North Cape bearing 150° one mile and ordered the course of the convoy to be altered to 270°. Actually, what the *Niger* had sighted was a large iceberg, but this was not realised for some time; at 2240, she blew up and sank with heavy loss of life, including Commander Cubison. Five minutes later a last signal from her, explaining the mistaken landfall and recommending a return to course 222°, was handed to Captain Hiss. But it was too late; already explosions were occurring among the merchant ships. The westerly course had led straight into the minefield. Considerable confusion prevailed, some thinking a U-boat attack was in progress, others imagining a surface raider. Four ships were sunk[225] and two seriously damaged.[226] Good rescue work was carried out by the escorts, especially the *Roseleys* (Lieutenant de vaisseau A. Bergeret). Though be had correctly appreciated that the convoy was in the minefield, Lieutenant Bergeret remained in these highly dangerous waters for 61 hours, during which time he picked up 179 survivors from various ships.

Meanwhile, the *Hussar*, which had obtained a shore fix, led out the remaining merchant ships, which reformed on a southerly course and in due course reached Reykjavik without further misadventure.

The Flag Officer, Iceland (Rear-Admiral Dalrymple-Hamilton) attributed this unfortunate occurrence to the change of plan, whereby a Commodore had to assume charge of the convoy, without full information of the conditions prevailing off the north-west coast of Iceland, i.e. the minefield and the apparent absence of any concerted arrangement between the SO, Escort and the Commodore as to what procedure should be adopted if land was not sighted when expected; to the thick weather, which prevented sights being taken for three days before making the land and the *Niger*'s unfortunate mistaking of ice for land, which dictated the alteration of course that led directly into the minefield; to the unreliability of the radar sets in the *Niger* and *Hussar*; and to the absence of any navigational aid such as a DF beacon to lead through the gap between the minefield and the shore.

CHAPTER V

Convoys PQ 18, QP 14, 15: September–November 1942

40

After the disaster to Convoy PQ 17 the Admiralty pressed for a suspension of the convoys until the season of perpetual daylight was over. As before, however, the political exigences were such as to render this most undesirable. Mr. Winston Churchill, who has recorded his inclination to increase the stakes on the principle of 'In defeat, defiance', suggested that a concentration of practically all our carriers, supported by heavy ships and other craft, should fight its way through with the next convoy. This plan 'which of course involved engaging a force vital to us out of proportion to the actual military importance of the Arctic Convoys'[227] could not be accepted by the Admiralty and the proposal was dropped.

In any case, the needs of Malta again intervened. Another operation to restock that sorely pressed island took place in August,[228] and the detachment of substantial forces from the Home Fleet in support postponed the running of the next pair of convoys to North Russia until September.[229] The fleet was further weakened by the gradual withdrawal of the American ships which were urgently required in the Pacific. The *Washington* with four destroyers left in July, followed in August by the *Wichita*, to which Rear-Admiral Giffen had shifted his flag.

During this interlude several steps were taken in preparation for their resumption. The first thing was to provide the Allied ships in North Russia with ammunition and provisions, much of which had been lost in the disaster to PQ 17. This was done by four destroyers, the *Marne, Martin, Middleton* and *Blankney*, which sailed on 20th July with replenishments for the escorts and merchant ships of QP 14 assembled at Archangel; though sighted by aircraft off Jan Mayen Island, they completed their passage without incident.

In August, two squadrons of Hampdens were flown to North Russia, in readiness to support Convoy PQ 18.[230] Their ground staff, stores and torpedoes were carried to Kola in the US cruiser *Tuscaloosa*, escorted by the destroyers *Rodman, Emmons* and *Onslaught*. A medical unit and stores, too, were sent in these ships in an attempt to alleviate the primitive conditions in the Russian hospitals, in which the sick and wounded of the convoy escorts and merchant ships were treated; but the medical unit was forbidden to land, on orders from Moscow and returned to the United Kingdom in the next westbound convoy.[231]

While the *Tuscaloosa* was at Archangel, the German pocket battleship *Scheer* carried out an operation between 18th and 25th August in search of Russian shipping to the north and east of Novaya Zemlya. She only succeeded in sinking one ice-breaker and after bombarding Dikson Island at the mouth of the Yenesei River, she returned to Narvik. To supplement this operation, it had been planned to mine the channel off the north-west coast of Novaya Zemlya, but the minelayer, the *Ulm*, while still south-east of Bear Island, was intercepted and sunk on 24th August by the *Marne, Martin* and *Onslaught*, which were sweeping to the southward of the *Tuscaloosa* on her return passage. After this operation the *Tuscaloosa* returned to the United States and the existence of Task Force 99 came to an end.[232]

41

When the strength of the Home Fleet permitted the resumption of the convoys to North Russia the operation differed in important respects from those before it. The events of July had shown the German readiness to send heavy ships to attack the convoys in the Barents Sea, where the Allied heavy ships could not operate without grave danger from hostile aircraft and submarines. Moreover, the value of the heavy covering force even west of Bear Island was much impaired through there being no large aircraft carrier available for duty with the Home Fleet.[233]

In these circumstances it was clear to the Commander-in-Chief, Home Fleet, that some radical change was necessary in the methods hitherto used for escorting the convoys. He was convinced by this time that we could always fight a convoy through – albeit with heavy loss – in the face of air and U-boat attacks, but that if the German surface forces were used intelligently, then there was considerable chance of a repetition of the PQ 17 disaster. He therefore decided that the counter to enemy surface attack must originate from the convoy escort itself and developed the idea of the 'fighting destroyer escort', which would remain with the convoy reinforcing the close escort for anti-submarine and anti-air purposes until the appearance of enemy surface craft, when it would be manoeuvred to attack them. He considered that a force of 12 to 16 Fleet destroyers would seem so formidable to the enemy as to deter him from forcing home an attack on the convoy;[234] if, on the other hand he persisted, it would be strong enough to defeat him.

Accordingly, instead of a weak destroyer escort, with a cruiser or a group of cruisers in more or less close support, the permanent escorts were augmented by a force of 16 Fleet destroyers and Rear-Admiral Burnett, flying his flag in the cruiser *Scylla*, which accompanied each convoy for the critical part of its passage, was placed in command of all the forces present with the convoy. For the first time, too, an aircraft carrier sailed with the convoys; this was the *Avenger*, one of the new 'escort' carriers, armed with 12 fighters and three anti-submarine aircraft and she had her own escort of two destroyers. In order that each convoy should receive the full protection, the merchant ships coming from Russia had to wait until the eastbound convoy reached the last stage of its voyage before they sailed, instead of the two convoys crossing near Bear Island as hitherto. This made the operation much longer than usual; and the time was increased by the length of the route, for the ice barrier in September permitted a more northerly passage than in any other month in the year (though still not far enough from Banak air station). In these circumstances a larger provision than usual was required for fuelling the escorts during the voyage; two oilers with their own destroyers were accordingly stationed in Lowe Sound, Spitzbergen (Force 'P') and two more sailed with the convoys (Force 'Q').[235]

For the first time the Commander-in-Chief, Home Fleet, did not go to sea, but directed operations from Scapa Flow. This, he subsequently remarked, enabled him to exercise more effective control and proved of considerable benefit. His second-in-command, Vice-Admiral Sir Bruce Fraser, with two battleships, the *Anson* (flag) and *Duke of York*, the *Jamaica* and a destroyer screen, was based at Akureyri (Iceland) and cruised for short periods north-west of Jan Mayen Island.

Additional cover was provided for Convoy QP 14 by a cruiser force under Vice-Admiral Bonham-Carter, consisting of the *Norfolk* (flag), *Suffolk* and *London* with two destroyers which operated to the westward of Spitsbergen between 17th and 20th September, in support of the *Cumberland, Sheffield* and *Eclipse* which were landing reinforcements and stores for the Norwegian post at Barentsburg.[236]

Four submarines were stationed close off the coast of Norway to intercept enemy ships going north from Narvik; and, joined by three more (the submarine 'covering force'), they afterwards formed a shifting patrol line to cover the passage of the convoys east of Bear Island.[237]

Besides the *Avenger's* aircraft and improved anti-submarine protection and reconnaissance by Coastal Command aircraft from Iceland and Russia, the convoys had the support of the two squadrons of torpedo-carrying Hampdens based in Russia against possible attack by surface ships in the Barents Sea.[238]

As it happened the German surface ships made no attempt on either convoy. Aircraft and U-boats, however, took a substantial toll. The east-going convoy, PQ 18, suffered very heavy torpedo bomber attacks, which sank ten of its 40 ships; two others were sunk by U-boats, a loss of 30 per cent. No warships were damaged, but four of the *Avenger's* Hurricanes were lost, the pilots of three being saved. Convoy QP 14 escaped air attack, but lost three ships out of 15 to U-boats, which in addition sank two of the escort and a fleet oiler.

42

Great importance was attached by the enemy to repeating their success of July against the next pair of convoys. Reports early in August had led them to suppose that PQ 18 had left Iceland on its easterly trip; bad weather and short visibility impeded special air reconnaissance for some days, but on the 12th and 13th August the whole sea area where the convoy might be was covered in perfect weather conditions. Practically a million litres of fuel were used by 140 aircraft flying for a total of 1,603 hours. Not until then did they come to the conclusion that something had delayed the sailing and revert to their routine reconnaissances.

On 8 September Convoy PQ 18 was located north of Iceland and between the 10th and 11th, three U-boats were disposed in longitude 3° W. between 76° 30' N. and 74° 30' N., four others as a second wave between Spitzbergen and Bear Island and five more were ordered to close the area. At the same time (10th September) the *Scheer, Hipper* and *Köln* with several destroyers left Narvik and proceeded to Altenfjord. They were sighted by all four submarines of the 'patrol force' and unsuccessfully attacked by one of them (the *Tigris*). There, however, the surface forces remained until the end of the operation. Group Command, North, wished to sail them on the 13th against QP 14; but the hand of Hitler again made itself felt and Grand Admiral Raeder, who that morning had received a reminder from him that the ships must not be unduly hazarded (in view of their importance to the defence of Norway), considered the risks too great and vetoed the operation.[239]

The German Air Force, elated by its success against PQ 17, the scattering of which was erroneously attributed to the air attack a couple of hours before, was ordered to make a great effort against PQ 18. By this time the torpedo bomber force had increased to 92 aircraft, whose attacks, it will be remembered, were to be synchronised with those of the bombers. Warning had been received that this convoy would be accompanied by an aircraft carrier with fighters and it was decided that she should be singled out for the whole strength of the initial attacks.

43

When the German ships left Narvik on 10th September, Convoy PQ 18 was passing Jan Mayen Island. To lessen the risk of detection the greater part of the convoy had sailed direct from Loch Ewe on the 2nd, only a few ships joining from Reykjavik as the main body passed up the west coast of Iceland on 8th September, though in fact the convoy was reported from the air that day. The Commodore was Rear-Admiral E.K. Boddam-Whetham (Ret.) and the convoy consisted of 39 merchant ships, with an oiler (*Atheltemplar*) and three motor minesweepers also bound for Russia, a rescue ship (the *Copeland*) and Force Q (the fleet oilers *Grey Ranger* and *Black Ranger*) (Plans 12 and 13). The close escort consisted of two destroyers, the *Malcolm* (Acting-Commander A. B. Russell, SO) and *Achates*, two A.A. ships, the *Ulster Queen* (Acting-Captain C. K. Adam) and *Alynbank* (Acting-Captain H. F. Nash), two submarines, *P614* and *P615* and 11 corvettes, minesweepers and trawlers.[240]

Rear-Admiral Burnett joined on 9th September south-west of Jan Mayen Island with the *Scylla*, half the Destroyer Force,[241] and the *Avenger* (Commander A. P. Colthurst) with her escort, the *Wheatland* and *Wilton* (the 'Carrier Force'); the other group of the Destroyer Force[242] had gone ahead to Lowe Sound (Spitsbergen) to oil from Force 'P'.[243] Two days later the *Scylla* and five destroyers parted company to oil there in their turn, leaving three ships of the Destroyer Force behind to fill up from Force 'Q'. On the 13th the second group of destroyers joined the convoy in the morning and the *Scylla* and her consorts in the afternoon, so the escort was complete.[244] They were then about 150 miles northwest of Bear Island, steering to pass 90 miles north of the island.

The convoy had already had several encounters with U-boats, apart from doubtful ASDIC contacts or U-boats forced to dive at a safe distance by the *Avenger*'s patrolling Swordfish. At mid-day on the 10th the *Harrier* and *Sharpshooter* attacked a contact astern of the convoy with

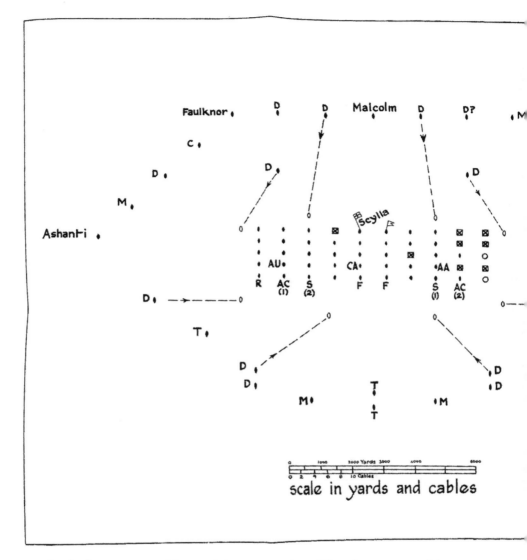

scale in yards and cables

depth charges in roughly 70° 40' N., 12° 30' W.;[245] in the evening of the 12th the *Malcolm* and *Impulsive* attacked one, reported at 2000 by the air patrol, the *Malcolm* dropping two patterns of depth charges without apparent result; and an hour later U 88 was sunk by the *Faulknor* ahead of the convoy in about 75° 15' N., 4° 50' E. On the 13th at least eight approached within 20 miles between 0600 and 1400, most of them being forced to dive out of range by the air patrols. At 0855 that morning, however, in about 75° 40' N., 7° 40' E. two ships – the

CONVOY PQ.18.
Cruising order with full escort.

Reference to letters and symbols.

⚑....Flagship of Rear-Adm: Burnett.

⚑..Commodore's ship.

AA⎫ anti-aircraft ships

AU⎭ ALYNBANK & ULSTER QUEEN.

AC(1) alternative stations for

AC(2) escort carrier AVENGER

C.............corvette

CA.........C.A.M. ship.

D.............destroyer.

F....Fleet oiler

M...minesweeper

R...rescue ship

S(1)⎫ alternative
⎬ stations for two
S(2)⎭ submarines and
escorting corvette

T......Trawler.

O   ships sunk by
submarine AM, 13 Sept.

⊠ do. by aircraft, PM do.

The destroyers named were ships of Captains (D) and of Senior Officer, permanent escort (MALCOLM) The station marked D? may not have been_____, occupied. Certain destroyers closed to the stations marked O, when attack from the air became imminent. The convoy was formed in ten columns, four cables apart, ships in column two cables apart——————.

, D

, C

, Onslow

—— , D

Stalingrad and *Oliver Elsworth* – in the starboard wing column of the convoy were torpedoed and sunk. The *Onslaught* foiled two more attacks made during the forenoon by U-boats that penetrated the outer screen on the starboard bow; and the *Sharpshooter* and *Tartar* attacked another astern of the convoy.

The German submarines had maintained touch with the convoy for three days in fog, rain and snow, which had shielded it from aircraft since its sighting on the 8th, while still west of Iceland. But shadowers,

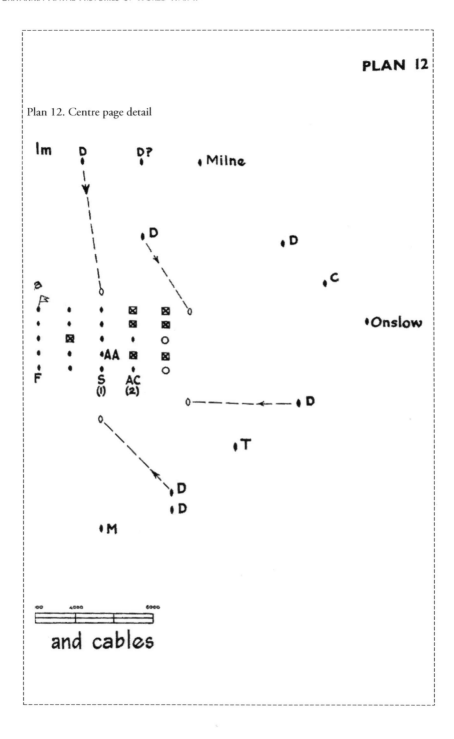

avoiding attack by the *Avenger*'s Sea Hurricanes, found it on the 12th and again on the 13th, while others shadowed the ships with Rear-Admiral Burnett returning from Bell Sound; thenceforward the convoy was continually under observation from the air. The shadowers were either Blohm and Voss 138 or Ju.88 aircraft and as they often worked in groups (as many as nine at a time were reported on the 14th), they were hard to deal with. Commander Colthurst of the *Avenger* remarked on 'the hopelessness of sending even four Sea Hurricanes to attack the heavily armed enemy shadowers.' More than once they protected submarines from attack by Swordfish and also, when the weather was clear enough, brought air striking forces to the convoy.

The first air attack came at 1500 on the 13th, while the screen was reforming on the return of the *Scylla* and the five destroyers, the convoy being then fully 450 miles from the German air stations. Some half a dozen to a dozen Ju.88 aircraft dropped bombs through gaps in the clouds, at a height of about 4,000 feet, without harm to the convoy or loss to themselves.

Directly after this, at 1530, over 40 torpedo aircraft came in from the starboard bow: Ju.88 and He.111, most of them armed with two torpedoes. Following their 'Golden Comb' tactique,[246] they approached in line abreast, in Commodore Boddam-Whetham's words like 'a huge flight of nightmare locusts,' flying 30 to 40 feet above the water and keeping such good station 100 to 150 yards apart that, said Rear-Admiral Burnett, it was impossible to break them up.[247] The main body attacked the starboard wing of the convoy, a few aircraft passing ahead and flying down either side of the *Scylla*, which steamed out ahead of the merchantmen. They were received by an intense fire from all guns in men-of-war and merchant ships. The Commodore ordered an emergency turn, 45° together, towards the enemy; but the two starboard columns either wheeled or did not turn at all (the whole affair lasted only seven or eight minutes) leading Rear-Admiral Burnett to suppose that the Commodore had purposely refrained from altering course. The aircraft pressed home their attack with great determination, dropping most of their torpedoes within 2,000 yards; they succeeded in sinking six of the seven merchant ships remaining in the two wing columns and two in the middle of the convoy – eight ships all told[248] – at a cost of five aircraft.

Three-quarters of an hour later, at 1615, a few He.115 appeared on the starboard beam. But the barrage fire of the escort foiled this attempt and the enemy dropped their torpedoes at long range without effect.

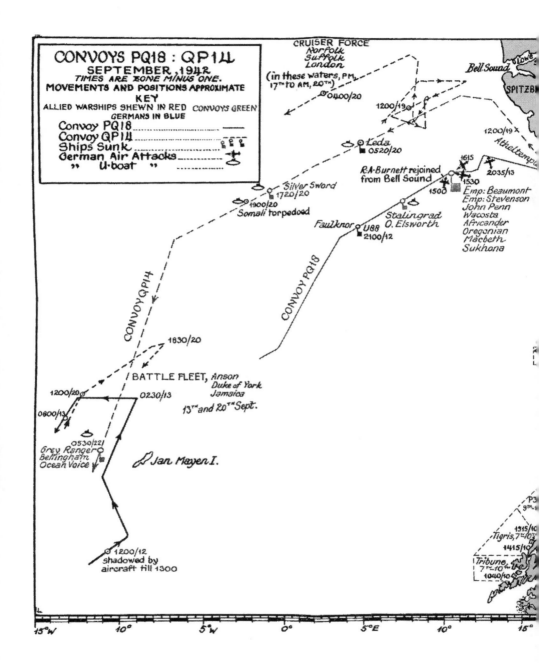

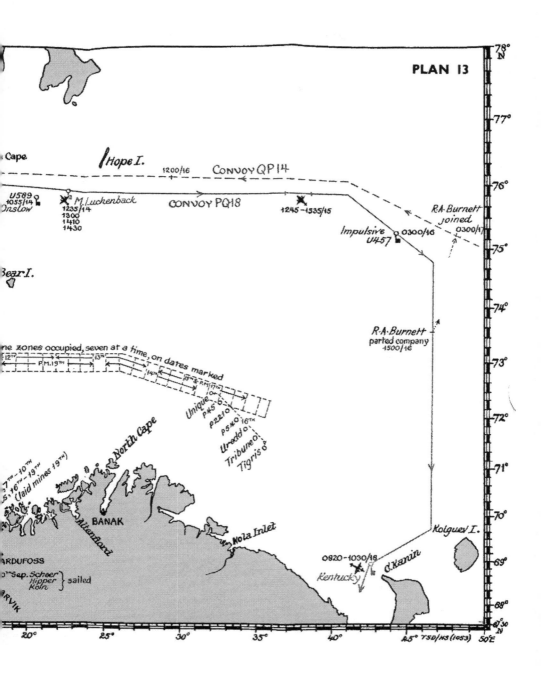

PLAN 13

Cape

Hope I.

1200/16

CONVOY QP 14

U 589
1055/14
Onslow

M.Luchenback
1235/14
1300
1410
1430

CONVOY PQ 18

1245 - 1535/15

R.A.Burnett
joined

Impulsive 0300/16
U457

0300/17

Bear I.

R.A.Burnett
parted company
1500/16

ne zones occupied, seven at a time, on dates marked

12ᵀᴴ

P.M.19ᵀᴴ

13ᵀᴴ

14ᵀᴴ

8 P.M 17ᵀᴴ

Unique
P 45

15ᵀᴴ 6 P.M.

16ᵀᴴ

P 221

P 54

Uredd
Tribune
Tigris

North Cape

7ᵀᴴ - 10ᵀᴴ
5, 16ᵀᴴ - 19ᵀᴴ
(laid mines 19ᵀᴴ)

BANAK

Altenfiord

Kola Inlet

Kolguev I.

Sep. Scheer
Hipper
Koln } sailed

ARDUFOSS

RVIK

C.Kanin

0820 - 1030/18

Kentucky

20°   25°   30°   35°   40°   45° TSD/HS (1053) 50°E

78°N
77°
76°
75°
74°
73°
72°
71°
70°
69°
68°
67°30'

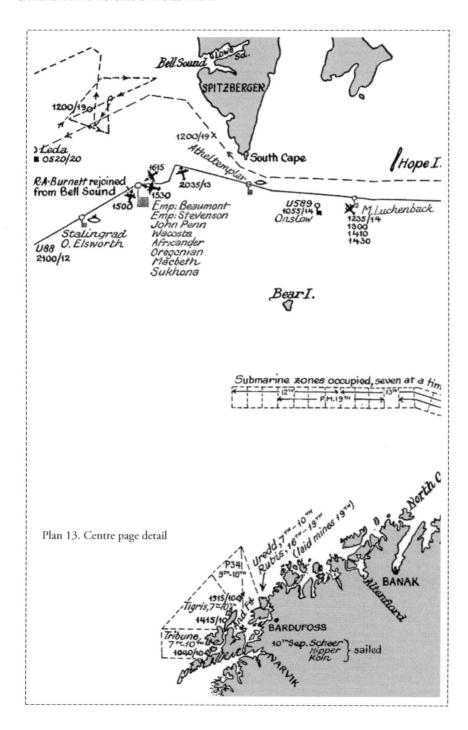

Plan 13. Centre page detail

Last of all that day, at 2035, when it was nearly dark, a dozen He.111 or He.115 aircraft approached from ahead, attacking in small groups during the next half hour or so, without damaging the convoy.

The Germans lost eight torpedo aircraft[249] in the three attacks, all destroyed by the ships' fire. The *Avenger* was caught at a disadvantage. She had been using her precious fighters in a vain endeavour to prevent shadowing since 0745 that morning and seems to have had two sections (four aircraft) in the air for that purpose, when the German striking force was reported 60 miles away at 1435. She flew off two more fighters, which with one of those already up engaged five Ju.88 aircraft as they retired after bombing the convoy; having spent their ammunition, the fighters made feint attacks on approaching torpedo aircraft. Thus, at the time of the enemy's principal attack, no British aircraft were ready to meet it; nor could more be flown off until an hour later, when four Hurricanes went up, only to have one shot down by a Blohm and Voss shadower. Commander Colthurst then realised the futility of sending even four Sea Hurricanes to attack the heavily armed shadowers and also the necessity of differentiating between reconnaissance groups and striking forces on the radar screen. 'I then decided,' he wrote:–

'that with the small number of obsolete fighters at our disposal and with their slow operation in an auxiliary carrier, we must use them only to break up large attacking formations rather than to destroy individuals; further, that we must endeavour to maintain a continual cycle of sections taking off, landing on to rearm and refuel and taking off again. The achievement of this would avoid congestion in the carrier and ensure that there were always some fighter sections ready to counter-attack striking forces.'[250]

The result was seen on the following day. In the meantime, however, the convoy was to suffer another loss from submarine attack. At 0330, the 14th, the oiler *Atheltemplar* was torpedoed in about 76° 10' N., 16° 40' E. and she had to be sunk, because 'there were at least five U-boats in the vicinity of the convoy' and ships could not be spared to tow and escort her to safety in Lowe Sound, some 120 miles away. This vessel, like the two oilers of Force 'Q', was stationed as the sternmost ship of a middle column in the convoy; her torpedoing was a lucky stroke for the German, as the *Impulsive* which was passing up the port side of the convoy after another hunt, had actually begun to attack the submarine before the torpedoes were fired. Some seven hours later, combined work by an aircraft and a destroyer ended in a success. The patrolling Swordfish sighted a U-boat to starboard of the convoy at 0940. The submarine (now known to have been *U-589*) dived and the Swordfish reported her by wireless and continued to shadow until driven off by two German aircraft. Rear-Admiral Burnett sent the *Onslow* to attack, using radio-telephony to get her 'quickly off the mark.' The destroyer sighted the enemy again on the surface at about 1020, but she dived while still six or seven miles off in about 75° 40' N., 20° 30' E.; at 1055 the *Onslow* made her first attack, continuing for nearly three hours, when the contact was lost after fuel oil, large bubbles of air and wreckage had come to the surface.

The day's battle in the air began at 1235, the 14th, when some 20 or more torpedo aircraft came in sight on the starboard bow, flying so low that there had been no radar warning of their approach. They divided into two groups, the larger of which 'made a dead set' at the *Avenger*, while the rest of the aircraft attacked the *Scylla* and the screen: on this day, it will be noticed, the enemy concentrated on the protecting men-of-war rather than on the merchant ships. The carrier left her station in rear of the convoy and pressed ahead to find fuller freedom to manoeuvre, sending up six fighters to meet the enemy. She was closely attended by her escorting destroyers, *Wheatland* and *Wilton*, whose handling was excellent, said Commander Colthurst: 'I always knew exactly where I should see them if I looked and I never had to give them a moment's thought.' The *Ulster Queen* also stood out from the convoy to support the *Avenger* with her six high-angle 4-inch guns. The fighters drove off some of the attackers and gunfire made others drop their torpedoes at long range; no ships were hit and the Germans lost 11 aircraft. 'It was a fine sight,' remarked Rear-Admiral Burnett:–

> 'to see *Avenger* peeling off Hurricanes, whilst streaking across the front of the convoy from starboard to port inside the screen with her destroyer escort blazing away with any gun which would bear and then being chased by torpedo bombers as she steamed down on the opposite course to the convoy to take cover ... Altogether a most gratifying action.'

Soon after this attack they had radar warning of another striking force, this time Ju.88 bombers. About 12 aircraft attacked between 1300 and 1410, coming down out of the cloud at 6,000 feet to drop their bombs at 2,000 feet, though one dive-bombed the *Avenger*, which had a narrow escape. Other ships of the escort had narrow escapes also and two bombs fell within the formation of the convoy; but no damage was done and one German was shot down.

Torpedo aircraft arrived again directly afterwards, coming from ahead and dividing into two groups as before and dropping torpedoes from 50 feet above the water at ranges of 2,000 to 3,000 yards. There were 25 aircraft all told and again their chief target was the *Avenger*, now on the starboard quarter of the convoy. By this time she had ten fighters in the air; they and the ships' guns accounted for nine of the enemy, one of which fell a victim to the little motor minesweeper No. 212. But a merchant ship in the starboard wing column, the *Mary Luchenbach*, was torpedoed and blew up, while three Hurricanes were lost, shot down by our own barrage. All three pilots were picked up by destroyers.

The last attack came at 1430, when about 20 bombers approached from astern dropping their bombs through gaps in the cloud at heights of 4,000 to 6,000 feet during the next hour or so, though a few made shallow dive-bombing attacks. Some bombs fell near, but they did no harm; and in spite of difficult cloud conditions, both for fighters and gunfire, one aircraft was hit.

It will be remembered that from the first the *Scylla* had moved out ahead of the convoy to clear her line of fire on the approach of torpedo aircraft. The *Ulster Queen* and *Alynbank*, on the other hand, had orders to remain in their stations, as Rear-Admiral Burnett considered the need for high-angle defence paramount, though it gave the ships little scope against aircraft flying low. On the 14th, however, profiting by experience like the *Avenger* in her sphere, Captain Adam of the *Ulster Queen* decided to make the most of his ship's good manoeuvring powers and turned out of the convoy to counter the torpedo attacks, regaining his station in time for the bombing attacks that followed.[251]

Next day, 15th September, bombers only attacked, about 50 passing above the convoy between 1245 and 1535. By this time the convoy was near 76° N., 36° E., well into the Barents Sea and 400 miles from Banak. The aircraft approached in groups of three generally and most of them dropped their bombs from within the clouds about 4,000 feet up. Whenever they came below the clouds or appeared in clear patches of sky, the ships received them with a heavy fire, while the fighters hunted them above. Some ships had narrow escapes, but none was hit. Towards the end of the battle the enemy seemed to keep circling overhead in cloud, waiting for the ships to pass clear from under it, perhaps, or for the fighters to run out of fuel. Rear-Admiral Burnett was considering altering course to keep beneath cloud when their leader was heard by radio-telephony to give orders to withdraw and having reached the limit of their fuel endurance they made off, jettisoning their remaining bombs. They lost three of their number in this attack, all falling to the ships' fire, although the devoted fighter pilots made 21 sorties during the afternoon. 'On this occasion,' reported Commander Colthurst:–

> 'the theory of continuing the cycle of take-offs and landings at about 25-minute intervals was put into practice with success. There were therefore always four sections available, with adequate fuel and ammunition, except during the short periods when two newly-fuelled sections were taking off and two waiting to land on to refuel.'[252]

This was the last attack from the air that Convoy PQ 18 had to face while the Destroyer Force and the carrier were in company. But they still had submarines to contend with. By this time, according to the German account, three were in contact (but could not break through the screen) and as many as 12 were in the vicinity. At 1340 on the 15th, in about 75° 50' N., 36° 30' E., during the air attack, two submarines revealed themselves by their exhaust smoke, some ten miles from the convoy and were forced to dive by the *Opportune*, sent to reconnoitre the smoke. This was a relief to Rear-Admiral Burnett, who had always to consider the danger of attack by surface ships. At 0300 on the 16th, in about 75° 15' N., 44° 15' E., the *Impulsive* attacked a submarine diving close on the port bow of the convoy, just outside the screen. After dropping her first depth charges she lost contact, the submarine passing under the wing column of merchantmen; but when the destroyer returned to the position of her attack she found fuel oil and wreckage on the surface, whilst an all-round sweep by ASDIC gave no result; the claim to have sunk the submarine (*U-457*) was afterwards confirmed. Again at 1040, the *Opportune* and *Offa* attacked another sighted on the surface five miles off. The U-boat dived at a range of 7,000 yards and depth charges were dropped, apparently without success. On this day, for the first time since the 12th, the *Avenger* had no anti-submarine patrol flying, the duty being taken over by Catalina aircraft, working from a Russian base. Later in the day the German Group Command North ordered the submarines to leave PQ 18 and to concentrate on QP 14.

In the afternoon of the 16th, Rear-Admiral Burnett parted company with PQ 18 to join QP 14, his forces leaving in three groups to lessen the risk of detection by the enemy. Besides the *Scylla* and the destroyers, the *Avenger* and the two oilers[253] of his own command, he took the anti-aircraft ship *Alynbank* and submarines *P615* and *P614*. Next morning, however, the Russian destroyers *Gremyashchi* and *Sokrushitelni* joined PQ 18 and early the following day two smaller Russian destroyers joined. They proved a useful reinforcement, especially the larger ships with their good long-range anti-aircraft armament,[254] for the convoy was again attacked whilst rounding Cape Kanin on 18th September. The first attack came at 0820, when 12 torpedo planes (He.111) approached from the starboard quarter, after a warning from the *Ulster Queen* that enemy aircraft were about. The Germans spread across the rear of the convoy in line abreast and flew in from astern, dropping torpedoes from 50 to 150 feet above the water at 3,000 to 4,000 yards range. The ships had 'a good chance' of avoiding the torpedoes, according to Commodore Boddam-Whetham, but No. 2 ship in the port wing column (the *Kentucky*), was hit. A similar attack took place an hour later, except that the enemy divided and attacked both sides of the convoy, one group dropping torpedoes at 4,000 yards, the other closing to 1,000 yards; and this time no ship was hit. Bombers (Ju.88) arrived with the first wave of torpedo aircraft and continued until 1030 to attack through the clouds at a height of some 2,500 feet. One bomb completed the destruction of the ship torpedoed in the first attack. The Germans lost four[255] aircraft, three by ships' gunfire and the fourth shot down by the Hurricane in SS *Empire Morn*, catapult-aircraft ship.[256] Commander Russell of the *Malcolm*, now senior officer of the escort, specially commended the services of the *Ulster Queen*, which manoeuvred astern of the convoy and seems to have accounted for two of the aircraft shot down.

The convoy reached the Dvina Bar in the evening of 19th September. Their troubles had not quite ended; for a dozen Ju.88 bombers attacked for about an hour the following afternoon, the 20th, as the ships were striving to find shelter from a full gale. Finally, two bombers attacked the *Ulster Queen* and three stranded merchantmen that she was guarding in the afternoon of the 21st, by which time the rest of the convoy had entered harbour. Luckily, no damage was done in these last attempts.

44

Convoy QP 14 went home unmolested from the air, except by shadowers, partly because at first the weather was thick and later because Rear-Admiral Burnett altered the route, steering up the west coast of Spitzbergen to increase the distance from Banak and Bardufoss. The convoy had sailed from Archangel on 13th September; 15 merchant ships under Commodore Dowding and two rescue ships, with an escort of two destroyers, the *Blankney* and *Middleton*, two A.A. ships, the *Palomares* and *Pozarica* and 11 corvettes, minesweepers and trawlers[257] under Captain Crombie of the *Bramble*.

Admiral Burnett joined early on the 17th in roughly 75° N., 48° E., one of the three groups of his force having been attacked unsuccessfully by a submarine the evening before. Compared with the outward passage, the next three days were uneventful. The *Avenger* kept anti-submarine patrols in the air whenever possible, though severe 'icing conditions' hindered their work on the 17th and 18th; and her Swordfish were also employed in searching for straggling merchantmen, two of which had parted company before the convoy met the Rear-Admiral. Shadowing aircraft appeared in the forenoon of the 18th, but lost touch in snow and thick weather in the afternoon. The first submarines appeared that evening, two being reported by a Catalina at 1700, a long way north-east of the convoy, while about the same time the patrolling Swordfish attacked another, which was shadowing the convoy from 20 miles astern, in about 76° N., 28° E. That evening, also, two destroyers were detached to Lowe Sound to bring out one of the oilers of Force 'P', as the two ships of Force 'Q' had exhausted their stock of fuel, having supplied 5,600 tons to ships of the escort since the operation began; the destroyers rejoined the following evening with the *Oligarch* and a destroyer belonging to the oilers' escort.[258]

The convoy rounded the South Cape, Spitzbergen, in the morning of the 19th and stretched along the coast north-westward. To prevent shadowing submarines from observing the change of route, Rear-Admiral Burnett arranged a special search by two aircraft and spread a distant screen of destroyers and minesweepers astern and on either quarter of the convoy an hour before altering course, the destroyers having orders to continue on the old course six miles past the turn to north-west and then to rejoin at high speed. Submarines were sighted by the Swordfish and forced to dive some seven, 20 and 12 miles from the convoy respectively between 0530 and 0800. No more was seen of the enemy that day, though an aircraft shadower arrived in time to watch the final alteration of course at 0820. On the other hand the return of a straggling merchant ship in the morning gave the Rear-Admiral an anxious moment at her first sighting. 'Our thoughts,' he wrote, 'again turned to the anchorage in Altenfjord.' The other straggler from the early days of the passage was found in the afternoon and taken by a destroyer to Bell Sound, whence they accompanied Force 'P' to British waters.

Then the luck changed, though not because of surface ships from Altenfjord. The German submarines had so far had only three successes to reward their persistency in following these two convoys. Now, between 20th and 22nd September, they sank two men-of-war, three merchant ships and a fleet oiler. The first ship lost was the minesweeper *Leda* (Commander A. H. Wynne-Edwards) stationed in the screen astern: she was torpedoed by *U-435* and sunk at 0520, the 20th, in about 76° 30' N., 5° E. By the end of the forenoon that day there appeared to be five submarines following the convoy and this gave opportunities for counter-attacks. At 1120 the Swordfish on patrol attacked one sighted 15 miles astern in about 76° 10' N., 2° 50' E.; two destroyers, on their way to assist in this attack, sighted and hunted two more without result. Then at 1230 the *Ashanti* attacked yet another which she had sighted first eight miles off on the bow of the convoy in roughly 76° N., 1° 30' E. Meanwhile, the two British submarines with the convoy being shortly due to part company to return to their base, the Rear-Admiral had detached them to patrol for a few hours in the path of the following enemy. *P614* unsuccessfully attacked *U-408* at 1520 in roughly 76° 20' N., 0° 30' E., having to make her attack by means of fleeting glimpses of the target through the periscope between snow squalls.

In the evening, however, the Germans gained further successes. They hit a merchant ship – the *Silver Sword*, one of the four survivors from PQ 17 – near the rear of the convoy at 1720 in about 75° 50' N., 0° 40' W. and she had to be sunk. Rear-Admiral Burnett then decided to send home the *Scylla* and *Avenger* independently (the danger of attack from the air was past), so the Admiral shifted his flag to the destroyer *Milne* and the two large ships parted company, the *Avenger* with three destroyers for escort. No sooner had they gone than the *Somali* (Lieut.-Commander C. D. Maud)[259] was hit. She was stationed abreast the convoy as port wing ship in the screen and was torpedoed by *U-703* at 1900 in roughly 75° 40' N., 2° W. But for the weather she might have been saved, for she made a great fight. The *Ashanti* took her in tow and provided electric power for her steering motors and submersible pump and they proceeded with three other destroyers and a trawler. Force 'P' appeared providentially on the 22nd, on its way home from Spitsbergen, which enabled the *Ashanti* to fill up with oil, of which she was running short. 'We presented,' wrote Captain Onslow of that ship, 'the somewhat unusual sight of three ships towing in line ahead while oiling was in progress.' Unluckily, the wind rose; and early on the 24th, when it had reached gale force, the *Somali* broke in two and sank after a tow of 420 miles in 80 hours.

To return to the convoy. A Catalina arrived in the morning of 21st September to give anti-submarine protection, but was lost a few hours later, while attacking a submarine that disabled the aircraft by gunfire before diving; the Catalina managed to keep going long enough to drop its depth charges when the submarine dived and then made a forced landing near the convoy. Soon afterwards, at 1115, in about 73° 50'N., 8° 20' W., the *Bramble* and *Worcester* prevented another attack on the convoy. Rear-Admiral Burnett in the *Milne* parted company early on the 22nd, leaving the convoy in charge of Captain Scott-Moncrieff of the *Faulknor*, who had now 11 destroyers and nine smaller ships for the screen. At 0630, an hour after the Rear-Admiral's departure, three ships were torpedoed and sunk by *U-435* within five minutes of each other – two merchantmen, the *Bellingham*, also a survivor of PQ 17 and the Commodore's ship the *Ocean Voice* and the oiler *Gray Ranger* of Force 'Q' – in position about 71° N., 11° W. Another submarine was sighted some miles away in the evening and attacked unsuccessfully by a destroyer. But that was the last event of the voyage. The destroyers parted company off Cape Wrath on the 26th to go to Scapa. Convoy QP 14 arrived in Loch Ewe the same day.

45

Rear-Admiral Burnett found it difficult to assess how far the measures adopted for the protection of convoys PQ 18 and QP 14 had contributed to the solution of this thorny problem. 'I do not know,' he wrote:–

'how far this operation may be considered to have been a success or failure, but I am convinced that had any of six circumstances been otherwise it must have been a tragic failure.

(a) Weather. Had the weather been bad the continual oiling could not have progressed and the supporting force would have had to withdraw ...

(b) Oilers. Had one or both of the oilers been torpedoed in the first attack, the supporting force would have had to withdraw or the convoy turned back.

(c) Had there been the least delay in getting into Bell Sound or had it been necessary to oil from Force 'P' at sea, the supporting force would not have been present during the most critical period and the losses in the first heavy torpedo bombing attack would have been immensely greater.

(d) Had surface and air attack been synchronised the convoy losses would have been very heavy.

(e) Had there been further torpedo bombing attacks, the ammunition shortage would have been serious and left the covering force with little to protect QP 14 on the return journey.

(f) Had we lost the '*Rangers*' at the far end we would have had to expose QP 14 to great danger by reducing the screen while we visited Bell Sound to oil on the return journey.'[260]

The Commander-in-Chief, Home Fleet, did not agree that weather too bad for oiling at sea or the loss of one of the convoy oilers would necessarily have entailed the return of PQ 18, provided it was still possible to fuel at Bell Sound; but it might have been necessary to cancel the sailing of QP 14.

Turning to enemy action, as mentioned previously the German Air Force made special efforts against PQ 18; during the three critical days, 13th to 15th September, the convoy had to endure rather more than 100 attacks by torpedo aircraft and rather under 100 by bombers and at the end of the voyage, when its escort had been reduced, 24 torpedo aircraft and an unrecorded number of bombers – on the direct orders of Reichs-Marschal Goering – continued the attack. In all they sank ten ships with torpedoes (for the one ship hit by a bomb was disabled already) and eight of them in the massed attack on the first day. This was a disappointment to them:–

'it was found that not only was it impossible to approach the aircraft carrier to launch an effective attack – on account of the fighters – but that a wide screen of warships made the launching of torpedoes against the inner merchant vessels an extremely hazardous undertaking. German aircraft losses were heavy ...'[261]

The whole operation cost the German Air Force 33 torpedo aircraft, six dive bombers and two long-range reconnaissance aircraft – a total loss of 41 aircraft. This was higher than the contemporary British analysis put it (37 – six by fighters and the remainder by ships' gunfire) and very much higher than had happened before. Exclusive of those shot down by fighters, this was ascribed to the better gunnery equipment of the fleet destroyers as compared with the ocean escort destroyers, improved control methods including intelligent use of radar and better close-range A.A. defences of merchant ships.[262]

As regards U-boat attack, the Commander-in-Chief, Home Fleet, remarked that:–

> 'the comparatively heavy losses they inflicted towards the end of the period were disappointing; but the surprising feature was their failure to achieve more in the earlier stages.'[263]

During the passage of these two convoys, their escorting ships and aircraft made 39 attacks on enemy submarines. Three U-boats were destroyed and five damaged,[264] against the loss of nine ships and a Catalina aircraft. A feature of the operations was the work done by the *Avenger's* three Swordfish aircraft, which had 16 sightings to their credit, including six attacks and the sinking of *U-589* by the *Onslow* owed much to prompt reporting by a Swordfish. Commander Russell of the *Malcolm* thought that the Germans tried to combine the work of submarines and aircraft, on 13th September, for instance, when he sighted a periscope during the big air-torpedo attack and on the 15th when the *Opportune* attacked two submarines on the horizon, while bombers were attacking Convoy PQ 18; but this was not the case, except as regards exchange of reconnaissance intelligence and there was some recrimination from U-boats which had been narrowly missed by the Luftwaffe attacks.

An aspect which must be borne in mind, common to all the Arctic convoys but especially when the operations were so prolonged as those under consideration, was the immense physical strain to which all taking part were subjected. All came through the ordeal triumphantly; the merchant ships though lacking speed and manoeuvrability to counter the vicious air and submarine attacks to which they were exposed for days on end and many of them carrying tons of high explosive;[265] the Royal Fleet Auxiliaries, with their arduous and continuous oiling duties; the submarines in their respective spheres and the aircraft crews of Coastal Command, whose work, especially of long distance and PRU reconnaissance, was 'invaluable', despite difficult weather conditions. The performance of the *Avenger* and the efforts to bring the damaged *Somali* back to harbour were specially singled out by the Commander-in-Chief for praise. But for sheer sustained effort the palm must go to the destroyers. 'For 18 days there was no let up,' to quote Rear-Admiral Burnett:–

'when there was no air attack in progress there were countless A/S hunts, counter attacks and investigations, continuous zig-zagging in formation, moving positions on a large screen to fill gaps of others away chasing contacts and, during lulls, topping up with oil or running alongside to take on or transfer survivors.'

The attacks on Convoys PQ 18 and QP 14 represented the high water mark of the German effort against the convoys to North Russia. Before the next pair sailed events in North Africa had compelled the German Air Force to transfer all the Ju.88 and He.111 torpedo forces from Norway to the Mediterranean, leaving only some dive bombers and the long range reconnaissance force, whose sole function was to report convoys for attack by U-boats and surface craft and the Naval He.115 torpedo-carrying seaplanes, whose slow speed restricted them to attacks on occasional stragglers.

46

For three months after Convoys PQ 18 and QP 14, the convoy traffic was interrupted. This was due to the demands on the resources of the Home Fleet in connection with the Allied landing in North Africa in November 1942. During this period no convoys sailed to North Russia, but at the end of October and beginning of November certain ships sailed independently between Iceland and Russia, 'taking advantage of the long nights and the passage north of Bear Island.'[266] The protection of these ships consisted of some trawlers spaced along the route for life saving and two submarines patrolling north of Bear Island (Operation 'FB').

In the latter part of November the light and ice conditions were more favourable than at any other time of the year; moreover the reduction of the German air forces warranted a corresponding reduction in the convoy escorts. It was therefore decided to run a westbound convoy, QP 15, from the White Sea. As the passage would be made in almost continual darkness and foul weather could be expected, the Commander-in-Chief, Home Fleet, wished to limit the convoy to 20 ships, but the Admiralty decided that 30 ships must be included.

Convoy QP 15 under Commodore W. C. Meeks sailed from Archangel on 17th November; one ship grounded and another failed to sail;[267] 28 ships put to sea. The escort consisted of five minesweepers,[268] four corvettes,[269] a trawler and the A.A. ship *Ulster Queen* and was to be reinforced in the Barents Sea by five destroyers, the *Faulknor, Echo,*

Impulsive, Intrepid and *Icarus*, under the command of Captain A. K. Scott-Moncrieff, which were to be relieved later by five others, the *Musketeer, Oakley, Orwell, Middleton, Ledbury*. Rear-Admiral Hamilton in the *London*, with the *Suffolk* and three destroyers, *Forester, Onslaught* and *Obdurate*, provided surface cover west of Bear Island. Four submarines, *Uredd, Junon, P312* and *P216*, operated off the exits to Altenfjord to discourage the *Hipper* and *Köln* from sailing.

The convoy met a succession of gales throughout its passage. These, with the almost complete lack of daylight caused it to become very scattered. Neither of the two destroyer forces succeeded in making contact with the main body; and by the time the convoy had reached Bear Island, it and its escort had broken up into a number of small groups, spread over a large area and without knowledge of each other's whereabouts. The route was adjusted to pass south of Bear Island to avoid the normal U-boat concentration between there and Spitzbergen, but many ships did not receive the signal. Fortunately after 18th November, when the convoy was sighted clearing the White Sea, the weather was entirely unsuitable for air reconnaissance and the enemy could get no clear picture of the situation.[270] In due course, all the merchant ships except two,[271] which were sunk by U-boats, arrived in Icelandic waters and were rounded up and taken straight on in two convoys to Loch Ewe.

This was the last of the well known series of PQ-QP convoys, as shortly afterwards for security reasons the titles of the convoys were changed to JW and RA respectively, both starting with the number 51.

Chapter VI

Convoys JW 51A, JW 51B–53, RA 51–53:
December 1942–February 1943
(AU times are Zone minus 1.)

47

The regular convoy system started again in mid-December 1942. Very different were the conditions from those under which Convoy PQ 8 had made its costly passage, both as regards the world-wide outlook and the particular problems of the convoys. For the three months which had elapsed had witnessed a dramatic change in the fortunes of the war. The Battle of El Alamein had finished the Axis hopes in the Middle East and their desert forces had been driven nearly 1,000 miles from the Egyptian frontier. To the west, General Eisenhower's Anglo-American forces controlled Morocco and Algeria and were moving on eastern Tunisia, the last enemy foothold in Africa. The Russian winter offensive – shortly to culminate in the elimination of some 330,000 men under Field-Marshal von Paulus at Stalingrad – was well under way. In the distant Pacific, the Japanese had been decisively defeated at Guadalcanal and the Americans had their feet firmly on the first rung of the ladder that led to Tokyo. Though a long road yet remained to be trodden, the prospects of the Axis in December 1942 seemed as gloomy as had those of the Allies the previous April. Only in the Atlantic was the issue still in doubt. There the U-boats and Luftwaffe continued to take a terrible toll of merchant shipping – though even there the peak had been reached and the Allied losses were very slowly but steadily diminishing, while those of the U-boats were markedly increasing.

Changed, too, were the conditions for the Arctic convoys. No longer did long hours of daylight invite constant air shadowing and attack. As in the previous winter the well-nigh perpetual darkness in itself afforded a large measure of protection. But this year a far larger number of U-boats and the German surface forces[272] based in Northern Norway were a very serious menace; and the Admiralty proposed to send out a convoy of 30 ships with 'an escort of summer dimensions.' This, however, was changed to two smaller convoys sailing a week apart, at the request of Admiral Tovey, who stated his views as follows:–

'From late November to mid-January the lack of daylight is such that air reconnaissance in the Arctic is virtually impossible. Provided that a convoy is of such a size that it can be handled and kept together, it therefore stands an excellent chance of evading both U-boat and surface attack and even of completing the passage without the enemy's knowing of its existence. A large convoy, on the other hand, is likely to fail to keep company and to split (as did QP 15) into a large number of small groups, covering a vast area and unaware of each other's position or composition. Such small groups would be more liable to detection by U-boats than a single concentrated convoy and would present the enemy surface forces with an ideal opportunity for an offensive sweep. Our own covering forces are always handicapped by having to identify a contact before they are free to attack; the enemy need not do so. The splitting of the convoy into a large number of scattered units would greatly add to this handicap.'[273]

Even as it was, with a convoy of 14 ships only, this handicap made itself felt. On 31st December, when the *Hipper* and *Lützow* attacked Convoy JW 51B in the Barents Sea, the 'covering' British cruisers were delayed in coming into action by having to identify a radar contact, which turned out afterwards to be stragglers from the convoy.

48
Convoys JW 51A and JW 51B sailed from Loch Ewe on 15th and 22nd December respectively. Each had a permanent escort of six or seven destroyers and some smaller vessels, the destroyers joining north-east of Iceland after filling up with fuel at Seidisfjord. Convoy RA 51 sailed from Murmansk on the 30th, with a similar escort, its destroyers being those that had brought out JW 51A; and it passed JW 51B in the eastern part of the Barents Sea on 1st January 1943. Besides their close escorts, the convoys had more distant protection by two cruisers and for part of the time two destroyers, under Rear-Admiral Burnett (Force 'R') which kept between the convoys and the coast of Norway. Owing to the danger of submarine attack, Admiral Tovey wished the cruisers to go no farther than 25° E., roughly the meridian of the North Cape, as the orders to

Rear-Admiral Hamilton had prescribed in July. 'The large number of U-boats,' said Admiral Tovey:–

> 'which usually surround and accompany these 7-knot convoys are a serious menace to covering cruisers so far from their base. The experience of the past year and especially the loss of the *Edinburgh*, had underlined this risk.'

The First Sea Lord, however, insisted on their going well to the eastward in the Barents Sea, as had Rear-Admiral Burnett's destroyer force in September; and this insistence was justified, as Admiral Tovey remarked afterwards, 'for otherwise the cruiser force would probably not have been present at the action on New Year's Eve.'[274]

As usual, since the coming of German surface ships to northern waters, British capital ships put to sea to support the convoys during their passage between Jan Mayen Island and Bear Island. The Home Fleet was still without an aircraft carrier; but a battleship, a cruiser and three destroyers patrolled a line some 300 to 400 miles north-westward of Altenfjord, then the base of the German heavy ships, on 21st and 22nd December and another force of the same strength repeated the patrol on the 28th and 29th. This was in support of the east-bound convoys. When RA 51 arrived west of Bear Island on 3rd January, two battleships and a cruiser with a screen of destroyers were patrolling as before, while two more cruisers worked further east, in effect replacing Rear-Admiral Burnett's force; the latter, being short of fuel, had stretched ahead of the convoy and was going to Seidisfjord to oil. Apart from surface protection, Allied submarines were stationed four at a time off the coast of Norway between Altenfjord and the North Cape.

49

Little need be said of Convoy JW 51A, which had fine weather and a completely uneventful passage. It consisted of 15 merchant ships and a fleet oiler under Rear-Admiral C. E. Turle (Ret.), as Commodore, escorted by seven destroyers, the *Faulknor* (Captain Scott-Moncrieff, SO), *Echo*, *Inglefield* and *Fury*, *Eclipse*, *Beagle* and *Boadicea*, two corvettes, a minesweeper and two trawlers. Commodore Turle introduced a useful variation in the normal cruising order; instead of leading one of the middle columns in the formation, as had been the usual practice, he took up a station ahead of the centre of the convoy, whence his signals could be seen at once by all the leaders of columns.

Convoy JW 51A sailed from Loch Ewe on 15th December. It was not sighted at all by the Germans and, passing south of Bear Island, arrived off Kola Inlet on Christmas day; there it divided, some ships going into harbour the same morning, the rest going on to Molotovsk in the Dvina River, where they arrived two days later.

Distant cover west of longitude 15° E. was provided by the *King George V* wearing the flag of the Commander-in-Chief, Home Fleet, the *Berwick* and three destroyers. Until the convoy passed Bear Island on 22nd December, Rear-Admiral Burnett in the *Sheffield*, with the *Jamaica, Opportune* and *Matchless* (Force 'R') cruised to the westward in the same general area as the battlefleet; then he accompanied the convoy to the eastward, sending his two destroyers to join the close escort and complete with fuel,[275] while the cruisers kept some 60 miles south of the convoy route. He arrived at Vaenga in Kola Inlet 24th December, a day ahead of the convoy.

50

Convoy JW 51B (Commodore, Captain R. A. Melhuish RIN) sailed from Loch Ewe on 22nd December (Plan 14). It numbered 14 merchant ships, with six destroyers, the *Onslow* (Captain R. St. V. Sherbrooke SO), *Oribi, Obedient, Orwell, Obdurate* and *Achates*, two corvettes, the *Rhododendron* and *Hyderabad*, the minesweeper *Bramble* and two trawlers, the *Vizalma* and *Northern Gem*, as close escort; and it followed the same route as the previous convoy.

Its passage at first was equally uneventful, except that a German aircraft probably reported it on the 24th, the day before the destroyers joined. During the night of the 28th-29th, however, the *Oribi*, the *Vizalma* and five merchant ships parted company in a strong gale and in thick weather half way between Jan Mayen Island and Bear Island; and the *Bramble* was detached the following afternoon to look for the missing merchantmen. The *Oribi* eventually reached Kola alone on the 31st after vainly searching for the convoy. Three of the merchant ships joined again independently on the 30th, the *Vizalma* returned with a fourth on 1st January and the last arrived at Kola on 5th January, two days after the main body. The *Bramble* – still separated from her consorts – was sunk by the enemy on 31st December.

Meanwhile Admiral Burnett had sailed from Kola with Force 'R' on the 27th to support the convoy, going as far west as 11° E. and overlapping the battlefleet's patrol line, before he turned back on the 29th, when the two destroyers of his force left him to go home. The cruisers kept well south of the convoy route as they went east again; and on reaching the meridian of Kola on the 30th, they turned north-west to cross the route early next day, the Rear-Admiral intending then to steer a parallel course a few miles north of the route and to cover the convoy from 40 to 50 miles astern.[276] This was the direction from which an attack was most likely to develop. Though the Germans were well aware of the approximate convoy route, they had no means of knowing how far along it the convoy would be[277] (apart from an occasional air or U-boat report).[278] In these circumstances – especially remembering the short visibility and Arctic dusk – a sweep along the route from ahead or astern was clearly indicated and in view of the position of Altenfjord the odds were heavily in favour of the sweep starting from astern.

Admiral Burnett seems to have thought that 31st December would be the critical day of the passage, for his objects in going north (after keeping south of the route hitherto) were to gain 'the advantage of light over any enemy that might appear' and to 'avoid air reconnaissance which would lead the aircraft on to the convoy.'[279] Against these factors had to be balanced the disadvantage of a position from which it would not be so easy to cut the enemy off from his base as from one further to the southward. This objection was more apparent than real; the position chosen was on the flank of the return route to Altenfjord and only a small alteration of course and high speed would be required to take the cruisers to an attack from any quarter.

The plan, however, was vitiated by the convoy being further to the south and much further to the west than Admiral Burnett supposed it to be,[280] with the result that instead of crossing the route behind it, as he had intended and shadowing from astern, he crossed ahead and was actually nearly 30 miles due north of it at 0830, 31st December. This ignorance of the relative position of the convoy exercised great influence on the Admiral's decisions throughout the action that ensued.[281]

Up to that morning, the 31st, there had been little sign that the Germans knew of the convoy's progress since the 24th; a merchant ship had intercepted what was possibly a submarine's homing signal in the night of the 27th and a destroyer sighted what was perhaps a submarine, which might have reported the convoy, in the night of the 30th, but that was all.

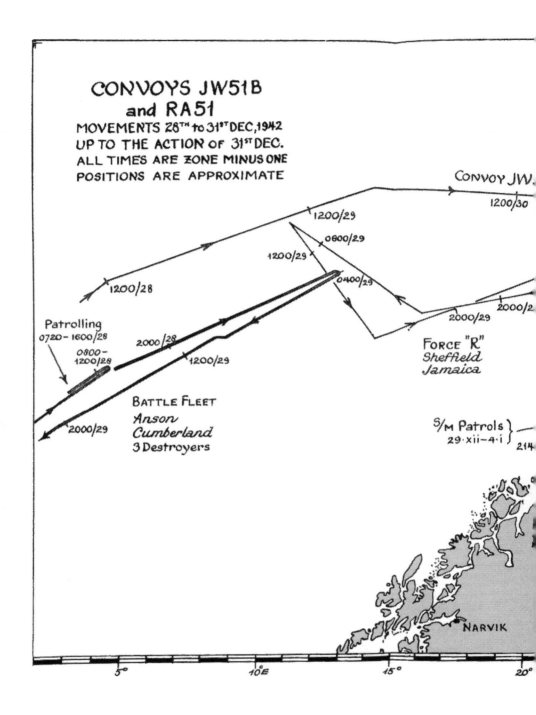

CONVOYS JW51B and RA51

MOVEMENTS 28ᵀᴴ to 31ˢᵀ DEC, 1942
UP TO THE ACTION of 31ˢᵀ DEC.
ALL TIMES ARE ZONE MINUS ONE
POSITIONS ARE APPROXIMATE

CONVOY JW.
1200/30

1200/29
0800/29
1200/29
0400/29
2000/2
2000/29
1200/28
2000/2

Patrolling
0720 - 1600/28

0800 -
1200/28
2000/28
1200/29

FORCE "R"
Sheffield
Jamaica

BATTLE FLEET
Anson
Cumberland
3 Destroyers

2000/29

S/M Patrols
29·xii–4·i
214

NARVIK

5°   10°E   15°   20°

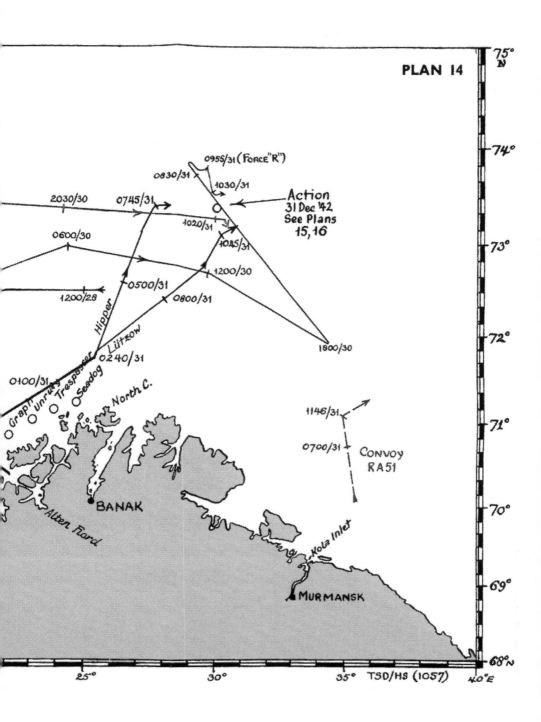

PLAN 14

0955/31 (Force "R")

0830/31

1030/31

Action
31 Dec '42
See Plans
15, 16

2030/30   0745/31

1020/31

0600/30

1045/31

1200/30

1200/28   0500/31

0800/31

Hipper

Lützow

1800/30

0240/31

0100/31

Graph
Unruh
Trespasser
Seadog

North C.

1146/31

0700/31   Convoy
RA 51

BANAK

Alten Fiord

Kola Inlet

MURMANSK

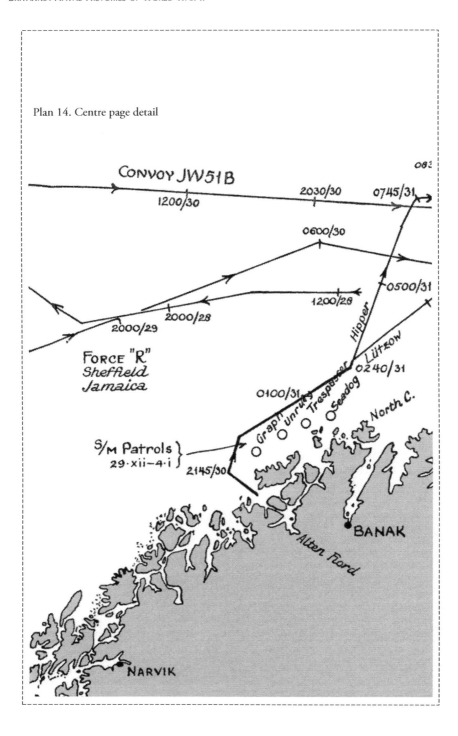

Plan 14. Centre page detail

CONVOY JW51B
1200/30
2030/30
0745/31
083

0600/30
0500/31

1200/28
2000/29
2000/28

FORCE "R"
Sheffield
Jamaica

Hipper
Lützow

0100/31
0240/31

Graph
Unruly
Trespasser
Seadog
North C.

S/M Patrols }
29·xii—4·i }
2145/30

BANAK

Alten Fiord

NARVIK

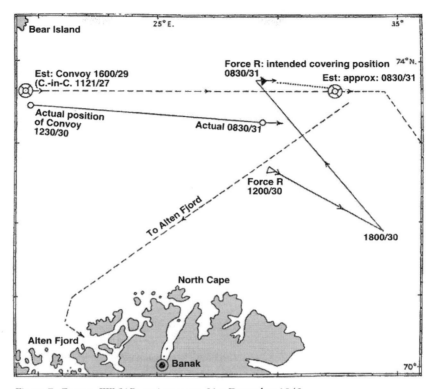

Figure 7. Convoy JW 51B; cruiser cover, 31st December 1942.

51

Actually, the convoy had been sighted south of Bear Island by a U-boat which reported it as 'weakly protected' at noon, 30th December and the squadron at Altenfjord, consisting of the *Hipper*, wearing the flag of Vice-Admiral Kummetz, the *Lützow* and six destroyers lost no time in putting to sea and steered for a position on the convoy route in the Barents Sea some 200 miles from Bear Island (Plan 14). Admiral Kummetz was not aware of the presence of Admiral Burnett's cruisers in the vicinity of the convoy, but he was hampered by orders from the Naval Staff not to risk his heavy ships and to avoid action with equal (or superior) enemy forces. Night attack was ruled out, as presenting too favourable an opportunity for the escort's torpedoes, so his actual attacks would be limited to about 2 ½ hours feeble daylight in the forenoon of the 31st.[282] Apart from the cramping effect of these restrictions, the German plan suffered from another serious defect. The *Lützow*, after the operations against Convoy JW 51B was to proceed to the Atlantic for commerce raiding. The plan

347

thus embraced two separate and unrelated aims. This split object, in addition to the overall orders to avoid risks, probably account for the singularly timid handling of the *Lützow* in the subsequent operations.

Admiral Kummetz decided to approach from astern of the convoy thereby obtaining advantage of light and to attack it from both sides, anticipating that the escort would be drawn off towards the first contact and that the convoy would turn away from it, thereby falling an easy prey to the other force. To give effect to this plan he divided his squadron into two forces, the *Hipper, Friedrich Eckholdt, Richard Beitzen* and *Z29* to attack from the north-west and the *Lützow, Z30, Z31* and *Theodor Riedel* to operate from the southward. During the night the *Lützow* was detached with orders to be 75 miles 180° from the *Hipper* (which would be in position 73° 40' N., 28° E.) at 0800, when a sweep to the eastward with the destroyers spread 15 miles apart on a line 15 miles ahead of the heavy ships would be ordered.

Admiral Kummetz has been criticised for adopting a plan which split his force and introduced complications such as timing difficulties, identification of own forces in the Arctic dusk and squalls, etc., but it is worth noting that his tactical dispositions did in fact work out exactly as he intended. The *Lützow* and her destroyers passed two or three miles south of the convoy while practically all its escorts were attending to the *Hipper* in the north and but for the extreme caution of Captain Strange of the *Lützow* there seems no reason why he should not have virtually annihilated the convoy.

52

To return to Convoy JW 51B, the situation at 0830 that New Year's Eve was thus approximately as follows. The convoy, temporarily reduced to 12 ships, with five destroyers, two corvettes and a trawler still in company, was on an easterly course in 73° 15' N., 29° E. (about 220 miles north-west of Kola Inlet). Some 45 miles to the northward was the trawler *Vizalma*, with one merchant ship in company and about 15 miles to the north-eastward was the *Bramble* (Commander H. T. Rust). Rear-Admiral Burnett in the *Sheffield* (Captain A. W. Clarke) with the *Jamaica* (Captain J. L. Storey) was about 30 miles north of the convoy and 15 miles south of the *Vizalma*. None of these four groups knew each other's relative positions and there was also one other straggler somewhere in the neighbourhood. Quite unknown to the British, for there had been no further sign that the enemy knew of their progress, still less that he was at sea in force, the *Hipper* had just crossed the wake of the convoy and was then within 20 miles to the north-westward, while the *Lützow*, still some 50 miles off, was closing in from the southward (Plans 15 and 16).

The weather was generally clear, the twilight visibility being about seven miles to the northward and ten miles to the southward, but at intervals much reduced by snow squalls; the sky was mostly covered with low cloud; the wind W.N.W., force 3, the sea slight, with no swell. There were 16 degrees of frost and there was ice on all the ships.

At 0830 the *Obdurate* (Lieut.-Commander C. E. D. Sclater) on the starboard beam on the convoy reported two destroyers to the south-west. Actually, they had been sighted ten minutes previously by the *Hyderabad* (on the starboard quarter of the convoy) but she had taken them for Russians coming to reinforce the escort and made no report. Captain Sherbrooke sent the *Obdurate* to investigate; they were steaming slowly to the northward across the wake of the convoy. A third destroyer soon came into sight. These were the *Eckholdt, Beitzen* and *Z29* gradually opening from the *Hipper* in anticipation of the order to turn and sweep to the eastward; they altered course away from the *Obdurate* to the north-west. At 0930 – an hour after she had first sighted them – the *Obdurate* had closed to 8,000 yards and they then opened fire on her, so she turned away and steered to rejoin the convoy. The enemy made no attempt to follow and disappeared to the north-westward. This was the beginning of a series of disconnected skirmishes fought in the gloom of the Arctic twilight, in which smoke screens and snowstorms made it often impossible for ships of either side to identify their opponents with certainty, or indeed even to be sure of their numbers.

Captain Sherbrooke had already turned the *Onslow* towards the gun flashes and he signalled to the *Orwell* (Lieut.-Commander N. H. G. Austen), *Obedient* (Lieut.-Commander D. C. Kinloch) and *Obdurate* to join him, leaving the convoy to the *Achates* (Lieut.-Commander A. H. T. Johns) and the three smaller ships of war, which moved out to lay a smoke screen between the enemy and the merchant ships in accordance with the operation orders.

A more formidable opponent, however, diverted Captain Sherbrooke's attention from the three destroyers. At 0939, he sighted a large ship eight miles to the north-westward, a little on his starboard bow, standing towards him; he had only the *Orwell* with the *Onslow*, for the *Obedient* had to come from the far side of the convoy. At 0941, the big German turned away to port to open fire on the *Achates*, then showing clearly to windward of her smoke and thus disclosed herself to be the *Hipper*, as her four symmetrically-placed gun turrets proved. The *Onslow*

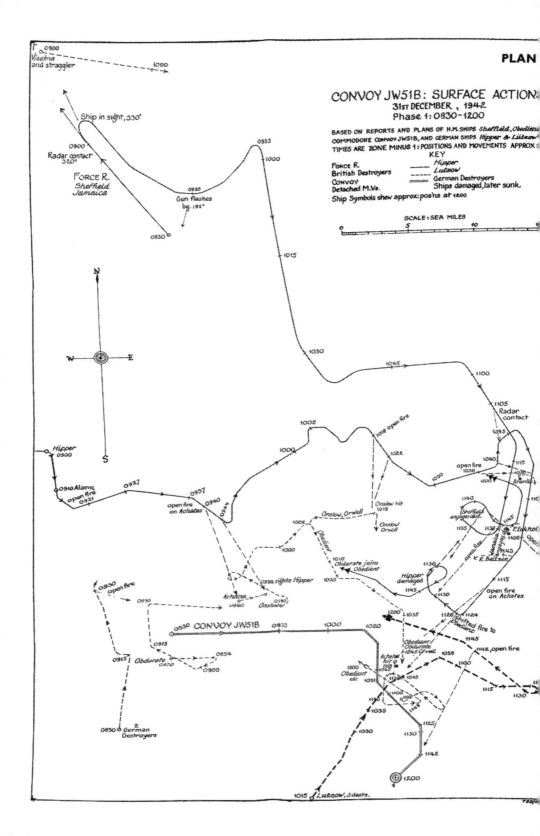

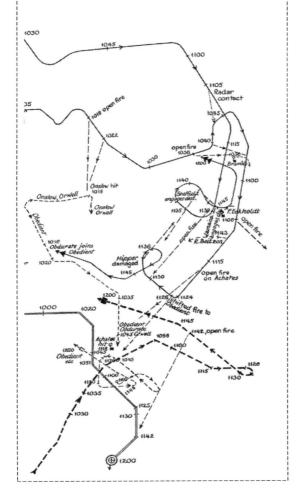

Plan 15. Centre page detail

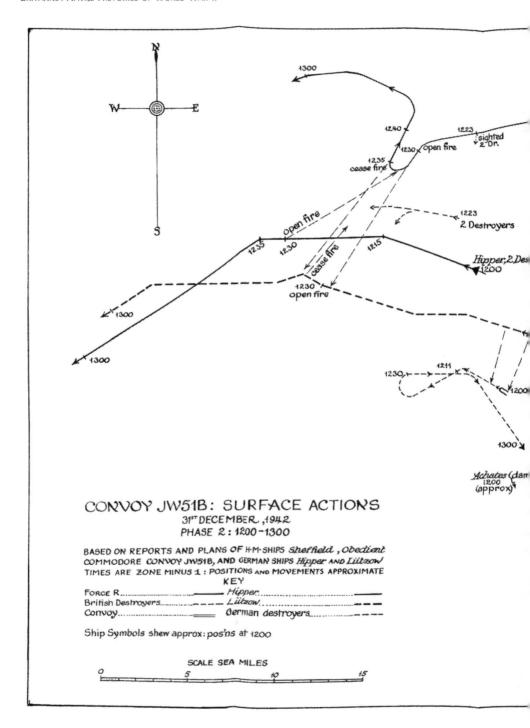

1300

N

W — E

S

1300

1240

1223
sighted
2 Dr.

1230 open fire

1235
cease fire

open fire

1235   1230

1223
2 Destroyers

1245

Hipper, 2 Des
1200

cease fire

1230
open fire

1300

1300

1230   1211

1200

1300

Achates (dam
1200
(approx)

CONVOY JW51B: SURFACE ACTIONS
31ST DECEMBER, 1942
PHASE 2: 1200-1300

BASED ON REPORTS AND PLANS OF H·M·SHIPS *Sheffield*, *Obedient*
COMMODORE CONVOY JW51B, AND GERMAN SHIPS *Hipper* AND *Lützow*
TIMES ARE ZONE MINUS 1: POSITIONS AND MOVEMENTS APPROXIMATE

KEY

Force R .... ——————— *Hipper* .... ———————
British Destroyers .... — — — — *Lützow* .... —— — ——
Convoy .... ════════ German destroyers ...... – – – – –

Ship Symbols shew approx: pos'ns at 1200

SCALE SEA MILES

0   5   10   15

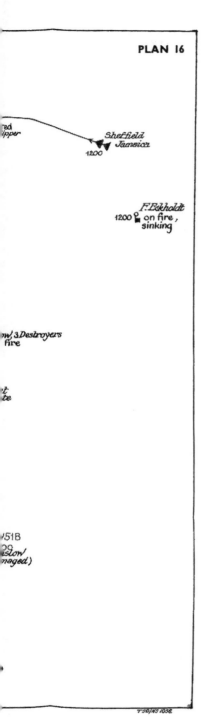

PLAN 16

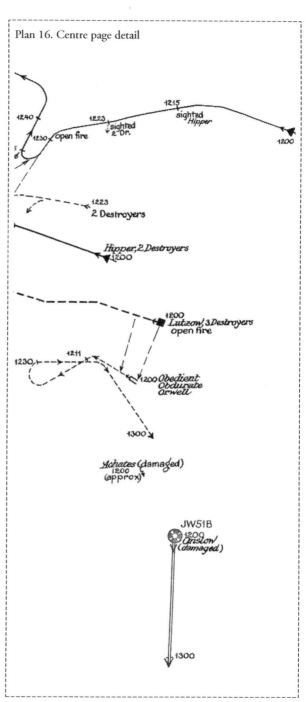

Plan 16. Centre page detail

T.SB/NS 1058.

and *Orwell* returned the fire, at a range of some 11,000 yards and followed round to a similar course. Captain Sherbrooke soon formed the opinion that the enemy was unwilling to face the risk of torpedo attack by the destroyers and made good use of the fact. For half an hour they skirmished fitfully, the British ships firing by radar, the *Hipper* sometimes hiding in smoke, sometimes firing towards the convoy and all the time edging to the north-east. Meanwhile, the convoy had turned from east to south-east at 0945,[283] and was going off at nearly nine knots, screened by smoke from the *Achates, Rhododendron* and *Northern Gem.* By 0955, the *Obedient* had joined Captain Sherbrooke and the *Obdurate* was in sight returning from the south-west. He ordered these two ships to join the convoy, anxious lest it should be attacked by the three German destroyers, which he had never seen himself and whose movements he could not trace. Actually they had been ordered to join the *Hipper* at 0933 (just after opening fire on the *Obdurate*). The *Obedient* steered away to the southward at 1008 and signalled to the *Obdurate* to join her, turning eastward later to lay a smoke screen across the wake of the convoy before joining it. A signal from the *Sheffield* that she was approaching on course 170° had been received 'with acclamation' a few minutes previously.[284]

At the same time as the *Obedient* turned south the *Hipper* hauled right up to the northward out of action and it was thought that she had received three hits.[285] Her firing had been 'aimless and erratic,' and whenever the range came within 11,000 yards she had turned away. This was partly in pursuance of the plan to lure the escort away to the northward and so leave the field clear for the *Lützow* and partly because Admiral Kummetz could form no clear picture of the situation owing to the smoke and poor visibility.

But a few minutes later she 'suddenly pulled herself together'[286] and turned back to fight the two remaining destroyers. After a few inaccurate salvos, she found the *Onslow*'s range and at 1020 scored four hits in rapid succession, inflicting considerable damage. A and B guns were put out of action, the fore superstructure and mess deck were set on fire, the main aerials and both radar sets were destroyed, the engine room holed and Captain Sherbrooke was severely wounded in the face, so that he could not see. Despite his wounds he continued to direct the flotilla and his ship until a further hit compelled him to disengage the *Onslow;* only then, after receiving reports as to her condition and assuring himself that the order to Lieut.-Commander Kinloch[287] of the *Obedient* to take

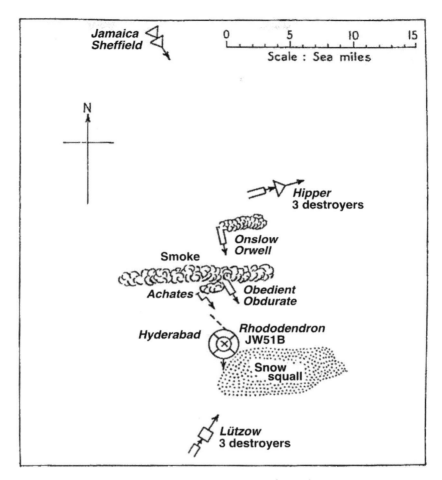

Figure 8. Convoy JW 51B: situation 1030, 31st December 1942.

charge of the destroyers was being acted on, didn't leave the bridge.[288] By the time Commander Kinloch learnt that he was in command (1035), a snowstorm had reduced the visibility to about two miles and the *Hipper* had disappeared. This was the end of the first action.[289]

By this time Rear-Admiral Burnett with the *Sheffield* and *Jamaica* was coming into the picture. Unfortunately he had been delayed from steering for the gunfire as early as he might have done by a radar contact picked up at 0858 of a ship some 15,000 yards ahead while he was still steering to the north-west. As the plot developed, at 0905 the stranger seemed to be going east at 25 knots, though it subsequently appeared that her speed had been greatly over estimated. Just before this 'a ship was dimly in sight' for a moment on the correct bearing and Rear-Admiral Burnett 'hauled away to the south-east and then closed' – at 0930 – 'in order to track and establish touch.'[290] It was, in fact, a merchant ship which had parted company from the convoy early on the 29th, with the trawler *Vizalma*; they were shortly to see the two British cruisers stretching away to the southward ten miles on their starboard bow, without knowing whether they were friend or foe. Two minutes later, at 0932, gun flashes were seen over the southern horizon and were taken for anti-aircraft fire. It must have been the skirmish between the *Obdurate* and the German destroyers that opened the day's fighting.

Rear-Admiral Burnett was in a perplexing position. He had no idea of the actual position of the convoy, whose safety was his prime objective and which he supposed to be well to the eastward of him. Past experience had taught him that stragglers were to be expected after the heavy gales; the brief exchange of gunfire seen at 0932 had soon died down and might well have come from one or a detached escort vessel. On the whole it seemed likely that the convoy was somewhere ahead of the *Vizalma* and her straggler (as to whose identity he was still uncertain) and with this in mind he continued to track them by radar steering to the east and north-east.

Then, at 0946,[291] 'heavy gunfire was observed to the southward and very shortly afterwards an enemy report of three destroyers was received'[292] from Captain Sherbrooke. Though by then suspecting that the convoy was considerably further south than anticipated, the Rear-Admiral held on for some minutes and it was not until 0955 that he altered course and increasing to 25 knots 'steamed towards the sight of the guns.'[293]

Knowing what we do now, it is clear that the cruisers could have intervened in the action earlier, had Admiral Burnett at once applied the two fundamental principles of British fighting policy, viz. 'when in doubt, steer for the sound of the guns' and 'the unfailing support given in battle by one British unit to another;'[294] on the other hand the 'safe and timely arrival' of the still unlocated convoy was his object,[295] and human reactions are known to be slow when subjected to the rigours of the bitter Arctic climate.

As the cruisers ran south they worked up to 31 knots and they could see through the smoke the later stages of the destroyers' first fight with the *Hipper*, though they could not distinguish the ships engaged. At about 1030, they had radar contacts of ships bearing 180° and 140°, at ranges of about 24,000 and 30,000 yards respectively, both ships apparently standing to the eastward at high speed. 'As the situation was not yet clear' Rear-Admiral Burnett turned eastward himself at 1035. A minute later there was a burst of firing on his starboard bow;[296] he continued to the eastward to close this, while taking care to preserve the light in his favour. At 1045 the nearer and western ship of the two radar contacts came in sight for a moment; she was 'larger than a destroyer, therefore necessarily an enemy,' but that was all that could be said of her.[297] The ships of the other contact, further east, altered course to the southward at 1054 and at 1055 the British cruisers turned to the southward in chase.

Ten minutes later they had a contact a little on the starboard bow at 19,000 yards and this was the ship they subsequently engaged. At 1112 she was seen to be firing to the eastward. Rear-Admiral Burnett then altered course towards her.

To return to the convoy.

The situation that Commander Kinloch had to cope with on taking over command of the escort at 1035 was by no means clear. The convoy, by this time steering 180°, was some three miles to the southward of the *Obedient* and *Obdurate*, which were closing it. The *Orwell*, somewhat to the north-east, was steering to join them. The *Achates* a little to the westward was continuing to lay smoke and the damaged *Onslow* was taking station ahead of the convoy from whence she could home Force 'R'. Just about this time, the *Rhododendron* from the port quarter of the convoy reported smoke to the southwest, followed ten minutes later by a report of a large vessel bearing 160° only two miles off, steering to the north-east. These reports necessarily engaged the attention of Commander Kinloch, but he did not accept them for want of corroboration by ships nearer the strangers and continued to follow the convoy to the southward, keeping between it and the direction in which the *Hipper* had disappeared. For some reason the *Hyderabad*, stationed on the starboard side of the convoy, which just previously had seen two destroyers and a large ship cross ahead from west to east, made no report. This was the *Lützow*'s force, but providentially a heavy snow-squall just then partially blotted out the convoy and her Captain, though aware of its presence, considered it too risky to attack and decided to stand off to the eastward until the weather should clear.

Meanwhile the *Hipper*, after disabling the *Onslow* had stood on to the E.N.E. at 31 knots. At 1036 she fell in with the *Bramble*, which no doubt had altered course towards the gunfire of the previous engagements and damaged her with a few salvos at short range.[298] At 1047 she altered course to the southward, detaching the *Friedrich Eckholdt* a few minutes later to finish off the *Bramble*.

Commander Kinloch with his three destroyers continued to the southward, gradually overhauling the convoy and passing down its port side. His last news of the *Hipper* had been a report from the *Orwell* placing her 038° eight miles from her at 1040. The weather cleared somewhat at about 1100 and the *Obedient* then sighted a cruiser and two destroyers bearing 060°. This was the *Lützow* waiting for the weather to clear; Commander Kinloch led round towards her and made smoke. She seemed to be steering about 150° and the British destroyers soon conformed, keeping between her and the convoy. At 1106 the enemy opened fire, but no fall of shot could be seen from the *Obedient*. Actually, the ship firing was the *Hipper*, which was approaching at 31 knots on course 190° on a bearing nearly the same as the *Lützow*'s; the *Hipper* at that time was firing on destroyers to the eastward, which she claimed to have set on fire. No British destroyers were in this position at the time; a possible explanation is that this was the unfortunate *Bramble* again, which in the murk and gloom had limped off to the southward or it may have been the *Friedrich Eckholdt* trying to rejoin. Be that it may, the *Hipper* continued at high speed on course 220° and at 1115 engaged the *Achates*, then just clearing her smoke screen in response to orders from Commander Kinloch to join the *Onslow* ahead of the convoy.[299] After three minutes, the *Achates* received a hit which crippled her, killing Lieut. -Commander A. H. T. Johns, her Commanding Officer and some 40 others. Lieutenant Peyton-Jones, who then took command, found he could only overtake the convoy very slowly, so he disregarded his orders and continued to lay smoke as before.

The *Hipper* then shifted her fire to the *Obedient*, which had led her destroyers to the northward again to keep between her and the convoy and had opened fire on her at a range of 8,500 yards at 1120.[300] At 1125 the *Hipper* hauled up to the north-westward (310°) and having straddled the *Obedient* and put her wireless out of action at 1128, altered course to 360° at 1130 in order to clear the torpedo menace. At the same time Commander Kinloch, as the range was rapidly opening, altered course to port to again close the convoy.

At this moment the *Hipper* received an unpleasant shock. Firing broke out from the northward and before it was realised what was happening, she received a hit which reduced her speed to 28 knots. Force 'R' had arrived. Her turn to the north-westward at 1125 had revealed her

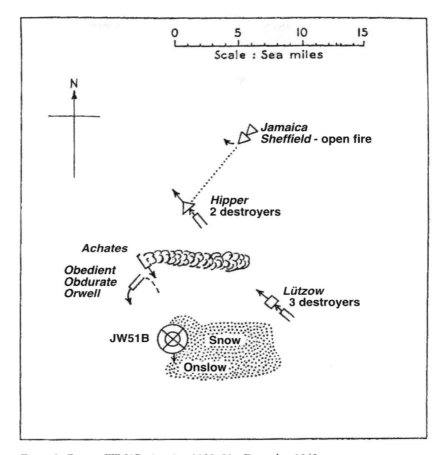

Figure 9. Convoy JW 51B: situation 1130, 31st December 1942.

broadside on to the approaching cruisers, then some seven or eight miles off.[301] Rear-Admiral Burnett led round to a roughly parallel course and at 1130 the *Sheffield* opened fire under helm at about 13,000 yards range, the *Jamaica* firing directly afterwards from her forward turrets. Taken completely by surprise, the *Hipper* failed to reply until after the fourth salvo had arrived; she made smoke and altered course towards them, swinging through east to 240° and receiving two more hits before she was round. This was too much for Vice-Admiral Kummetz, who thus found himself between Commander Kinloch's destroyers to the southward and an unknown force engaging him from the northward and at 1137 he made a general signal ordering all ships to break off action and retire to the west.

The British ships conformed with her turn and the range at one stage fell as low as 8,000 yards; unluckily, the *Hipper* then became obscured and the *Sheffield* had to cease fire from 1136 to 1139, losing three precious minutes at short range. At 1143, when both sides were pointing southward again, two German destroyers appeared in an ideal position to attack with torpedoes at 4,000 yards range. The *Sheffield* reversed her helm and headed for one destroyer; this was the *Friedrich Eckholdt*, which had mistaken the British cruisers for the *Hipper* and *Lützow*, which she was trying to rejoin. The *Sheffield* engaged her with all guns down to pompoms passing within half a mile of her and reducing her to a shambles in ten minutes. The *Jamaica* astern fired first at the other destroyer, which was further off and which turned away seemingly unharmed;[302] then she shifted her aim to the *Sheffield's* target, but refrained from firing on the blazing wreck, which the enemy subsequently admitted had been sunk. Meanwhile the *Hipper*, having completed the full circle of her turn passed out of sight to the westward. She had suffered three hits in the brief action; her No.3 boiler room was flooded and her hangar on fire; the only salvo she got off at her opponents had fallen harmlessly in the sea.

Before the British cruisers found the enemy again, the *Obedient* and her consorts had one more fight. After disengaging from the *Hipper* at 1130, they had stood to the southward to close the convoy. The flashes of Rear-Admiral Burnett's guns to the north-eastward had been a welcome sight; though they had known he was on his way, they could not know when he would arrive. They also saw another engagement further east at 1138, apparently between a large ship and a much smaller one, the latter firing a single gun. This may have been the *Friedrich Eckholdt* sinking the *Bramble*.[303] Then, some three minutes later, a large ship began shelling the convoy from the north-east at a distance of about nine miles; some of the merchant ships were not yet screened by the smoke the destroyers had been laying and one of them, the *Calobre*, was damaged – the only casualty they suffered in the whole battle. This was the *Lützow* (as was deduced at the time from the size of the shell splashes), which seeing no possibility of attacking the convoy from the east, had altered course at 1126 to the north-westward, in order to maintain contact with the *Hipper*, which she had seen firing and identified by exchange of recognition signals ten minutes previously.

The convoy made an emergency turn to 225°, while Commander Kinloch hauled round to the eastward to cover it with smoke and opened fire; according to the *Lützow* all shots fell short. One of the German destroyers following the *Lützow* fired a few ineffective rounds – the only part, apparently, that they took in the whole day's fighting. After about five minutes, the smoke screen became effective and the *Lützow* ceased fire. Immediately afterwards Commander Kinloch sighted the *Hipper* and her two destroyers on a south-westerly course four or five miles to the northward. The three British destroyers turned together to the north-west which put the *Obdurate* – to whom Commander Kinloch had turned over the direction of the destroyers when his own wireless was disabled – at the head of the line and steered between the convoy and the new enemy. The Germans altered away to a similar course; but by this time the *Lützow* was steaming to join the *Hipper* at 24 knots and she opened an accurate fire on the *Obdurate* at 1155, to which the British destroyers replied. At 1202, after the *Obdurate* had been damaged by a near miss, they turned away to keep between the convoy and the most likely direction of attack (should the enemy close again) while the *Lützow* continued to the westward. But this was the last attempt the Germans made; Vice-Admiral Kummetz had repeated his signal to withdraw at 1149 and no more was seen of them by the destroyers. At 1240, with no enemy in sight and night drawing on, they steered south to overtake the convoy.

All this time the crippled *Achates*, her bows deep in the water and listing ominously, had continued to screen the convoy with smoke. By 1300 the list had increased to about 60° and a quarter of an hour later she lost steam. Lieutenant Peyton-Jones then signalled for assistance and the *Northern Gem* closed her at once. She capsized suddenly and sank at 1330, 81 of her crew being saved by the trawler.[304]

Meanwhile the *Sheffield* and *Jamaica* to the northward had turned through east nearly to north as they engaged the German destroyers and on ceasing fire at 1154 they had altered to the westward. At 1215 they sighted the *Hipper* for a moment 12 miles away on the port bow going also to the westward. Then at 1223 two destroyers came in sight four or five miles to the southward in a good position for firing torpedoes. Rear-Admiral Burnett turned towards them to engage; as the guns were training on the target, however, the *Sheffield* sighted a larger ship (the *Lützow*) further away on about the same bearing. At 1229 the British cruisers opened fire on her at a range of some 14,000 yards. She replied at once; and the *Hipper* joined in the fight two or three minutes later from further ahead. The *Lützow*'s shots fell consistently short, but the *Hipper*'s fire was dangerously accurate, so the Rear-Admiral hauled up to the northward to avoid being engaged 'from both sides at once' and to lessen the risk from torpedoes, fired by the destroyers, which were not being engaged. By 1236 the fight was over, the *Jamaica* claiming one hit on the *Lützow*.[305] The Germans continued to the westward and the British ships soon turned west also, tracking the enemy by radar until at 1400 they lost contact. By this time the radar operators in the *Sheffield*, who had been operating their apparatus in an exposed position in a temperature well below freezing point for hours, were completely exhausted.[306] Moreover, Rear-Admiral Burnett did not wish to get too far from the convoy, of whose position he was still very uncertain. The *Hipper* and *Lützow* had been driven off, but it was known that the *Nurnberg* had been with them in Altenfjord and she was believed to be at sea somewhere in the vicinity. He accordingly swept to the southward, between the convoy and the *Hipper* and *Lützow* 'still with the advantage of what little light remained.'[307]

So the fighting ended. The British forces had lost the *Achates* and the *Bramble*, but the convoy was intact and they had sunk the *Friedrich Eckholdt* and seriously damaged the *Hipper*.[308] As a result of these actions, too, the Germans abandoned the plan for the *Lützow* to break out into the Atlantic, which was deemed impossible of fulfilment and thoroughly discouraged,[309] they steered for Altenfjord.

53

Convoy JW 51B had no more encounters with the enemy after the action on 31st December. In the afternoon of 2nd January, two minesweepers and two Russian destroyers joined, the Russians taking charge of the ships bound for Archangel, which then parted company. The main body of the convoy entered Kola Inlet on the 3rd and the Archangel detachment arrived on the 6th (Plan 17).

Rear-Admiral Burnett had patrolled with the *Sheffield* and *Jamaica* to the westward of Convoy JW 51B up to 1830, 31st December, when he followed it to the south-east and finally turned north early on 1st January to give protection to the westbound convoy, RA 51. Having arrived north of the latter's route, he turned westward and stretched ahead. Next day, 2nd January, he proceeded to Seidisfjord, where he arrived on the 4th, cover for the convoy then being provided by Rear-Admiral Hamilton in the *Kent* with the *Berwick*, detached for the purpose by the Commander-in-Chief, Home Fleet, who on receipt of the action reports on the 31st December had put to sea with them and the *King George V* (flag), *Howe*, *Bermuda* and six destroyers[310] to give additional cover. But in fact this was an unnecessary precaution; the German squadron had made straight for Altenfjord. The *Hipper* was sighted by the *Graph*, the westernmost of the patrolling submarines, soon after 0100, 1st January, but she was too far off and moving too fast to allow an attack. Some three hours later the *Graph* unsuccessfully attacked two destroyers, one of them apparently in tow of the other and that was the last seen of the enemy. The battlefleet cruised to the eastward of Jan Mayen Island until noon, 3rd January and then steered for Scapa Flow, followed by Rear-Admiral Hamilton's cruisers next day.

Convoy RA 51, under Commodore Turle, had sailed from Murmansk in a strong north-westerly gale on 30th December (Plan 17). It consisted of 14 merchant ships escorted by six destroyers,[311] a minesweeper,[312] and four trawlers[313] under Captain Scott-Moncrieff of the *Faulknor*. On the day of the action it was over 150 miles to the south-east of JW 51B and so well clear of danger; on 1st January it safely avoided three patrolling U-boats, of which warning had been received before sailing. Otherwise Captain Scott-Moncrieff's passage home was as uneventful as had been his passage out with Convoy JW 51A and the ships of RA 51 all reached Loch Ewe on 11th January 1943.

54

The operations in connection with these three convoys and especially the surface action of 31st December, were recognised by both sides as a notable success for the British. Admittedly they took place when the long hours of darkness afforded much protection against U-boats and aircraft, but, as Admiral Tovey remarked:–

> 'that an enemy force of at least one pocket battleship, one heavy cruiser and six destroyers, with all the advantage of surprise and concentration, should be held off for four hours by five destroyers and driven from the area by two 6-inch cruisers without any loss to the convoy is most creditable and satisfactory.'[314]

The basic reasons for the British success are not far to seek. Paradoxically, though the initiative was entirely in the hands of the Germans, their aim was confused and their tactics were primarily defensive, whereas the convoy escorts – whose role was essentially defensive – invariably carried it out by boldly taking the offensive.[315]

Thus the tactics of both Captain Sherbrooke and Commander Kinloch were governed throughout by their clear grasp of their objective, i.e., the safety of the convoy and were characterised by offensive action

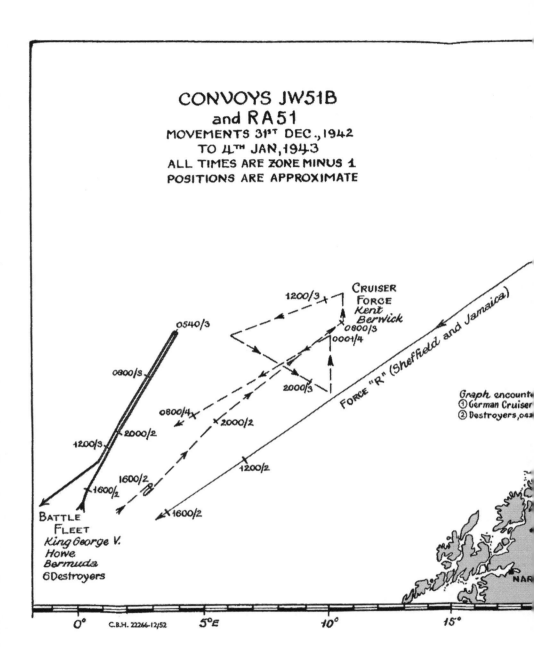

CONVOYS JW51B
and RA51
MOVEMENTS 31ST DEC., 1942
TO 4TH JAN, 1943
ALL TIMES ARE ZONE MINUS 1
POSITIONS ARE APPROXIMATE

CRUISER
FORCE
Kent
Berwick

1200/3

0800/3
0001/4

0540/3

FORCE "R" (*Sheffield and Jamaica*)

0800/3

2000/3

Graph encounte
① German Cruiser
② Destroyers, 04

0800/4

2000/2

1200/3

2000/2

1600/2

1200/2

1600/2

1600/2

BATTLE
FLEET
King George V.
Howe
Bermuda
6 Destroyers

NAR

0°   C.B.H. 22266-12/52   5°E   10°   15°

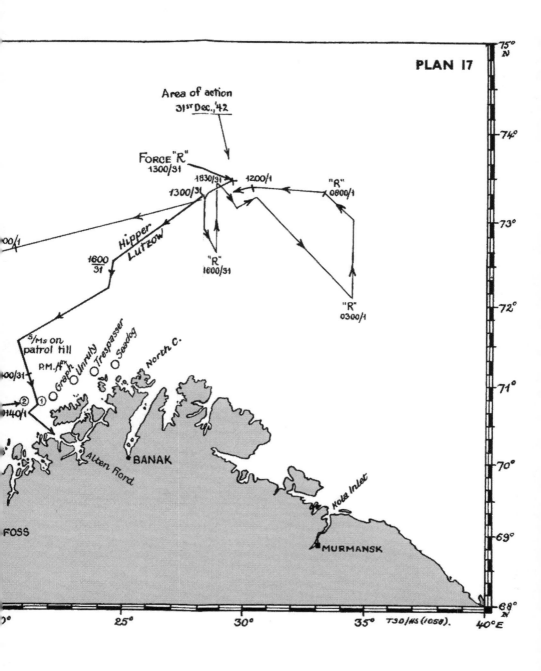

PLAN 17

Area of action
31st Dec., '42

Force "R"
1300/31

1830/31   1200/1

1300/31   "R"
                          0800/1

00/1

Hipper
Lutzow

1600
31

"R"
1600/31

"R"
0300/1

S/Ms on
patrol till

P.M./31

00/31   Graph Unruly Trespasser Seadog   North C.

② ①

140/1

Alten Fiord   BANAK

FOSS

Kola Inlet

MURMANSK

T30/HS (1058).

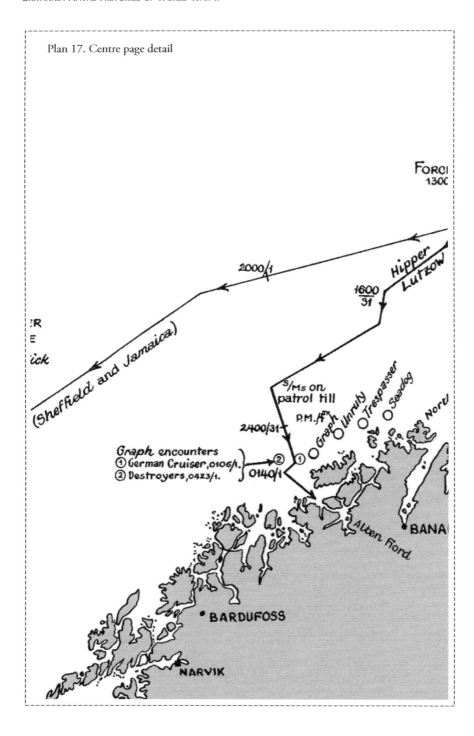

Plan 17. Centre page detail

whenever an enemy threatened it. But whatever the difficulties and distractions of the moment, they never forgot the convoy – witness Captain Sherbrooke's detachment of the *Obedient* and *Obdurate* at 1008, because, while holding off the *Hipper* did not know the whereabouts of the German destroyers and Commander Kinloch's invariable turn to close the convoy as soon as each attempt of the enemy to close the convoy had been foiled for the time being.

The German tactics, on the other hand, were vitiated throughout by lack of clear definition of their object. 'The result of this engagement was obviously unsatisfactory for the Germans but a complete success for the British,' writes the German Vice-Admiral Weichold. 'Tactically this was due to poor visibility and the problems inherent in a night action, but primarily the Germans were paralysed by the stringency of their operation orders.'[316] It has already been suggested that the proposed commerce raiding foray of the *Lützow* was a weakness in the German plan, in laying down two objects for their operation; but reading their war diaries and reports of the action, it is difficult to avoid the conclusion that once in contact a third and overriding object supervened, viz., to avoid damage to their ships and get safely back to harbour.

Thus, except on one occasion,[317] the German destroyers tamely followed their respective heavy ships and took no part whatever in the actions, much to the mystification of Commander Kinloch.[318] Vice-Admiral Kummetz explained their inactivity as follows:–

'To make a destroyer attack was out of the question, owing to possible confusion with the enemy. As the action developed I should no longer have been able to assemble our own destroyers round *Hipper* before darkness and would thus have left her without destroyer protection at a difficult period ...'[319]

Captain Strange of the *Lützow* held similar views, which in due course received the overall approval of Admiral Schniewind – in view of the important part 'played by the amount of consideration that had to be given to the limiting factor of risk.'[320] Nevertheless, it can hardly be doubted that a resolute attack on the convoy by the *Lützow's* destroyers about 1045 – just after they had passed a few miles ahead of it – would have paid handsome dividends.

As a result of the action all the German naval authorities realised that no Commander at sea could possibly succeed in the face of such binding conditions and subsequently new directives were issued, giving the

Commander afloat freedom to use all his resources, once an operation had been approved by the shore command. But it was long before the effect of this greater freedom was to be tested, for the action of 31st December 1942 had repercussions in the highest Nazi circles quite out of proportion to its intrinsic merits (or demerits) and by the time they had calmed down the convoys to North Russia had been temporarily discontinued. Hitler, curiously ignorant of the principles of maritime strategy, had long suffered under a sense of grievance that more spectacular results had not been achieved by the surface forces of his fleet. He first heard of the action through BBC reports. A delay in the German reports reaching his headquarters[321] so infuriated him, that without waiting to receive them he informed Grand Admiral Raeder on 1st January – that it was his 'firm and unalterable resolve' to have these useless ships laid up and to do away with the German Fleet. This led to the resignation by Admiral Raeder of his post as Commander-in-Chief of the Navy and the appointment of Admiral Dönitz in his place.

55

Less than a week after the arrival of Convoy RA 51 the next east-going convoy JW 52 started from Loch Ewe. Delays in unloading prevented the sailing of the corresponding west-going convoy RA 52, so its departure was postponed until about 29th January, when JW 52's escort would be available to bring it home.

Convoy JW 52 sailed on 17th January and was routed east of the Faroes. The Commodore was Vice-Admiral Sir Malcolm Goldsmith (Ret.) and the convoy consisted of 14 ships, escorted by three 'Hunt' class destroyers, the *Blankney, Middleton* and *Ledbury*, one minesweeper, two corvettes and two trawlers.3[322] The 'Hunts' were relieved to the northeast of Iceland by seven destroyers from Seidisfjord – the *Onslaught* (Commander W. H. Selby SO), *Beagle, Musketeer, Offa, Matchless, Bulldog* and ORP *Piorun*. A cruiser force under Rear-Admiral Hamilton consisting of the *Kent* (flag), *Glasgow* and *Bermuda*, covered the convoy from longitude 10° E. to Kola Inlet; and Vice-Admiral Sir Bruce Fraser, wearing his flag in the *Anson*, with the *Sheffield* and four destroyers, cruised south-west of Bear Island while the convoy was passing through the area deemed most liable to surface attack, i.e., between the meridians 24° and 32° E.

Throughout the passage the weather was favourable and the convoy made remarkably good progress, after one particularly slow ship – the

Empire Baffin – had been sent back by the Commodore. Both the *Anson*'s force, then northeast of Iceland and the convoy were sighted by enemy aircraft on 23rd January. The next day U-boats made contact west of Bear Island.

Skilful evasive alterations of course[323] and energetic counter-attack based on HF DF prevented them from scoring any success; and an abortive air attack by four He.115 torpedo aircraft that afternoon cost the enemy two of the attackers. The convoy, escort and cruiser covering force reached Kola safely on 27th January.

After two days spent in resting the escorts, the westbound convoy, RA 52, under Commodore Melhuish sailed on 29th January. Only 11 ships, instead of the 24 hoped for, were ready. These had an unusually large escort; nine destroyers – the *Forester* and *Icarus* in addition to those which had brought out JW 52 – two minesweepers, four corvettes, four trawlers[324] and the damaged *Onslow*. Battleship and cruiser cover was provided by the same forces as had covered JW 52.

Intermittent U-boat attacks were experienced from 1st February onwards; the last of these succeeded in sinking one merchant ship – the American SS *Greylock* – on the 3rd. 'This occurred on what was the nineteenth consecutive day in these wintry northern waters for the majority of the escort and it is not to be expected that personnel and materiel were then at their best.'[325] No lives were lost, the entire crew being rescued by the *Harrier, Oxlip* and the four trawlers.

The remaining ten ships of the convoy duly arrived at Loch Ewe on 8th February.

56

It had been planned to sail the next convoy, JW 53, from Loch Ewe on 11th February, but loading delays deferred the date until the 15th and then only 25 ships out of 30 were ready. These under Rear-Admiral E. W. Leir (Ret.) as Commodore, were escorted by three 'Hunt' class destroyers – the *Pytchley, Middleton* and *Meynell* – three corvettes, two minesweepers and two trawlers,[326] all under Commander H. G. A. Lewis of the *Jason*. The *Musketeer, Matchless* and *Bryony* followed next day with three additional merchant ships, but heavy weather compelled all three to turn back.

By the time the convoy reached Bear Island, there would be almost as much daylight – with all the advantages it conferred on the enemy air operations – as darkness, so a very strong escort was detailed to take over north-east of Iceland. This consisted of the *Scylla*, 13 destroyers,[327] and the escort carrier *Dasher*, with two attendant destroyers,[328] all under the command of Captain I. A. P. MacIntyre of the *Scylla*.

Cruiser cover was provided by Rear-Admiral Burnett, wearing his flag in the *Belfast*, with the *Sheffield* and *Cumberland* and heavy cover by the Commander-in-Chief in the *King George V* with the *Howe, Norfolk* and six destroyers.

Strong gales and very heavy seas were encountered by all ships during the first four days after the convoy sailed. The *Dasher* was damaged and returned to port, the *Sheffield* lost the roof of 'A' turret and her place was taken by the *Norfolk*,[329] and several destroyers suffered damage; one merchant ship was seriously injured and put in to Scapa, escorted by the *Matchless*, while five others returned to Loch Ewe. The remaining 22 merchant ships were delayed 48 hours and scattered, but were rounded up north-east of Iceland and thenceforward made good progress. During this four days' gale the *Scylla* and Home Fleet destroyers were not in company and the work of Commander Lewis in keeping the convoy together in such conditions was subsequently described by the Commander-in-Chief as 'admirable.'

During the night of 19th/20th February, the battlefleet – then on its way to Akureyri – passed within radar range of the partially scattered convoy, whose position and grouping the *King George V* was able to determine with some accuracy. This information was passed by 'special method'[330] at 0812, 20th, to the forces[331] sailing that day from Seidisfjord and proved 'invaluable' to Captain Campbell, the Senior Officer.

Convoy JW 53 was sighted by enemy aircraft on 23rd February and daily for the rest of the trip; U-boats made contact west of Bear Island on the 24th. But the enemy showed little inclination to attack. Two bombing attacks were entirely without success, while the U-boats were so discouraged by the aggressive tactics of the escort based on HF DF reports, that they failed to bring off any attack at all.

The convoy divided off the Murman Coast, 15 ships arriving at Kola Inlet on 27th February and the other seven entering the White Sea two days later.

The return convoy, RA 53, consisting of 30 ships under Sir Malcolm Goldsmith, left Kola Inlet on 1st March. The escort consisted of the *Scylla* and her 13 destroyers, four corvettes and two trawlers.[332] The battleship and cruiser covering forces were the same as for JW 53, except that the *Glasgow* replaced the *Berwick* with the battlefleet.

The U-boats which had followed JW 53 to the eastward gained contact with RA 53 the day after it sailed and accompanied it all the way to Iceland. After an ineffective attack by 12 Ju.88 bombers in the Barents Sea, one ship, the *Executive*, was sunk and one, the *Richard Bland*, was damaged by U-boats near Bear Island. Then the weather increased to a full gale and the convoy, far behind its schedule, began to straggle; this gave the U-boats their chance and they sank the damaged *Richard Bland* and one other, the *Puerto Rican*. A fourth, the *J. L. M. Curry* foundered in the gale and the *J. H. Latrobe* almost followed suit, but was towed into Seidisfjord by the *Opportune*, 'an excellent bit of work.'[333]

57

The passages of the January and February convoys could be regarded with satisfaction; the losses had been small and, as the Commander-in-Chief remarked, were due rather to the weather than to enemy action. But with the increasing daylight hours as the Spring advanced, he viewed the prospect with much anxiety; and when it became known in March that the *Tirpitz* had moved from Trondheim and with the *Scharnhorst* (which had arrived in Norway in February) and *Lützow*[334] was based at Altenfjord, he informed the Admiralty that he did not consider the continuance of the convoys justifiable, since such a powerful enemy concentration would compel the battlefleet to accompany them into the Barents Sea – a proceeding to which he was strongly averse.[335]

As things turned out, the matter was never put to the test. The Atlantic convoys were at this time suffering such heavy losses from U-boats that the Admiralty decided that their escorts must be increased. This could only be done at the expense of the Arctic convoys. All their escorting craft, except a bare minimum of destroyers as a screen for the battlefleet, were accordingly transferred temporarily to the Western Approaches and the convoys scheduled to sail to and from North Russia in March – JW 54 and RA 54 – were postponed indefinitely. By the time the convoys were re-started, the strategical situation had undergone a change and they were never again confronted by such menacing conditions.

Chapter VII

Convoys JW 54–66, RA 54, 67, November 1943 to May 1945
(All times are Zone minus 1)

58

By the autumn of 1943, the problem of the Atlantic convoys had been solved by the provision of long range aircraft for their protection. The German heavy ship concentration remained at Altenfjord, but on 22nd September midget submarines succeeded in crippling *Tirpitz*[336] and when this was known the Admiralty at once decided to resume the convoys to North Russia. The threat from surface craft was further reduced by the departure of the *Lützow* about this time for a long refit in Germany, leaving only the *Scharnhorst* and six destroyers in Northern Norway.

The Admiralty had undertaken to send 40 merchant ships a month to North Russia, but Admiral Sir Bruce Fraser, who had succeeded Sir John Tovey as Commander-in-Chief, Home Fleet, shared the opinion of his predecessor that this was far to great a number to be included in one convoy in Arctic winter conditions. It was therefore decided that the convoys should be run in two parts, each containing 20 ships and separated by about a fortnight. His policy for their protection was based a through escort of destroyers and escort vessels, with a local escort at each end of the sea passage; close cover by cruisers while the convoys were in the danger area south of Bear Island and battle ship cover from a position in 10° E. Longitude about 200 miles south-west of Bear Island.

Four east-going and four west-going convoys were run in November and December 1943, without the loss of a single merchant ship. The weather was generally favourable to all these convoys, considering the locality and the time of the year and no enemy interference other than occasional U-boat attacks took place until Christmas, when an attempt by surface forces resulted in the sinking of the *Scharnhorst*.

59

The first convoy of this series – RA 54A – consisted of 13 ships which had been languishing in Kola Inlet since the previous spring. The outgoing escort[337] for these ships sailed from Seidisfjord on 23rd October, taking with them five Russian minesweepers and six Russian motor launches. Convoy RA 54A sailed from Archangel on 1st November. It was delayed by thick fog, which concealed it from the enemy and arrived in the United Kingdom ports on 13th and 14th November without loss and undetected.

Rear-Admiral Burnett in the *Belfast*, with the *Kent* and *Norfolk* covered the convoy route between the meridians 31° 32' E. And 0° 55' W.; and heavy cover was provided by a force under Vice-Admiral Sir Henry Moore (Second-in-Command, Home Fleet) consisting of the *Anson* (flag), *Formidable, Jamaica* and six destroyers which operated from Akureyri while the convoy was in the danger area.

Convoy JW 54A, 18 merchant ships, sailed from Loch Ewe on 15th November, followed a week later (22nd November) by JW 54B, 14 ships. In addition a tanker sailed with each of these convoys. The usual escorts of Home Fleet and Western Approaches destroyers and escort craft[338] accompanied them and they arrived at their destinations without loss or damage. As unloading was a slow process only one return convoy of eight ships was run, RA 54B, which sailed from Archangel on 26th November and arrived in the United Kingdom ports on 9th December.

The cruiser covering Force composed of the *Kent* (flag, Rear-Admiral Palliser, who had succeeded Rear-Admiral Hamilton), *Jamaica* and *Bermuda* covered JW 54A right through to Kola Inlet and RA 54B and JW 54B while they were in the danger area south of Bear Island.

Heavy cover under Vice-Admiral Moore was provided by the *Anson*, USS *Tuscaloosa* and screen for JW 54A; for JW 54B and RA 54B, the *Belfast* took the place of the *Tuscaloosa*. This force worked from Akureyri as before.

60

The third group of convoys was run in December. By this time the convoy cycle had settled down and both east and west-going convoys were divided into two parts, the whole cycle occupying 27 days (i.e. from 12th December to 8th January 1944).

Cruiser cover for this group was provided by Vice-Admiral Burnett[339] in the *Belfast*, with the *Norfolk* and *Sheffield*, while the Commander-in-Chief in the *Duke of York* with the *Jamaica* and four destroyers provided heavy cover.

Convoy JW 55A left Loch Ewe on 12th December. Eight[340] Home Fleet destroyers under Captain Campbell in the *Milne* escorted it from the north-east of Iceland, in addition to the *Westcott*, a minesweeper and a corvette.[341]

Hitherto, the Germans had shown no interest in the convoys since their resumption. The Commander-in-Chief, Home Fleet, presumed that their inactivity arose from ignorance of what was going on. When, therefore, he heard that JW 55A had been sighted and reported by aircraft, he then felt sure that some attempt by surface craft would ensue and accordingly he decided to extend the battleship cover right through to the Russian ports.

This he did, visiting Vaenga between 16th and 18th December, where he made personal contact with the Russian Commander-in-Chief, Admiral Golovko and informed himself of local conditions. He then proceeded to Akureyri to fuel, while JW 55A completed its passage unmolested, 12 ships arrived at Kola on 21st December and seven ships at Archangel on 22nd December.

That day Convoy RA 55A (22 ships) sailed from Kola, escorted by Captain Campbell's eight fleet destroyers, the *Westcott, Beagle*, three corvettes and a minesweeper.[342] JW 55B (19 ships) under Rear-Admiral M. W. S. Boucher as Commodore had left Loch Ewe two days previously (20th) and was expected to pass Bear Island on Christmas Day about the same time as RA 55A. Its escort consisted of eight Home Fleet destroyers[343] under Captain J. A. McCoy of the *Onslow* and the *Whitehall, Wrestler*, two corvettes and a minesweeper.[344]

Cruiser cover was provided east of Bear Island by Vice-Admiral Burnett's three cruisers, *Belfast* (Captain F. R. Parham), *Sheffield* (Captain C. T. Addis), *Norfolk* (Captain D. K. Bain) which sailed from Kola on 23rd December and the Commander-in-Chief left Akureyri the same evening for the usual heavy ship covering position.

Meanwhile Convoy JW 55B had been reported by enemy aircraft and during the morning of 24th December was continuously shadowed. Through the German surface forces had never operated so far west, such a contingency was possible; the Commander-in-Chief therefore ordered the convoy to reverse its course for three hours that afternoon so that if the enemy were in that area they would be unable to make contact with it before dark.

On Christmas Day RA 55A passed Bear Island apparently undetected by the enemy and the Commander-in-Chief had ordered its course to be diverted to the north-westward, clear of the area and four Fleet destroyers – the *Musketeer* (Commander R. C. Fisher SO), *Matchless* (Lieut.-Commander W. S. Shaw), *Opportune* (Commander J. Lee-Barber) and *Virago* (Lieut.-Commander A. J. R. White) – to be detached from its escort to reinforce JW 55B.[345]

Early on 26th December (0319) the Admiralty signalled that the *Scharnhorst* was at sea. She had, in fact, left Altenfjord with five destroyers the previous evening and was then some 200 miles to the eastward of the *Duke of York*, steering to the northward.

61

The Germans had received reports of the resumed sailings of the convoys as early as the middle of November, but both the Naval War Staff and Group Command, North, considered that in view of the superiority of British radar the employment of the *Scharnhorst* against them would be too risky in the winter darkness. But for political reasons Grand Admiral Döenitz was anxious to show Hitler the value of the capital ship and on 19th December he obtained his sanction to attack the next convoy with the *Scharnhorst* and destroyers.

When JW 55B was located on 22nd December, preparations were put in hand. Eight U-boats, then off Bear Island, were re-disposed further to the westward and the surface forces were brought to short notice for steam. Reliance was placed on the Luftwaffe for continuous reconnaissance in the vicinity of the convoy and in particular to search for any covering force of warships which might be within 300 miles of it.

Contact with the convoy was lost after 1600, 24th December, but regained by a U-boat early next forenoon; and from then on U-boats continued to shadow, the weather being bad for aircraft. The British escort was believed to comprise three cruisers, five destroyers and four smaller craft; there were no indications of a heavier covering force being at sea.

Under these circumstances the operation was launched. In the absence of Vice-Admiral Kummetz, who was on leave, the execution of the project was committed to Rear-Admiral Bey, who hoisted his flag in the *Scharnhorst* and with five destroyers put to sea in the evening of 25th December.

The Germans intended to intercept the convoy in approximately the longitude of North Cape, when the *Scharnhorst* and two destroyers would stand off while the remaining three shadowed until twilight broke and visibility improved sufficiently to enable the most effective use to be

SINKING OF THE SCHARNHORST

CRUISER OPERATIONS.
0840 – 1500 26th. Dec., 1943.

(Based on Chart accompanying C. in C. H. F.'s despatch, and German Staff Records. Movements approx: only.

Track of *Scharnhorst* _____ ___ ___
   "   " *German Destroyers* ___ ___ ·___ ·
   "   " *Force I* _____
   "   " *36ᵀᴴ Div* ___ ·· ___ ·· ___ ·· ___ ··
   "   " *Convoy JW55B* ___ ___ ___

Radar contacts, Ranges, etc ___ ___ ___ ___
Ship symbols show positions at times of
opening fire (0929 and 1221)

1200
1221
1300
1100

1418   1400

1000

1100 1300

0929

0900 ✕

36ᵗʰ Div.
detached
to join
C.S.10.

1000

1040

0900

0840
Convoy
JW55B

0929

0840

1500

36ᵗʰ Div.
0840

0929

1027

CAUTION
This chart is based on a series of
plan projections. Meridians will
necessarily be distorted, and are
therefore omitted. Bearings,
except between units in immediate
vicinity of one another will be unreliable.

0   5   10   15

SCALE·MILES

1027

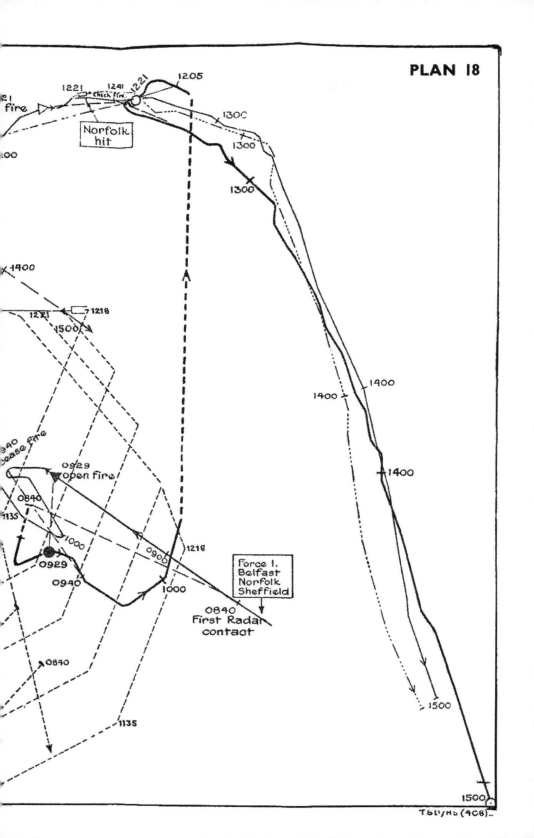

PLAN 18

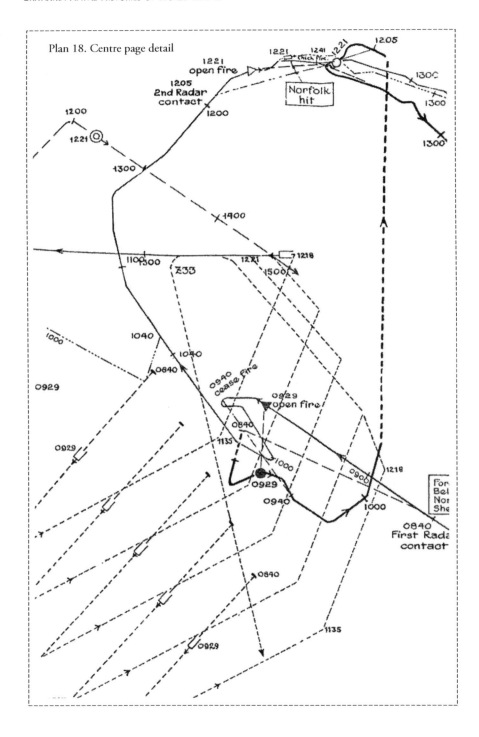

Plan 18. Centre page detail

1221
open fire

1221 1241 1221 1205
check fire

1205
2nd Radar
contact

1300

1300

Norfolk
hit

1300

1200

1221

1200

1300

1400

1100 1500

Z33

1221

1218

1500

1000

1040

1040

0929

0840

0940
cease fire

0929
open fire

0929

0840

1135

1000

0929

0940

0900

1218

1000

For
Bel
Nor
She

0840
First Rada
contact

0840

0929

1135

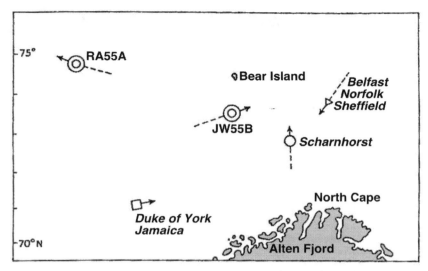

Figure 10. Convoy JW 55B, RA 55A; situation 0400, 26th December 1943

made of the battlecruiser's guns. If any enemy heavy ships should appear, the action was to be broken off immediately by the *Scharnhorst* and the destroyers were to fight a delaying action covering her retirement.

On clearing the land very heavy weather was encountered, which would so reduce the fighting efficiency of the destroyers, that Admiral Bey asked for instructions as to whether the operation should proceed. The matter was referred to Grand Admiral Dönitz himself, who ordered it to continue; if the destroyers could not remain at sea, the *Scharnhorst* might complete the task alone at Rear-Admiral Bey's discretion.

This left the Rear-Admiral no choice but to continue to the northward throughout the night, the eight shadowing U-boats keeping him supplied with valuable reports on the progress of the convoy.

62

The situation in the Bear Island area at 0400, 26th December,[346] was thus as follows:–

The westbound convoy, RA 55A, of whose existence the enemy was aware, was some 220 miles to the westward of Bear Island, in approximate position 74° 42' N., 5° 27' E., steering 267°, 8 knots.

Convoy JW 55B, its escort by then increased to 14 destroyers and three smaller craft all under Captain McCoy, was about 50 miles south of Bear Island, steering 070°, 8 knots.

Vice-Admiral Burnett's cruisers were about 150 eastward of JW 55B, steering 235°, 18 knots and the Commander-in-Chief in the *Duke of York* (Captain the Hon. G. H. E. Russell) with the *Jamaica* (Captain J. Hughes-Hallett) and four destroyers, the *Savage* (Commander M. D. G. Meyrick), *Scorpion* (Lieut.-Commander W. S. Clouston), *Saumarez* (Lieut.-Commander E. W. Walmsley) and the Norwegian *Store* (Lieut.-Commander S. Storeheill), was some 350 miles to the south-west of the Vice-Admiral, steering 080° at 24 knots.

The *Scharnhorst* was steering 000° approximately 90 miles south-west of Admiral Burnett and just over 100 miles to the south-eastward of the convoy.

At this time the Commander-in-Chief, Home Fleet – accepting the disability of breaking wireless silence – directed Vice-Admiral Burnett and Captain McCoy to report their positions and at 0628 ordered the convoy to steer 045° (to increase the enemy's difficulties in finding it) and the Vice-Admiral to close it for mutual support.

Meanwhile Admiral Bey had held his northernly course until 0800, when he altered to 230°, probably acting on a U-boat report which led him to suppose he was too far north and swept to the south-westward, with his destroyers spread five miles apart ten miles ahead of the *Scharnhorst* (Plan 18).

While on this course she came within radar range of Vice-Admiral Burnett's cruisers approaching from the eastward, which picked her up at 0840 at 35,000 yards bearing 295°. She was almost exactly between the cruisers and the convoy, which the Vice-Admiral's reckoning placed 30 miles beyond her.

The range decreased rapidly and just before 0930 an engagement commenced in which the *Norfolk* hit with her second or third salvo; the *Scharnhorst*, taken by surprise, at once increased speed and turned to the south-eastward, later altering to a north-easterly course. This Admiral Burnett took to mean that she was endeavouring to work around to the northward of the convoy for a second attempt and as her speed in the existing heavy weather seemed to be four to six knots higher than his cruisers, he broke off the action and steered to the north-westward close on the convoy. The enemy was last seen at 1020 bearing 078°, 36,000 yards and steering to the north-eastward at 28 knots.

Meanwhile the Commander-in-Chief had ordered Captain McCoy to turn the convoy to the northward at 0930 and a few minutes later to send four destroyers to reinforce Admiral Burnett. These, the *Musketeer, Opportune, Matchless* and *Virago* under Commander Fisher joined the

Vice-Admiral a few minutes after her enemy had disappeared. The convoy, which had altered back to 045° at 1030 was picked up 20 minutes later and the cruisers commenced zigzagging ten miles ahead of it, with Commander Fisher's four destroyers disposed ahead of them as a green. The convoy remained on this course until just before noon, when Captain McCoy, who had by then received orders from the Commander-in-Chief to use his discretion as to course, altered to 125°.

Just then (1205), while the convoy was turning, the *Belfast*'s radar again picked up the enemy. The Vice-Admiral's appreciation had been correct and a quarter of an hour later the *Scharnhorst* hove in sight on a westerly course. The cruisers immediately opened fire and the destroyers were ordered to attack with torpedoes, but the enemy at once turned away to the south-eastward and they could not reach a firing position.

This second action lasted about 20 minutes and again the *Scharnhorst* was 'most effectively driven off the convoy' by the cruisers' 'determined attach.'[347] Several hits on her were claimed by the cruisers, but the *Norfolk* received two hits and the *Sheffield* was straddled and suffered minor damage from fragments.

By 1241 the range had opened considerably and as the German was retiring on a course favourable for interception by the Commander-in-Chief, Vice-Admiral Burnett decided to check fire and shadow with his whole force.

Shortly after this, unknown to anybody on either side, the convoy nearly fell in with the German destroyers. These had continued to sweep to the south-westward until 1030[348] when orders came through from Admiral Bey to alter course to 070°, 25 knots. They were then, of course, widely separated from their flagship, which was steaming hard to the northward after her first engagement; and in fact they never regained contact. An hour later the Admiral ordered a further change to 030° and at 1218, as the result of a delayed U-boat report, he ordered them to operate in an area considerably further to the westward.

For the run to the new area, they concentrated on the northern destroyer, which steered 280° – a course on which they passed about eight miles to the southward of the convoy coming down on its south-easterly course just after 1300. Had Admiral Bey's orders been delayed ten minutes, a contact could hardly have been avoided; as it was, they held on to the westward for an hour and a quarter, when orders were received to break off the operation and return to harbour.

Throughout the afternoon the *Scharnhorst* held a southerly or south-easterly course, shadowed by Vice-Admiral Burnett's radar from a position some seven or eight miles astern. All unsuspected by the Germans, the Commander-in-Chief's force was closing them rapidly from the south-westward; and at 1650 she was suddenly illuminated by a star shell and came under the fire of the main armament of the *Duke of York* and the *Jamaica* the surprise and consternation were complete. She at once altered to port to the northward followed by the *Duke of York* and then to the eastward; a long chase ensued, in which both ships obtained hits on each other, but the *Scharnhorst* checked fire, as did the *Duke of York* four minutes later. But just then the *Scharnhorst*'s speed dropped and the British forces closed on her from all directions.

The *Savage* and *Saumarez, Scorpion* and *Sword* which had been following her at their best speed on either quarter brought off gallant torpedo attacks, further reducing her speed with at least three hits and five minutes later (1901) the *Duke of York* and the *Jamaica* re-engaged at a range of 10,400 yards. Hits were immediately scored, while the *Norfolk* and later the *Belfast* joined in from the northward. In less than 20 minutes the *Scharnhorst* was reduced practically to a standstill and was finished off by torpedoes from the *Belfast, Jamaica* and Commander Fisher's four destroyers.

Little more remains to be told. That evening all British forces proceeded to Kola Inlet, where they arrived next day without incident. Convoy JW 55B and RA 55A finished their voyages unmolested, the latter after having been dispersed by a gale.

Convoy RA 55B (eight ships), which left Kola Inlet on 31st December escorted by the same ships under Captain McCoy which had brought out JW 55B,[349] reached the United Kingdom 8th January, after being subjected to a few half-hearted U-boat attacks.

63

The sinking of the *Scharnhorst* left the Germans with no effective heavy ships in North Norway and greatly eased the situation for the Home Fleet bat the beginning of 1944. Battleship cover could be dispensed with and all efforts directed to countering the U-boat menace, which, assisted by the gradually improving light conditions, constituted the main German effort against the convoys. Through the damaged *Tirpitz* and some destroyers remained at Altenfjord, they never again put to sea against the convoys; nor until the end of 1944 did the German Air Force attempt to intervene and then it was on a much smaller scale than in 1942.

Four east-going and four west-going convoys were run between

January and April, with a loss of only five merchant ships and two escorts – all torpedoed by U-boats. Then increasing daylight, coupled with the demands on the fleet for the landings in Normandy, brought about another cessation of the convoys until August, when they started again and continued to the end of the War. During this latter period nine east-going and nine West-going were run; only eight merchant ships and three escorts were sunk. The U-boat losses on the other hand, were severe, 22[350] being destroyed in the whole of 1944 and three[351] in the first four months of 1945, as against one in 1943 and five in 1942.

All these convoys were very heavily escorted and threw a great strain on ships and men; but throughout 1944 their passages were uneventful compared with the earlier ones. It is therefore unnecessary to recount their fortunes in detail and they will only be mentioned briefly in order to show the development and variations of defence measures to meet the changed and changing conditions.

In December 1944, however, the Germans intensified their efforts. Torpedo bombers of the German Air Force were once more based at Bardufoss; and the advent of schnorkel[352] enabled the U-boats to concentrate in the restricted waters and particularly poor ASDIC conditions in that area. This renewed offensive culminated in the attacks on Convoys JW 64 and RA 64 in February 1945 whose story will be told in some detail.

64

The first convoy to sail from Loch Ewe after the sinking of the *Scharnhorst*, JW 56A (20 ships) started its voyage on 12th January. There was a strong escort similar to that of the previous convoy and cruiser cover in the danger area was provided by Vice-Admiral Palliser in the *Kent*, with the *Berwick* and *Bermuda*.

JW 56A was unlucky from the start. A heavy gale off the Faeroes forced five ships to put back and the remainder were considerably delayed. In the Bear Island area determined U-boats attack sank three ships.

In these circumstances the Commander-in-Chief postponed the sailing of RA 56A and ordered the escorts of this convoy to meet the approaching JW 56B in the danger area. All the returning ships were to sail in one convoy, RA 56, supported by the combined escorts of both outward convoys and three extra destroyers from Scapa.[353]

These measures were successful. Convoy JW 56B reached Kola Inlet undamaged in spite of heavy U-boat attack during the later part of the journey, in the course of which HMS *Hardy* (Captain W. G. A. Robson) was torpedoed and sunk. RA 56 consisting of 37 ships made the passage to the United Kingdom under an escort which never fell below 26 ships, without counting the cruiser cover and arrived safely without serious molestation.

As a result of the successful passage of this large convoy, the Commander-in-Chief decided to change his policy and instead of dividing the convoys into two parts, to run large single convoys, each with a big escort as possible.

Convoy JW 57, consisting of 42 merchant ships[354] and six Russian light craft left Loch Ewe on 20th February. A cruiser, the *Black Prince* (Captain D. M. Need), in which Vice-Admiral I. G. Glennie (VA(D)), who was in command of the whole complicated escort, wore his flag, was added to the close escort, which contained an increased number of destroyers. For the first time since the *Avenger* had proved her worth with Convoy PQ 18 eighteen months before, an escort carrier, the *Chaser* (Captain H. V. P. McClintock) was available[355] and in addition a Western Approaches Support Group (B.1) accompanied the convoy as far as Bear Island.[356] The usual cruiser cover was provided by the *Berwick* (Captain N. V. Grace SO), Jamaica (Captain J. Hughes-Hallett) and ORP *Dragon*.

Three days after Loch Ewe, the convoy was sighted and shadowed and shortly afterwards the *Mahratta* (Lieut.-Commander E. A. F. Drought) was torpedoed and sunk. The enemy seemed determined on a vigorous offensive. But in this he was frustrated – mainly by aircraft. On 24th February the *Keppel* (Commander I. J. Tyson) sank *U-713* with depth charges and the next day a Catalina operating at its extreme range from Sullom Voe sank a U-boat *U-601* in the vicinity of the convoy. Following this, a swordfish from the *Chaser* carried out numerous attacks with rocket projectiles on others, damaging several and forcing them to dive and lose contact, while her Wildcats damaged and drove off shadowing aircraft. These operations completely disorganised the German attack and JW 57 finished its journey practically unmolested.

The return convoy, RA 57, left Kola on 2nd March. Admiral Fraser had expected that the U-boats, having been thwarted in their attempts on the outward convoy, would wait for RA 57 in the approaches to Kola. He therefore arranged for a special Russian air patrol to cover the area to seaward and keep the U-boats submerged and ordered a wide diversion of the convoy route to the eastward. These measures had the desired effect; the convoy was not detected until it was two days out from harbour and the advantage thus gained was never lost. Air attacks by

Chaser's Swordfish prevented the U-boats from getting ahead and sank three of them with rocket projectiles. One ship of the convoy was sunk, but the remainder reached the United Kingdom safely.

The next pair of convoys, JW 58 and RA 58, were modelled on the same pattern, but two escort carriers, the Activity (Captain G. Willoughby) and *Tracker* (Captain J. H. Huntley and two Western Approaches support groups (Nos. 2 and 8) were included in the escort. The whole operation was commanded by Vice-Admiral Dalrymple-Hamilton[357] who flew his flag in the *Diadem* (Captain E. G. A. Clifford). The USS cruiser *Milwaukee*, which was being turned over to the Russians, was included in the Convoy JW 58.

By this time there were indications that the *Tirpitz* might again be seaworthy. An attack on her in Altenfjord by aircraft of the Fleet Air Arm from the *Victorious, Furious* and three escort carriers under the general direction of Vice-Admiral Sir Henry Moore with his flag in the *Anson* was synchronised with the passage of Convoy JW 58 and heavy cover for both operations was furnished by the *Duke of York* (flag, Commander-in-Chief) and *Anson*. The attack on the *Tirpitz*,[358] which took place on 3rd April, was a conspicuous success, and heavy cover for the convoys was no longer necessary.

Convoys JW 58 and RA 58 reached their destinations unscathed; the enemy on the other hand, lost three U-boats and six shadowing aircraft.

Convoy JW 58 completed the stipulated convoy quote for the spring, but one more west-going convoy, RA 59, was run, in order to bring back some merchant ships which had not been unloaded when RA 58 sailed and also the crew of USS *Milwaukee*, now re-named *Murmansk*. There were besides over 2,300 Soviet officers and ratings to be brought tenth United Kingdom to take over HMS *Royal Sovereign* and other British ships into the Russian service. The transport *Net Hellas* was sailed with the outward-bound escorts to assist in bringing back this large number of passengers; she developed engine trouble, however, was forced to return: Rear-Admiral McGrigor,[359] who was in command of the operation with his flag in the *Diadem* took the convoy escort on and reached North Russia apparently undetected.

The American and Soviet parties were embarked in the merchant ships and escorts and Convoy RA 59 sailed on 28th April. U-boats attacked off Bear Island and sank one merchant ship, but lost three of their number to Swordfish from *Fencer* (Captain W. W. R. Bentinck), a remarkable achievement especially in view of the bad flying weather and for the remainder of there passage the large escort, assisted by her aircraft and those from the *Activity* (Captain Willoughby) kept the enemy well at arm's length.

> 'With the return of RA 59,' wrote the Commander-in-Chief, 'the convoy season may be said to have come to a close ... Taken as a whole the campaign can be claimed as a success. A large volume of valuable supplies has reached Russia almost intact and the enemy has sustained far greater losses in attempting to hinder them than he has inflicted on our forces.'[360]

65

From May to July, 1944, the naval effort in home waters was centred on the Allied landings in Normandy. By the beginning of August, however, the situation there was sufficiently stabilised to allow the convoys to North Russia to be resumed.

Admiral Sir Henry Moore had succeeded Sir Bruce Fraser as Commander-in-Chief, Home Fleet, in June. He found the convoy situation much the same as that which obtained in early April. The bulk of the German Air Force was fully occupied in other theatres, but there was a strong concentration of U-boats in Northern Norway and the *Tirpitz* with five destroyers was still at Altenfjord, and was believed to be sufficiently battle-worthy again to constitute a serious threat to the convoys. Several attempts during the summer months to cripple her permanently by carrier-borne aircraft had failed, chiefly owing to the greatly improved German smoke screening organisation.

The first convoy of the new series, JW 59, consisted of 33 merchant ships, one rescue ship and 11 Russian submarine chasers, which sailed from Loch Ewe on 15th August. It was escorted by the *Jamaica* (Captain J. Hughes-Hallett), the escort carriers *Vindex* (Captain H. T. T. Bayliss) and *Striker* (Captain W. P. Carne) and 18 escorting craft.

Vice-Admiral Dalrymple-Hamilton conducted the operation. Instead of flying his flag in the A.A. cruiser, as had been customary, he embarked in the escort carrier *Vindex*. This was a great success, as the carrier had better 'action information' accommodation and he was also able more readily to assess the risk and decide on the scale of the air effort, to meet the frequently changing weather conditions.

An operation by carrier-borne aircraft against the *Tirpitz* was synchronised with the running of the convoy and the strong forces[361] so employed also served as heavy cover for the convoy. The Russian battleship *Archangel* (formally the *Royal Sovereign*) and eight destroyers sailed from Scapa and overtaking the convoy west of Bear Island, proceeded through to Kola.

Convoy JW 59 had an uneventful passage. Continuous daylight enabled a full flying programme to be carried out and U-boats were given no chance of closing the convoy; but the sloop *Kite* (Lieut.-Commander A. N. G. Campbell) was torpedoed and sunk with heavy loss of life, only nine being saved. A shadower was shot down by Wildcats and a U-boat was sunk by a Swordfish. Another U-boat was destroyed two days later by the *Mermaid* (Lieut.-Commander J. P. Moses), *Loch Dunvegan* (Commander E. Wheeler RNR), *Keppel* (Commander I. J. Tyson) and *Peacock* (Lieut.-Commander R. B. Standard VC RNR). This hunt lasted 12 hours.

The return of convoy, RA 59A, sailed from Kola on 28th August and arrived at Loch Ewe 5th September. The U-boat attacks were on an even smaller scale than against JW 59. Only one was sighted; she was forced to dive by a Swordfish and hunted to destruction after six hours by the *Keppel, Peacock, Mermaid* and *Whitehall* (Lieut.-Commander P. J. Cowell).

The next pair of convoys, JW 60 and RA 60, ran between 15th September and 6th October. Rear-Admiral McGrigor, flying his flag in the *Campania* (Captain K. A. Short) was in charge. As the state of other *Tirpitz* was uncertain, the *Rodney* (Captain the Hon. R. O. Fitzroy) was included in the escort, in case she attempted a sortie.

Actually the precaution was unnecessary. On 15th September – just as JW 60 was starting its voyage – RAF heavy bombers working from North Russia hit her with a 12,000lb. Bomb, inflicting such damage that it was decided not to attempt to repair her, but use her as a fixed battery to strengthen the defences of Northern Norway. Further attacks by the bombers eventually capsized and sank her on 12th November. Seldom, if ever, has a single ship 'in being' exerted greater strategical influence, though inflicting – in her whole inglorious career – practically no material damage on her enemy.[362]

Convoy JW 60 accomplished the passage apparently undetected. The return convoy lost two ships to U-boats, one of which was damaged.

The next east-going convoy, JW 61, left Loch Ewe on 20th October. Vice-Admiral Dalrymple-Hamilton conducted the operation, with his flag in the *Vindex*. This convoy differed from previous ones, in that the normal supporting forces were supplemented by two support groups and an additional escort carrier, with the subsidiary object of the destruction of U-boats. No U-boats were encountered until east of Bear Island, when

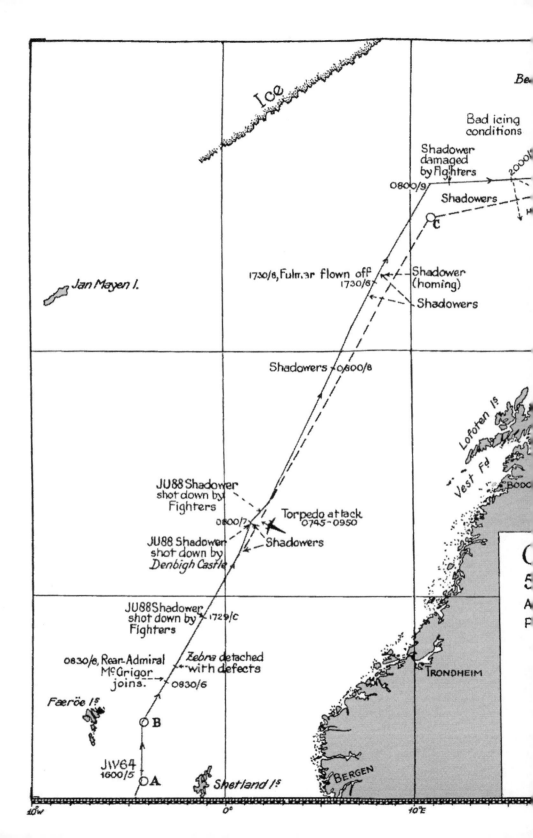

Ice

Be—

Bad icing
conditions

Shadower
damaged
by Fighters
0800/9

2000/

Shadowers

C

Shadower
(homing)

1730/6, Fulmar flown off
1730/6

Shadowers

Jan Mayen I.

Shadowers 0800/8

Lofoten Is

Vest Fd

BODO

JU88 Shadower
shot down by
Fighters

Torpedo attack
0745-0950

0800/7

JU88 Shadower
shot down by
Denbigh Castle

Shadowers

C
5
A
P

JU88 Shadower
shot down by
Fighters

1729/6

0830/6, Rear-Admiral
M?Grigor
joins.

Zebra detached
with defects

0830/6

Faeröe Is

TRONDHEIM

B

JW64
1600/5

A

Shetland Is

BERGEN

10°W   0°   10°E

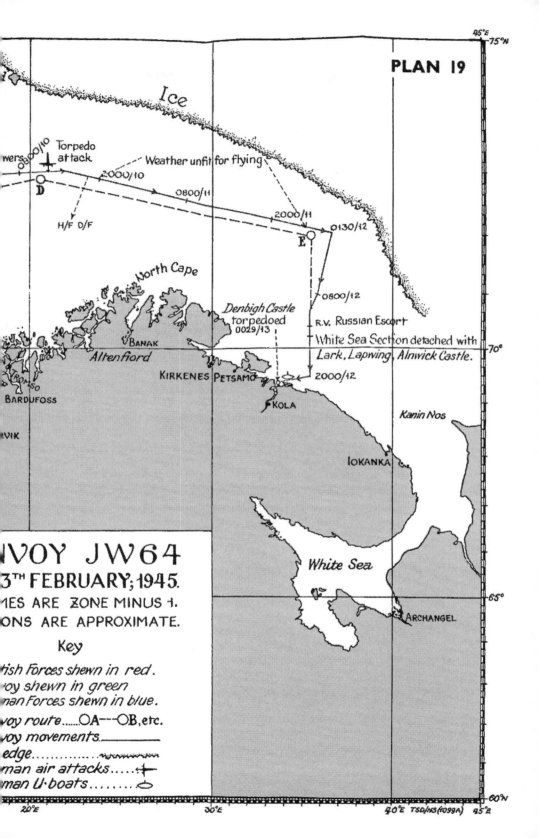

PLAN 19

Ice

Torpedo
attack

wers 0800/10

Weather unfit for flying

2000/10

0800/11

D

2000/11

0130/12

H/F D/F

E

0800/12

North Cape

R.V. Russian Escort

Denbigh Castle
torpedoed
0029/13

White Sea Section detached with
Lark, Lapwing, Alnwick Castle.

BANAK

Altenfiord

KIRKENES PETSAMO

2000/12

Kanin Nos

BARDUFOSS

KOLA

IOKANKA

RVIK

White Sea

ARCHANGEL

NVOY JW 64

3ᵀᴴ FEBRUARY, 1945.

MES ARE ZONE MINUS 1.

ONS ARE APPROXIMATE.

Key

ish Forces shewn in red.
oy shewn in green
man Forces shewn in blue.

oy route......OA---OB, etc.
oy movements_____
edge..............〰〰〰
man air attacks.....✈
man U·boats........⬡

20°E   30°E   40°E TSD/HS(1099A) 45°E

45°E
75°N

70°

65°

60°N

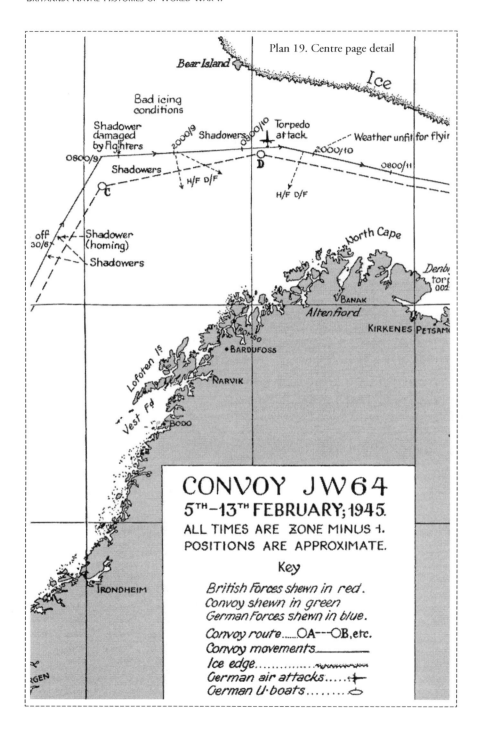

Plan 19. Centre page detail

Bear Island

Ice

Bad icing conditions

Shadower damaged by Fighters

2000/9 Shadowers 0000/10 Torpedo attack

Weather unfit for flyir

0800/9

2000/10

0800/11

Shadowers

C

D

H/F D/F

H/F D/F

off 30/6

Shadower (homing)

Shadowers

North Cape

Denb torp 002

BANAK

Altenfiord

KIRKENES PETSAM

BARDUFOSS

Loforen Is

NARVIK

Vest Fd

BODO

TRONDHEIM

RGEN

CONVOY JW64
5TH–13TH FEBRUARY; 1945.
ALL TIMES ARE ZONE MINUS 1.
POSITIONS ARE APPROXIMATE.

Key

British Forces shewn in red.
Convoy shewn in green
German Forces shewn in blue.
Convoy route......OA---OB,etc.
Convoy movements_____
Ice edge............
German air attacks.....
German U-boats........

the support groups were sent ahead to keep down any which might be patrolling off the approaches to Kola. This manoeuvre was successful and the convoy arrived intact; a number of U-boats was sighted, but none was destroyed, owing to bad ASDIC conditions. Similar tactics were adopted in the case of Convoy RA 61, when three escort groups were sent out ahead of it from Kola, to break up possible U-boat patrol lines. Contacts occurred, but again U-boats were destroyed. RA 61 negotiated the danger area safely and arrived home without loss; but the *Mounsey* was damaged by an explosion and forced to return to Kola.

A special fast convoy, JW 61A, of two large ships escorted by the *Berwick* (Captain N. V. Grace), *Campania* (Captain K. A. Short) and four destroyers was run at the beginning of November, to repatriate about 11,000 Russian ex-prisoners of war. A token Norwegian Force to take part in the Russian advance into North Norway took passage in the *Berwick*.

The last two convoys in 1944, JW 61A and RA 62, met with stiffer resistance than of late. Torpedo bombers again made their appearance, after an absence of over two years and a heavy concentration go U-boats in the approaches to Kola had to be met.

JW 62 sailed from Loch Ewe on 29th November with the normal escort and two additional support groups, the whole under the direction of Rear-Admiral McGrigor with his flag in the *Campania* and despite the U-boat concentration off Kola arrived without loss.

RA 62 left Kola on 10th December. Hunting groups were again sent out ahead to keep down the U-boats. About 24 hours after sailing, the *Cassandra* (Lieutenant G. C. Leslie), had her bows blown off by a torpedo and was escorted back to Kola for temporary repairs. The convoy was subjected to torpedo bomber attacks in addition to the U-boats, but suffered no damage. Two Ju.88 were shot down; one U-boat was destroyed and several were damaged. The lack of night fighters to deal with shadowers was keenly felt.

The first pair of convoys to run in 1945, JW 63 and RA 63, under the direction of Vice-Admiral Sir Frederick Dalrymple-Hamilton in the *Vindex* (Captain J. D. L. Williams), was remarkable in that no contact was made with the enemy on either outward or homeward passages. Entry into Kola Inlet was made in fog and heavy snowstorms. Bad weather was encountered on both passages, and a gale north-east of the Faeroes scattered RA 63 and caused superficial damage. The Vice-Admiral put in to the Faeroes to reassemble the convoy, which then completed its passage without further incident.

66

In contrast with the convoys run in January 1945, the next pair, JW 64 and RA 64, were in almost continual contact with the enemy. Very heavy weather, culminating in a hurricane which scattered Convoy RA 64 south-east of Jan Mayen, was again encountered.

Convoy JW 64 (Plan 19) sailed from Greenock[363] on 3rd February 1945, escorted by Fleet destroyer *Zebra* and elements of the 7th and 8th Escort Groups[364] of the Western Approaches Command under Commander A. H. Thorold of the *Cygnet* and proceeded through the Minches to the northward. The oiler *Black Ranger*, escorted by the *Serapis* and *Denbigh Castle* joined on the 5th and next afternoon Rear-Admiral McGrigor, flying his flag in the *Campania* (Captain K. A. Short), with the *Nairana* (Captain V. N. Surtees), *Bellona* (Captain G. S. Tuck) and eight Fleet destroyers[365] made contact north-east of the Faeroes.

An hour or so later the convoy was sighted by an enemy aircraft making a routine meteorological flight from Trondheim and that afternoon the first shadower appeared. The latter – a Ju.88 – was soon shot down by two Wildcats from the *Campania*, one of which was lost with its pilot, Sub-Lieutenant Smyth, in the fight; from then on the convoy was shadowed by aircraft at intervals, day and night, until the day before reaching Kola.

Early next morning, 7th February, the convoy was again shadowed and Rear-Admiral McGrigor, anticipating a dawn torpedo attack ket the scree in its night cruising disposition, 'which proved very suitable with its two concentric circles of escorts.'[366] A number of Ju.88 torpedo bombers was detected at 0745,[367] one of which was speedily shot down by the *Denbigh Castle* (Lieut.-Commander G. Butcher RNVR). The Rear-Admiral altered course 90° to starboard towards the dawn, so as to bring the enemy's most favourable attacking sector astern. Radar indicated that about a dozen aircraft were operating in two groups from the north-west and south-west, but they did not press home their attacks and withdrew at about 0900. Low cloud and bad light prevented two Wildcats sent up by the *Nairana* from intercepting them; but the Wildcats later set on fire a shadower.

During 8th and 9th February, shadowers were much in evidence and seemed to be making homing signals for U-boats. An attempted attack on the shadowers in the evening of the 8th by the only night fighter with the force failed owing to the darkness and poor R/T communication. In landing on the *Campania* the fighter – an antique Fulmar – crashed into the barrier and was damaged beyond repair. But no attacks, either by submarines or aircraft, materialised. Air searches and patrols were flown to try to find the U-boats, but none was sighted. The Rear-Admiral had proceeded slightly to the northward of the route before turning to the eastward and it seemed from HF DF bearings that the convoy passed round the northern flank of a submarine patrol line. In the evening of the 9th all flying from the carriers was stopped by the weather.

On 10th February the convoy spent a lively forenoon. Shadowers appeared at 0340, when it was south of Bear Island and only about 250 miles from Bardufoss. Shortly before 1000 an aircraft was thought to be Russian, on the strength of a corrupt message from the SBNO, North Russia, button minutes later the *Sioux* recognised it as a Ju.88 and drove it off with one engine on fire, but not before it had dropped a torpedo. This was the only warning received of the torpedo attack which was the on its way; the Rear-Admiral subsequently remarked that 'it was fortunate ... as it gave the screens time to start moving into their anti-aircraft positions and brought everyone to the alert.'[368]

The weather and light were poor with low 10/10ths cloud, rain-squalls and between whiles visibility of about 5 miles.

At 1019 the main attack started to appear on the radar, approaching from the starboard bow. The *Whitehall* (Lieut.-Commander P. J. Cowell), the righthand ship of the extended screen ahead, sighted two groups of about eight Ju.88s each closing at sea level. One of them was coming straight for her. She and the *Lark* (Commander H. Lambton) broke up the formation with their gunfire, causing it to take violent evasive action:
–

'When three aircraft detached themselves to attack the *Whitehall* with torpedoes, she sent one away damaged, shot down the second, shared the third with the *Lark* and successfully avoided all torpedoes. Fine work by veteran with a close range armament of only two Oerlikons each side.'[369]

The *Orwell* (Lieut.-Commander J. R. Gower) and the *Nairana's* fighters also shot down aircraft; the latter, with the *Cynet, Sioux* and *Onslow* each got 'probables' or inflicted damage.

Meanwhile Rear-Admiral McGigor had turned the convoy 90° away from these attacks by emergency turns and more fighters were flown off from the carriers. Further attacks then developed from all directions, the

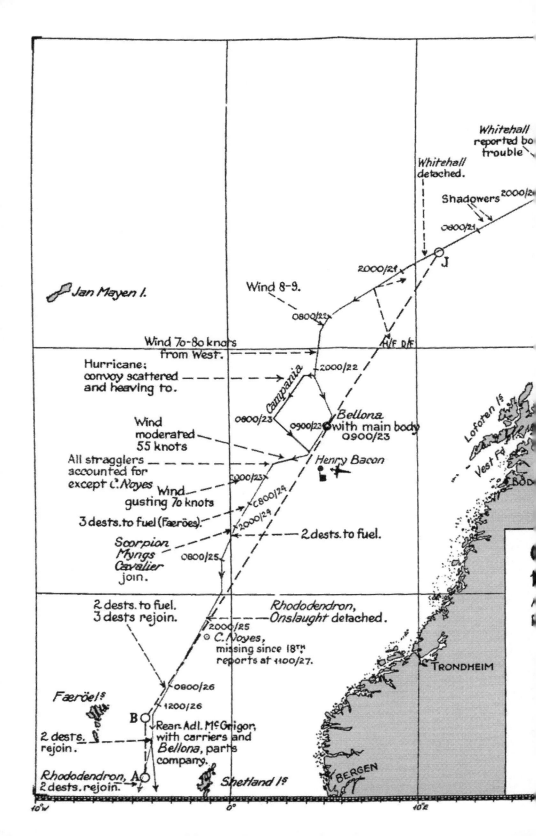

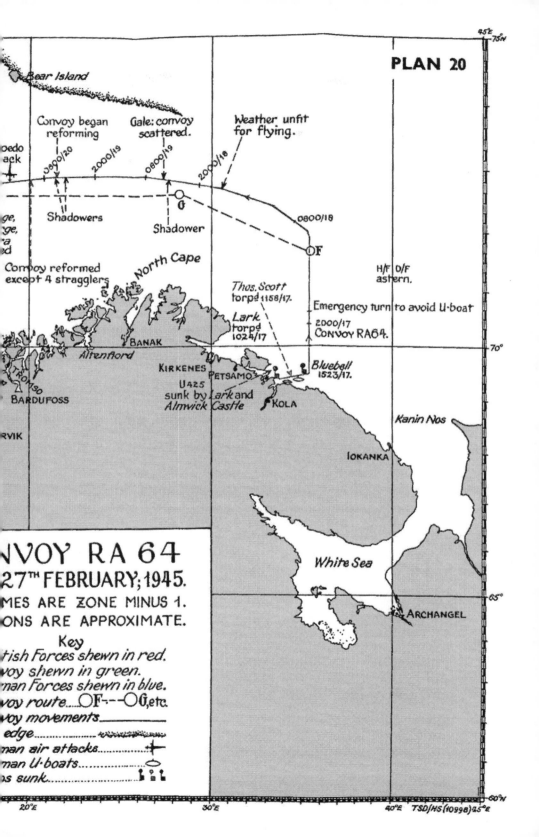

PLAN 20

Bear Island

Convoy began reforming

Gale: convoy scattered.

Weather unfit for flying.

rpedo
ack

0800/20

2000/19

0800/19

2000/18

0800/18

G

F

Shadowers

Shadower

H/F D/F astern.

ge,
ge,
ea
d

Convoy reformed except 4 stragglers

North Cape

Thos. Scott torpd 1158/17.

Emergency turn to avoid U-boat

2000/17 Convoy RA64.

Lark torpd 1024/17

BANAK

Altenfiord

TROMSÖ

BARDUFOSS

RVIK

KIRKENES

PETSAMO

KOLA

Blueball 1523/17.

U425 sunk by Lark and Almwick Castle

Kanin Nos

IOKANKA

White Sea

ARCHANGEL

NVOY RA 64

27ᵀᴴ FEBRUARY; 1945.

MES ARE ZONE MINUS 1.

ONS ARE APPROXIMATE.

Key

tish Forces shewn in red.

voy shewn in green.

man Forces shewn in blue.

voy route.....OF----OG, etc.

voy movements_____

edge.................

man air attacks...............

man U-boats...............

s sunk.............

20°E

30°E

40°E

TSD/HS (10998) 25°E

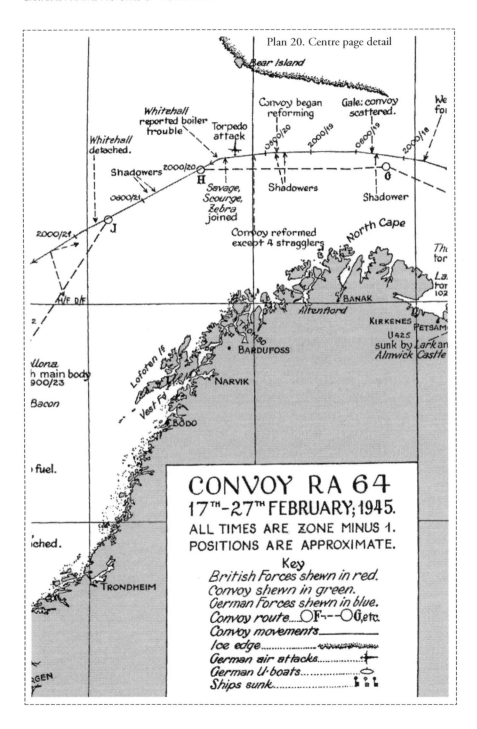

Plan 20. Centre page detail

Bear Island

Convoy began
reforming

Gale: convoy
scattered.

We
for

Whitehall
reported boiler
trouble

Torpedo
attack

0800/20

2000/19

0600/19

2000/18

Whitehall
detached.

Shadowers 2000/20

H

0800/21

Shadowers

G

Shadower

J

2000/21

*Savage,
Scourge,
Zebra*
joined

Convoy reformed
except 4 stragglers

North Cape

*Th
for*

*La.
tor
102*

A/F D/F

BANAK

2 /

Altenflord

KIRKENES PETSAM

*llona
h main body
900/23*

TROMSO

BARDUFOSS

*U425
sunk by Larkan
Almwick Castle*

Bacon

Loforen Is

NARVIK

fuel.

Vest Fd

BODO

ched.

CONVOY RA 64
17ᵀᴴ–27ᵀᴴ FEBRUARY; 1945.
ALL TIMES ARE ZONE MINUS 1.
POSITIONS ARE APPROXIMATE.

Key
British Forces shewn in red.
Convoy shewn in green.
German Forces shewn in blue.
Convoy route.... O F---O G, *etc.*
*Convoy movements*_____
Ice edge................
German air attacks............ +
German U-boats............
Ships sunk............

TRONDHEIM

GEN

biggest threat coming from the starboard bow. These torpedoes were combed by other emergency turns, some of them exploding in the wakes inside the convoy. The Admiral remarked that reports of approaching torpedoes received from the screen were most useful.

These attacks cost the enemy further aircraft. The *Campania*'s fighter got one 'probable' and damaged another; the *Onslaught* (Commander the Hon. A. Pleydell-Bouverie), shot one down and the port wing of the convoy with the help of the *Campania* and escorts 'dropped their Ju.88 neatly among the rear ships;'[370] a number of aircraft was damaged by other escorts. Unfortunately friendly fighters returning damaged to the carrier were also fired at indiscriminately by escorts and merchant ships, in spit of a warning about them by convoy R/T.[371]

After 1110 there was all, but at 1130 more Ju.88s came in. One was probably shot down by the *Nairana*'s fighters, escorts and convoy and that finished the attacks. The total score was assessed at seven Ju.88s shot down, four 'probables,' eight damaged out of 20 – 25 which took part. The British lost one fighter, the pilot of which was saved and suffered no other damage, despite sweeping claims subsequently put out by the Germans.

Little more remains to be told of the passage of JW 64. No further air attacks occurred. Icing, heavy snow-showers and short visibility hampered air operations; but whenever the weather permitted A/S patrols were flown during the approach to Kola Inlet. On 12th February the Russian escort was met and the Archangel section of the convoy was detached, with the *Lark*, *Lapwing* and *Alnwick Castle* as extended screen as far as the entrance of the White Sea. The remainder arrived at Kola Inlet that night and proceeded up to the harbour in pitch darkness, snow-squalls and short visibility. Soon after midnight when the last merchant ship was well on its way in, the *Denbigh Castle* was torpedoed just outside the entrance. 'Greatly to the credit of her officers and ship's company' she was kept afloat and 'the *Bluebell* (Lieutenant G. H. Walker) did excellent work in towing her in.'[372] She had, however, to be beached before reaching the anchorage and later turned over on her side, becoming a total loss.

The next day (14th February) two merchant ships arrived from the White Sea under Russian escort were torpedoed in almost exactly the same position as the *Denbigh Castle*.

While the escorting force was at Kola Inlet, Captain Allison in the *Zambezi*, with the *Zealous*, *Zest* and *Sioux*, was sent to evacuate some

Norwegians who were being attacked by the Germans in Soroy (off the entrance to Altenfjord). About 500 men, women and children were successfully taken off without incident and distributed among merchant ships of Convoy RA 64 for passage to the United Kingdom.

67

Meanwhile the problem of getting Convoy RA 64 (Plan 20) through the U-boat infested waters off Kola Inlet was occupying Rear-Admiral McGrigor's attention. 'It is clear,' he wrote afterwards:–

'That on sailing RA 64 would have to force its way through a strong concentration of U-boats ... one U-boat was working right in the entrance, where it had torpedoed three ships in the last few days, while HF DF fixes and Russian reports showed that others were clustered along the first 40 miles of the convoy route and could not be avoided. Russian countermeasures were confined to day flying and a few small craft patrolling the entrance and were quite ineffective. There was no night flying, no hunting groups and no thought on their part of taking the offensive against the U-boats so handily placed.'

In these circumstances he decided to send all suitable escort vessels to hunt the approaches as far as 35° E. The night before sailing and arranged for Russian craft to flood there area on the day of sailing so as to keep the U-boats down; Russian escorts were to follow the convoy until dark to take charge of any damaged ships and Russian tugs were to stand by.

Accordingly, the *Cygnet* (Commander A. H. Thorold), *Lark, Lapwing, Alnwick Castle* and *Bamborough Castle* sailed at dusk 16th February, to sweep the approaches. The sweep was not unfruitful and *U-425* was sunk by the *Lark* and *Alnwick Castle* during the night.

Convoy RA 64, 34 ships, sailed from Kola Inlet next morning, 17th February. The leading ships passed Toros Island at 0745,[373] but the convoy was slow getting out and two hours later eight ships were still in the Inlet.

It was not long before trouble started. At 1024 the *Lark*, then sweeping ahead of the convoy, was torpedoed and had her stern blown off. She managed to keep afloat and later that day was towed back to Kola. About an hour and a half later a merchant ship, the *Thomas Scott*, was torpedoed within sight of her; the crew 'immediately abandoned ship although the ship was floating on a even keel with little sign of damage, in a calm sea surrounded by escorts;'[374] she sank later while being towed back to harbour.

A third success was scored by the U-boats before the day was over. At 1523, half an hour after the convoy had altered course to the northward, the *Bluebell* was hit by a torpedo and blew up; there was only one survivor. Apart from a contact at 1830, which was unsuccessfully hunted, nothing was seen of the U-boats.

All this time the escort had been short-handed, as Commander Thorold with four escort vessels was standing by the damaged *Lark*. The Russians eventually took her over at 1740 and succeeded in towing her into harbour; and Commander Thorold's vessels overtook the convoy early next morning, 18th February. That day was uneventful and there were no signs of U-boats. In the afternoon the weather deteriorated and all flying had to be stopped and that night a gale blew up, with a big swell and sea and wind of 60 knots between gusts from ahead. By the morning of the 19th the convoy was scattered; the gale continued throughout the day, moderating about 2300 and at first light in the morning of the 20th the task of reforming the convoy was started. This was a matter of urgency, as enemy aircraft had started shadowing at 0420 and a torpedo attack was expected to follow. The escorts did well[375] and by 0900, 20th, 29 ships were in station, leaving four stragglers, two of which were coming up from astern.

An hour later groups of aircraft were detected coming from the port bow and crossing ahead of the convoy, which was steering 270°. The sea was still very rough with a strong wind, but the *Nairana*[376] flew off fighters to intercept. Rear-Admiral McGrigor manoeuvred the convoy to the southward to bring the aircraft on the quarter and it was from this direction that most of the attacks developed, though some came in from ahead. A large number of the torpedoes exploded prematurely, apparently on breaking surface in the trough of the rough seas and there were no casualties, either in the convoy or among the stragglers, one of which was attacked. By 1140 the last enemy aircraft had been driven off by Wildcats. Over 25 aircraft had taken part. Of these the *Onslow*, *Zealous* and fighters each shot down one; the fighters and the *Bamborough Castle* each got a 'probable' and four were damaged by the *Rhododendron*, *Sioux* and *Lapwing*. The returning Wildcats were again fired on by some merchant ships, 'fortunately without fatal results, in spite of warning by R/T and all that was said at the convoy conference. There was no excuse for it whatsoever.'[377]

Soon after noon, the escort was reinforced by the *Savage, Scourge* and *Zebra*, which had been sent by the Commander-in-Chief from Scapa to replace the casualties suffered off Kola. By that evening 31 ships of the convoy out of 33 were in station; one of the two stragglers was found and gathered in next afternoon (21st February). The other, the *Crosby Noyes*, was not heard of until she reported her position nearly a week later (27th) some 300 miles astern of the convoy, which was then in the latitude of the Shetlands.

During 21st and 22nd February the convoy was shadowed at intervals and a few HF DF bearings of U-boats were obtained, but no attacks occurred. On the 22nd another strong gale reaching 70-80 knots blew up from ahead. 'These constant gales ... which persisted throughout the voyage,' wrote Rear-Admiral McGrigor:–

'Caused much difficulty in keeping stragglers with the convoy. Engine trouble, defective steering, ice chipped propellers, shifting cargoes and splitting decks were among the very genuine reasons for dropping astern and at times stopping.'[378]

In the evening things got much worse and the convoy became badly scattered. Some ships followed the Commodore on a course 160°, while others hove to – amongst the latter the flagship *Campania* after rolling 45° each way.

At 0515, 23 February, though it was still blowing a full gale, an enemy aircraft appeared and must have reported a badly scattered convoy. A slight improvement of the weather enabled the *Campania* to rejoin the convoy some 40 miles to the eastward at 1045; there were then 20 merchant ships in company and a considerable proportion of the escorts. By 1700 all but one of the missing ships had been collected and course was resumed to the south-westward. Fortunately no air attack on the convoy in its unformed state followed the early morning sighting; but one straggler, the *Henry Bacon*, was attacked by part of a formation of about 19 torpedo bombers and sunk that afternoon. A DF bearing of her enemy report enabled Wildcats to find her, nearly 50 miles to the east of the convoy. Captain Allison in the *Zambezi* with the *Zest* and *Opportune*, was sent to rescue survivors and pick up 65, including Norwegian refugees from Soroy.[379]

For the next two days the gale continued strong with gusts up to 70 knots limiting the convoy's speed to about 3 ½ nots. There was much trouble with stragglers and their defects and by this time the *Bellona* and most of the destroyers were running short of fuel.[380] The latter were dispatched as necessary to the Faeroes to fill up and rejoin as soon as possible; the *Whitehall* had already been sent there with feed water trouble. In the evening of 23rd February, three fresh destroyers, the *Mynas, Scorpion* and *Cavalier*, arrived from Scapa; two of these were ordered to escort defective stragglers astern direct to the Faeroes.

During the night of 25th and 26th February, the wind though still very strong, shifted to the north-west, which allowed the convoy to make about seven knots for a few hours – the fastest speed for very many days; later in the day, it had by the evening of 26th February, they had passed the Faeroes and Rear-Admiral McGrigor with the two carriers, the *Bellona* and four destroyers proceeded to Scapa, leaving Commander R. F. Jessel of the *Zealous* in charge of the convoy which arrived at the Clyde in due course without further incident.

68

Convoys JW 64 and RA 64 were the last convoys to encounter serious enemy resistance. Rear-Admiral McGrigor's remarks on the operations are therefore of particular interest as enshrining the lessons of experience at the end of the long series of convoys. 'The outstanding features of JW 64 and RA 64,' wrote the Admiral:–

'Were the continuous heavy seas and adverse gales which persisted during the easterly run of JW 64 and for practically the whole passage of RA 64, the increased part ... played by enemy aircraft, the concentration of U-boats outside Kola when RA 64 sailed and the absence of U-boats during the remainder of the passage.'[381]

After briefly commenting on the effect of the weather – the reduction of RA 64's speed between three and six knots for most of the passage, its dispersal on two occasions and the impossibility of fuelling the escorts at sea[382] – the Admiral remarked on the increased enemy air effort.

Both convoys were shadowed at intervals day and night from just north of the Faeroes to one day out from Kola. Shadowers used radar to pick up the convoy at about 20 to 25 miles. By day they usually left very quickly, presumably by three or four aircraft flying about 25 miles apart in the middle or morning watch; when found the convoy would be shadowed and reported for two or three hours and homing signals made if in U-boat waters. 'I have already in my report on JW 62 and RA 62,'

A Type 277 radar which is a parabolic reflector made of wire mesh, this lowers its weight and wind resistance.

wrote Rear-Admiral McGrigor:–

> 'Drawn attention to the need for night fighters in the winter convoys, to the great chances they would have in suitable weather and to the healthy effect it would have on the enemy if some of his night shadowing aircraft were shot down. The one night fighting Fulmar provided was too obsolete and too full of defects to be of use ...'[383]

Turning to the Ju.88 torpedo attacks, the Rear-Admiral first stressed the extreme importance of having good radar communications in the flagship, remarking that he was fortunate in the *Campania* in having Type 277, through a blind arc of some 25° either side astern was always an anxiety.[384] Enemy torpedo bombers approached at sea level, visibility was usually poor and it was on information provided by Type 277 that the convoy had to be manoeuvred, the screening ships kept informed of the directions from which attacks were developing and fighters vectored to intercept. Moreover Type 277 almost always gave the first warning of the attack.

The enemy tactics seemed to be to send out a main group of perhaps 16 torpedo aircraft, accompanied by one or two smaller groups, all flying out at sea level. On finding the convoy these split up to attack in pairs from different bearings, afterwards retiring and attacking again later with their second torpedoes.

In practice the co-ordination of the attacks was poor. Groups would be broken up by the fighters and by gunfire from the outer screen and some of the aircraft would break away to attack screening ships, who proved quite capable of looking after themselves. Of the remainder, many would fire their torpedoes at too long range when they came under fire from the inner screen. A number of torpedoes, however, did enter the convoy. 'Against these,' the Admiral stated:–

> 'I have found it quite practicable to manoeuvre the convoy by
> emergency turns of 45°, although it is advisable to do a second turn
> of 45° before too long on account of station keeping. It takes time to
> get signals through, in practice at least two or three minutes,
> depending on visibility and even then it is advisable on turning to
> pass the course by Convoy R/T as some ships always miss the signal.
> With a large convoy it is obviously impossible for ever ship to be
> combing torpedoes, but much can be done to reduce the targets
> presented.'[385]

He also recommended an initial turn to bring the dawn or dusk ahead of the main attack astern, which undoubtedly upset the enemy and caused him either to fire his torpedoes from an unfavourable position (if committed to the attack) or to circle round at about 15 miles range trying to reach a better one; this was easily prevented by another emergency turn at the right moment. But for the smaller subsidiary attacks reliance had to be placed on the gunfire of the screen and in the last resort, that of the convoy.

Stragglers were in great danger and heavy casualties might have been incurred if the attacks on 20th and 23rd February had developed before the convoy was reformed after its dispersal by weather.

The Rear-Admiral gave great credit to the carrier fighters for their share in the operations, but considered their number inadequate. On this occasion they started with ten between two carriers, but after the attack on 20th February these were reduced at one time to four serviceable in the *Nairana* and one in the *Campania*. Each carrier needed its full complement of eight and this would be the more necessary as the hours of daylight increased.

As regards the problem of entering or leaving Kola without losses (or even the safety of ships in harbour there,[386] the position was most unsatisfactory. The approach was confined to a 40 mile passage running eastward along the shore before turning north; this was perfectly well known by the enemy and U-boats were stationed every few miles along it. The damage to the *Denbigh Castle* and a day later to two merchant ships proved that they were also operating in the actual entrance to the inlet.[387]

How to get an unformed convoy through these U-boats the Rear-Admiral described a major problem, to which the only answer would seem to be so to hunt and harry them as to force them to withdraw further from the coast. For this reason he considered it most important that each convoy should be so strong in long endurance escort vessels as to enable a continual offensive to be undertaken the approaches for the whole period the convoy was at Kola. The numbers needed for A/S and A.A. protection on passage were eight on the inner screen and ten on the outer; if possible one or two extra should be provided to replace casualties either from enemy action or weather damage, machinery defects, etc. In order to carry out the offensive against the U-boats off Kola, there should be as many long endurance sloops, frigates and modern corvettes as possible; Fleet destroyers were not suitable for this work, but a few should be included in the escort for their speed and surface armament.

Rear-Admiral McGrigor briefly summed up the results of JW 64 and RA 64 operations as follows:–

'We lost badly in the U-boat war. One U-boat was sunk against two escorts and one merchant ship sunk and one escort damaged.

All escorts had a most gruelling and uncomfortable time with the constant bad weather. Their effectiveness as A.A. screens was very encouraging. Aircraft[388] shot down during JW 64 and RA 64 totalled:–

Fighters	4 confirmed,	5 probables,	2 damaged
Gunfire	8 confirmed,	2 probables,	13 damaged
Total	12 confirmed,	7 probables,	15 damaged

Against this we lost one merchant ship straggler sunk by torpedo aircraft and two fighters, the pilot of one which was saved. The main convoy suffered no damage.'

69

No subsequent convoys had to cope with such onslaughts by either the enemy or the elements as those so finely surmounted by Convoys JW 64 and RA64, and the story of their passages can be told in a few words.

The late arrival of Convoy RA 64 and storm damage to its escorts (out of a total of 16 destroyers, no fewer than 12 required docking for minor hull damage caused by the weather) delayed the sailing of the next convoy, JW 65, until 11th March. Vice-Admiral Dalrymple-Hamilton, flying his flag in the *Campania*, with *Trumpeter* (Captain K. S. Colquhoun), *Diadem* and 19 escorts was in command. The convoy was routed so as to pass at least 300 miles from Trondheim and Bardufoss airfields. There were no incidents on the passage and excellent weather was experienced until arrival off Kola. At the instance of the Commander-in-Chief, Home Fleet, a new channel had been swept to the entrance, but this was not used in order to avoid compromising it for the departure of RA 65. Russian air cover was augmented by aircraft from the escort carriers, but unfortunately a snowstorm stopped flying for 1 ½ hours during the most dangerous period of the approach and two merchant ships and the *Lapwing* (Act.-Commander E. C. Hutton) were sunk by U-boats.

The frigates sailed ahead of the Convoy RA 65 and carried out harrying tactics off the entrance, while four Fleet destroyers proceeded at high speed along the old route, dropping depth charges and firing star shell, before turning to join the convoy, which meanwhile had taken a new route. No U-boats were encountered and after being joined by the ships from the White Sea at a rendezvous, RA 65 completed its passage without incident in good weather.

One more pair of convoys was run before the conclusion of hostilities. Rear-Admiral Cunninghame-Graham, who had succeeded Vice-Admiral Sir Frederick Dalrymple-Hamilton, was in command of the operations, with his flag in the *Vindex* (Captain J. D. L. Williams). In view of the U-boat threat off Kola, an extra Escort Group (the 19th) was made available, bring the total number of escorts up to 22, in addition to the *Premier* (Captain R. J. Gardiner) and *Bellona* (Captain Tuck). Convoy JW 66, consisting 26 ships,[389] sailed from the Clyde on 17th April; it was undetected by the enemy until arrival off Kola Inlet and all ships arrived safely.

The sailing of the return convoy was simulated the day before departure to mislead the U-boats and the 7th and 9th Escort Groups hunted them off the entrance. One U-boat was destroyed and another damaged, but the *Goodall* was torpedoed and sunk. RA 66 left by the new route unscathed; though shadowed intermittently by aircraft for two days, somewhat surprisingly no attack developed and the passage was completed without interference.

Although hostilities in Europe had ceased before the next convoy (JW 67) of 26 ships[390] sailed from the Clyde on 12th May, there was still a number of U-boats at sea, whose intentions were uncertain; the attitude of the German High Command in North Norway, too was unknown. A reduced escort under Captain Browning in the *Onslow*, with the *Obdurate, Queen* (Captain K. J. D'Arcy) and ten escorts of the 4th and 9th Escort Groups[391] therefore accompanied it as an insurance against 'accidents.'

When the convoy was north-east of the Faeroes, a report was received from HNorMS *Store* that she had met a convoy of 16 U-boats and five merchant ships in Vestfjord proceeding to Trondheim. The 9th Escort Group was accordingly detached to escort the U-boats to Loch Eriboll – a pleasant variation from the role they had so long carried out. The remainder of JW 67's passage and the return trip of RA 67 were without incident. Thus need the story of the long series of convoys to and from North Russia.

Chapter VIII

Comments and Reflections

70

Between August 1941 and May 1945, 40[392] outward bound convoys had carried the Hugh total of £428,000,000 worth of material, including 5,000 tanks, over 7,000 aircraft and quantities of munitions from Britain to North Russia.[393] Of the 811 ships which sailed in these convoys, 720 completed their voyage; 33 turned back for various reasons and 58 (or 7.2%) were sunk. The 34 westbound convoys fared better, losing 29 ships (or 4%) out of the 717 which sailed.[394] A total of 829 officers and men of the British and Allied merchant navies lost their lives.

Of the protecting forces, 18 ships (including two cruisers) of the Royal Navy and Polish submarine *P551* were sunk, with a loss of 1,815 officers and men; in addition, 129 were killed in various actions.

It was a heavy price to pay – but the goods were delivered. Nor did the enemy despite his advantage come off scathe less; the battlecruiser *Scharnhorst*, three large destroyers, 38 U-boats and an unknown number of aircraft were destroyed in action against the convoys.

Few will deny that the continuance of the traffic constituted an achievement unique in the history of convoy. The physical conditions alone imposed a well-nigh intolerable strain on both ships and men; the ever present proximity of ice, the bitter cold, the tempests and darkness of winter and perpetual daylight of summer – all introduced perils and problems peculiar to this Polar waters.

Moreover, the enemy held all the strategical cards. Fortunately, he did not know how to play them. To recapitulate – throughout the whole passage ships were liable to submarine attack. The route, severely restricted by ice on the shore-based aircraft for some 1,400 miles from Russian terminal ports. Such variations as could be made in it could usually be deduced by the enemy, even if the convoy was not located by air reconnaissance early in its passage forces could operate lay on its flank.

With the fate of the *Prince of Wales* and *Repulse* fresh in mind, it was not surprising that Sir John Tovey was reluctant to expose his capital ships to heavy air attack by shore-based aircraft and in addition U-boats in waters beyond the radius of effective action by destroyers.[395]

Should the enemy supplement his air and submarine offensive by surface attack[396] in the Barents Sea, it seemed as if it would be all too easy for him to inflict such losses as to bring the traffic to a complete standstill.

The succeeding sections seek to trace out how the difficulties were overcome and how it proved possible to keep the convoys running with such a remarkable degree of success.

71

Of the three forms of attack which had been met, surface attack presented the knottiest problem. The U-boat menace was much the same as in the Atlantic; suitable close escorts in sufficient numbers should be able to cope with this. Air attack (particularly with torpedoes) from the nearby shore-bases was more serious, but that again could be mitigated by suspending the convoys during the all-daylight summer months, by increasing powerful A.A. fire from escort and merchant ships and by fighters from the escort carriers when they became available. So long as escorts and convoys could keep together, it should be possible to confine losses from air and U-boat attack to reasonable limits.

But as regards surface attack, the answer was not apparent. The crux of the problem was how to protect the A/S and A.A. escorts from being overwhelmed in the Barents Sea. An answer was sought by providing cruiser cover in varying strengths (according to the latest intelligence), while heavy ships – with a fleet carrier, when available – cruised to the westward of 14° E. Longitude in support; but it was always doubtful whether the latter force would be able to intervene effectively should the occasion arise.[397] So long as the *Tirpitz* was battle worthy, the problem was never really solved, though in practice things worked out better than could have been expected. But this was due to the restrictions imposed on the German surfaces forces by Hitler, rather than to the intrinsic value of the British protective measures. To this cause must be ascribed the fact that whenever the German surface forces made contact they accomplished so little. Commander Richmond's bold defence of Convoy QP 11 and there fine tactics of Captain Sherbrooke and Commander Kinloch with Convoy JW 51B could hardly have saved their convoys had the enemy resolutely pressed home his attacks; nor could the appearance of Admiral Burnett's two light cruisers have caused the *Hipper* and *Lützow* to withdraw from the scene of action, but the determination of the Germans to accept no risk to their ships.

Turning to air attack, this was very effective in 1942 and caused serious casualties. Fortunately, the German Air Force was reduced and all its torpedo bombers were withdrawn at the end of that year; and by the time they attempted a come-back, escort carriers invariably accompanied the convoys. After 1942 the air attacks were on a greatly reduced scale and accomplished little; but it must be remembered that the convoys were discontinued during the all-daylight months in 1943 and 1944.

Throughout the whole period, U-boats kept up a sustained offensive. This followed the pattern of that in the Atlantic. At first patrols were established which would attack at sight; later, when the number of U-boats in Norway was increased they favoured 'pack' tactics, waiting until several submarines were in contact and then attacking together. The introduction of HD DF, enabling the escort craft to locate and keep them at a distance, was responsible for their first serious check; but they could not be properly hunted (owing to the necessity for the destroyers to conserve fuel and stand by for A.A. defence) until Escort Carriers and Support Groups from the Atlantic became available; they then sustained very sever losses. As already mentioned, their final tactics were to concentrate in the approaches of Kola Inlet, a difficult move to counters which inflicted losses on both escorts and merchant ships; but heavy depth charging and sweeping the area and action by air patrols kept the situation in hand.

72

The development of the tactics of the convoys and close escorts from the small beginnings of the winter of 1941-42 to their final form in Spring of 1945 is of interest.

It was in the last nine months of 1942 that far the heaviest scale of attack had to be met, when U-boat and air attack was well-nigh continuous and surface attack was frequently attempted. At this time there was a serious shortage of escort craft of all sorts. These had to be provided as and when they could be spared from other duties and consequently seldom constituted a well-drilled team, accustomed to work with each other. This makes the overall success of their efforts the more remarkable.

In the first place, there were the 'through' escorts, consisting of destroyers, corvettes and trawlers from the Western Approaches

Command which joined the convoy at the assemble port. These ships had good endurance and were well equipped and trained for anti-submarine work, but were weak in fire power. Minesweepers, too, though unsuitable for anti-submarine, air or surface protection, sometimes acted as escorts on their way to and from the White Sea minesweeping force. Later on, off Iceland or the Faeroes, they were joined by Home Fleet destroyers – not so experienced in A/S work as the Western Approaches escorts and with shorter endurance, but strong in fire power and speed; they too would join the anti-aircraft cruiser and escort carriers, when they became available.

As regards tactics, a rather close, almost circular screen was found to be best. This had several advantages. It kept the convoy together, stragglers being easily detected; it permitted visual signalling (in clear intervals between fog, snow, hail and spray); it allowed of maximum concentration of fire over the convoy; it conserved fuel; and any newcomer detected was certain to be an enemy.[398]

The Fleet destroyers were disposed with a view to easy concentration towards any quarter threatened by surface forces, with the A.A. cruiser in support. Under air attack, the A.A. cruiser usually came out to traverse the front of the convoy, in order to give freedom of manoeuvre for bringing her maximum gunpowder to bear. The other escorts were placed so to leave the anti-submarine screen intact on the departure of the Fleet destroyers.

When escort carriers were present, they normally occupied suitable stations within the convoy. While operating their aircraft, they steamed appropriate courses within the anti-submarine screen. If they had to break out, the two nearest Fleet destroyers accompanied them, to provide anti-submarine protection and to stand by for aircraft crashes.

The aircraft carried were Swordfish or Avengers and Sea Hurricanes or Wildcats. The Swordfish, fitted with rocket assisted take-off gear and armed with depth charges and rocket projectiles were used for anti-submarine search, patrols and attack; Wildcats for day fighter defence and in support of anti-submarine strikes. Most of the heavy toll of U-boats taken in 1944-45 was due to the fine offensive spirit of the carrier aircraft in rocket and depth charge attacks on surfaced submarines trying to gain bearing 20 miles or more from the convoy.[399] Radar (3 cm. ASV) was of great value to the Swordfish for the detection of the U-boats and the natural phenomenon of the Northern Lights greatly facilitated their operations in the darkness of the Arctic winter.

But it was strenuous work. The aircraft were operated on a schedule of 12 hours flying and 12 hours maintenance, in light varying from full daylight to full darkness; in extreme cold, with frozen deck gear and in seas from calm to mountainous. Some ships buckled the fore end of their flying decks, 60 feet above the water line and one recorded sea rolling the whole length of the flight deck.

73

Frequent reference has been made in the foregoing pages to the severe climatic conditions with which the convoys had to cope. They were indeed formidable.

Gales of unusual violence were of frequent occurrence and weather damage was often severe. In the merchant ships deck cargo, tanks, wagons and locomotives would sometimes shift and necessitate return to port. There was not much cargo bring back from Russia and the light ships with bows ballasted up so as to submerge the propellers became sometimes unmanageable in a bow or beam wind. Escorts, too, suffered badly, losing boats, davits and men on many occasions. Eventually destroyers used to leave their boats behind and in later classes flying bridges were fitted to allow fore and aft traffic.

Ice was never far off and ice in any shape or form was always a menace, as was stressed by Captain Denny in the early days of the convoys;[400] later, special ice reports were issued for the information of the escorts. Approach to the ice edge or large floes could be sensed by ice-blink and an intenser cold. Small floes could not be detected easily and it was preferable to be some 40 miles clear of the ice edge. The temptation to elude U-boats by entering ice leads had to be resisted; they would usually end in blind alleys and were apt to close in behind, leaving ships in a veritable maze, with resulting damage to forepeaks, propellers and steering gear. Experienced officers preferred to accept almost any hazard – such as turning a convoy off the ice edge by light signals in darkness when U-boats were known to be about – to risking such an encounter.

Heavy snow and ice on the upper deck and top hamper were dangerous if allowed to accumulate and once formed increased in bulk very rapidly. Whenever possible hands had to set to with picks and mauls; later special steam hoses were employed. Working parts, muzzles and chases of guns, torpedo tubes, etc., were kept ice free by special grease, steam and electric heating and jacketing; generally speaking these measures were effective, but they involved a lot of extra maintenance.

74

The Royal Navy and the Allied Navies which assisted it and the Mercantile Marines which took part may legitimately be proud of the story of the Arctic Convoys. As in all operations of war, their success ultimately hinged on the human element. This came through the ordeal triumphantly, though tested almost to the limit of endurance.

At a comparatively early stage, Rear-Admiral Burnett stressed the severe strain imposed on the destroyers.[401] This did not diminish as time went on; the later double convoys frequently involved as much as 28 days steaming for most of them, with no respite except for two or three days at Kola. And the prolonged strain on the smaller escort vessels – minesweepers and trawlers, sloops and corvettes – was no less. Nor should the fine work of the Fleet oilers, two of which were lost by enemy action and the rescue ships be forgotten. It was a service which called for a degree of endurance and hardihood from officers and men for which it would be hard to find a parallel.

But for sheer fortitude and courage perhaps the palm should go to the merchant ships. As Rear-Admiral Bonham-Carter remarked, 'We in the Navy are paid to do this sort of job ... We may be able to avoid bombs and torpedoes with our speed, a six or eight knot ship has not this advantage ... Nevertheless year after year the six or eight-knot ships, laden largely with lethal cargoes, continued to plod backwards and forwards on that grim 2,000 mile journey.

The skill and seamanship of the Commodores and Masters in handling their ships in these large convoys – in fog, darkness and storm, hampered by ice or under enemy attack – is attested by the remarkable fact that not a single merchant ship was lost through collision. And the skill the officers was matched by the fortitude and grit of the ships' companies and guns' crews.

'The Russian Convoys,' said M. Musky, the Soviet Ambassador in London, in 1943, 'are a Northern Saga of heroism, bravery and endurance.' With this dictum we can unreservedly agree.

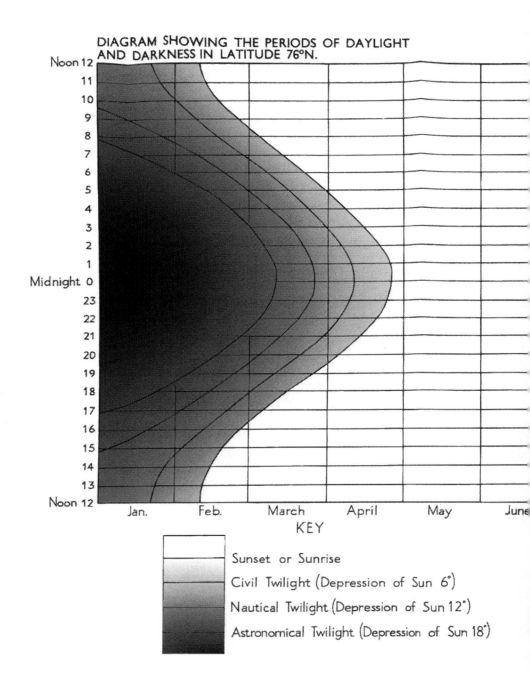

DIAGRAM SHOWING THE PERIODS OF DAYLIGHT
AND DARKNESS IN LATITUDE 76°N.

KEY

Sunset or Sunrise
Civil Twilight (Depression of Sun 6°)
Nautical Twilight (Depression of Sun 12°)
Astronomical Twilight (Depression of Sun 18°)

PLAN 21

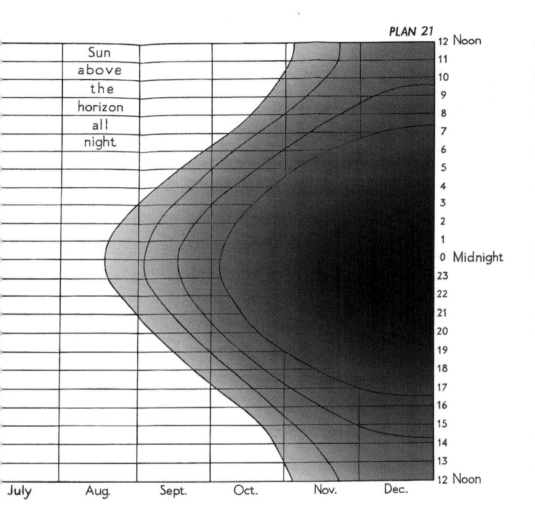

Endnote

1. Operation 'Dervish.' After this first convoy, the eastbound convoys were known by the letters PQ and the westbound QP, the convoys being numbered consecutively. At the end of 1942, for security reasons, the nomenclature was altered to JW and RA respectively, the new series starting at number 51.

2. While the issue of their 1941 offensives, by which they hoped to force Russia to sue for an early peace, was in doubt, these convoys of course had not the importance they acquired when the prospect of a long war confronted them.

3. 162 ships sailed during this period, but four turned back.

4. Twelve eastbound PQ 1-11 and 'Dervish'; seven westbound, QP 1-7. See App. A(f).

5. In addition, an oiler sailed with PQ 12.

6. Roughly from Jan Mayen Island to 150 miles west of Bear Island

7. Special patrols, designed to spot the departure of the German heavy ships from Trondheim, were flown by Coastal Command when the Arctic convoys where at sea in the danger area. These patrols were not so effective as they might have been, owing to the serious shortage of aircraft from which Coastal Command was suffering, and the difficult weather conditions, which frequently rendered their efforts nugatory.

8. M. 050799/42.

9. About 200 miles east of Jan Mayen Island.

10. *Faulknor* (D8), *Eskimo, Punjabi, Fury, Echo* and *Eclipse*. The three last named sailed seven hours before the remainder, with orders to fuel at Seidisfjord and to join at sea.

11. *Onslow* (D 17), *Ashanti, Intrepid, Icarus, Lookout* and *Bedouin*.

12. *Berwick* could only steam 27 knots and was to have been replaced by the *Sheffield* from the Iceland-Faroes patrol. The latter, however, on her way to join the fleet struck a mine on 4th March and had to go to Seidisfjord, escorted by the *Faulknor* and *Eskimo*, which were sent to her aid by Vice-Admiral Curteis. On the same day the *Bedouin* parted company with the C.-in-C. to pick up a man overboard; owing to the rendezvous signal being incorrectly received, she missed the fleet. These three destroyers did not rejoin until some days later.

13. The *Gossamer* and one whaler arrived in Russia independently; the fourth whaler capsized in the Barents Sea.

14. One battleship or 8-inch cruiser in position 64° 26z N. 10° 18' E. course 045° at 1801A/6.

15. For the air reconnaissance, see Admiralty Messages 1623A/4, 1752A/5 and 1823A/6 and C.-in-C., Rosyth, 1751/4, 2151/5 and 1757/6 March.

The French submarine *Minerve* was returning to her base, on relief by the *Seawolf*, but was ordered on the 6th to a station some 200 miles down the coast.

On 18th March, while going from this 'heart-breaking patrol', as the captain of her flotilla called it, the *Seawolf* had her reward by sinking a German submarine.

16. At noon, 7th, according to the *Kenya*, visibility was one mile; two hours later, it was 30 miles (to the north-westward). At 1130 that day, the C.-in-C., H.F., altered course to the south-westward (away from the enemy, as it happened) to 'search for clearer weather'.

17. At noon, 7th, the *Tirpitz* was on a north-westerly course, about 70 miles to the S.S.W. of the two convoys, which were then passing each other and roughly the same distance to the E.S.E. of the Home Fleet, which had altered course to the south-west half an hour previously. She passed some 40 miles ahead of QP 8 on a northerly course at about 1330 and 70 miles astern that evening on an easterly course. She was then about 65 miles astern of PQ 12 and was actually within 120 miles of this convoy until she abandoned the operation in the evening of the 8th March.

18. *Hazard* (SO), *Salamander*, *Oxlip* and *Sweet Briar*. Local escort was provided by the minesweepers *Harrier* and *Sharpshooter* until daylight, 3rd March and by the U.S.S.R. destroyers *Gremyaschi* and *Gromki* as far as longitude 30° E.

19. 'Enemy surface forces may be in vicinity of PQ 12. Convoy is to steer 360° unless other orders have been received from C.-in-C., Home Fleet.' 1519A/7 (to convoy escort, repeated to C.-in-C.).

20. The observer in the Walrus had these orders from Captain Denny: 'On no account a signpost to the convoy. Course steered in sight of anything was to be at right angles to the bearing of the convoy and the track out and home to include a 90-degree alteration of course ... Enemy report to be made on Fleet wave and to include position, course and speed of PQ 12.'

21. The composition of the convoy and escort were correctly given, but the position is some 60 miles to the westward of that estimated by the *Kenya* at the time (70° 05' N. 6° 09' W.); and the convoy was making good nearer eight knots than six. These errors combined to cause the *Tirpitz* subsequently to place the convoy further west than it actually was.

22. Approximate positions were:–
(a) 73° N. 0° 30' E. (U-134)
(b) 72° 28'N. 1° 20'E. (U-584)
(c) 71° 50'N. 2° 50'E. (U-454)
(d) 71° 15'N. 3° 55'E. (U-589)

23. *Tirpitz, Scheer*, 5th Destroyer Flotilla (*Z25, Hermann Schuemann, Paul Jacobi* and *Friedrich Ihn*), 2nd Torpedo Boat Flotilla (*T5, T12*).
   After consideration, it was decided that the slow speed of the *Scheer* would probably hamper the *Tirpitz* and the operation against the convoys was limited to the latter and three destroyers.

24. *Hermann Schuemann, Friedrich Ihn* and *Z25*. Local A/S escort through *Fro Havet* was provided by the *Paul Jacobi, T5* and *T12*.

25. This position was about 40 miles to the westward of PQ 12's actual position at this time.

26. *Tirpitz* war diary, 6th March 1942.

27. The destroyers were eventually to form a reconnaissance screen from 72° 25' N. 11° 30' E. to 71° 50' N. 6° 30' E. (approximately 100 miles) and to steer 350 at 25 knots from 1430, rejoining the *Tirpitz* at 1900 in 72° 45' N. 9° 30' E.; but these orders were cancelled, as the result of the sinking of the *Ijora*.

28. C.-in-C., Home Fleet's report (M.050801).

29. Ibid

30. C.-in-C., Home Fleet's report (M.050801/42).

31. It was not until 1815 that evening that the Fleet was thought to be at sea.

32. German account. The Germans placed the sinking in 72° 40' N. 10° 30' E., only about five miles north-west of the *Ijora*'s signalled position (72° 35' N., 10° 50' E.).

33. Admiral Ciliax had decided to abandon the search that evening (8th), on account of inadequate air reconnaissance, uncertainty of enemy dispositions and the unfavourable weather. All three destroyers were ordered to rejoin him at 0700, 9 March, in 68° 13' N. 10° 32' E. (some 145 miles due west of Narvik).

34. QP 8.

35. C.-in-C., Home Fleet's report (M.050801/42).

36. *Onslow, Punjabi, Fury, Ashanti, Echo* and *Eclipse*. Only the Lookout remained with the battle fleet, as the *Intrepid* and *Icarus* had been sent to Seidisfjord for fuel (at 2000, 7th).

37. A Fokker Wulf 200 made contact with the *Tirpitz* at 1120 and was ordered to search to the westward, but it sighted nothing.

38. She was then in approximately 72° 25' N. 13° 17' E.

39. The C.-in-C. subsequently remarked, 'Although this was not my object in breaking wireless silence, there was a good chance that to do so might be the means of saving PQ 12'.

40. *Kent* which was on patrol in Denmark Strait, was relieved by USS *Quincy* and two American destroyers.

41. *Kent* and *Landon*, 70° N. Long. 0°; *Trinidad* and *Liverpool*, 69° N. 1° W.

42. *Tirpitz*: Course 082° thought at the time to be 040°, speed about 26 knots.
Aircraft: Course 115° at 90 knots.
Wind from 070° at 35 knots.

43. Actually, the *Tirpitz* had sighted them at 0858 (Log of *Tirpitz*).

44. The *Tirpitz* reported that the aircraft attacked with great determination and dash, some of them, after dropping their torpedoes, attacking the ship's bridge with guns.

45. The *Tirpitz*'s aircraft became involved with two Albacores some 25 miles astern before the torpedo attack. When later it came across some Swordfish, it had run out of ammunition.

46. At 0948, a Heinkel 115 joined her as close escort, this aircraft reported a submarine attacking at 1038 and the *Tirpitz* took avoiding action. Actually, no submarine was in this area, but the Germans did not know this and this incident received consideration when the policy for the future employment of the *Tirpitz* was under review by the German Naval Staff.
She finally arrived at Narvik without further incident at 1620, 9th March.

47. According to German sources the shadower reported an aircraft carrier, one light and three heavy cruisers in 65° 55 N. 8° 53 E. at 1015. The Luftwaffe unit operating in this area sent all available aircraft, six in number, to attack; of these two only succeeded in doing so. No torpedo aircraft were available.

48. *Faulknor, Eskimo, Bedouin* and *Tartar*.

49. *Javelin, Inconstant, Ledbury, Grove, Woolslon, Verdun, Wells* and *Lancaster*.

50. The return, of the *Tirpitz* to Trondheim, does not seem to have been certainly known in England until the 18th, the first day since the 11th on which air reconnaissance was possible.

51. M.050799/42.

52. On this latter point he added that he understood there might be a desire to operate the concentrated heavy ships to the eastward of Bear Island in the future and stated that he was not prepared to take them beyond longitude 14° E. without a full destroyer screen, except on definite information of an enemy ship in that area.

53. The Admiralty considered it unsound to base any plan on the supposition that the enemy did not wish to fight and doubted whether a covering force of two heavy ships was sufficient, in view of the experience of the *Hood* and *Prince of Wales* against the *Bismarck*. They agreed that the Fleet should not proceed east of 14° E. without a screen and that the destruction of the *Tirpitz* should be his primary object, but considered that this latter could best be brought about by giving strong close support to the convoys. No reply seems to have been sent to the C.-in-C., however.

54. *German Surface Ships, Policy and Operations, etc.*, p. 105.

55. This could not be effected before the autumn of 1944, owing to labour shortages. Actually, work was again suspended in the spring of 1943 and the ship was never completed.

56. G.H.S./4. *German Surface Ships, Policy and Operations.*

57. Two Russian and HMS *Oribi*.

58. C.-in-C., Home Fleet's signal H45A/16 March 1942. These orders were subsequently included in Home Fleet 'Instructions for Escorts of North Russian Convoys' (Mem. HY, in M.08483/42).

59. The *Lanierton* with the oiler *Oligarch* (Force Q) parted company at 0200, 24 March, and proceeded in accordance with previous orders for a rendezvous in which to fuel the destroyers accompanying the heavy ship covering force.

60. Sulla, Sumba and Silja.

61. HMS Harrier and four minesweepers of the 1st and 6th M.S. Flotillas based at Kola Inlet accompanied QP 9 until 0400, 23 March. A Russian destroyer, which was intended to have remained in company until dusk 23rd, lost contact during the night 22nd/23rd.

63. Admiralty Message 1336/23. The C.-in-C., Home Fleet, subsequently questioned the wisdom of this new route, involving a long passage within effective range of the enemy bombers at Banak, 'particularly during periods of long daylight, when air operations are facilitated and U-boats attacks rendered correspondingly difficult' (M.07411/42).

64. In the evening of 25 March, Captain Saunders reluctantly decided to break wireless silence to report the situation to the Admiralty, C.-in-C., Home Fleet and SBNO, North.

Russia, and also to order the scattered merchant ships to rendezvous in position E (73° 10' N. 15° 20'E.) on 27th, in order that the convoy might be reformed before making the Bear Island passage. The C.-in-C., Home Fleet, subsequently stated that he did not consider the breaking of wireless silence justified on this occasion.

65. The situation was not helped by the fact that the Commodore of the convoy (Commodore Casey) was embarked in a tanker, SS *River Afton*, which found herself unable to steer within 5 points of the wind, and after drifting towards the Lofoten Islands until noon, 27th, completed the voyage independently.

The Commanding Officer, HMS *Trinidad*, in his report of proceedings, stressed the importance of the Commodore being embarked in the best found ship of a convoy.

66. The *Sumba* reported herself unable to make headway and short of fuel in a position 50 miles S.W. of Bear Island, i.e., 120 miles N.E. of the *Fury*; DF bearings, however, placed her to the S.W. of her. Accordingly, she steered 240° and made contact at 1600.

Commenting on this incident, the Commanding Officer, *Fury*, described the presence of these whalers (whose endurance was insufficient to make the passage without fuelling) as 'a source of constant anxiety to the Senior Officer of the escort, and not only anxiety, but on this occasion a menace through causing one of the two destroyer escorts to be absent from the convoy for twelve hours.' It also necessitated the breaking of wireless silence that it was so important to preserve.

67. This general situation only became known to the *Trinidad* gradually in the course of the day.

68. Admiralty Messages 0001/27, 2146/27, 2219/27.

69. According to a report by the Second Officer of SS *Induna*, then in company with the *Empire Starlight*, *Ballot* and *Silja*, a Blohm-Voss reconnaissance plane sighted this group at close range as early as the forenoon of 26th March. The aircraft was engaged and seen to be hit; it then disappeared into a snowstorm. Since no report appears to have been received by the Germans at this time it seems that it subsequently crashed.

70. Sunset, 28th, 1754; Civil twilight (sun 6° below horizon) ended 1907. Sunrise, 29th, 0416; Civil twilight commenced 0304.

71. The U-boat was sighted in a haze about four miles on the starboard bow. Fire was opened on her, but as she did not immediately dive, it was thought it might be a boat under sail from the *Empire Ranger* and cease fire was ordered after three salvoes. She then submerged, and the *Trinidad* altered course to 280° to avoid the area.

72. They had been picked up by the German destroyers. *See* Sec. 15.

73. The *Oribi* was ordered to sweep 20 miles astern of the group to look for possible stragglers, before taking her place in the screen.

74. They were reported by the Russians in 71° 10' N., 31° 40' E. at 2000, 28th March.

75. This position is some 60 miles to the eastward of that given in B.R.1337 (72° 30' N., 27° 00' E.), but is probably fairly accurate.

76. Actually, they were approximately 40 miles E. by S. of the *Eclipse*'s group and some 70 miles to the westward of the easternmost group. The *Trinidad* and *Fury* were not very far to the south-westward of them.

77. This position agrees remarkably closely with the position given by the German destroyer *Z25*. According to her account, however, fire was opened at 0947 (German time: 0847A). British times have been used in this Narrative.

78. This is not confirmed by the Germans.

79. Actually no torpedoes were fired by the *Trinidad* at *Fury* during this encounter.

80. HMS *Trinidad*'s report.

81. The torpedo seemed to come from about half a mile to the left of *Z26*, and it was thought at the time that it had been fired from another destroyer, invisible in the mist. It is now known that this was not the case (see Sec. 20). Both the other German destroyers were some five to six miles to the north-eastward during this action.

82. HMS *Eclipse*'s report.

83. Ibid.

84. Ibid.

85. The C.O. Eclipse (Lieut. Commander Mack) was still of the opinion that this ship was the *Trinidad*, of whose torpedoing he was by then aware, and informed the *Oribi* that he was going to join her. He also knew that there was a damaged enemy destroyer about, which 'might be worth beating up.'

86. The Germans evidently mistook the *Eclipse* for one of her consorts, as she flashed her call-sign at her on first sighting.

87. 'A' gun was out of action, owing to ice.

88. Three had unfortunately been fired in local control owing to an error on the part of the Gunner (T), who was under the impression that bridge communications had broken down.

89. Commenting on this action the C.-in-C., Home Fleet, subsequently remarked:–
'HMS *Eclipse* was most ably handled by Lieut. Commander Mack, and she was gallantly fought under the most severe conditions ... I consider Lieut. Commander Mack was entirely correct in retiring in the face of this superior force and handled his ship cleverly to avoid more serious damage.'

90. A signal from the *Trinidad* ordering the *Eclipse* to join her and act as A/S screen was not received.

91. The *Harrier, Gossamer, Hussar* and *Speedwell* had left Kola Inlet on 28th March to patrol the last part of the convoy route in the vicinity of positions B and U (see Plan 4) and look out for stragglers from PQ 13. The *Harrier* was on her way to search for the *Empire Ranger*'s boats, which were thought to be making for the coast, when she heard that the *Trinidad* had been torpedoed; she then steered to close her.

An interesting sidelight is thrown on some of the difficulties under which the SBNO, North Russia (Rear-Admiral R. H. Bevan) laboured by the fact that on this occasion the minesweepers had orders specially to look out for SS *River Afton* and *Empire Cowper*, from which two officers and a rating were to be taken off to avoid their being incarcerated by our Russian Allies on arrival – as had happened in the case of three officers shortly before.

92. The *Silja* was found next day (30th) by the *Oribi*, and eventually completed her voyage in tow of the *Harrier*.

93. Her survivors, several of whom died of exposure in her boats, were rescued by a Russian minesweeper on 2nd April.

94. It is to be noted that the ships lost were all proceeding independently of the convoy at the time of their loss.

95. M.051479/42.

96. G.H.S./4. *German Surface Ships, Policy and Operations.*

97. M.051479/42.

98. Ibid.

99. *See* App. A.

100. Destroyers *Bulldog, Beagle, Beverley, Amazon* and *Newmarket*. Corvettes *Campanula, Oxlip, Saxifrage* and *Snowflake*. The *Newmarket* developed condenser trouble and did not join up.

101. *Hebe* and *Speedy.*

102. Rear-Admiral Bonham-Carter's report on this passage was not encouraging. After referring to the 'large escort, which was intended for 25 ships' he remarked: 'Under present conditions with no hours of darkness, continually under air observation for the last four days, submarines concentrating in the bottlenecks, torpedo attack to be expected, our destroyers unable to carry out a proper hunt or search owing to the oil situation, serious losses must be expected in every convoy.

The remains of PQ 14 were extremely lucky in the weather in that when the first heavy air attack developed on Friday 17th April, fog suddenly came down ... on the following day ... when a combined surface, submarine and air attack was expected, the weather again was on our side, fog and snow showers persisting all day and on the final run in to Kola Inlet a strong gale from the north-west sprang up. I consider it was due to the fine work of the A/S Escort Force (under Commander M. Richmond) that only one ship was lost ...' (M.06950/42).

103. These figures are from German sources.

104. This distance was chosen as being clear of the area believed to be covered by the enemy coastal air patrols.

The only submarines available for these covering operations were the French *Minerve*, the Norwegian *Uredd* and the Polish *P551* and *P43*. The *Sturgeon*, after leaving the convoy in 5° E. proceeded to the south-westerly zone, the remainder having moved to the north-eastward by then.

106. A US squadron, known as Task Force 39, under Rear-Admiral R. C. Giffen, USN, had joined the Fleet at Scapa on 3rd April. It consisted of the new 16-inch gun battleship *Washington*, the carrier *Wasp*, the 8-inch gun cruisers *Wichita* and *Tuscaloosa* and six destroyers.

107. *See* App. A.

108. Approximate position 73° 03' N. 33° E.

109. The C.-in-C., Home Fleet, subsequently remarked that his instructions to the Rear-Admiral were 'that the *Edinburgh* was to protect Convoy PQ 11 against surface attack by destroyers ... The provision of this protection necessitated the *Edinburgh* being within close supporting distance of the convoy and therefore exposed her to considerable risk of attack by U-boats operating against the convoy. The smallness of the A/S escort available for QP 11 did not enable me to provide Edinburgh herself with any A/S screen' (M.06931/42).

110. Owing to the lack of a supporting force, it had been decided not to operate destroyers against PQ 15 and QP 11.

111. Zone minus 2.

112. This was the first time the German Air Force had attacked a convoy with torpedoes.
The Germans had been slow to appreciate the potentiality of this form of attack. From the outbreak of war until the autumn of 1941 the German Fleet air arm maintained about a couple of dozen torpedo-carrying seaplanes, which were used spasmodically with poor results. In 1941 the improvement of the defensive A.A. armament of merchant ships led the Luftwaffe to consider the use of the torpedo as an alternative to bombing. After friction with the Navy, which considered the torpedo as its own preserve, Goering obtained leave in December 1941 for the Luftwaffe to develop torpedo aircraft. He.111 and Ju.88 aircraft were found suitable and by April 1942 twelve crews had been trained. These were sent to Bardufoss and thereafter the arm was rapidly expanded.

113. It had been decided at the convoy conference and at a meeting of C.O.s, Escort Vessels, 'that in event of surface attack the destroyers would interpose themselves between the enemy and the convoy, while the latter turned away or scattered; the corvettes were to manoeuvre with the convoy.

114. The German destroyer *Hermann Schoemann* mounted 5–5-inch HA/LA guns; *Z24* and *Z25*, 5–5.9-inch each: total 5–5-inch, 10–5.9-inch guns.

The *Bulldog, Beagle* and *Amazon* had been stripped of 50 per cent of their main armament to fit additional A/S devices for the Battle of the Atlantic and mounted only 2–4.7-inch guns each; the *Beverley*, 3–4-inch guns, of which only two could be fired on a broadside: total, 6–4.7-inch, 3–4-inch guns.

115. Commanding Officer, HMS *Bulldog*'s report, in M.08568/42.

116. It was thought at the time that some hits might have been scored on the Germans during the last two engagements, but this is not confirmed by the German records.

117. To a congratulatory signal made by Commander Richmond to the destroyers after the actions, he received the instant reply from one of them, 'I should hate to play poker with you!'

118. 'This tortuous track could be seen winding astern, indicated by the oil and occasionally the ship got completely out of control and swept round in a complete circle. The engine room register shows that in one watch, 64 engine orders were executed on one shaft alone.' – C.O., HMS *Edinburgh*'s report, in M.06931/42.

119. This signal had not reached the SO, Minesweepers, when the attack took place next day. Admiral Bonham-Carter subsequently remarked that this was fortunate, as had it been acted on the minesweepers would not have been in a position to take off the ship's company of the *Edinburgh*.

120. The *Niger* had been detached during the night to meet the two Russian destroyers which were supposed to be sailing from Kola to the *Edinburgh*'s assistance. They did not sail until long after expected and the *Niger* rejoined the British force at 1020, 2nd May.

121. 'The minesweepers were like three young terriers going in and firing when they could.' Rear-Admiral Bonham-Carter's Report, App. II (in M.06931/42).

122. Logs of *Hermann Schoemann* and *Z24* (P.G.74466, P.G.74635).

123. Commanding Officer, HMS *Foresight*'s report (in M.06931/42).

124. Four torpedoes had been fired by *Z24*.

125. Lieutenant J. Bitmead, who had taken command of the *Forester* on the death of the Commanding Officer, remarked in his report: '*Foresight*'s appearance was just in the nick of time and undoubtedly saved us from further hits and had a great heartening effect, on the ship's company.'

126. About 60 men in boats and rafts were left behind; these were subsequently rescued by U-38.

127. Despite having been hit by three torpedoes and being abandoned in the middle of an action, only two officers and 55 ratings were lost and 23 ratings wounded out of a total complement of about 760. Fortunately the wind and sea had gone down, before the minesweepers went alongside.

128. *Gremyaschi* and *Sokrushitelni*: 4–5.1-inch, 2–3-inch A.A. guns.

129. Ship fitted with catapult aircraft. On this occasion the aircraft was not flown off, as it was desired to reserve it for use against the attacks expected off Kola Inlet. As things turned out, these did not materialise, owing to bad weather.

130. *See* App. A.

131. The *King George V* left Scapa for Liverpool for repairs and refit on 8th May. The Commander-in-Chief transferred his flag to the *Duke of York* and the Vice-Admiral, 2nd in command shifted to the *Nelson*.

132. The convoy was then in approximately 73° 17' N., 8° 25' E. Admiral Burrough described the attack as 'ragged and very poorly executed – possibly due to the intense cold ... The volume of fire put up by the escort and convoy, who were keeping excellent station, was impressive ...' – Report by R.A. 10th C.S. (in M.06826).

133. As all the enemy destroyers in the North had been sunk or damaged in the final action with the *Edinburgh*, the C.-in-C., Home Fleet, instructed the *Nigeria* and *London* to leave PQ 15 west of Bear Island and not to proceed into the U-boat waters further east, unless the convoy was threatened by enemy cruisers or larger vessels.

134. 'The feeling of being shadowed day and night with such efficiency is uncomfortable and considering the efficiency of the shadowing, I am surprised that more air attacks did not take place ... It is surprising also that there is only evidence that one submarine attack took place ...' – C.O., HMS *Bramble*'s Report (in M.08491/42).

135. *See* Chapter II.

136. The pocket battleship *Scheer* was found to have moved to Narvik, the remainder being still at Trondheim.

137. *Inglefield* (D.3), *Escapade, Onslow* and *Icarus*.

138. Six Hurricanes had been promised for the first 60 miles and three PE3 fighters for 200 miles. Only three Hurricanes arrived, which covered the ships for three-quarters of an hour and then returned to base.

139. The ship was then in 73° 37' N., 23° 26' E. (about 70 miles S.E. of Bear Island).

140. One officer, 60 ratings and 20 merchant seamen taking passage lost their lives.

141. Churchill, W. S., *The Second World War* (English edition). Vol. IV, pp. 230-234.

142. The *Scheer* was at Narvik and on 16th May the *Lützow* left the Baltic for Trondheim, joining the *Scheer* at Narvik on the 26th.

143. *Duke of York* (flag, C.-in-C.), *Washington* (flag, Rear-Admiral Giffen), *Victorious, Wichita, London* and nine destroyers.

144. Owing to the evident inability of the Russians to provide air cooperation in the Barents Sea, the C.-in-C., Home Fleet, had asked for RAF reconnaissance and long range fighter aircraft to be stationed in North Russia. These would provide the convoys during the worst part of their passage with A/S patrols, fighter protection and reconnaissance against surface attack. But the number of aircraft in Coastal Command was insufficient to meet any of these requirements.

145. *St. Elstan, Lady Madeleine, Retriever* and *Northern Spray*. The *Retriever* considered her speed insufficient and returned to Iceland on 24th May.

146. *Honeysuckle, Starwort, Hyderabad* and FFS *Roselys*.

147. The *Garland* lost touch in the fog and subsequently joined up with Admiral Burrough.

148. For this purpose. Captain (D) **17** in the *Onslow* placed himself and his destroyers under the orders of Commander Onslow, the Senior Officer of the close escort.

149. 'I was greatly impressed by the spirit and determination of the Master and crew of the *Carlton*, also by the calm acceptance by *Northern Spray* of a long and difficult voyage with no hope of support against air attack.' – Commanding Officer, HMS *Ashanti*'s report (in M.08408/42).

150. According to German sources, 101 Ju.88s and seven He.111 were used; three Ju.88s were lost.

151. Four bombs fell in a group abreast the bridge about 20 feet off. There was no underwater damage, but the *Garland* was riddled from stem to stern with splinter holes; 'A' and 'B' guns, one Oerlikon and No. 1 boiler room were put out of action and a fire was started in the forecastle. Casualties amounted to 25 killed and 43 wounded. It was thought that this unusual splinter damage was caused by the first bomb exploding on striking the water and detonating the other three in the air.

152. Seventy-four officers and 397 men were rescued in this way from the seven ships sunk in the course of the passage.

153. The convoy was then in 73° 30' N. 22° 40' E., about 80 miles south-east of Bear Island.

154. Commanding Officer, HMS *Ashanti*'s report in M.08408/42.

155. Ibid.

156. *Bramble* (SO), *Leda, Seagull, Niger, Hussar* and *Gossamer*.

157. Commanding Officer, HMS *Ashanti*'s report in M.08408/42.

158. *See* App. A.

159. Except for one Russian merchant ship, which had been unable to keep up and had returned to Kola on 22nd May.

160. Döenitz War Diary, 3rd June 1942.

161. This curious error that heavy air attack would force the convoys to scatter persisted for some time and received some colour when the next convoy (PQ 17) scattered some two hours after its first air attack for quite different reasons.

162. The total strength of the German Air Forces in the area of the North Cape at this time stood at:–

LR Bombers (Ju.88) 103

Torpedo Bombers (He.111) 42

Torpedo Floatplanes (He.111) 15

Dive Bombers (Ju.87) 30

LR Reconnaissance (Fw.200 Condor) 8

LR Reconnaissance (Ju.88) 22

LR Reconnaissance (Bv.138) Fleet Air Arm 44

163. Operation 'Harpoon.' The cruiser *Kenya*, flying the flag of Vice-Admiral Curteis, *Liverpool* and eight destroyers left Scapa on 4th June. The *Liverpool* and *Matchless* were damaged and the *Bedouin* sunk in the course of the operation; the remainder rejoined the Home Fleet on 24th June.

164. This attitude had a most serious effect on the whole conduct of operations. It is hardly too much to say that once the heavy ships were at sea, their object became their safe return to harbour, rather than to inflict damage on the enemy. On this occasion, for example, after Hitler's approval had been obtained, Grand Admiral Raeder deemed it necessary to warn Group Command, North, that a Naval reverse at this juncture would be particularly undesirable; whereupon Group Command, North, signalled to Admiral Schniewind: – 'Better short-lived operations with partial success than a prolonged attempt at complete success. Should the situation appear doubtful, do not hesitate to disengage. On no account allow the enemy to score success against the main body of the fleet.'

Instructions more damping and cramping to the Commander of an operation can scarcely be imagined.

165. *See* Sec. 11.

166. C.-in-C., Home Fleet's despatch, London Gazette, 17th October 1950, pp. 5144, 5145.

167. Idem.

168. Admiralty Message O157B of 27 June 1942.

169. C.-in-C., Home Fleet's despatch, London Gazette, 17th October 1950, p. 5145.

170. i.e. a force that did not include the *Tirpitz*.

171. *See* Secs. 2, 11, 12, 13 (note 5.)

172. The telephone between the Fleet Flagship at Scapa Flow and the Admiralty was much used for the exchange of views on many important questions. No verbatim record of these conversations was kept.

173. *See* Home Fleet memo. HY4, dated 21st June 1942, App. VI (in M.08483/42).

174. Vice-Admiral Sir Bruce Fraser succeeded Vice-Admiral Sir A. Curteis as Vice-Admiral 2nd in command. Home Fleet, on 28th June.

175. Hitler's sanction was particularly important from the point of view of air cover, which, owing to the jealousy between the Luftwaffe and the Navy, could not be relied on except by Hitler's orders.

176. Commander Broome subsequently remarked on the difference between the North Russia and Atlantic convoys: in the Atlantic, he said, 'with one main threat, sighting a U-boat is a clear lower deck affair, followed by determined and prolonged hunting, whereas with air attack as probably the greater threat, all one can afford to do is to throw something at the U-boats as they appear.'

177. Report of proceedings, R.A.1st C.S., in T.S.D.3288/42.

178. They were accompanied by six destroyers, *Z24, Z27, Z28, Z29, Z30* and *Richard Beitzen.*

179. *Hans Lady, Theodor Riedel* and *Karl Galsler.* This left only the *Friedrich Ihn* with the group.

180. 'Immediate. Reference Admiralty message 0157, 27th, para, (i) – unless otherwise ordered by C.-in-C., H.F., you may proceed eastward of 25° E. should situation demand it.

(ii) This is not to be taken as urging you to proceed eastward against your discretion. T.O.O. 1230B/4 July.'

181. 'Immediate. Reference Admiralty's 1230/4. Once the convoy is to the eastward of 25° E. or earlier at your discretion you are to leave the Barents Sea unless assured by Admiralty that *Tirpitz* cannot be met. My position at 1500B/4 75° 46' N.» 10° 40z E. course 332° altering at 1600B to south-westward ... T.O.O.1512B/4.'

182. 'Immediate. Your 1512B/4. Intend withdrawing to westward about 2200B/4 on completion of destroyer oiling. T.O.O. 1809B/4.'

183. 'Most immediate. C.-in-C., H.F.'s 1512/4 and your 1520/4. Further information may be available shortly. Remain with convoy pending further instructions. T.O.O. 1858B/4.'

184. 'I had very carefully weighed the pros and cons, of being in or out of the convoy now that it had entered the most dangerous area for air attack and 1 had come to the conclusion that the only advantage of being in the convoy was increased anti-aircraft protection to the convoy. Against this was the very great risk of damage to my force, either from air attack or U-boats, while fulfilling a duty for which, at this stage, it was not intended. I decided, therefore, to keep clear of the convoy; and in the light of events I am more than ever convinced that it is correct for cruisers never to be restricted in movement and speed by stationing them in the convoy.' (Report of Proceedings, R.A.1st C.S.)

185. Report of Commanding Officer, HMS *Keppel.*

186. Ibid.

187. According to the Germans three aircraft were shot down and one damaged.

188. It is now known that this was emphasised in the German operation orders.

189. *See* Sec. 34.

190. Technically, the term 'disperse' meant that ships would break formation and proceed at convenient speed towards their port of destination, i.e. for some hours they would be in close proximity to each other. The term 'scatter' meant that they would start out on different bearings in accordance with a scheme laid down in the convoy instructions.

191. It will be remembered that these laid down emphatically that in event of surface attack by a force overwhelmingly superior to the escort, the primary object of the latter was to shadow the enemy and, should a favourable opportunity occur, to attack them (*see* Sec. 12).

192. *See* Sec. 37.

193. The aircraft later fell in with the *Palomares*, by whom its crew was rescued.

194. Report of proceedings, R.A.C. 1st C.S. (in M.7591).

195. Ibid.

196. *See* Naval Staff History, *Battle Summary No. 32. Malta Convoys*, 1942.

197. *See* Sec. 34, Rear-Admiral Hamilton was unaware of the hint the 1st Sea Lord had given Sir John Tovey over the telephone and consequently was entirely unprepared for the order to scatter the convoy.

198. My final brief instructions to PQ 17 and remaining escorts were as follows. 'Convoy scatter and proceed to Russian ports. Remaining escorts proceed independently to Archangel. Submarines remain to attack if enemy approaches before convoy dispersed, then act under orders of Senior Officer.'
    '*Palomares* has doubtless taken charge but I feel I let my excellent escort down by leaving them thus and therefore submit these hurried and inadequate instructions, requesting they may be readjusted or amplified as necessary at the first opportunity.'
    Actually, he was still in the U-boat zone which had caused the Admiralty order to him to use high speed for his withdrawal to the westward, but of this he was not aware.

199. Actually, he was still in the U-boat zone which had caused the Admiralty order to him to use high speed for his withdrawal to the westward, but of this he was not aware.

200. Report of proceedings, R.A. 1st C.S. (in T.S.D.3288/42).

201. The C.-in-C. subsequently remarked:– 'The decision to concentrate the escorting destroyers on the cruiser force was, in these circumstances, correct, but once he was clear of the convoy and in default of information that the *Tirpitz* was near, Rear-Admiral commanding 1st Cruiser Squadron should have released these destroyers and instructed them to rejoin the scattered convoy: their value for anti-U-boat purposes, for rounding up scattered ships and, if the *Tirpitz* had appeared, for diverting and delaying her, would have been considerable …' (C.-in-C.'s despatch in M.052452/43).

202. No mention of any attack by a hostile submarine appears in the *Tirpitz* war diary and she suffered no damage.

203. *See* Plan 10.

204. Submarines *P614* and *P615*, coming from their escort duties astern of the convoy to stations south-east of the *Trident* did not arrive until the afternoon of the 6th.

205. Sic. It was actually the *Scheer*.

206. They had put into Langfjord on account of fog on the way from Altenfjord to Narvik.

207. Commodore Dowding's report (in M.011511/42).

208. Commander Broome subsequently reported:– 'I would like to place on record the cheerful way this ship took on an unexpected task (relieving the *Grey Ranger*) and dealt with it. Oiling destroyers was almost continuous and to handle the gear it was necessary to clear lower deck on each occasion, in order to keep the A.A. armament manned … There were no complaints. The spirit of that ship was shown in a signal made to *Keppel* after the *Christopher Newport* was torpedoed in which the Captain volunteered to take the ship in tow.'

It is satisfactory to record that the Master (Captain A. Hobson) and all his ship's company were picked up by the *Salamander* almost immediately after abandoning ship.

209. *Bolton Castle, Fairfield City, Pan Kraft, Peter Kerr, Washington* and *Paulus Potter*.

210. *Earlston, Empire Byron, River Afton* (Commodore), *Carlton, Daniel Morgan* and *Honomu*.

211. Four ships were sunk by aircraft in about 77° N., 36°-38° E., some 450 miles from Banak. This gives point to Commander Broome's argument that it made little difference whether the convoy was 300 or 500 miles from enemy air station, but that it was important to keep on to the eastward. (*See* Sec. 34.)

212. *Pan Atlantic*.

213. *John Witherspoon, Hartlebury, Alcoa Ranger* and *Olopana*.

214. The Commanders of the two anti-aircraft ships remarked on the danger to ships of being hemmed in on the edge of an icefield where submarines and aircraft might attack, Captain Jauncey of the *Palomares* saying that the German submarines 'made full and effective use of their knowledge of the southern ice barrier, the position of which was unknown to the British and Russian authorities. This may partly explain the loss of the four ships torpedoed whilst trying to reach Matochkin Strait or Moller Bay on 6th to 8th July (M.11511/42).

215. *Lord Austin, Lord Middleton* and *Northern Gem*.

216. She subsequently reached Archangel. *See* postea.

217. A day or so after the convoy left, a U-boat arrived and finding no ships, bombarded the signal station at Gusini Nos.

218. From German sources. It was thought at the time that nine had been destroyed.

219. In some cases U-boats had administered the coup de grace to ships already damaged by air attack.

220. C.-in-C., Home Fleet's despatch, (M.052452/43) (Case 7607).

221. Corvettes *Starwort, Honeysuckle* and *Hyderabad*. FFS *Roselys*; minesweepers *Niger, Hussar* and two trawlers. The submarine *Trident* accompanied the convoy as far west as 23° E. and three Russian destroyers as far as 30° E.

222. Admiralty signal 2246 B/2 July.

223. The *Inglefield* and *Intrepid*, which had been with this part of the convoy, parted company early on 5th July to fuel at Seidisfjord.

224. By soundings.

225. The American *Hybert, Heffron, Massmar* and the Russian *Rodina*.

226. The American *John Randolph* and Panamanian *Exterminator*.

227. Churchill W. S., The Second World War (English edition). Vol. IV, p.239.

228. Operation 'Pedestal'. The Victorious (flag, Rear-Admiral Lyster), *Nigeria* (flag, Rear-Admiral Burrough, C.S.10), *Kenya, Manchester, Sirius* and 11 destroyers. The *Manchester* and *Foresight* were sunk during the operation and the *Nigeria* and *Kenya* were damaged. The remaining Home Fleet ships returned at the end of August.

229. The possibility of running the westbound convoy alone during this interval was examined, but adequate submarine cover could not be provided. At the request of the Soviet Government two Russian merchant ships sailed from Iceland independently in August and after a long passage extending well into the Kara Sea, arrived unscathed.

230. After the passages of PQ 18 and QP 14, the Hampdens were presented to the Russians, their crews being brought back by three destroyers in October.

231. 'The reason for this astonishing decision by our Allies could not be discovered; but I renewed my representations for the strongest pressure to be brought to bear to induce them once more to change their minds. That British seamen, wounded while carrying supplies to Russia, should be exposed unnecessarily to the medieval treatment prevalent in Russian hospitals, was intolerable.' – C.-in-C., Home Fleet's despatch in M.052452/43.

232. 'This force had provided a welcome reinforcement to the Home Fleet at a time when its strength was much reduced. The conduct of officers and men had been admirable and the ships displayed a very high degree of weapon efficiency. In Admiral Giffen I had a loyal and enthusiastic colleague whose tact and good humour never failed. I was very sorry to see them go.' – C.-in-C., Home Fleet's despatch in M.052452/43.

233. The *Victorious* on her return from Operation 'Pedestal' was taken in hand for refitting at Rosyth, where she remained until 20th September.

234. The events of 31st December 1942 confirmed this view, though on that occasion there were not nearly so many destroyers present. The winter darkness of December was however, a factor operating against the German surface forces. *See* Secs. 51, 52.

235. A spare oiler was also kept in Iceland in case of emergency.

236. Operation 'Gearbox II'. This operation was synchronised with the running of the Arctic convoys, as affording a good opportunity of carrying it out unobserved by the G.A.F., when the latter would be fully occupied against the convoys.

237. The cruising areas and submarine patrol stations are shown in Plan 13.

238. Admiral Tovey subsequently remarked:–

'This higher scale of air support was most valuable; but a further increase is still required, particularly in the number of aircraft available for the anti-submarine escort of all forces when within range of our air bases. Nor is one auxiliary carrier a full solution of the problem of air attack: her fighters are too few to deal with the great forces which the enemy brings against these convoys. Moreover, the weather, which on this occasion was exceptionally favourable to the *Avenger*, will frequently make it impossible to operate aircraft from her small flying deck.'

239. Admiral Tovey listed the probable reasons for the enemy's inaction as follows:–

(i) The strength of the destroyer force.

(ii) The presence of Allied submarines off the north coast of Norway, emphasised by the attack by the *Tigris* and of two submarines with the convoys.

(iii) The presence of torpedo-carrying aircraft in North Russia.

(iv) The knowledge that their forces were constantly being reconnoitred by British aircraft.

(v) The sighting of the British battlefleet on 12th September, north-east of Iceland and steering to the north-east and doubt as to its subsequent movements.

240. Corvettes *Bryony, Bergamot, Bluebell* and *Camelia*; minesweepers *Harrier, Gleaner* and *Sharpshooter*; trawlers *St. Kenan, Cape Argona, Daneman* and *Cape Mariato*.

241. Force 'B' *Milne* (D.3), *Marne, Martin, Meteor, Faulknor* (D.8), *Intrepid, Impulsive* and *Fury*.

242. Force 'A' *Onslow* (D.17), *Onslaught, Opportune, Offa, Eskimo, Somali* and *Ashanti* (D.6) and *Tartar*.

243. Force 'P' *Oakley, Cowdray, Worcester, Windsor*, RFAs *Oligarch* and *Blue Ranger*.

244. The cruising disposition of PQ 18 with its full escort is shown in Plan 12.

245. According to the Germans, no U-boat made contact with PQ 18 until 12th September.

246. *See* Sec. 30.

247. The C.-in-C., Home Fleet subsequently remarked that the short visibility and cloud of the last few days had prevented 'the early and comparatively small scale air attacks which had been directed against previous convoys; and thus had the unexpected and unfortunate result of depriving the guns and fighters of the practice and experience which would have helped them to deal with the first massed attack.' – C.-in-C.'s Despatch in M.052452/43.

248. *Empire Beaumont, John Penn, Empire Stevenson, Wacosta, Africander, Oregonian, Macbeth* and *Sukhona*.

249. According to German sources. Thirteen were claimed by the British at the time.

250. This account of the *Avenger's* services on 13th September is based on her 'Diary of Events' and on Rear-Admiral Burnett's 'Summary of Air Attack' (both in M.051890/42) and on the Minutes in T.S.D. 1309/42.

251. *See* M.015134/42 for *Scylla* and JI.052050/42 for *Ulster Queen*. Captain Adam remarked that his ship was considerably handier than the *Alynbank*.

252. It is not clear how many Hurricanes the *Avenger* had ready for service. She had only eight left four sections–after the fighting on the 14th; but she may have already fitted out some of her six spare aircraft.

253. The *Gray Ranger* and *Black Ranger* had been employed throughout the passage in 'topping up' destroyers with oil.

254. The two large Russian destroyers each mounting four 5-inch guns with an elevation of 45° besides two regular 3-inch high-angle guns were stationed one on either beam of the convoy, where according to Captain Adam of the *Ulster Queen* they were 'a great help and excellently handled.'

255. According to German sources three aircraft were shot down and one damaged.

256. The *Empire Morn* was No. 3 in the 5th column in the middle of the convoy. The pilot of her aircraft remarked on the difficulty he had in avoiding the balloon cables of other ships.

257. Corvettes *Lotus, Poppy, Dianella* and FFS *La Malouine*; minesweepers *Bramble, Leda* and *Seagull*; trawlers *Lord Middleton, Lord Austin, Ayrshire* and *Northern Gem*.

258. Force 'P' had oiled the destroyers of Vice-Admiral Bonham-Carter's cruiser force at a rendezvous near 77° N., 5° E., on the 17th and 18th.

259. Lieut.-Commander Maud whose own ship, the *Icarus*, was refitting, had taken command of the *Somali* temporarily in the absence of Captain Eaton owing to sickness.

260. Rear-Admiral Burnett's Report (in M.051890/42).

261. Air Ministry pamphlet No. 248, The Rise and Fall of the German Air Force.

262. The ships in PQ 18 carried between them 167 Oerlikon guns, 11 Bofors, 17–3-inch or 12-pdr. HA/LA; and the Oerlikon ammunition supplies were (for the first time) on an adequate scale.

263. C.-in-C., Home Fleet's despatch.

264. Sunk, *U-88, U-457* and *U-589*; damaged, *U-251, U-255, U-403, U-405* and *U-255* (T.S.D./ F.D.S./X/375751).

265. Rear-Admiral Boddam-Whetham in a private letter to Rear-Admiral Burnett remarked, 'It's a funny feeling to realise one is sitting on top of 2,000 tons of T.N.T., but we nearly all carry between that and 4,000 tons. I don't think the bigger amount would make more than some tiny fraction of a second difference to the time one entered the next world.' In addition, *U-253*, while waiting for QP 14 off Iceland, was sunk by a Catalina.

266. C.-in-C., Home Force's despatch (in M.052901/43). The details are as follows:–
Ships sailed to Russia 13, from Russia 8.
Ships turned back to Russia 3, from Russia –.
Ships sunk to Russia 4, from Russia 1.
Ships wrecked to Russia 1, from Russia –.
Ships arrived to Russia 5, from Russia 7.
267. The American *Meanticut* and *Ironclad*.
268. *Halcyon, Britomart, Hazard, Sharpshooter* and *Salamander*.
269. *Bryony, Bergamot, Bluebell* and *Camelia*.

270. FO Northern Waters, rightly judging that the convoy would be weakly escorted while the British Naval forces were supporting the landings in North Africa, had intended to send the *Hipper* and destroyers against QP 15 in the Barents Sea; but the weather was such as to limit the use of the cruiser's guns and too bad for the destroyers to put to sea so no surface operations took place.

271. *Goolistan* and *Kusnetz Lesov*.

272. *Tirpitz, Lützow, Hipper, Köln* and *Nurnberg*. In December 1942, unknown to the British, the *Tirpitz* was suffering from defects to her fire control, the *Köln* was considered unseaworthy in rough weather and the Nurnberg was being used for training purposes.

273. C.-in-C., Home Fleet's despatch (in M.052901/43).

274. Ibid.

275. It had been intended that Force 'R' should fuel at Seidisfiord before undertaking the latter part of the passage, but thick fog prevented the cruisers from entering.

276. The C.-in-C., Home Fleet's instructions at this time laid down that the cruisers were not to close within 50 miles of the convoy, on account of the U-boat danger, unless or until the enemy surface craft had been located.

277. cf. the *Tirpitz*'s attempts to find PQ 12, *see* Secs. 5 to 7.

278. Actually on this occasion JW 51B was reported 50 miles south of Bear Island by *U-354* in the forenoon of 30th December. This was the only report received by the Germans during the whole passage.

279. Rear-Admiral Burnett's Report in M.052455/43. The importance attached to the advantage of light received justification in the event, when the cruisers completely surprised the *Hipper* and hit her before she had any idea of their presence (*see* Sec. 52).

280. From a signal made by the C.-in-C., Home Fleet, timed 1121A/27, estimating that the convoy would pass the longitude of Bear Island at 1600A, 29th. The convoy actually passed this point some 20 hours later at about 1200, 30th, i.e., was about 150 miles further to the westward than expected. It was also some 20 miles to the southward of the route originally laid down.

281. Admiral Burnett never sighted the convoy or escort throughout the day. He consequently never really knew where it was and whether it was in formation, or – as he rather suspected after the gales and from the radar contact he soon picked up in the north – split up.

282. In latitude 73° N. the sun was at no time less than 6° below the horizon (Civil twilight). Nautical twilight (12° below horizon) started at about 0809 and ended about 1450. The moon (3rd quarter) set about 1110.

283. From the *Obedient*'s report (in M.052539/43). The Commodore's report, however, states that the convoy altered course to south-east at 1020.

284. In view of the faulty estimate of the convoy's position given in the C.-in-C., Home Fleet's signal 1121A/27 and of the fact that the convoy was to the southward of the route ordered, up until then Force 'R' had been imagined about 100 miles to the north-east (HMS *Obedient*'s report).

285. The German records make no mention of her being hit at this stage.

286. HMS *Obedient*'s report (in M.052539/43).

287. Lieutenant-Commander Kinloch was promoted to Commander that day, 31st December 1942. He will therefore be referred to in his new rank hereafter in this account of the actions.

288. HM The King approved the award of the Victoria Cross to Captain Sherbrooke for his bravery.

289. The Hipper's log pays the following tribute to Captain Sherbrooke's tactics :– 'The (British) destroyers conducted themselves very skilfully. They placed themselves in such a position between *Hipper* and the convoy that it was impossible to get near the ships. They also made very effective use of smoke screens ... Their relative position forced *Hipper* to run the risk of a torpedo attack, while trying to use her guns on the ships.'

290. Rear-Admiral Burnett's Report. The primitive nature of the radar in 1942 should be borne in mind. In the *Sheffield* bearings and ranges were passed by voice-pipe and the operators were using a virtually new machine, in which their training and experience was very limited.

291. The German and destroyer reports place the time of the *Hipper* opening fire on the *Achates* as 0941. This discrepancy cannot be reconciled.

292. Rear-Admiral Burnett's Report.

293. Ibid.

294. *Fighting Instructions*, 1947, Ch. IV, par. 108. The same instruction appeared in F.I., 1939 (Sec. I, Clause 3).

295. *Fighting Instructions*, 1939, Sec. XX, p. 110, as amended by C.A.F.O. P373/41. These instructions called attention to 'the possibility of the enemy endeavouring to draw the escort away from the convoy in order to leave it open to attack by other enemy forces.'

296. The *Bramble* being engaged by the *Hipper* (*see* postea).

297. It is difficult to account for this western sighting, as no ship is known to have been in these positions at the times. It must be remembered that in 1942 radar was comparatively in its infancy, but this contact was checked by a visual glimpse. In the analysis after the action, these contacts were taken to be the *Lützow* and the *Hipper* and in contemporary plans the two ships were shown some miles apart, both attacking from the northward. It was not until the German reports became available in 1945 that it was realised the attack was from both flanks.

298. The *Bramble* made an enemy report 'one cruiser bearing 300°' at 1039. This was taken in by the *Hyderabad* only and did not reach the Senior Officer of the escort until some days later.

299. Commander Kinloch had at first ordered the *Achates* to join his three destroyers of the 17th Flotilla, but on learning that her speed had been reduced to 15 knots by a hit in the previous engagement, he told her to join the *Onslow*.

300. Commander Kinloch does not seem to have been aware that the ship which engaged the *Achates* and *Obedient* was a different enemy to the one he had been dealing with at 1100. This is quite understandable, when the conditions of darkness and smoke are remembered. The *Lützow*, meanwhile, had passed to the eastward.

301. Both the *Sheffield* and *Jamaica* judged her to be the *Lützow* and she was so described in the contemporary reports, though some in the *Sheffield* identified her correctly.

302. The *Richard Beitzen*, another of the *Hipper*'s group.

303. As the *Friedrich Eckholdt* was so soon afterwards herself destroyed with all hands, nothing is known with certainty of what she did after being detached to sink the *Bramble*, or whether she actually fell in, with her.

304. The C.-in-C., Home Fleet, subsequently remarked:– 'I consider the action of Lieut.-Commander A. H. T. Johns RN and subsequently Lieutenant L. E. P. Jones RN, to have been gallant in the extreme. They only had one idea, to give what protection they could to the convoy and this they continued to do up to the moment of sinking. The behaviour of all officers and ratings was magnificent.' The Admiral also highly commended Lieutenant Aisthorpe, RNR, for the 'courageous and seamanlike handling of the *Northern Gem*' which resulted in the rescue of so many survivors.

305. This is not substantiated by German sources.

306. The *Jamaica*'s radar had been smashed by her own gunfire.

307. Rear-Admiral Burnett's Report.

308. This was the last appearance of the *Hipper* in an operational capacity. After repairs in Norway, which lasted most of January 1943, she was used for training in the Baltic for a few weeks and then paid off until April 1944; then after a refit she was again used for training.

309. 'As we withdrew (from the scene of action, the unsatisfactory feeling reigned that in spite of the general position, which was apparently favourable at first we had not succeeded in getting at the convoy or in scoring any successes at all ... The sad truth remains that *Friedrich Eckholdt* was lost.' Extract from *Lützow*'s War Diary.

310. *Raider, Queenborough, Musketeer, Piorun, Montrose* and *Worcester*.

311. *Faulknor, Fury, Echo, Eclipse, Inglefield* and *Beagle*.

312. *Gleaner*.

313. *Cape Argona, St. Kenan, Daneman* and *Cape Mariato*.

314. C.-in-C., Home Fleet's Despatch, London Gazette, 17th October 1950.

315. cf. QP 11, Commander Richmond's tactics: *see* Sec. 24.

316. G.H.S.4. German Surface Ships. Policy and operations.

317. The *Friedrich Eckholdt*, which was detached for the specific purpose of sinking the isolated and crippled *Bramble*.

318. 'The inactivity of the German destroyers is inexplicable. They made no attack on the convoy and in two engagements were following astern of their cruiser without taking any part.' Commander Kinloch's report (in M.052539/43).

319. N.I.D.24/X9/45. Extract from Log of *Hipper*.

320. N.I.D.24/X9/45. Appreciation by Admiral, Nordmeer. Admiral Schniewind was under no delusion as to the impossible position the officers afloat were placed in. In the 'Appreciation' referred to above which is really his covering letter to Admiral Kummetz' report and takes up no more than half a sheet of foolscap, he referred no less than three times to the 'limiting factor of risk,' which he finally recommended should be disregarded in future.

321. Admiral Kummetz had maintained wireless silence during his withdrawal after the action. He was much annoyed to find that as the result of a U-boat report a rumour of a great German naval success had got about before his own report was received.

325. C.-in-C., Home Fleet's remarks (in M.02715/43).

326. Minesweepers, *Jason* (SO), *Halcyon*; corvettes *Dianella, Poppy* and *Bergamot*; trawlers *Lord Middleton* and *Lord Austin*.

327. *Milne* (Captain I. M. R. Campbell SO A/S screen), *Faulknor* (Captain A. K. Scott-Moncrieff, Second-in-Command A/S screen), *Boadicea, Inglefield, Orwell, Opportune, Obedient, Obdurate, Fury, Intrepid, Impulsive, Eclipse* and ORP *Orkan.*

328. *Blankney* and *Ledbury.*

329. The *Berwick* relieved the *Norfolk* with the battlefleet.

330. A method which reduced to the minimum the risk of giving away their position to the enemy.

331. *Milne* and seven destroyers.

332. Corvettes, *Poppy, Bergamot, Lotus* and *Starwort*; trawlers, *St. Elstan* and *Northern Pride.*

333. C.-in-C.'s despatch, in M.053313/43.

334. Grand Admiral Doenitz very soon after taking over as C.-in-C. had persuaded Hitler to modify his orders to lay up the fleet and the *Scharnhorst* and *Tirpitz* were kept in northern waters until they were eventually sunk, with the *Lützow* in addition until mid-1943.

335. *See* Secs. 11, 32.

336. *See* Naval Staff History, *Battle Summary No. 29.*

337. Fleet destroyers, *Milne* (Captain Campbell SO), *Musketeer, Mahratta, Matchless, Savage, Scorpion, Scourge, Saumarez* and *Westcott*; minesweepers, *Harrier* and *Seagull*; corvette, *Eglantine.*

338. Through escorts:– Convoy JW 54A; *Onslow* (Captain J. A. McCoy SO), *Onslaught, Orwell, Impulsive, Iroquois, Haida, Huron, Inconstant, Whitehall, Heather* and *Hussar.*

Convoy JW 54B; *Saumarez, Savage, Scorpion, Stord, Scourge, Venus, Vigilant, Hardy, Beagle, Rhododendron, Poppy* and *Halcyon.*

Convoy RA 54B; same as JW 54A, but *Harrier* took the place of *Hussar.*

339. Promoted Vice-Admiral 9th December 1943.

340. *Milne, Musketeer, Meteor, Matchless, Opportune, Ashanti, Virago* and *Athabaskan.*

341. *Acanthus* and *Speedwell.*

342. Corvettes, *Acanthus, Pianella* and *Poppy*; minesweeper, *Speedwell.*

343. *Onslow, Onslaught, Orwell, Impulsive, Scourge, Iroquois, Huron* and *Haida.*

344. Corvettes, *Oxslip* and *Honeysuckle*; minesweeper, *Gleaner.*

345. Commander-in-Chief, HF 1201 of 24th December to RA(D).

346. For further details of the operations which ensued see Naval Staff History, *Battle Summary No. 24.*

347. Commander-in-Chief's despatch.

348. A breakdown in communications between the *Scharnhorst* and the destroyers had occurred shortly after 0800 and no signals were exchanged for about a couple of hours.

349. In addition the *Rhododendron*.

350. These figures refer to those sunk in tactical contact with the convoys. Seven others were sunk in the Arctic area when no convoy was at sea and two by the Russians in the Kara Sea.

351. Ibid.

352. In effect a breathing pipe which enabled the diesel engines to run without surfacing.

353. At the same time he made preliminary arrangements with the Commander-in-Chief, Western Approaches, for the loan of escort carriers and support groups for future convoys.

354. In addition, a tanker was included.

355. The *Dasher* had started with Convoy JW 53, but had been unable to accompany it owing to weather damage. *See* Section 56.

356. One or more escort carriers and support groups accompanied all subsequent convoys.

357. VAC 10th Cruiser squadron.

358. *See* Naval Staff History, *Battle Summary No. 27*.

359. RAC, 1st Cruiser Squadron.

360. Commander-in-Chief's despatch (in M.07458/44).

361. Operation 'Goodwood.' *Duke of York* (flag, Commander-in-Chief), *Indefatigable* (flag, RAC, 1st Cruiser Squadron, Rear-Admiral McGrigor), *Formidable, Furious, Trumpeter, Nabob, Berwick, Devonshire, Kent* and 19 destroyers.

362. Except in self-defence against submarines and air attack, her guns were only fired in anger on one occasion, when her main armament fired 46 rounds at installations at Spitsbergen in the course of a raid on 8th September 1943.

363. In order to save manpower it had been decided to close down Loch Ewe as a convoy assembly port in favour of the Clyde.

364. Destroyer, *Whitehall*; sloops, *Cygnet, Lapwing* and *Lark*; corvettes; *Bamborough Castle, Alnwick Castle, Bluebell* and *Rhododendron*.

365. *Onslow* (D.17) (Captain J. H. Alison), *Zest* and *Zealous*. The *Zebra* had to be detached to the Faeroes with defects.

366. Rear-Admiral McGrigor's report (in M.02639/45).

367. All times are Zone minus 1.

368. Rear-Admiral McGrigor's report.

369. Ibid.

370. Ibid

371. The Rear-Admiral subsequently remarked;- 'This showed a quite inexcusable lack of fire discipline even taking into account the bad visibility, low cloud and pace of events. There is little resemblance between a Ju.88 and a Wildcat and none with a Swordfish.'

Captain Tuck of the *Bellona* recommended that a 'recognition exercise' should be carriers out as soon as possible after the carriers joined the convoys, in order to familiarise guns' crews with friendly aircraft in different aspects of approach.

372. Rear-Admiral McGrigor's report.

373. All times are Zone minus 1.

374. Rear-Admiral McGrigor's report.

375. Some idea of what this work entailed may be gathered from the following quotation from Captain Allison's report on the *Zambezi*'s activities 24 hours later. 'It is noteworthy that it took *Zambezi* 12 hours continuous steaming at the highest possible speed over an area of nearly 1,000 square miles to round up nine stragglers …'

376. The *Campania* had only one fighter serviceable, which was not flown off.

377. Rear-Admiral McGrigor's report. The Admiral gave the 'highest credit' to the *Nairana* and her Wildcats. 'They operated with great success and landed on safely in a really rough sea with a wind over the deck on landing of over 50 knots.'

378. Ibid.

379. The survivors' story makes it clear that between 30 and 40 of the *Henry Bacon*'s crew deliberately sacrificed their chance of escape in one of the boats to their Norwegian passengers. This unselfish act cost most of them their lives; all those in boats were picked up.

380. Rear-Admiral McGrigor subsequently remarked that it was 'fortunate that none of the usual short-legged escorts like *Beagle* and *Bulldog* were present.'

381. Rear-Admiral McGrigor's report.

382. All but four of the destroyers had to be detached to the Faeroes to fuel.

383. Rear-Admiral McGrigor's report.

384. When the enemy Air Force seemed to be taking special interest in the convoy a corvette fitted with Type 277 was placed on the inner screen with instructions to pay particular attention to stern bearings.

385. Rear-Admiral McGrigor's report.

386. Apart from the U-boat menace in the approaches, the Rear-Admiral thought it most probable that later in the year when there was no longer loose ice in the inlet, a U-boat would proceed up the harbour and attack ships at Vaenga. There was nothing to stop it and he recommended that the Russians should be encouraged to take more adequate measures to protect ships there.

387. It was at first thought that these ships had been mined, but sweeping operations undertaken at Rear-Admiral McGrigor's request by the feeble Russian minesweeping forces available failed to find any mines.

388. The German figures for aircraft casualties in these operations are one lost, 13 missing, one damaged.

389. Twenty two merchant ships, one rescue ship, one tanker, two Norwegian relief ships.

390. Twenty three merchant ships, one rescue ship, two Norwegian relief ships.

391. 4th Escort Group, *Bentinck, Obdurate, Board, Pasley, Bazeley* and *Drury*.
9th Escort Group, *Matane, Loch Alvie, St. Pierre, Monnow* and *Nene*.

392. *See* Appendix A.

393. Cargo.
Approximate amount despatched from UK or USA (tons)
1941 300,00 **1942** 1,350,000 **1943** 450,000 **1944** 1,250,000 **1945** 650,000
Total 4,000,000
Approximate amount lost *enroute* from UK or USA (tons)
1941 10,000 **1942** 270,000 **1943** – **1944** 10,000 **1945** 10,000
Total 300,000

394. These figures do not include ships that sailed independently. For comparison, the losses in the Atlantic convoys from all causes amounted to 0.7%.

395. The circumstances under which Admiral Sir Bruce Fraser took the *Duke of York* right through to Kola in the operations which culminated in the sinking of the *Scharnhorst* were different from those which Admiral Tovey had to cope. At the time of the *Scharnhorst* episode, the *Tirpitz* was known to be out of action, so a small, compact force of one battleship and a cruiser was sufficient. The operation, too, took place at the darkest period of the year, when the German Air Force would be least effective.

396. The arm 'surface attack' throughout is used to denote attack by surface forces which include or are closely supported by heavy ships too powerful for the convoy escorting vessels to be able to engage with a reasonable chance of success.

397. The knowledge (or even suspicion) of such a force 'in being,' however, exercised great influence on the enemy plans. *See* Sections 33 and 35.

398. It must be remembered that the conditions of the Arctic convoys were quite different from those in the Atlantic. The latter were not exposed to the continuous threat of air attack, nor, usually, to surface attack. Nor, in the Atlantic, relatively far from enemy bases, was the breaking of wireless silence likely to be fraught with such immediate consequences.

399. Each carrier had up to 12 Swordfish and eight Wildcats. Anything up to three Swordfish were on patrol at a time, with strikes of two Swordfish and one or two Wildcats in support and by night two Swordfish alone; but it was not until 1945 that continuous night flying was carried out. Fighters operated in sections of two, with one section up when shadowers were about; these would be increased when air attack was expected.

400. *See* Section 3.

401. *See* Section 45.

Appendix A

Convoys to North Russia (PQ:JW)

Convoy

Dervish, Commodore Captain J. C. K. Dowding DSO, RD, RNR, Hvalfjord 21.08.41, sailed 7, arrived 7, Archangel 31.08.41

PQ 1, Commodore Captain D. Ridley, Master SS *Atlantic*, Hvalfjord 29.09.41, sailed 10, arrived 10, Archangel 11.10.41

PQ 2, Scapa 17.10.41, sailed 6, arrived 6, Archangel 30.10.41

PQ 3, Hvalfjord 09.11.41, sailed 8, arrived 7, Archangel 28.11.41, 1 ice damaged

PQ 4, Hvalfjord 17.11.41, sailed 8, arrived 8, Archangel 28.11.41

PQ 5, Hvalfjord 27.11.41, sailed 7, arrived 7, Archangel 12.12.41

PQ 6, Hvalfjord 08.12.41, sailed 7, arrived 2, Murmansk 20.12.41 and 5 Molotovsk 23.12.41

PQ 7, Hvalfjord 26.12.41, sailed 2, arrived 1, Murmansk 12.01.42, 1 sunk by U-boat

PQ 7B, Hvalfjord 31.12.41, sailed 9, arrived 9, Murmansk 11.01.42

PQ 8, Commodore Captain R. W. Brundle Master SS *Harmatris*, Hvalfjord 08.01.42, sailed 8, arrived 8, Murmansk 17.01.42, 1 torpedoed towed by HMS *Matabele*

PQ 9, Hvalfjord 01.02.42, sailed 7, arrived 7, Murmansk 10.02.42

PQ 10, Hvalfjord 01.02.42, sailed 3, arrived 3, Murmansk 10.02.42, PQ 9 and PQ 10 joined up and sailed in company from Reykjavik

PQ 11, Commodore Master S. S. *Kingswood*, Loch Ewe 06.02.42, sailed 13, arrived 13, Murmansk 23.02.42

PQ 12, Commodore Captain H. D. Hudson RD, RNR, Reyjavik 01.03.42, sailed 16, arrived 16, Murmansk 12.03.42 HMS *Shera* capsized

PQ 13, Commodore Captain D. A. Casey CBE, DSO, DSC, RD, RNR, Reyjavik 20.3.42, sailed 19, lost 5, arrived 14, Murmansk 31.03.42, 2 bombed and sunk, 2 sunk by U-boat, 1 by surface craft, HMS *Trinidad* torpedoed: German destroyer *Z26* sunk

PQ 14, Commodore Captain E. Rees DSC, RD, RNR killed inaction 16.04.43, Reyjavik 08.04.42, sailed 24, lost 1, arrived 7, Murmansk 19.04.42, 1 sunk by U-boat, 16 returned to harbour weather and ice damage

PQ 15, Commodore Captain H. J. Anchor OBE, RD, RNR, Reyjavik 26.04.42, sailed 25 plus 2 icebreakers, lost 3, arrived 22, Murmansk 05.05.42, 3 torpedoed by aircraft and sunk, ORP *P551* (95 miles out of position) sunk by escort HMS *Punjabi* with battlefleet sunk in collision.

PQ 16, Commodore Captain N. H. Gale DSO, RD, RNR, Reyjavik 21.05.42, sailed 35, 1 returned to harbour damaged, 7 lost, arrived 27, Murmansk 30.05.42 Archangel 01.06.42, 5 bombed, 1 torpedoed by aircraft, 1 sunk by U-boat

PQ 17, Commodore Captain J. C. K. Dowding DSO, RD, RNR, Reyjavik 27.06.42, sailed 36 including 1 RFA oiler. Oilers are included when they carriers cargo or part cargo of oil for Russia, 2 returned to harbour, lost 23, arrived 11, 4 Archangel 11.07.42 6 Archangel 25.07.42 1 Molotovsk 28.07.42, 1 grounded, 10 bombed, 3 torpedoed by aircraft, 10 by U-boats, figures do not include 3 rescue ships 1 of which was bombed and sunk

PQ 18, Commodore Rear-Admiral E. K. Boddam-Whetham DSO (ret.), Loch Ewe 02.09.42, sailed 40, lost 13, arrived 27, Archangel 17.09.42, 3 sunk by U-boats, 10 by torpedo bombers

JW 51A, Commodore Rear-Admiral C. E. Turle DSO (ret.), Loch Ewe 15.12.42, sailed 16 plus 1 RFA Oiler, arrived 16 plus oiler Kola Inlet 25.12.42 Molotovsk 27.12.42

JW 51B, Commodore Captain R. A. Melhuish RIN (ret.), Loch Ewe 22.12.42, sailed 14, arrived 14, Kola Inlet 03.01.43 White Sea 06.01.43, HMS *Achates* and *Bramble* sunk by German surface ships, German destroyer *Friedrich Eckholdt* sunk

JW 52, Commodore Vice-Admiral Sir M. L. Goldsmith KBE, DSO (ret.), Loch Ewe 17.01.43, sailed 14, arrived 13, Kola Inlet 27.01.43, 1 returned to Iceland through lack of speed

JW 53, Commodore Rear-Admiral E. W. Leir DSO (ret.), Loch Ewe 15.02.43, sailed 28, arrived 22, Kola Inlet 27.02.43 White Sea 02.03.43, 6 returned to Iceland due to weather

JW 54A, Commodore Captain B. B. Grant RD, RNR, Loch Ewe 15.11.43, sailed 18, arrived 18, Kola Inlet 24.11.43 White Sea 28.11.43

JW 54B, Commodore Captain E. C. Denison MVO, RN (ret.), Loch Ewe 22.11.43, sailed 14, arrived 14, Kola Inlet 02.12.43 White Sea 04.12.43

JW 55A, Commodore Captain W. J. Mills RD, RNR, Loch Ewe 12.12.43, sailed 19, arrived 19, Kola Inlet 20.12.43 White Sea 22.12.43

JW 55B, Commodore Rear-Admiral M. W. S. Boucher DSO, Loch Ewe 20.12.43, sailed 19, arrived 19, Kola Inlet 29.12.43 White Sea 31.12.43, *Scharnhorst* sunk by covering forces 26.12.43

JW 56A, Commodore Captain I. L. Whitehorn RN (ret.), Loch Ewe 12.01.44, sailed 20, arrived 12, Kola Inlet 28.01.44, convoy put into Akureyri owing to weather 5 returned 3 sunk by U-boats, HMS *Hardy* sunk by U-boat

JW 56B, Commodore Captain M. J. D. Mayall RD, RNR, Loch Ewe 22.01.44, sailed 16, arrived 16, Kola Inlet 01.02.44

JW 57, Commodore Captain R. D. Binks OBE, RD, RNR, Loch Ewe 20.02.44, sailed 42, arrived 42, KolaInlet 28.02.44, HMS *Mahratta* sunk by U-boat

JW 58, Commodore Captain J. O. Dunn RD, RNR, Loch Ewe 27.03.44, sailed 49, arrived 48, Kola Inlet 05.04.44, 1 Ship ice damaged returned to Iceland

JW 59, Commodore Captain G. H. Creswell CB, DSO, DSC, RN (ret.), Loch Ewe 15.08.44, sailed 33, arrived 33, Kola Inlet 25.08.44 White Sea 27.08.44, HMS *Kite* sunk by U-boat

JW 60, Commodore Captain J. Smith RD, RNR, Loch Ewe 15.09.44, sailed 30, arrived 30, Kola Inlet 23.09.44 White Sea 25.09.44

JW 61, Commodore Rear-Admiral M. W. S. Broucher DSO, Loch Ewe 20.10.44, sailed 29, arrived 29, Kola Inlet 28.10.44 White Sea 30.10.44

JW 62, Commodore Captain E. Ullring RNorR, Loch Ewe 29.11.44, sailed 30, arrived 30, Kola Inlet 07.12.44 White Sea 09.12.44

JW 63, Commodore Rear-Admiral M. W. S. Broucher DSO, Loch Ewe 30.12.44, sailed 35, arrived 35, Kola Inlet 08.01.45 White Sea 09.01.45

JW 64, Commodore Captain E. Ullring RNorR, Clyde 03.02.45, sailed 26, arrived 26, Kola Inlet 13.02.45 White Sea 15.02.45

JW 65, Commodore Captain W. C. Meek RD, RNR, Clyde 11.03.45, sailed 24, lost 2, arrived 22, Kola Inlet 21.03.45, 2 merchant ships and HMS *Lapwing* sunk by U-boats off Kola Inlet

JW 66, Commodore Captain Sir Roy K. Gill KBE, RD, RNR, Clyde 16.04.45, sailed 22, arrived 22, Kola Inlet 25.04.45 White Sea 28.04.45

JW 67, Commodore Captain G. E. Sutcliffe RN (ret.), Clyde 12.05.44, sailed 23, arrived 23, Kola Inlet 20.05.45 White Sea 22.05.45

Convoys from North Russia

QP 1, Commodore Captain J. C. K. Dowding DSO, RD, RNR, Archangel 28.09.41, sailed 14, arrived 14, Scapa 09.10.41

QP 2, Archangel 02.11.41, sailed 12, arrived 12, Kirkwell 17.11.41

QP 3, Archangel 27.11.41, sailed 10, arrived 8, Seidisfjord 07.12.41, 2 returned owing to weather

QP 4, Archangel 20.12.41, sailed 13, arrived 11, Seidisfjord 16.01.42 2 put into Murmansk

QP 5, Murmansk 13.01.42, sailed 4, arrived 4, Reykjavik 24.01.42

QP 6, Commodore Captain Davitt (Master, *Empire Redshank*), Murmansk 24.01.42, sailed 6, arrived 6, UK 02.02.42

QP 7, Murmansk 12.02.42, sailed 8, arrived 8, Seidisfjord 22.02.42

QP 8, Murmansk 01.03.42, sailed 15, arrived 14, Reykjavik 11.03.42, 1 straggler sunk by surface craft

QP 9, Commodore Captain H. T. Hudson RD, RNR, Murmansk 21.03.42, sailed 19, arrived 19, Reykjavik 03.04.42

QP 10, Commodore Captain D. A. Casey CBE, DSO, DSC, RD, RNR, Murmansk 10.04.42, sailed 16, arrived 11, Reykjavik 21.04.42, 1 returned to Murmansk, 2 sunk by U-boats 2 bombed and sunk

QP 11, Commodore Captain W. H. Lawrence (Master, SS *Briarwood*), Murmansk 28.04.42, sailed 13, arrived 12, Reykjavik 07.05.42, 1 straggler sunk by surface craft, HMS *Edinburgh* torpedoed by U-boat and subsequently sunk

QP 12, Murmansk 21.05.42, sailed 15, arrived 14, Reykjavik 29.05.42, 1 returned to Murmansk

QP 13, Commodore Captain N. H. Gale DSO, RD, RNR, Archangel 26.06.42, sailed 12, Murmansk 27,06,42, sailed 23, lost 5, arrived 30, Loch Ewe 16 07.07.42, Reykjavik 14 07,07.42, 4 sunk 1 damaged and part beached, HMS *Niger* sunk in British minefield

QP 14, Commodore Captain J. C. K. Dowding DSO, RD, RNR, Archangel 13.09.42, sailed 15, lost 3, arrived 12, Loch Ewe 26.09.42, 3 sunk by U-boats, HMS *Somali, Leda* and RFA *Gray Ranger* (Force Q) sunk by U-boats

QP 15, Commodore Captain W. C. Meek RD, RNR, Archangel 17.11.42, sailed 28, lost 2, arrived 26, Loch Ewe 30.11-03.12.42, scattered by gales, 2 sunk by U-boats

RA 51, Commodore Rear-Admiral C. E. Turle DSO (ret.), Kola Inlet 30.12.42, sailed 14, arrived 14, Loch Ewe 11.01.43

RA 52, Commodore Captain R. A. Melhuish RIN (ret.), Kola Inlet 29.01.43, sailed 11, lost 1, arrived 10, Loch Ewe 08.02.43, 1 sunk by U-boat

RA 53, Commodore Vice-Admiral Sir M. L. Goldsmith KBE, DSO (ret.), Kola Inlet 01.03.43, sailed 30, lost 4, arrived 26, Loch Ewe 14.03.43, 2 stragglers sunk by U-boats, 1 floundered in a gale

RA 54A, Commodore Captain W. L. P. Cox RNR, Archangel 01.11.43, sailed 13, arrived 13, Loch Ewe 14.11.43

RA 54B, Commodore Master SS *Empire Scott*, Archangel 26.11.43, sailed 9, arrived 9, Loch Ewe 0912.43

RA 55A, Commodore Captain B. B. Grant RD, RNR, Kola Inlet 23.12.43, sailed 22, arrived 21, Loch Ewe 01.01.44, 1 ship returned to Kola Inlet

RA 55B, Commodore Captain E. C. Denison MVO, RN (ret.), Kola Inlet 31.12.43, sailed 8, arrived 8, Loch Ewe 08.01.44

RA 56, Commodore Rear-Admiral M. W. S. Boucher DSO (ret.), Kola Inlet 03.02.44, sailed 37, arrived 37, Loch Ewe 11.02.44

RA 57, Commodore Captain M. J. D. Mayall RD, RNR, Kola Inlet 02.03.44, sailed 31, lost 1, arrived 30, Loch Ewe 10.03.44, 1 sunk by U-boat

RA 58, Commodore Captain R. D. Binks OBE, RD, RNR, Kola Inlet 07.04.44, sailed 36, arrived 36, Loch Ewe 14.04.44

RA 59, Commodore Captain J. O. Dunn RD, RNR, Kola Inlet 28.04.44, sailed 45, lost 1, arrived 44, Loch Ewe 06.05.44, 1 sunk by U-boat

RA 59A, Kola Inlet 28.08.44, sailed 9, arrived 9, Loch Ewe 06.09.44

RA 60, Commodore Captain G. H. Creswell CB, DSO, DSC, RN (ret.), Kola Inlet 28.09.44, sailed 30, lost 2, arrived 28, Loch Ewe 05.10.44, 2 sunk by U-boats

RA 61, Commodore Rear-Admiral M. W. S. Boucher DSO (ret.), White Sea 30.10.44 Kola Inlet 02.11.44, sailed 33, arrived 33, Loch Ewe 09.11.44 Clyde 10.11.44

RA 62, Commodore Captain E. Ullring RNorR, Kola Inlet 10.12.44, sailed 28, arrived 28, Loch Ewe 19.12.44 Clyde 20.12.44, Torpedo bomber attacks recommence

RA 63, Commodore Rear-Admiral M. W. S. Boucher DSO (ret.), Kola Inlet 11.01.45, sailed 30, arrived 30, Loch Ewe 21.01.45 Clyde 23.01.45

RA 64, Commodore Captain E. Ullring RNorR, Kola Inlet 17.02.45, sailed 34 excluding 2 sunk off KolaInlet before joining RA 64, lost 4 including 2 sunk off KolaInlet before joining RA 64, arrived 31, Loch Ewe 28.02.45 Clyde 01.03.45, 1 returned to Kola Inlet, 1 sunk by U-boat, 1 straggler by torpedo aircraft, HMS *Bluebell* sunk by U-boat

RA 65, Commodore Captain W. C. Meek RD, RNR, Kola Inlet 23.03.45, sailed 25, arrived 25, Kirkwell 31.03.45 Clyde 01.04.45 Belfast 01.04.45

RA 66, Commodore Captain Sir Roy K. Gill KBE, RD, RNR, Kola Inlet 29.04.45, sailed 24, arrived 24, Clyde, HMS *Goodall* sunk by U-boat

RA 67, Commodore Captain G. E. Sutcliffe RN (ret.), Kola Inlet 23.05.45, sailed 23, arrived 23, Clyde 31.05.45

Independent Sailing (Operation FB)

Eastbound
29.10.42-02.11.42, sailed Reykjavik 13, turned back 3, lost 4 sunk by U-boat 1 wrecked, arrived Russian ports 5

Westbound
29.20.42-24.01.43, sailed Russian ports 28, lost 1 to surface ship, arrived Akureyri 27

Nominal list of Merchant Ship losses

(a) In or ex-convoys to North Russia (PQ:JW).
(b) In or ex-convoys from North Russia (QP:RA).
(c) Independent sailings.
(d) Sunk in Russian ports.
(e) Other Non-Combatant ships in connection with convoy traffic.

(a) Convoys to North Russia (PQ:JW)

Convoy PQ 7
Waziristan Gross Tons 15,135 British, convoy PQ 7 sunk by U-boat
Total Gross Tons 15,135

Convoy PQ 13
Empire Ranger (Straggling or separated from convoy) Gross Tons 7,008 British,
    sunk by A/C bombs
Induna (Straggling or separated from convoy) Gross Tons 5,086 British, sunk by U-boat
Effingham Gross Tons 6,421 USA, sunk by U-boat
Bateau (Straggling or separated from convoy) Gross Tons 6,487 Panamanian,
    sunk by Destroyer
Raceland (Straggling or separated from convoy) Gross Tons 4,815 Panamanian,
    sunk by A/C bombs
Total Gross Tons 129,817

Convoy PQ 14
Empire Howard Gross Tons 6,985 British, sunk by U-boat
Total Gross Tons 6,985

Convoy PQ 15
Botavon Gross Tons 5,8481 British, sunk by A/C torpedo
Cape Corso Gross Tons 3,807 British, sunk by A/C torpedo
Jutland Gross Tons 6,153 British, sunk by A/C torpedo
Total Gross Tons 15,808

Convoy PQ 16
Empire Lawrence Gross Tons 7,4301 British, sunk by A/C bombs
Empire Purcell Gross Tons 7,049 British, sunk by A/C bombs
Lowther Castle Gross Tons 5,171 British, sunk by A/C torpedo
Alamar Gross Tons 5,689 USA, sunk by A/C bombs
City of Joliet Gross Tons 6,167 USA, sunk by A/C bombs
Mormacsul Gross Tons 5,481 USA, sunk by A/C bombs
Syros Gross Tons 6,191 USA, sunk by U-boat
Total Gross Tons 43,178

Convoy PQ 17
Aldersdale (RFA) (Straggling or separated from convoy) Gross Tons 8,4021 British,
    sunk by A/C bombs
Bolton Castle (Straggling or separated from convoy) Gross Tons 5,203 British,
    sunk by A/C bombs

Earlston (Straggling or separated from convoy) Gross Tons 7,130 British, sunk by U-boat

Empire Byron (Straggling or separated from convoy) Gross Tons 6,645 British, sunk by U-boat

Hartlebury (Straggling or separated from convoy) Gross Tons 5,082 British, sunk by U-boat

Navarino Gross Tons 4,841 British, sunk by A/C torpedo

River Afton (Straggling or separated from convoy) Gross Tons 5,479 British, sunk by U-boat

Alcoa Ranger (Straggling or separated from convoy) Gross Tons 5,116 USA, sunk by U-boat

Carlton (Straggling or separated from convoy Gross Tons 5,172 USA, sunk by U-boat

Christopher Newport Gross Tons 7,191 USA, sunk by A/C torpedo

Daniel Morgan (Straggling or separated from convoy) Gross Tons 7,177 USA, sunk by U-boat

Fairfield City (Straggling or separated from convoy) Gross Tons 5,686 USA, sunk by A/C bombs

Honomu (Straggling or separated from convoy) Gross Tons 6,977 USA, sunk by U-boat

Hoosier Gross Tons 5,060 USA, sunk by A/C bombs

John Witherspoon (Straggling or separated from convoy) Gross Tons 7,191 USA, sunk by U-boat

Olopana (Straggling or separated from convoy) Gross Tons 6,069 USA, sunk by U-boat

Pan Atlantic (Straggling or separated from convoy) Gross Tons 5,411 USA, sunk by A/C bombs

Pan Kraft (Straggling or separated from convoy) Gross Tons 5,644 USA, sunk by A/C bombs

Peter Kerr (Straggling or separated from convoy) Gross Tons 6,476 USA, sunk by A/C bombs

Washington (Straggling or separated from convoy) Gross Tons 5,564 USA, sunk by A/C bombs

William Hooper Gross Tons 7,177 USA, sunk by A/C torpedo

Paulus Potter (Straggling or separated from convoy) Gross Tons 7,168 Dutch, sunk by A/C bombs

El Capitan Gross Tons 5,255 Panamanian, sunk by A/C bombs

Total Gross Tons 141,116

Convoy PQ 18

Atheltemplar Gross Tons 8,992 British, sunk by U-boat
Empire Beaumont Gross Tons 7,044 British, sunk by A/C torpedo
*Empire Stevenso*n Gross Tons 6,209 British, sunk by A/C torpedo
John Penn Gross Tons 7,177 USA, sunk by A/C torpedo
Kentucky Gross Tons 5,446 USA, sunk by A/C torpedo
Mary Luchenback Gross Tons 5,049 USA, sunk by A/C torpedo
Oliver Elsworth Gross Tons 7,191 USA, sunk by U-boat
Oregonian Gross Tons 4,862 USA, sunk by A/C torpedo
Wacosta Gross Tons 5,432 USA, sunk by A/C torpedo
Africander Gross Tons 5,441 Panamanian, sunk by A/C torpedo
Macbeth Gross Tons 4,885 Panamanian, sunk by A/C torpedo
Stalingrad Gross Tons 3,559 Russian, sunk by U-boat
Sukhoma Gross Tons 3,124 Russian, sunk by A/C torpedo
Total Gross Tons 74,411

Convoy JW 56A

Fort Bellingham Gross Tons 7,153 British, sunk by U-boat
Andrew G. Curtin Gross Tons 7,200 USA, sunk by U-boat
Penelope Barker Gross Tons 7,177 USA, sunk by U-boat
Total Gross Tons 21,530

Convoy JW 65

Horace Bushnell Gross Tons 7,176 USA, sunk by U-boat
Thomas Donaldson Gross Tons 7,210 USA, sunk by U-boat
Total Gross Tons 14,386

(b) Convoys from North Russia (QP:RA)

Convoy QP 8

Ijora (Straggling or separated from convoy) Gross Tons 2,815 Russian, sunk by
　　Destroyer
Total Gross Tons 2,815

Convoy QP 10

Empire Cowper Gross Tons 7,164 British, sunk by A/C torpedo
Harpalion Gross Tons 5,486 British, sunk by A/C torpedo
El Occidente Gross Tons 6,008 Panamanian, sunk by U-boat
Kiev Gross Tons 5,823 Russian, sunk by U-boat
Total Gross Tons 24,481

Convoy QP 11

Tsiolkovsky (Straggling or separated from convoy) Gross Tons 2,847 Russian, sunk by
　　Destroyer
Total Gross Tons 2,847

Convoy QP 13
Heffron Gross Tons 7,611 USA, sunk by Mine (British)
Hybert Gross Tons 6,120 USA, sunk by Mine (British)
Massmar Gross Tons 5,828 USA, sunk by Mine (British)
Rodina Gross Tons 4,441 Russian, sunk by Mine (British)
Exterminator Gross Tons 6,073 Panamanian, sunk by Mine (British)
Total Gross Tons 30,073

Convoy QP 14
Ocean Voice Gross Tons 7,174 British, sunk by U-boat
Bellingham Gross Tons 5,345 USA, sunk by U-boat
Silver Sword Gross Tons 4,937 USA, sunk by U-boat
Total Gross Tons 17,456

Convoy QP 15
Goolistan (Straggling or separated from convoy) Gross Tons 5,851 British, sunk by
U-boat
Kuznetz Lesov (Straggling or separated from convoy) Gross Tons 3,974 Russian, sunk by
U-boat
Total Gross Tons 9,825

Convoy RA 52
Greylock Gross Tons 7,460 USA, sunk by U-boat
Total Gross Tons 7,460

Convoy RA 53
Executive Gross Tons 4,978 USA, sunk by U-boat
J. L. M. Curry Gross Tons 6,800 USA, sunk by Floundered
Puerto Rican (Straggling or separated from convoy) Gross Tons 6,076 USA, sunk by
U-boat
Richard Bland (Straggling or separated from convoy) Gross Tons 7,191 USA, sunk by
U-boat
Total Gross Tons 25,045

Convoy RA 57
Empire Tourist Gross Tons 7,062 British, sunk by U-boat
Total Gross Tons 7,062

Convoy RA 59
William S. Thayer Gross Tons 7,176 USA, sunk by U-boat
Total Gross Tons 7,176

Convoy RA 60
Samsuva Gross Tons 7,219 British, sunk by U-boat
Edward H. Crockett Gross Tons 7,167 USA, sunk by U-boat
Total Gross 14,395

Convoy RA 64

Thomas Scott Gross Tons 7,176 USA, sunk by U-boat

Henry Bacon (Straggling or separated from convoy) Gross Tons 7,177 USA, sunk by A/C torpedo

Horace Grey (Straggling or separated from convoy) Gross Tons 7,200 USA, sunk by U-boat (before joining convoy)

Norfjell (Straggling or separated from convoy) Gross Tons 8,129 Norwegian, sunk by U-boat (before joining convoy)

Total Gross Tons 29,682

(c) Independent Sailings (OPN.FB)

East Going

Empire Gilbert Gross Tons 6,640 British, sunk by U-boat

Empire Sky Gross Tons 7,455 British, sunk by U-boat

Chulmleigh Gross Tons 5,445 British, sunk by wrecked Spitsbergen

William Clarke Gross Tons 7,176 USA, sunk by U-boat

Dekabrist Gross Tons 7,363 Russian, sunk by U-boat

Total Gross Tons 34,979

West Going

Donbass Gross Tons 7,925 Russian, sunk by Destroyer

Total Gross Tons 7,925

(d) Sunk in Russian Ports

Empire Starlight Gross Tons 6,850 British, ex-PQ 13 sunk by Bombed or Mined

Lancaster Castle Gross Tons 5,172 British, ex-PQ 12 sunk by Bombed or Mined

New Westminster City Gross Tons 4,747 British, ex-PQ 13 sunk by Bombed or Mined

Alcoa Cadet Gross Tons 4,823 USA, ex-PQ 15 sunk by Bombed or Mined

Steel Worker Gross Tons 5,686 USA, ex-PQ 16 sunk by Bombed or Mined

Total Gross Tons 27,278

(e) Non Combatant Ships other than Foregoing

Zaafaran (Straggling or separated from convoy) Gross Tons 1,559 British, PQ 17 (Rescue Ship) sunk by A/C Bombs

Gray Anger RFA Gross Tons 3,313 British, PQ 14 sunk by U-boat

Total Gross Tons 4,872

Abstract of Merchant Ship Losses

(a) Convoy to North Russia
British 21, USA 29, Panamanian 5, Russian 2, Dutch 1, Total 58, **Gross Tons 353,366**
(b) Convoys from North Russia
British 6, USA 15, Panamanian 2, Russian 5, Norwegian 1, Total 29,
   Gross Tons 178,317
(c) Independents
British 3, USA 1, Russian 2, Total 6, **Gross Tons 42,004**
(d) In Russian Ports
British 3, USA 2, Total 5, **Gross Tons 27,278**
(e) Other than above
British 2, **Gross Tons 4,872**

Grand Total of Numbers Lost
British 35, USA 47, Panamanian 7, Russian 9, Dutch 1, Norwegian 1, Total 100,
   Gross Tons 604,837

Analysis of Merchant Ship Losses

Ships sailed in Convoy
Surface Attack East Going PQ:JW 1, West Going QP:RA 2, Straggling or Separated 3
   Independent Sailing West Going 1
Submarine East Going PQ:JW 23, West Going QP:RA 18 (including 2 ships lost off
   Kola before joining RA 64), Under Escort 24, Straggling or Separated 17 (including
   2 ships lost off Kola before joining RA 64)
Bombed by Aircraft East Going PQ:JW 17, West Going QP:RA 2, Under Escort 9,
   Straggling or Separated 10
Independent Sailing East Going 4
Torpedoed by Aircraft (Torpedo bombers were operating in force only from May to
   September 1942, and on a reduced scale from December 1944 to February 1945)
East Going PQ:JW 17, West Going QP:RA 1, Under Escort 17, Straggling or
   Separated 1
Mined West Going QP:RA 5 (in British minefield), Under Escort 5 (in British
   minefield)
Floundered West Going QP:RA 1, Under Escort 1
Wrecked *Independent Sailing East Going 1*

Grand Total of Numbers Lost
East Going PQ:JW 58, West Going QP:RA 29, Total 87
Under Escort 56, Straggling or Separated 31, Total 87
Independent Sailing East Going 5, West Going 1 Total 6

Note - In addition 1 rescue ship was sunk by bombs. 1 Fleet oiler by submarine and 5
   merchant ships by air attack or mines after arrival in Russian ports, bringing the
   total of non-combatant ships lost in connection with the convoy traffic to 100.

Losses of Protecting Ships of War

Trinidad Cruiser Damaged by own torpedo supporting PQ 13, 29.03.1942; sunk by
dive bombers 14.05.1942

Edinburgh Cruiser Damaged by U-boat's torpedo, 30.04.1942; sunk by destroyers
02.05.1942 (QP 11)

Matabele Destroyer Sunk by U-boat, 17.01.1942 (PQ 8)

Punjabi Destroyer Sunk in collision, 01.05.1942 (with battle fleet supporting PQ 15
and QP 11)

Somali Destroyer Sunk by U-boat, 20.09.1942 (QP 14)

Achates Destroyer Sunk by *Hipper*, 31.12.1942 (JW 51B)

Hardy Destroyer Sunk by U-boat, 1.44 (JW 56A)

Mahratta Destroyer Sunk by U-boat, 2.44 (JW 57)

Kite Sloop Sunk by U-boat, 8.44 (JW 59)

Lapwing Sloop Sunk by U-boat, 3.45 (JW 65)

Goodall Frigate Sunk by U-boat, 4.45 (RA 66)

Denbigh Castle Corvette Sunk by U-boat, 2.45 ((JW 64)

Bluebell Corvette Sunk by U-boat, 2.45 (RA 64)

Gossamer Minesweeper Sunk by bombs, Kola Inlet, 24.06.1942

Niger Minesweeper Mined and sunk, 05.07.1942 (QP 13)

Leda Minesweeper Sunk by U-boat, 20.09.1942 (QP 14)

Bramble Minesweeper Sunk by surface craft, 31.12.1942 (JW 51B)

Shera Armed Whaler Capsized and sunk, 09.03.1942 (PQ 12)

P551 Submarine Sunk by escort of PQ15, 02.05.1942

Losses 2 Crusiers, 6 Destroyers, 2 Sloops, 1 Frigate, 2 Corvettes, 4 Minesweepers, 1
Whaler, 1 Submarine **Total 19**

Appendix B

Allied Warships with Main Armament and Commanding Officers

I. January 1942 – March 1943 (Chapters I–VI)

Note – Ships are listed alphabetically according to type. Names of C.O.s are taken from appropriate Navy Lists.

Capital Ships

HMS *Anson* 10 14-in, 16 5.25-in Captain H. R. G. Kinahan CBE, Flag, Vice-Admiral Sir Bruce A. Fraser KBE CB VA (2) 28.06.1942

HMS *Duke of York* 10 14-in, 16 5.25-in Captain C. H. J. Harcourt CBE, Captain G. E. Creasy DSO MVO –.09.1942

HMS *Howe* 10 14-in, 16 5.25-in Captain C. H. L. Woodhouse CB

HMS *King George V* 10 14-in, 16 5.25-in Captain W. R. Patterson CB CVO, Captain P. J. Mack DSO –.05.1942, Flag, Admiral Sir John C. Trovey KCB KBE DSC C-in-C Home Fleet

HMS *Nelson* 9 16-in, 12 6-in, 6 4.7-in, Captain H. B. Jacomb

HMS *Renown* 6 15-in, 20 4.5-in, Captain C. S. Daniel CBE DSO, Flag, Vice-Admiral A. T. B. Curteis CB VA (2)

USS *Washington* 9 16-in, 20 5-in, Flag, Rear-Admiral R. C. Giffen USN

Aircraft Carriers
(a) Fleet Carriers

HMS *Victorious* 16 4.5-in, 21 Albacores, 12 Fulmars, Captain H. C. Bovell CBE, Captain L. D. Macintosh DSC 30.09.1942

USS *Wasp* 8 5-in, 76 Aircraft
(b) Escort Carriers

HMS *Avenger* 3 4-in, 12 Hurricanes (+ 6 spare), 3 Swordfish, Commander A. P. Colthurst

HMS *Dasher* 3 4-in, Act. Captain C. N. Lentaigne DSO

A.A. Ships

HMS *Alynbank* 8 4-in, Act. Captain H. F. Nash

HMS *Palomares* 6 4-in, Act. Captain J. H. Jauncey

HMS *Pozarica* 6 4-in, Act. Captain E.D.W. Lawford

HMS *Ulster Queen* 6 4-in, Act. Captain C. K. Adam

Cruisers

HMS *Belfast* 12 6-in, 12 4-in, Captain F. R. Parkham, Flag,
    Rear-Admiral R. L. Burnett CB DSO OBE (JW 53)

HMS *Bermuda* 12 6-in, 8 4-in, Captain T. H. Back

HMS *Berwick* 8 8-in, 8 4-in, Captain G. H. Faulkner DSC

HMS *Cumberland* 8 8-in, 8 4-in, Captain A. H. Maxwell-Hyslop AM

HMS *Edinburgh* 12 6-in, 12 4-in, Captain H. W. Faulkner, Flag, Rear-Admiral
    S. S. Bonham-Carter CB CVO DSO (PQ 14, PQ 11) Sunk, 02.05.1942

HMS *Glasgow* 12 6-in, 8 4-in, Captain E. M. Evans-Lombe

HMS *Jamaica* 12 6-in, 8 4-in, Captain J. L. Story

HMS *Kent* 8 8-in, 8 4-in, Captain A. E. M. B. Cunninghame-Graham

HMS *Kenya* 12 6-in, 8 4-in, Captain M. M. Denny CB, Captain A. S. Russell
    01.04.1942

HMS *Liverpool* 12 6-in, 8 4-in, Captain W. R. Slater DSC

HMS *London* 8 8-in, 8 4-in, Captain R. M. Servaes CBE, Flag,
    Rear-Admiral L. H. K. Hamilton CB DSO

HMS *Manchester* 12 6-in, 8 4-in, Captain H. Drew DSC

HMS *Nigeria* 12 6-in, 8 4-in, Captain J. G. L. Dundas CBE, Flag,
    Rear Admiral H. M. Burrough CB DSO

HMS *Norfolk* 8 8-in, 8 4-in, Captain E. G. H. Bellars

HMS *Scylla* 8 4.5-in, Captain I. A. P. Macintyre CBE, Flag,
    Rear-Admiral R. L. Burnett CB DSO OBE (PQ 18, QP 14)

HMS *Sheffield* 12 6-in, 8 4-in Captain A. W. Clarke, Flag,
    Rear-Admiral R. L. Burnett CB DSO OBE (JW/RA 51)

HMS *Suffolk* 8 8-in, 8 4-in, Captain R. Shelley

HMS *Trinidad* 8 8-in, 8 4-in, Captain L. S. Saunders, Sunk, 14.05.1942

USS *Tuscaloosa* 9 8-in, 8 5-in, Captain N. C. Gillette USN

USS *Wichita* 9 8-in, 8 5-in, Captain H. W. Hill USN

Destroyers

HMS *Achates* 2 4.7-in, 1 3-in, Lieut.-Com. A. H. T. Johns, killed in action,
    sunk ((JW 51)

HMS *Amazon* 2 4.7-in, 1 3-in, Lieut.-Com. The Lord Teynham

HMS *Ashanti* 8 4.7-in, 2 4-in, Commander R. G. Onslow

HMS *Badsworth* 6 4-in, Lieutenant G. T. S. Gray

HMS *Beagle* 2 4.7-in, 1 3-in, Commander R. C. Medley DSO

HMS *Bedouin* 6 4.7-in, 2 4-in, Commander B. G. Scurfield OBE AM

HMS *Beverley* 3 4-in, Lieutenant R. A. Price

HMS *Blankney* 6 4-in, Lieut.-Com. P. F. Powlett DSO DSC

HMS *Boadicea* 3 4.7-in, 1 3-in, Lieut.-Com. F. C. Brodrick

HMS *Bramham* 6 4-in, Lieutenant E. F. Baines

HMS *Broke* 2 4.7-in, 1 3-in, Lieut.-Com. A. F. C. Layard

HMS *Bulldog* 2 4.7-in, 1 3-in, Commander M. Richmond DSO OBE

HMS *Campbell* 2 4.7-in, 1 3-in, Act. Commander E. C. Coats DSO DSC

HMS *Cowdrey* 6 4-in, Lieut.-Com. C. W. North

HMS *Douglas* 2 4.7-in, 1 3-in, Lieut.-Com. R. B. S. Tennant

HMS *Echo* 4 4.7-in, 1 3-in, Lieut.-Com. N. Lanyon

HMS *Eclipse* 4 4.7-in, 1 3-in, Lieut.-Com. E. Mack DSO

USS *Emmons*

HMS *Escapade* 4 4.7-in, 1 3-in, Commander E. N. V. Currey DSO,
    Lieut.-Com. E. C. Peake 01.12.1942

HMS *Eskimo* 6 4.7-in, 2 4-in, Commander E. G. Le Geyt

HMS *Faulkner* 5 4.7-in, 1 3-in, Captain A. K. Scott-Moncrieff

HMS *Foresight* 3 4.7-in, 1 3-in, Commander J. S. Salter

HMS *Forester* 3 4.7-in, 1 3-in, Lieut.-Com. G. P. Huddart killed in action,
    Lieut.-Com. J. A. Burnett DSO 04.08.1942

HMS *Fury* 4 4.7-in, 1 3-in, Lieut.-Com. C.H. Campbell

ORP *Garland* 3 4.7-in, 1 3-in

USRS *Gremyaschi* 4 5.1-in, 2 3-in

USRS *Gromki* 4 5.1-in, 2 3-in

HMS *Grove* 6 4-in, Lieut.-Com. J. W. Rylands

USRS *Grozni* 4 5.1-in, 2 3-in

HMS *Icarus* 4 4.7-in, 1 3-in, Lieut.-Com. C. D. Maud DSC,
    Lieut.-Com. E. N. Walmsley DSC 27.10.1942

HMS *Impulsive* 4 4.7-in, 1 3-in, Lieut.-Com. E. G. Roper DSC

HMS *Inconstant* 4 4.7-in, 1 3-in, Lieut.-Com. W. S. Clouston

HMS *Inglefield* 5 4.7-in, 1 3-in, Commander A. G. West

HMS *Intrepid* 4 4.7-in, 1 3-in, Commander J. H. Lewes,
    Commander C. A. de W. Kitcat –.06.1942

HMS *Javelin* 6 4.7-in, 1 4-in, Commander G. E. Fardell

HMS *Keppel* 2 4.7-in, 1 3-in, Lieut.-Com. J. E. Broome

USRS *Kuibyshev* 4 4-in

HMS *Lamerton* 6 4.7-in, Lieut.-Com. C. R. Purse DSC

HMS *Lancaster* 3 4-in, 1 12-pdr., Act. Commander N. H. Whatley

HMS *Leamington* 1 4-in, 1 12-pdr., Lieutenant B. M. D. l'Anson

HMS *Ledbury* 6 4-in, Lieut.-Com. R. P. Hill

HMS *Lookout* 6 4.7-in, 1 4-in, Lieut.-Com. C. P. F. Brown DSC

HMS *Mackay* 3 4-in, 1 3-in, Lieutenant J. B. Marjoribanks

HMS *Malcolm* 2 4-in, 1 3-in, Act. Commander A. B. Russell

HMS *Marne* 6 4.7-in, 1 4-in, Lieut.-Com. H. N. A. Richardson DSC

HMS *Martin* 6 4.7-in, 1 4-in, Commander C. R. P. Thompson DSO

HMS *Matabele* 6 4.7-in, 2 4-in, Commander A. C. Stanford DSC,
    sunk (PQ 8) 17.01.1942

HMS *Matchless* 6 4.7-in, 1 4-in, Lieut.-Com. J. Mowlam DSO

USS *Mayrant* 4 5-in

HMS *Meteor* 6 4.7-in, 1 4-in, Lieut.-Com. D. J. B. Jewett

HMS *Meynell* 4 4-in, Lieutenant B.M.D. l'Anson

HMS *Middleton* 6 4-in, Lieut.-Com. D. C. Kinloch,
    Lieut.-Com. C. S. Battersby –.08.1942

HMS *Milne* 6 4.7-in, 1 4-in, Captain I. M. R. Campbell

HMS *Montrose* 3 4.7-in, 1 3-in, Act. Commander W. J. Phillips

HMS *Musketeer* 6 4.7-in, 1 4-in, Commander E. N. V. Currey DSC

HMS *Newmarket* 3 4-in

HMS *Oakley* 6 4-in, Lieut.-Com. Lieut.-Com. R. C. V. Thomson (ret.), Lieut.-Com. T.
    A. Pack-Beresford –.06.1942

HMS *Obdurate* 4 4-in, Lieut.-Com. C. E. L. Sclater DSC

HMS *Obedient* 4 4-in, Lieut.-Com. D. C. Kinlock, promoted Commander 31.12.1942

HMS *Offa* 4 4.7-in, 1 4-in, Lieut.-Com. R. A. Ewing

HMS *Onslaught* 4 4.7-in, 1 4-in, Commander W. H. Selby

HMS *Onslow* 4 4.7-in, 1 4-in, Captain H. T. Armstrong,
    Captain R. St. V. Sherbrooke DSO –.09.1942

HMS *Opportune* 4 4in, Commander M. L. Power OBE, Commander J. Lee-Barber
    DSO 26.09.1942

HMS *Oribi* 4 4.7-in, 1 4-in, Commander J. E. H. McBeath DSO DSC

ORP *Orkan* 6 4.7-in, 1 4-in

HMS *Orwell* 4 4in, Lieut.-Com. N. H. G. Austen DSO

ORP *Piorun* 6 4.7-in, 1 4-in

HMS *Punjabi* 6 4.7-in, 2 4-in, Commander The Hon. J. M. Waldegrave DSO (ret.),
    sunk in collision

HMS *Pytchley* 4 4-in, Lieut.-Com. H. Unwin DSC

HMS *Quadrant* 4 4.7-in, Lieut.-Com. W. H. Farrington

HMS *Queensborough* 4 4.7-in, E. P. Hinton DSO MVO

HMS *Raider* 4 4.7-in, Lieut.-Com. K. W. Mitchell

USS *Rhind* 4 5-in

USS *Rowan* 4 5-in

HNorMS *St Albans* 3 4-in, Commander S. V. Storeheill RNorN

USSRS *Sokrushitelni* 4 5.1-in, 2 3-in

HMS *Somali* 6 4.7-in, 2 4-in, Captain Lieut.-Com. J. W. M. Eaton DSO DSC

HMS *Tarter* 6 4.7-in, 2 4-in, Commander R. T. White DSO,
    Commander St. J. R. J. Tyrwhitt DSC 05.06.1942

HMS *Venomous* 4 4.7-in, Commander H. W. Falcon-Steward

HMS *Verdun* 4 4-in, Lieut.-Com. W. S. Donald DSC

HMS *Volunteer* 3 4.7-in, 1 12-pdr., Lieut.-Com. A. S. Pomeroy,
    Lieut.-Com. G. J. Luther 03.12.1942

USS *Wainwright* 4 5-in, Lieut.-Com. R. H. Gibbs USN

HMS *Wells* 3 4.7-in, 1 12-pdr., Lieutenant L. J. Pearson,
    Lieutenant F. W. M. Carter –.11.1942

HMS *Wheatland* 6 4-in, Lieut.-Com. R. De L'Brooke

HMS *Wilton* 6 4-in, Lieutenant A. P. Northey DSC

HMS *Windsor* 4 4-in, 1 12-pdr., Lieut.-Com. D. H. F. Hetherington DSC

HMS *Woolston* 4 4-in, Lieut.-Com. W. K. Mitchell

HMS *Worcester* 4 4.7-in, 1 12-pdr., Lieut.-Com. W. A. Juniper DSO

Minesweepers

HMS *Bramble* 2 4-in, Captain J. H. F. Crombie DSO,
    Commander H. T. Rust DSO 16.11.1942, killed in action 31.12.1942

HMS *Britomart* 2 4-in, Lieut.-Com. S. S. Stamwitz

HMS *Gleaner* 2 4-in, Lieut.-Com. F. J. G. Hewitt DSC

HMS *Gossamer* 2 4-in, Lieut.-Com. T. C. Crease, bombed and sunk, Kola

HMS *Halcyon* 2 4-in, Lieut.-Com. C. H. Corbet-Singleton DSC

HMS *Harrier* 2 4-in, Commander A. D. H. Jay DSO

HMS *Hazard* 2 4-in, Lieut.-Com. J. R. A. Seymour

HMS *Hebe* 2 4-in, Lieutenant A. L. Gulvin

HMS *Hussar* 2 4-in, Lieutenant R. C. Biggs DSO DSC

HMS *Jason* 2 4-in, Commander H. G. A. Lewis
HMS *Leda* 2 4-in, Commander A. H. Wynne-Edwards
HMS *Niger* 2 4-in, Commander A. J. Cubison DSC, mined and sunk (QP 13)
HMS *Salamander* 2 4-in, Lieutenant W. R. Muttram
HMS *Seagull* 2 4in, Lieut.-Com. C. H. Pollock
HMS *Sharpshooter* 2 4-in, Lieut.-Com. W. L. O'Mara
HMS *Speedwell* 2 4-in, Lieut.-Com. T. E. Williams
HMS *Speedy* 2 4-in, Lieut.-Com. J. G. Brooks DSC

Corvettes

HMS *Bergamot* 1 4-in, Lieutenant R. T. Horan RNR
HMS *Bluebell* 1 4-in, Lieutenant H. G. Walker RNVR
HMS *Bryony* 1 4-in, Lieut.-Com. J. P. Stewart DSC RNR
HMS *Camelia* 1 4-in, Lieutenant R. F. J. Maberley RNVR
HMS *Campanula* 1 4-in, Lieut.-Com. B. A. Rogers RNR
HMS *Dianella* 1 4-in, Lieutenant J. G. Rankin RNR
HMS *Honeysuckle* 1 4-in, Lieutenant H. H. D. MacKillican DSC RNR
HMS *Hyderabad* 1 4-in, Lieutenant S. C. B. Hickman RNR
FFS *La Malouine* 1 3.7-in, Lieutenant V. E. H. Bidwell RNR
HMS *Lotus* 1 4-in, Lieutenant H. J. Hall RNR
HMS *Oxlip* 1 4-in, Lieutenant C. W. Leadbetter RNR
HMS *Poppy* 1 4-in, Lieutenant N. K. Boyd RNR
HMS *Rhododendron* 1 4-in, Lieut.-Com. L. A. Sayers RNR
FFS *Roselyn* 1 4-in, Lieutenant de Vaisseau B. Bergeret
HMS *Saxifrage* 1 4-in, Lieutenant N. L. Knight RNR
HMS *Snowflake* 1 4-in, Lieutenant H. G. Chesterman RNR
HMS *Starwort* 1 4-in, Lieut.-Com. N. W. Duck RNR
HMS *Sweetbriar* 1 4-in, Lieutenant J. W. Cooper RNR

Trawlers

HMS *Ayrshire* 1 4-in, Lieutenant L. J. A. Gradwell RNVR
HMS *Blackfly* 1 4-in, Lieutenant A. P. Hughes RNR
HMS *Cape Argona* 1 4-in, Lieutenant E. R. Pato RNR
HMS *Cape Mariano* 1 4-in, Lieutenant T. S. Clouston RNVR
HMS *Daneman* 1 4-in, Lieutenant G. O. T. D. Henderson RNVR
HMS *Lady Madeleine* 1 4-in, Lieutenant W. G. Ogden RNVR
HMS *Lord Austin* 1 4-in, Lieutenant O. B. Egjar
HMS *Lord Middleton* 1 4-in, Lieutenant R.H. Jameson RNR
HMS *Northern Gem* 1 4-in, Skipper-Lieutenant H. C. Aisthorpe RNR
HMS *Northern Pride* 1 4-in, Lieutenant A. L. F. Bell RNR
HMS *Northern Spray* 1 4-in, Lieutenant G. T. Gilbert RNVR
HMS *Northern Wave* 1 4-in, Lieutenant W. G. Pardoe-Mathews RNR
HMS *Paynter* 1 4-in, Lieutenant R. H. Nosier DSC RANVR
HMS *Retriever* 1 4-in, Lieut.-Com. G. E. Greeve RNR
HMS *St. Elstan* 1 4-in, Lieutenant R. M. Roberts RNR
HMS *St. Kenan* 1 4-in, Lieutenant J. Mackay RNR
HMS *Vizalma* 1 4-in, Lieutenant R. J. Angleback

Whalers

HMS *Shera* Lieutenant W. E. Bulmer RNR, capsized

HMS *Shusa* Sub.-Lieutenant J. B. Powell RNR

HMS *Silja* Lieutenant H. C. Farmer RNVR

HMS *Stefa* Lieutenant T. Costley RNVR

HMS *Sulla* Skipper T. Meadows RNR

HMS *Sumba* Lieutenant W. E. Peters RNR

HMS *Svega* Lieutenant F. P. Maitland RNVR

Submarines

HMS *Graph* 5 torp. tubes, Lieutenant P. B. Marriott

FFS *Junon* 7 torp. tubes, Capitaine de Fregate Querelle DSC

FFS *Minerve* 9 torp. tubes, Capitaine de Corvette P. M. Sonneville DSC

RNN *014* 4 torp. tubes, Lieut.-Com. H. A. W. Goossens RNethN

HMS *P43* 4 torp. tubes, Lieutenant A. C. Halliday

HMS *P45* 4 torp. tubes, Lieutenant H. B. Turner

HMS *P54* 4 torp. tubes, Lieutenant C. E. Oxborrow DSO

HMS *P212* 7 torp. tubes, Lieutenant J. H. Bromage DSC

HMS *P221* 7 torp. tubes, Lieutenant M. F. R. Ainslie DSC

ORP *P551* 4 torp. tubes, Lieut.-Com. K. Romanowski

HMS *P614* 5 torp. tubes, Lieutenant D. J. Beckley

HMS *P615* 5 torp. tubes, Lieutenant P. E. Newstead

FS *Rubis* 5 torp. tubes, 32 mines, Capitaine de Corvette H. Rousselot DSC

HMS *Seadog* 7 torp. tubes, Lieutenant D. S. R. Martin

HMS *Sealion* 7 torp. tubes, Lieut.-Com. G. R. Colvin

HMS Seanymph 7 torp. tubes, Lieutenant G.D.N. Milner DSC

HMS *Seawolf* 7 torp. tubes, Lieutenant R. P. Raikes

ORP *Sokol* 4 torp. tubes, Lieut.-Com. G. Koziolkowski

HMS *Sturgeon* 6 torp. tubes, Lieut.-Com. M. R. G. Wingfield

HMS *Taurus* 11 torp. tubes, Lieut.-Com. M. R. G. Wingfield

HMS *Tigris* 6 torp. tubes, Lieutenant L. W. Napier,
  Lieut.-Com. G. R. Colvin 15.04.1942

HMS *Torbay* 11 torp. tubes, Lieutenant R. J. Clutterbuck

HMS *Trespasser* 11 torp. tubes, Lieutenant R. M. Favell

HMS *Tribune* 10 torp. tubes, Lieutenant N. J. Coe DSC,
  Lieutenant M. C. R. Lumby 07.07.1942 Lieutenant S. A. Porter DSC 20.12.1942

HMS *Trident* 10 torp. tubes, Commander G. M. Sladen DSO DSC

HMS *Tuna* 10 torp. tubes, Lieutenant M. B. St. John,
  Lieutenant R. P. Raikes DSO 26.08.1942

HMS *Ursula* 6 torp. tubes, Lieutenant R. B. Lakin DSC

HMS *Unique* 4 torp. tubes, Lieutenant E. R. Boddington

HMS *Unruly* 4 torp. tubes, Lieutenant J. P. Fyfe

HNorMS *Uredd* 4 torp. tubes, Lieutenant R. O. Rören RNorN

II. November 1943 – May 1945 (Chapters VII)

Note - Ships are listed alphabetically according to type. Names of C.O.s are taken from appropriate Navy Lists.

Capital Ships
HMS *Anson* 10 14-in, 16 5.25-in, Captain E. D. B. MaCarthy DSO, Flag, Vice-Admiral Sir Henry Moore KCB CVO DSO VA (2)

HMS *Duke of York* 10 14-in, 16 5.25-in Captain The Hon. G. H. E. Russell CBE, Flag, Vice-Admiral Sir Bruce A. Fraser GCB KBE C-in-C Home Fleet 15.06.1944. Flag, Vice-Admiral Sir Henry Moore KCB CVO DSO C-in-C Home Fleet

HMS *Rodney* 9 16-in, 12 6-in, 6 4.7-in, Captain The Hon. R. O. Fitzroy, Flag, Admiral Sir Henry Moore KCB CVO DSO

Fleet Carriers
Aircraft complements are typical: types varied from time to time

HMS *Formidable* 16 4.5-in, 21 TBR, 6 2-seater Fighters, 12 1-seater Fighters, Captain P. Rucke-Keene CBE

HMS *Furious* 10 4.5-in, 15 TBR, 6 2-seater Fighters, 12 1-seater Fighters, Captain G. T. Phillips DSO DSC

HMS *Indefatigable* 16 4.5-in, 27 TBR, 9 2-seater Fighters, 18 1-seater Fighters, Captain Q. D. Graham CBE DSO

HMS *Victorious* 16 4.5-in, 21 TBR, 12 Fighters, Captain M. M. Denny CB CBE

Escort Carriers
HMS *Activity* 2 4-in, 7 Wildcat, 3 Swordfish, Captain G. Willoughby

HMS *Campania* 2 4-in, 4 Wildcat, 12 Swordfish, 3 Fulmars (JW 60, 62), 1 Fulmar (JW 64), 3 additional Wildcats (JW 65), Flag, Rear-Admiral R. R. McGregor CB DSO (Convoys JW/RA 60, 62, 64), Flag, Vice-Admiral Sir Frederick H. G. Dalrymple-Hamilton KCB (JW/RA 65)

HMS *Chaser* 2 4-in, 11 Swordfish, 11 Wildcat, Captain H. V. P. McClintock DSO

HMS *Fencer* 2 4-in, 11 Swordfish, 9 Wildcat, Act. Captain W. W. R. Bentinck

HMS *Nabob* 2 5-in, Act. Captain H. N. Lay RCN

HMS *Nairana* 2 4-in, 14 Swordfish, 6 Wildcat, Captain H. N. Surtees DSO

HMS *Premier* 2 5-in, 12 Avenger, Act. Captain R. J. Gardiner

HMS *Queen* 2 5-in, 8 Avenger, 8 Wildcat, Act. Captain K. J. D'Arcy DSO

HMS *Striker* 2 4-in, 12 Swordfish, 10 Wildcat, Captain W. P. Carne

HMS *Tracker* 2 4-in, 10-12 Avenger, 6-7 Wildcat, Act. Captain J. H. Huntley

HMS *Trumpeter* 2 5-in, 8 Avenger, 8 Wildcat, Act. Captain K. S. Colquhoun

HMS *Vindex* 2 4-in, 12 Swordfish (JW 59, 61, 63), 8 Swordfish (JW 66), 6 Hurricane (JW 59), 4 Wildcat (JW 61), 7 Wildcat (JW 63), 12 Wildcat (JW 60), Captain H. T. T. Bayliss, Captain J. D. L. Williams 26.12.1944, Flag, Vice-Admiral Sir Frederick H. G. Dalrymple-Hamilton KCB (Convoys JW/RA 59, 61, 63), Flag, Rear-Admiral A. E. M. B. Cuninghame-Graham (Convoys JW/RA 66)

Cruisers

HMS *Belfast* 12 6-in, 12 4-ins, Captain F. R. Parham, Flag, Vice-Admiral R. L. Burnett
CB DSO OBE (Convoys RA 54A, JW/RA 55A, 55B)

HMS *Bellona* 8 5.25-in, Captain G. S. Tuck DSO

HMS *Bermuda* 12 6-in, 8 4-ins, Captain T. H. Back

HMS *Berwick* 8 8-in, 8 4-ins, Captain H. J. Eberton Captain N. V. Grace –.01.1944

HMS *Black Prince* 8 5.25-in, Captain D. M. Lees DSO, Flag, Vice-Admiral I. G.
Glennie CB (Convoy JW 57)

HMS *Devonshire* 8 8-in, 8 4-ins, Captain D. K. Bain DSO 29.02.1944

HMS *Diadem* 12 8 5.25-in, Captain E. G. A. Clifford, Flag, Vice-Admiral Sir Frederick
H. G. Dalrymple-Hamilton KCB (JW/RA 58), Flag, Rear-Admiral R. R.
McGregor CB DSO (Convoy RA 59)

ORP *Dragon* 5 6-in, 2 4-ins

HMS *Jamaica* 12 6-in, 8 4-ins, Captain J. Hughes-Hallett DSO

HMS *Kent* 8 8-in, 8 4-ins, Captain G. A. B. Hawkins DSO MVO, Flag, Rear-Admiral
A. F. E. Palliser CB (Convoy JW 54A, 54B, RA 54B, JW 56A, 57)

HMS *Norfolk* 8 8-in, 8 4-ins, Captain D. K. Bain Captain J. G. Y. Loveband
01.09.1944

HMS *Sheffield* 12 6-in, 8 4-ins, Captain C. T. Addis

USS *Tuscaloosa* 9 8-in, 8 5-in

Destroyers

HMS *Ashanti* 2 4.7-in, 1 3-in, Lieut.-Com. J. R. Barnes

HMCS *Athabaskan* 6 4.7-in, 2 4-in, Lieut.-Com. J. H. Stubbs DSO RCN

HMS *Beagle* 2 4.7-in, 1 3-in, Lieut.-Com. N. R. Murch

HMS *Cassandra* 4 4.5-in, Lieutenant G. C. Leslie

HMS *Cavalier* 4 4.5-in, Lieut.-Com. D. T. McBarnet DSC

HMCS *Haida* 6 4.7-in, 2 4-in, Commander H. G. De Wolf RCN

HMS *Hardy* 4 4.7-in, Captain W. G. A. Robson DSO DSC, sunk (JW 56B)

HMCS *Huron* 6 4.7-in, 2 4-in, Lieut.-Com. H. S. Rayner DSC RCN

HMS *Impulsive* 4 4.7-in, 1 3-in, Lieut.-Com. P. Bekenn

HMS *Inconstant* 4 4.7-in, 1 3-in, Lieut.-Com. J. H. Eaden DSC

HMCS *Iroquois* 2 4-in, Commander J. C. Hubbard DSC RCN

HMS *Keppel* 2 4.7-in, 1 3-in, Commander I. J. Tyson DSC RD RNR

HMS *Mahratta* 6 4.7-in, 1 4-in, Lieut.-Com. E. A. F. Drought DSC, sunk (JW 57)

HMS *Matchless* 6 4.7-in, 1 4-in, Lieut.-Com. W. S. Shaw

HMS *Meteor* 6 4.7-in, 1 4-in, Lieut.-Com. D. J. P. Jewitt

HMS *Milne* 6 4.7-in, 1 4-in, Captain I. M. R. Campbell DSO, (D) 3

HMS *Musketeer* 6 4.7-in, 1 4-in, Commander R. L. Fisher DSO OBE

HMS *Myngs* 4 4.5-in, Captain P. G. L. Cazalet DSC, (D) 23

HMS *Obdurate* 4 4-in, Lieut.-Com. R. D. Franks DSO OBE

HMS *Onslaught* 4 4.7-in, 1 4-in, Commander W. H. Selby DSC Commander the Hon.
A. Pleydell-Bouverie 14.02.1944

HMS *Onslow* 4 4.7-in, 1 4-in, Captain J. W. McCoy DSO Captain H. W. S. Browning
OBE 09.09.1944 (D) 17

HMS *Opportune* 4 4-in, Commander J. Lee-Brber DSO Commander R. E. D. Ryder
VC 14.08.1944

HMS *Orwell* 4 4-in, Lieut.-Com. Lieut.-Com. J. M. Hodges DSO Lieut.-Com. J. R. Gower DSC 15.07.1944

HMS *Saumarez* 4 4.7-in, Lieut.-Com. E. W. Walmsley DSC

HMS *Savage* 4 4.5-in, Commander M. D. G. Meyrick Lieut.-Com. C. W. Malins DSO DSC –.06.1944

HMS *Scorpion* 4 4.7-in, Lieut.-Com. W. S. Clouston Commander C. W. McMullen DSC –.10.1944

HMS *Scourge* 4 4.7-in, Lieut.-Com. G. I. M. Balfour

HMS *Serapis* 4 4.7-in, Lieut.-Com. E. L. Jones DSC

HMCS *Sioux* 4 4.7-in, Lieut.-Com. E. E. G. Boak RCN

HNorMS *Stord* 4 4.7-in, Lieut.-Com. S. Storeheill RNorN

HMS *Venus* 4 4.7-in, Commander J. S. M. Richardson DSO

HMS *Vigilant* 4 4.7-in, Lieut.-Com. L. W. L. Argles

HMS *Virago* 4 4.7-in, Lieut.-Com. A. J. R. White

HMS *Westcott* 4 4-in, Commander H. Lambton (ret.)

HMS *Whitehall* 4 4.7-in, Lieut.-Com. P. J. Cowell DSC

HMS *Wrestler* 4 4-in, Lieutenant R. W. B. Bacon DSC

HMS *Zambesi* 4 4.5-in, Captain J. H. Allison (D) 2

HMS *Zealous* 4 4.5-in, Commander R. F. Jessel DSO DSC

HMS *Zebra* 4 4.5-in, Lieut.-Com. E. G. Peake

HMS *Zest* 4 4.5-in, Lieut.-Com. R. B. N. Hicks DSO

Sloops

HMS *Cygnet* 6 4-ins, Commander A. H. Thorold

HMS *Kite* 6 4-ins, Lieut.-Com. A. N. G. Campbell, sunk (JW 59)

HMS *Lapwing* 6 4-ins, Act. Commander E. C. Hutton (ret.), sunk (JW 65)

HMS *Lark* 6 4-ins, Commander H. Lambton

HMS *Mermaid* 6 4-ins, Lieut.-Com. J. P. Mosse

HMS *Peacock* 6 4-ins, Lieut.-Com. R. B. Stannard VC

Frigates

HMS *Bazely* 3 3-ins, Lieut.-Com. J. W. Cooper DSC RNR

HMS *Bentinch* 3 3-ins, Lieutenant P. R. G. Worth

HMS *Byard* 3 3-ins, Lieut.-Com. J. I. Jones DSO DSC RNR

HMS *Drury* 3 3-ins, Lieut.-Com. N. J. Parker

HMS *Goodall* 3 3-ins, Lieut.-Com. J. V. Fulton RNVR, sunk (JW 66)

HMCS *Loch Alvie* 1 4-ins, 2 2-pdr, Lieut.-Com. E. G. Old RCN

HMS *Loch Dunvegan* 1 4-ins, 2 2-pdr, Commander E. Wheeler RNR

HMCS *Matane* 2 4-ins, Lieutenant J. J. Coates

HMCS *Monnow* 2 4-ins, Commander E. G. Skinner DSC RD RCNR

HMS *Mounsey* 3 3-ins, Lieutenant F. A. J. Andrew

HMCS *Nene* 2 4-ins, Lieut.-Com. E. R. Shaw RCNR

HMS *Pasley* 3 3-ins, Lieutenant P. R. G. Mitchell

HMCS *St. Pierre* 2 4-ins, Lieut.-Com. J. A. Tullis

Corvettes

HNorMS *Acanthus* 1 4-ins, LA

HMS *Alnwick Castle* 1 4-ins, HA/LA, Lieut.-Com. H. A. Stonehouse RNR

HMS *Bamborough Castle* 1 4-ins, HA/LA, Lieutenant M. S. Work DSC RNR

HMS *Bluebell* 1 4-ins, HA/LA, Lieutenant G. H. Walker DSC, sunk (RA 64)

HMS *Denbigh Castle* 1 4-ins, HA/LA, Lieut.-Com. G. Butcher DSC RNR, sunk (JW 64)

HMS *Dianella* 1 4-ins, LA, Lieutenant J. F. Tognola RNR

HNorMS *Eglantine* 1 4-ins, LA

HMS *Heather* 1 4-ins, LA, Lieutenant W. L. Turner RNR

HMS *Honeysuckle* 1 4-ins, LA, Lieutenant H. H. D. MacKilligan DSC RNR

HMS *Oxlip* 1 4-ins, LA, Lieut.-Com. C. W. Leadbetter RNR

HMS *Poppy* 1 4-ins, LA, Lieutenant D. R. C. Onslow RNR

HMS *Rhododendron* 1 4-ins, LA, Lieutenant L. A. Sayers Lieutenant G. L. F. Melville RNR 03.08.1944 Lieutenant R. S. Mortimer RNR 21.01.1945

Appendix C

Warship Dispositions for Selected Convoys

I. PQ 12 and PQ 8; March 1942

Battle Fleet
King George V (Flag, C.-in-C.)
Duke of York
Renown (Flag, V.A. Curtis)
Victorious
Berwick
Onslow
Bedouin Parted company p.m. 4th March, rejoined p.m. 9th March.
Intrepid
Lookout
Ashanti
Icarus
Faulkner Parted company p.m. 4th March, rejoined p.m. 9th March.
Eskimo Parted company p.m. 4th March, rejoined p.m. 9th March.
Punjabi
Fury
Echo
Eclipse
Tartar Joined the Fleet p.m. 9th March.
Javelin Joined the Fleet a.m. 10th March.
Inconstant Joined the Fleet a.m. 10th March.
Grove Joined the Fleet a.m. 10th March.
Ledbury Joined the Fleet a.m. 10th March.
Lancaster Joined the Fleet a.m. 10th March.
Wells Joined the Fleet a.m. 10th March.
Woolston Joined the Fleet a.m. 10th March.
Verdun Joined the Fleet a.m. 10th March.

Submarines

Seawolf
Trident
Minerve (Fr.) Left her patrol p.m. 7th March.
Uredd (Nor.) Arrived on patrol, night 12th/13th March.
Junon (Fr.) Arrived on patrol, night 9th March.
Sealion Arrived on patrol, night 9th March.

Escort for Convoy PQ 12

Kenya
Oribi
Offa
Gossamer Never joined the convoy.

Escort for Convoy QP 8

Nigeria (Flag, R. A. Hamilton) Never joined the convoy.
Hazard
Salamander
Oxlip
Sweetbriar

Destroyer Oiling Operations

London Went to rendezvous 70° N. To oil destroyers.
Kent Went to rendezvous 70° N. To oil destroyers.
Liverpool Went to rendezvous 69° N., 1° W.
Trinidad Went to rendezvous 69° N., 1° W.

II. PQ 17 and QP 13; June–July 1942

Battle Fleet

Duke of York (Flag, C.-in-C.)
Washington (Flag, R. A. Griffen)
Victorious (Flag, V. A. Fraser)
Nigeria (Flag, R. A. Burrough)
Cumberland
Faulknor
Onslaught
Middleton
Escapade
Blankney
Martin
Marne
Wheatland
Onslow
Ashanti
Mayrant
Rhind
Manchester (Flag, V. A. Bonham-Carter) Joined the Fleet on 3rd July.
Eclipse Joined the Fleet on 3rd July.

Cruiser Force

London (Flag, R. A. Hamilton)
Norfolk
Tuscaloosa (USA)
Somali
Wainwright (USA)
Rowan (USA)

Submarine 'Covering Force'

Ursula
Tribune
P212
Sturgeon
Minerve (Fr.)
P45
P54
Seawolf
Trident Joined the patrol 2nd July, having left the escort of convoy QP 13 on 30th June.

Escort for Convoy PQ 17

Keppel
Fury
Offa
Ledbury
Wilton
Leamington
Palomares
Pozarica
Lotus
Poppy
La Malouine
Dianella
Halcyon
Britomart
Salamander
Lord Middleton
Lord Austin
Ayrshire
Northern Gem
P615
P614

Force Q

Douglas
Grey Ranger Replaced *Aldersdale* on 2nd July

Escort for Convoy QP 13

Inglefield
Intrepid
Achates
Volunteer
Garland (Polish)
Alynbank
Starwort
Honeysuckle
Hyderabad
Roselyn (Fr.)
Niger
Hussar
Lady Madeleine
St. Elstan

III. PQ 18 and QP 14; September 1942

Battle Fleet

Anson (Flag, V. A. Fraser)
Duke of York
Jamaica
Keppel
Montrose
Campbell
Mackay
Bramham The *Broke* replaced the *Bramham* with the Fleet on the second
    occasion of going to sea.
Broke

Cruiser Force

Norfolk (Flag, V. A. Bonham-Carter)
Suffolk
London
Cumberland Absent from the force, landing men and gear in Spitzbergan,
    16th/18th September.
Sheffield Absent from the force, landing men and gear in Spitzbergan,
    17th/19th September.
Bulldog
Amazon
Echo
Eclipse Absent from the force, landing men and gear in Spitzbergan,
    16th/19th September.

Submarine 'Covering Force'

Tribune
Tigris
P54
Uredd (Nor.)

Minelayer

Rubis (Fr.)

Escort Force

Scylla (Flag, R. A. Burnett)

Destroyer Force
Group A

Onslow
Offa
Onslaught
Opportune
Ashanti
Somali
Tarter
Eskimo

Group B

Milne
Meteor
Martin
Marne
Faulknor
Fury
Intrepid
Impulsive

Carrier Force

Avenger
Wheatland
Wilton

Force P

Oakley
Cowdray
Worcester
Windsor
Oligarch
Blue Ranger

Force Q
Gray Ranger
Black Ranger

Close Escort for PQ 18
Malcolm
Achates
Ulster Queen
Alynbank Parted company with Convoy PQ 18 on 16th September and joined
QP 14 on 17th September.
Bryony
Bergamot
Bluebell
Camelia
Harrier
Gleaner
Sharpshooter
St. Kenan
Cape Argona
Daneman
Cape Mariato
P615 Parted company with Convoy PQ 18 on 16th September and joined
QP 14 on 17th September.
P614 Parted company with Convoy PQ 18 on 16th September and joined
QP 14 on 17th September.

Close Escort for QP 14
Blankney
Middleton
Palomares
Pozarica
Lotus
La Malouine
Poppy
Dianella
Bramble
Leda
Seagull
Lord Middleton
Lord Austin
Ayrshire
Northern Gem

IV. JW 51A and RA 51; December 1942

Battle Fleet

All Battle Fleet ships cruised during passages of Convoys JW 51A, JW 51B
  and RA 51 respectively.

King George V (Flag, C.-in-C.)
Anson (Flag, V. A. Fraser)
Howe
Berwick
Cumberland
Bermuda
Musketeer
Quadrant
Raider
Forester
Impulsive
Icarus
Queensborough
Montrose
Worcester
Piorun (Polish)

Cruiser Force

(Passage of RA 51 only)
Kent (Flag, R. A. Hamilton)
Berwick

Force R

Sheffield (Flag, R. A. Burnett)
Jamaica
Opportune Not present in action of 31st December.
Matchless Not present in action of 31st December.

Submarines

(During passage of JW 51A)
Taurus (late P339)
Torbay
Seaymph (P223)
Sokol (Polish)

Submarines

(During passage of JW 51B and RA 51)
Trespasser (P312)
Seadog (P216)
Graph
Unruly (P49)

Escort for Convoy JW 51A

Faulknor
Fury
Echo
Eclipse
Inglefield
Beagle
Boadicea
Honeysuckle
Oxlip
Seagull
Northern Wave
Lady Madeleine

Escort for Convoy JW 51B

Onslow
Oribi
Obedient
Obdurate
Orwell
Achates
Rhododendron
Hyderabad
Bramble
Visalia
Northern Gem

Escort for Convoy RA 51

The destroyers of the escort for JW 51A except
Boadicea
Gleaner
Cape Argona
St. Kenan
Daneman
Cape Mariato

Appendix D

German Surface Forces Stationed in Norway

Battleship
Tirpitz 8 15-in, 12 6-in, 16 4-in, January 1942 – November 1944 out of action, September 1943 – March 1944, April – July 1944, destroyed by RAF November 1944

Battle Cruiser
Scharnhorst 9 11-in, 12 5.9-in, 14 4.1-in, February 1943 – December 1943, sunk by Home Fleet forces, 26th December 1943

Pocket Battleships
Scheer 6 11-in, 8 6-in, 6 4-in, February – November 1942
Lützow 6 11-in, 8 6-in, 6 4-in, May – August 1942, December 1942 – September 1943

Cruisers
Hipper 8 8-in, 12 4-in, March 1942 – February 1943
Prinz Eugen 8 8-in, 12 4-in, March – May 1942. Torpedoed by *Trident* on arrival and under repair the whole time
Köln 9 6-in, 6 3.5-in, July 1942 – February 1943
Nurnberg 9 6-in, 8 3.5-in, November 1942 – May 1943

Destroyers
Friedrich Eckholdt 5 5-in, HA/LA, sunk by *Sheffield*
Friedrich Ihn 5 5-in, HA/LA
Hans Lody 5 5-in, HA/LA
Hermann Schoemann 5 5-in, HA/LA, sunk by *Edinburgh*, *Foresight* and *Forester*
Karl Galster 5 5-in, HA/LA
Paul Jacobi 5 5-in, HA/LA
Richard Blitzen 5 5-in, HA/LA
Theodor Riedel 5 5-in, HA/LA
Z24 5 5.9-in, HA/LA
Z25 5 5.9-in, HA/LA
Z26 5 5.9-in, HA/LA, sunk by *Trinidad* and *Eclipse*
Z27 5 5.9-in, HA/LA
Z28 5 5.9-in, HA/LA
Z29 5 5.9-in, HA/LA   *The number of destroyers kept in Norwegian ports varied,*
Z30 5 5.9-in, HA/LA   *the highest at any one time from the end of May 1942,*
Z31 5 5.9-in, HA/LA   *being nine or ten.*

Appendix E

German U-boat Submarines Sunk in Arctic Convoy Operations

1942

U-655 Rammed, 24th March, HMS *Sharpshooter* (QP 9)

U-585 Depth charge, 29th March, HMS *Fury* (PQ 13)

U-589 Depth charge, 12th September, HMS *Faulknor* (PQ 18)

U-88 Depth charge, 14th September, HMS *Onslow* (PQ 18)

U-457 Depth charge, 16th September, HMS *Impulsive* (PQ 18)

U-253 Depth charge, 23rd September, Catalina

1943

U-644 Torpedoed, 7th April, HMS *Tuna* (patrol S.E. Jan Mayen)

1944

U-314 Depth charge, 30th January, HM ships *Whitehall* and *Meteor* (JW 56B)

U-713 Depth charge, 24th February, HMS *Keppel* (JW 57)

U-601 Depth charge, 25th February, Catalina (JW 57)

U-472 Rocket, gunfire, 4th March, Swordfish (*Chaser*) and *Onslaught* (RA 57)

U-366 Rocket, gunfire, 5th March, Swordfish (*Chaser*) (RA 57)

U-973 Rocket, gunfire, 6th March, Swordfish (*Chaser*) (RA 57)

U-961 Depth charge, 29th March, HMS *Starling* (JW 58)

U-355 Depth charge, 1st April, HMS *Beagle*, Avenger (*Tracker*) (JW 58)

U-360 Hedgehog, 2nd April, HMS *Keppel* (JW 58)

U-288 Depth charge, 3rd April, Aircraft (*Tracker* and *Activity*) (JW 58)

U-277 Depth charge, 1st May, Swordfish (*Fencer*) (RA 59)

U-674 Depth charge, 2nd May, Swordfish (*Fencer*) (RA 59)

U-959 Depth charge, 2nd May, Swordfish (*Fencer*) (RA 59)

U-361 Depth charge, 17th July, Liberator (patrol)

U-347 Depth charge, 17th July, Catalina (patrol)

U-742 Depth charge, 18th July, Catalina (patrol)

U-354 Depth charge, 22nd August, Swordfish (*Vindex*) (JW 59)

U-344 Depth charge, 23rd August, E.G.20; *Keppel, Mermaid, Peacock* and *Loch Dunvegan* (JW 59)

U-394 Rocket, Depth charge, 2nd September, Swordfish (*Vindex*) E.G.20; *Keppel, Whitehall, Mermaid* and *Peacock* (RA 59A)

U-921 Depth charge, 30th September, Swordfish (*Campania*)

U-387 Depth charge, 9th December, HMS *Bamborough Castle* (RA 62)
U-365 Depth charge, 13th December, Swordfish (*Campania*) (RA 62)

1945
U-425 Squid, 17th February, E.G.8; *Lark* and *Alnwick Castle* (off Kola Inlet)
U-307 Gunfire, 29th April E.G.19; *Loch Inch* (RA 66)
U-286 29th April, E.G.19; *Loch Shin, Anguilla* and *Cotton* (RA 66)

Numbers of U-boats in Northern Norwegian Waters
In January 1942, only four U-boats were assigned to Northern Norwegian waters. By April 1942 the number had risen to 20 and from then until the end of 1943 the average number was 21. During 1944 this average rose to 28 (maximum 32 in July); but in January 1945 the number was down to 20.

Appendix F

German Air Forces in Northern Norway, 1942

1. In February 1942 the GAF had the following aircraft in Northern Norway:–

60 long range bombers
30 dive bombers
30 single engined fighters
In addition the German Fleet Air Arm had 18 floatplanes, carrying torpedoes.

2. In March 1942 Reichs Marshal Goering ordered the GAF units to co-operate with the Navy against the convoys. From then on the available bomber forces shadowed and attacked them when the weather permitted.

3. The GAF had been slow to appreciate the potentiality of torpedo caring aircraft. In 1941, as a result of the increased defensive armament of merchant ships, the GAF began to take an interest in the torpedo as an alternative to bombing and in December of that year it was decided to develop this form attack.

4. He.111 and Ju.88 aircraft were found suitable and by April 1942 12 crews had been trained. Thy were sent to Bardufoss and arrived in May, together with 60 Ju.88 bombers.

5. By June 1942, the Air Forces in Northern Norway had risen to:–

German Air Force	Naval
103 long range bombers (Ju.88)	44 long range reconnaissance
30 dive bombers	(BV.138)
42 torpedo bombers (He.111)	15 torpedo carrying floatplanes
8 long range reconnaissance (Fw.200 Condor)	(He.115
22 long range reconnaissance (Ju.88)	**Total 264**

6. By October 1942, torpedo bombers had been increased by the addition of 35 Ju.88 to 92.

7. After the Allied landings in North Africa, most of the GAF in the north including the whole of the Ju.88 and He.111 torpedo bombers, was transferred to the Mediterranean, leaving only the LR Reconnaissance Force, whose sole function was to report convoys for attack by surface craft and U-boats, some dive bombers and the slow He.115 naval floatplanes.

Sources

General
Admiralty Historical Section War Diary
C.-in-C. Home Fleet, War Diaries
1st, 10th, 18th Cruiser Squadrons War Diaries
FO Submarines, War Diaries
FO Submarines, Summaries of Operations
SBNO North Russia, Monthly Reports
Monthly A/S Reports
Convoy Signal Packs (Trade Division)
C.-in-C. Home Fleet, Dispatches, 1941 – 31st May 1945 (RO. Cases 7607, 8941)
C.-in-C. Home Fleet, Protection of Russian Convoys (M.050799/42)
C.-in-C. Home Fleet, Instructions for Convoy Escorts (M.08483/42)
C.-in-C. Home Fleet, North Russian Convoy Instructions (M.011219/42)
RAC 10th CS, Recommendations: additional convoy protection (M.03384/42)
1st Sea Lord's Papers, Vols. 14, 21, 22
Air Ministry Pamphlet No. 248, The Rise and Fall of the German Air Force
German Surface Ships Ships, Policy and Operations (GHS 4)
Admiral Doenitz War Diary
Führer Conferences
Air Ministry Historical Section (Translations of GAF Reports)
Naval Staff History, Operations of British Submarines, Volume I
Naval Staff History, Development of British Naval Aviation
Navy Lists
Pink Lists
War Vessels and Aircraft, British and Foreign
Ships' Logs and Signal Logs (as necessary)
History of US Naval Operations, World War II, Vol. I; Captain S. E. Morison
The Second World War, Vols. IV and V; The Rt. Hon. W. S. Churchill OM PC CH MP
RUSI Journal, May 1946; Lecture by Captain I. M. Campbell DSO RN

Chapter I – PQ 11, QP 8
March 1942
C.-in-C., Home Fleet, Reports M.050799, 050800, 050801/42
HMS *Victorious*, Air attack on *Tirpitz* M.05027/42
HMS *Faulkner*, Report of Proceedings, 11th – 14th March 1942 M.05116/42
HMS *Kenya*, Report of Proceedings, 3rd – 12th March 1942 M.04471/42
RAC 10th CS Report of Proceedings, 24th February – 8th March 1942 M.04185/42
1st Cruiser Squadron, War Diary TSD.3280/42

Commodore, PQ 12 Report of Proceedings M.04033/42
HMS *Hazard*, Report of Proceedings M.05070/42
Submarines, Reports of Proceedings M.04475, 04953, 050000, 05142/42
Tripitz log PG.48531

Chapter II – PQ 13, QP 9
March 1942
HMS *Trinidad*, Report of Proceedings, 21st – 30th March 1942 M.07411/42
HMS *Trinidad* and *Fury*, Action Report, 29th March 1942 M.08061/42
HMS *Eclipse*, Action Report, 29th March 1942 M.07411/42
HMS *Eclipse*, Action Damage Report M.05577/42
SO 6th MS Float. Report of local Escort, PQ 13 M.06682/4
C.-in-C., Western Approaches, RA(D) HF M.08251/42
HMS *Kenya*, Report of Proceedings, 12th – 29th March 1942 M.05063/42
HMS *Offa*, Report of Proceedings, 24th – 31st March 1942 M.06286/42
HMS *Sharpshooter*, Report of Proceedings, 21st – 29th March 1942 M.05742/42
HMS *Trinidad*, Report on being torpedoed M.051139/42
HMS *Trinidad*, Board of Enquiry NL.10827/42
German destroyer, *Z25*, War Diary PG.74655

Chapter III – PQ 14, PQ 16, QP 10, QP 12
April and May 1942
Rear-Admiral, 18th CS, Report on PQ 14 M.06950/42
HMS *Bulldog*, Report of Proceedings, PQ 14, QP 11 M.08568/42
Vice-Commodore, Report of Proceedings, PQ 14 M.06704/42
Commodore, Report of Proceedings, QP 10 M.05842/42
HMS *Liverpool*, Report of Proceedings, QP 10 M.06400/42
HMS *Marne*, Air attacks, 11th and 13th April 1942 M.05868/42
HMS *Blackly*, Air attack, 12th April 1942 M.05898/42
HMS *Orbi*, Report of Proceedings, 10th – 21st April, QP 10 M.06020/42
HMS *Speedwell*, Air attack, 11th April 1942 M.06253/42
Rear-Admiral, 18th CS with enclosures (torpedoing of *Edinburgh*, 30th April. Action reports, 2nd May 1942) M.06931/42
Rear-Admiral, 10th CS, Report of Proceedings, 23rd April – 5th May 1942, PQ 15 M.06826/42
Rear-Admiral, 10th CS, Report of Proceedings, 20th – 29th May 1942, PQ 16, QP 12 M.07941/42
Captain (D) 6, SO 1st MSF, Report of Proceedings, M.08491/42
Commodore, Report of Proceedings, PQ 15 M.06940/42
Force Q, Report of Proceedings, 24th April – 9th May 1942 M.08078/42
HMS (MV) *Ulster Queen*, Report of Proceedings, PQ 15 M.07824/42
Rear-Admiral, 18th CS, Remarks on the sinking of *Trinidad* M.06900/42
HMS *Trinidad*, Report of Proceedings, loss by air attack M.07976/42
HMS *Ashanti*, Report of Proceedings, 24th – 30th May 1942, PQ 16 M.08408/42, 08761/42
Captain D (3), Report of Proceedings, 21st – 29th May 1942, QP 12 M07591/42
Logs, German destroyer *Hermann Schoeman* and *Z24* PG.74466, 74635

Chapter IV – PQ 17, QP 13
June and July 1942
RAC, 1st CS, Report of Proceedings TSD.3288/42
HMS *Keppel*, Report of Proceedings M.09823/42 (bound in 1st SL's papers)
Commodore, Report of Proceedings, PQ 17 M.011511/42
HMS *Pozarica*, Report of Proceedings M.012741, 011478/42
Rescue ships *Rathlin* and *Zamalek*, Reports of Proceedings M.014513/42
Report of losses, QP 13 M.051361/42
HMS *Inglefield*, Report of Proceedings M.010678/42

Chapter V – PQ 18, QP 14, QP 15
September and November 1942
C.-in-C., Home Fleet's Report, with enclosures M.051890/42
SBNO, Archangel report M.052050/42
Commodore, Report of Proceedings, PQ 18 M.014755/42
Naval Air Division, minute on HMS *Avenger*'s report TSD. 1309/42
Appendix (Gunnery) to Report of RA(D) M.01534/42
HMS *Malcolm, Achates* and close escort, Reports of Proceedings M.014415/42
HMS (MV) *Ulster Queen*, Report of Proceedings M.015645/42
SS *Temple Arch*, Report of Proceedings M.014755/42
Loss of HMS *Leda* M.01492/42

Chapter VI – JW 51A, JW 51B, JW 53, RA 51, RA 53
December 1942 to February 1943
C.-in-C., Home Fleet's Report, JW 51A, 5, RA 51 M.052714/43
SO Force 'R' (Rear-Admiral Burnett) Action report, 31st December 1942
    M.052455/43
HMS *Obedient*, Action report, 31st December 1942 M.052539/43
HMS *Achates*, Report of Proceedings and Action report, 31st December 1942
    M.052557/43
HMS *Achates*, Board of Enquiry into loss M.02711/43
C.-in-C., Home Fleet's Report, JW/RA 52 (with enclosures) M.02715/43
C.-in-C., Home Fleet's Report, JW/RA 53 (with enclosures) M.04046/43
HMS Graph, Report of Proceedings M.0865/43
Operation 'Rainbow' (Regenbogen) NID.24/X9/45
Vice-Admiral Kummetz War Diary PG.48737/NID
Lützow War Diary PG.48243/NID

Chapter VII – JW 54, JW 66, RA 54, RA 66
November 1943 to May 1945
C.-in-C., Home Fleet's Report, JW/RA 54A, B (with enclosures) RO. Case 8538
C.-in-C., Home Fleet's Report, Operation 'Hotbed,' JW 1, RA 64 (with enclosures)
    RO. Case 9073
Naval Staff History, BS No. 24, Sinking of *Scharnhorst*

Vice–Admiral Sir Simon Lister KCB OBE

Simon Lister joined the Royal Navy in 1978. After training at the Royal Naval Engineering College at Manadon and the Royal Naval College, Greenwich gaining an MSc in Nuclear Engineering in 1986, was subsequently appointed the marine engineer officer of the submarine *Odin*. He went on to be marine engineer officer of *Torbay* and then *Trenchant* in 1993. He became Naval Assistant to the Chief Executive of the Ship Support Agency in 1994 and, after attending the London Business School in 1996, he became Director, Naval Plans at the Ministry of Defence in 1997 and then Naval Attaché in Moscow in 2001.

He became head of the team responsible for phase one of the internal restructuring programme at the Defence Logistics Organisation in 2004. Lister went on to be Commander, HM Naval Base Plymouth in 2005, Senior Naval Member on the Directing Staff at the Royal College of Defence Studies in 2008 and Director, Submarines in 2009. Lister became Chief of Materiel (Fleet) and Chief of Fleet Support with promotion to the rank of Vice-Admiral in 2013. In 2017, he was appointed as interim head of the Submarine Delivery Agency (SDA) and given the title of Chief of Materiel (Submarines).

Appointed Officer of the Order of the British Empire (OBE) in the 2001 Birthday Honours, Companion of the Order of the Bath (CB) in the 2013 New Year Honours, and Knight Commander of the Order of the Bath (KCB) in the 2017 Birthday Honours.

In 2017 Lister took a sabbatical from his Royal Navy Career to lead the Aircraft Carrier Alliance delivering the nation's new Queen Elizabeth Class carriers. He retired from active naval service in 2019.

Following his retirement, Lister became Managing Director of BAE Systems's naval ships business. In 2021, he additionally became a non-executive director on the board of the Office for Nuclear Regulation. Recently he has been a member of the Scottish Government's National Strategy for Economic Transformation Delivery Board.

G. H. Bennett

G H Bennett, is Associate Professor at Plymouth University where he has taught history, including that of the Second World War since 1992. Author of more than 20 volumes on Military, Diplomatic and Political history he has appeared in documentaries on the Second World War as well as historical series such as *Who Do You Think You Are* and *Combat Ships*. He is also a regular contributor to BBC National, Local Radio and to Gem Collector TV.

Richard Porter

Dr Richard Porter is the Hon. Curator at the Britannia Museum and an Associate Lecturer with the University of Lincoln at Britannia Royal Naval College. He joined the College in 1989 as a Senior Lecturer in the Department of Marine Environmental Sciences, having read Geology at the University of Sheffield. After completing his PhD, his career began in the museum world. He became Head of the Education Department at The Manchester Museum and was Assistant Keeper at Sheffield City Museums, prior to that, where he had been involved in the production of both permanent and temporary exhibitions.

At Dartmouth, he was instrumental in setting up a permanent museum at the College which opened in 1999. Since then, he had been Curator of the Britannia Museum, until 2014. In 2005, he co-authored, with Dr Jane Harrold, *Britannia Royal Naval College 1905–2005: One hundred Years of Officer Training at Dartmouth*. For this history of the College, they were awarded the Sir Robert Craven Trophy by the Britannia Naval Research Association, for their outstanding contribution to naval research. A revised, updated edition was published in 2007, re-titled *Britannia Royal Naval College Dartmouth: An Illustrated History*, reprinted in 2012.

Michael Pearce

Mike Pearce served with the Ministry of Defence (Navy) for nearly 40 years and was on the staff of the Britannia Royal Naval College, Dartmouth for 12 years. Closely involved with the Royal Navy throughout his career, he held management and planning roles within many different fields of MoD activity and on numerous projects for the Royal Navy in London, Hampshire and at the Naval Base at Devonport in addition to BRNC. As a naval historian, he has been a trustee of the Britannia Museum since its inception in 2008 and is a series editor for the Britannia Naval Histories of World War II. In 2012 he co-authored, with Dr Richard Porter, the introduction to *Fight for the Fjords, the Battle for Norway 1940*, and in 2013 wrote the introduction to *Between Hostile Shores, Mediterranean Convoy Battles 1941-42*, both BNHWW2 titles. Following the series re-launch in 2019, he wrote the introduction to *Confronting Italy, Mediterranean Surface Actions in 1940* and, in 2020, to *Dunkirk, Operation Dynamo 26th May – 4th June 1940, An Epic Of Gallantry*, published to mark the 80th anniversary, followed in 2021 by contributing in-depth picture research to *Rise of the Aircraft Carrier, Pacific Naval Strategy 1941-1945*. His particular area of expertise is the period 1860-1960 and he continues to undertake research, both on behalf of the Trust and in his own areas of interest.

He traces his first spark of interest in naval matters back to the age of four, when his father lifted him shoulder-high on the Isle of Wight ferry so that he could see HMS *Vanguard*, the last British battleship. His interest in naval history took off in his teens when he started reading and buying naval history books – he has never stopped. At school, he was often found tucked away in corners, avidly reading naval history and he counts himself fortunate that his career enabled him to put his knowledge to effective use.

Married to Anne, they have two grown-up children and live in South Devon where Mike is also a qualified watchkeeper with the National Coastwatch Institution at Prawle Point.

Index

Britannia
Naval
Histories of
World War II

Historical material, newly commissioned commentary, maps, plans
and first–hand accounts of specific battles. Each foreword is written
by naval veterans of the highest order.

Never previously published in this format, World War II Battle
Summaries are documents once stamped 'restricted' or
'confidential' and held in the archive of Britannia Royal Naval College
in Dartmouth, South West England. They are unique records written
up by naval officers during the conflict, and soon after 1945. Events
are recorded in minute detail, accompanied by maps and plans
drawn up during the period by serving officers. These historical
texts have been reorganised into a contemporary format. The first–
hand accounts are from worldwide sources and contain reactions,
emotions and descriptions, making fascinating reading.

Introduction by
M J Pearce

Confronting Italy
Mediterranean Surface Actions in 1940. Exploding the Myth of Mussolini's 'Mare Nostrum'

Paperback
ISBN 978–1–84102–439–4
Hardback
ISBN 978–1–84102–442–4
ebook
Amazon B086M6J66F
Number of Pages
192 pages

Foreword
Admiral Sir John Cunningham Kirkwood 'Jock' Slater, GCB, LVO, DL. A former first Sea Lord and great–nephew of Admiral Sir Andrew Cunningham, Commander–in–Chief of the Mediterranean fleet during this period when the actions covered in this volume took place.

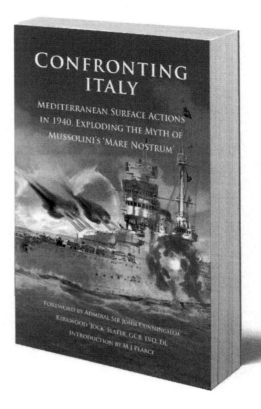

※ Contains both an Italian and British first-hand account.
※ Includes tracking maps drawn when the Battle Summary was compiled.
※ Includes the supplement to the *London Gazette*

Actions in the Mediterranean were fought when the Royal Navy was still evolving its use of naval air power and when radar at sea was primitive and fitted to only a few ships, while Italy's Regia Marina was handicapped by having access to neither.

Introduction by
M J Pearce

Dunkirk
Operation "Dynamo"
26ᵗʰ May – 4ᵗʰ June 1940
An Epic of Gallantry

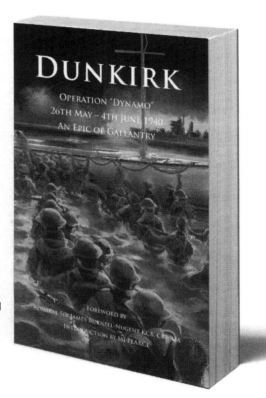

Paperback
ISBN 978-1-83801-070-6
Hardback
ISBN 978-1-83801-071-3
eBook
Amazon B0888T89RY
Number of Pages
420 pages

Foreword
Admiral Sir James Burnell–Nugent KCB, CBE, MA. He became Second Sea Lord and Commander–in–Chief Naval Home Command with responsibility for all personnel matters. He flew his flag in HMS Victory, making frequent use of Nelson's Great Cabin.

- Declassified content records events in minute detail.
- Includes maps drawn when the Battle Summary was compiled.
- Unpublished photographs of the beaches, town, and harbour is included.

The Royal Navy achieved what it set out to do, despite grievous losses, in the teeth of determined opposition. The loss of the main British field army would have enfeebled the nation militarily and psychologically, potentially resulting in a negotiated peace with Nazi Germany.

Introduction by
G H Bennett

Rise of the Aircraft Carrier

Pacific Naval Strategy 1941–1945

Paperback
ISBN 978-1-83801-073-7
Hardback
ISBN 978-1-83801-074-4
eBook
Amazon B09LZ6LLCS
Number of Pages
340 pages

Foreword
James Bergeron, Chief Political
Advisor for NATO Maritime
Command in Northwood, United
Kingdom. Previously in support
of NATO as a member of the US
Government Service, he is
considered to be one of NATO's
most experienced foreign policy
advisors in the fields of
maritime operations.

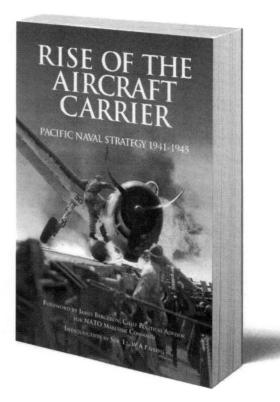

- Declassified content records events in minute detail.
- Includes detailed maps drawn when the Battle Summary was compiled.
- 192 photographs of carriers and aircraft both USN, IJN and HMS included.

Unmatched US industrial capacity enabled the design and construction of large numbers of highly capable carriers, their escorts and new naval aircraft. Despite early losses, the USN swiftly outstripped the IJN in numbers and capability, leaving the Japanese to rely on converting aircraft carriers from all manner of other vessels.

Japanese aircraft carrier IJN *Akagi* in April 1942 during the Indian Ocean Raid as seen from an aircraft that has just taken off from her deck. The aircraft on the flight deck preparing for taking off are Aichi D3A Type 99 dive bombers.

Rise of the Aircraft Carrier: Pacific Naval Strategy 1941–1945

BMT Press

Britannia Museum Trust Press

Printed in Great Britain
by Amazon